THE MYTH OF
ACHIEVEMENT
TESTS

THE GED AND THE
ROLE OF CHARACTER
IN AMERICAN LIFE

The Myth of Achievement Tests

EDITED BY

JAMES J. HECKMAN,

JOHN ERIC HUMPHRIES,

AND TIM KAUTZ

THE UNIVERSITY OF CHICAGO PRESS

Chicago and London

The University of Chicago Press, Chicago 60637
The University of Chicago Press, Ltd., London
© 2014 by The University of Chicago
All rights reserved. Published 2014.
Paperback edition 2015
Printed in the United States of America

23 22 21 20 19 18 17 16 15   2 3 4 5 6

ISBN-13: 978-0-226-10009-8 (cloth)
ISBN-13: 978-0-226-32480-7 (paper)
ISBN-13: 978-0-226-10012-8 (e-book)
DOI: 10.7208/chicago/9780226100128.001.0001

Library of Congress Cataloging-in-Publication Data

The myth of achievement tests : the GED and the
role of character in American life / edited by James J.
Heckman, John Eric Humphries, and Tim Kautz.
     pages ; cm
  Includes bibliographical references and index.
  ISBN 978-0-226-10009-8 (cloth : alk. paper) —
  ISBN 978-0-226-10012-8 (e-book)
  1. GED tests.   2. Academic achievement—
United States—Testing.   3. Educational tests and
measurements—Standards—United States.
4. Personality development.   I. Heckman, James J.
(James Joseph), editor.   II. Humphries, John Eric,
editor.   III. Kautz, Tim, editor.
  LB3060.33.G45M98 2012
  373.126'2—dc23

                                        2013025706

♾ This paper meets the requirements of
ANSI/NISO Z39.48-1992 (Permanence of Paper).

We must remember that intelligence is not enough.

Intelligence plus character—that is the goal of true education.

— MARTIN LUTHER KING, JR.,

  "The Purpose of an Education," 1947

Character is higher than intellect.

— RALPH WALDO EMERSON,

  Nature, Addresses, and Lectures, 1849, reprinted 1979

CONTENTS

COMMENT FROM A GED INSTRUCTOR

As a GED teacher, I found your abstract very informative. I rarely see my students after they graduate (or not). My assumption has been that they go on to some form of success. However, I have wondered what level of success can be attained by students who barely meet the minimum requirements of the test or must retake sections numerous times.

I know this wasn't a focus of your paper, but another barrier to GEDs is the manner in which they are taught. Rather than a learning environment which motivates these individuals to reach their full potential, they are held captive in a classroom of pre-tests, assessments, and mounds of published workbooks. Many "teachers" do nothing more than assess and assign a course of study through endless mundane workbooks. The bottom line is that these students don't really master the material. (Actually, I have been in workshops with some GED teachers that had no grasp of the material.) . . .

What you opened my eyes to was the need to engage the whole person. Since reading your abstract, I have been talking to the principal about the need to include life skills, counseling, and motivational videos and speakers. Tomorrow I'm going to show a short video by Dewitt Jones on passion.

Thank you for your work,

Norm Frankenberger
Charles A. Jones Career and Education Center
Sacramento, CA
July 2010

In the early 1990s, one of us—James Heckman—visited a job training center in Corpus Christi, Texas. He witnessed a miracle in progress. High school dropouts with roughly six years of schooling were—in the course of a few months—converted into high school graduates. This miracle was produced by the General Educational Development testing program, the GED program for short. The GED exam is an achievement test designed to capture *general knowledge,* the concept that underlies all achievement tests. The miracle seemed too good to be true—and it was.

Stephen Cameron and James Heckman investigated the miracle using data that followed GED recipients over time, both before and after they received the GED. They also had data on dropouts who do not GED certify. For their sample of young men, GED recipients perform in the labor market much more like other dropouts than high school graduates. Adjusting for their greater cognitive ability, GED recipients perform the same as dropouts (see Cameron and Heckman, 1993). Concurrently, Lois Quinn conducted evaluations of the effectiveness of GEDs in Wisconsin postsecondary schools and in the labor market. Her conclusions were identical (Pawasarat, Reynolds, and Quinn, 1986; Quinn, 1986; Quinn and Pawasarat, 1986).

The national press featured this research (see Frank, 1992; Marriott, 1993; Murphy, 2001; Peterson, 1992a, 1992b). A five-minute special on the GED ran on prime-time television (Blakemore and Jennings, 1993).[1] Despite the widespread media coverage of the ineffectiveness of the GED, the credential persists as a major factor in American education. The American Council on Education (ACE), along with Pearson Education, Inc., currently promotes GED certification. ACE is the major lobbying organization that represents the interests of American colleges in Washington. ACE brought the GED to scale some 60 years ago.

To counter the early academic research, ACE launched a blizzard of responses that obscured the negative evidence on the effects of GED certification. However, scholarly articles agree that GED recipients do not perform at the level of high school graduates, a finding confirmed in this book.

For decades, ACE has attempted to prevent careful evaluations of its exam. It successfully lobbied to block the United States Census from

---

1. Available at http://tvnews.vanderbilt.edu/program.pl?ID=149754.

distinguishing GED recipients from high school graduates, and it has prevented large-sample evaluations of the effectiveness of the certificate (see Quinn, 1990). In response to the accumulating evidence against the benefits of GED certification, ACE raised the passing standards for the GED exam but did not change the nature of the test. These reforms reduced the number of GED certificates issued, but even after the reforms were implemented, GED certificates comprise more than 12% of all high school credentials issued in 2012.

While ACE was raising passing standards, it also expanded the GED program into high schools, inducing low-performing students to drop out. Until recently, GED certification was a welcome addition to the portfolio of strategies available to states and schools hard pressed to show performance under the No Child Left Behind Act. Low-performing students could be shunted into GED programs and purged from the books without penalty.

This book establishes in a definitive way that, *as a group,* GED recipients are not equivalent to high school graduates. After controlling for their greater cognitive ability, most GED recipients perform at the level of high school dropouts in the labor market, in marriage, in the military, and in society at large. Counting GED recipients as high school graduates conceals major social problems.

The findings in this book extend well beyond the GED program. The widespread use of the GED test is a consequence of a pervasive belief that achievement tests are effective measures of human capabilities. The studies in this book demonstrate that achievement tests fail to capture many capabilities that produce human flourishing. *Character skills*—conscientiousness, perseverance, social skills, and the like—matter greatly for success in life. Raw smarts are rarely enough.

Inadvertently, the GED testing program has produced a natural experiment in American society that demonstrates the power of character. GED recipients are relatively smart dropouts, who, as a group, lack character skills. Most GED recipients consistently fail in tasks in life. Although some GED recipients are successful, they are few and far between.

The evidence assembled in this book challenges a central premise of America's test-oriented society. In the mid-nineteenth century, Horace Mann, the father of the Common School Movement in the United States and a creator of a precursor to the modern achievement test, recognized that successful schools produce character and that tests do not capture many skills that matter:

To value schools, by length instead of quality, is a matchless absurdity. Arithmetic, grammar, and the other rudiments, as they are called, comprise but a small part of the teachings in a school. The rudiments of feeling are taught not less than the rudiments of thinking. The sentiments and passions get more lessons than the intellect. Though their open recitations may be less, their secret rehearsals are more. —Horace Mann (1838, 58)

This message has been lost in contemporary analyses of educational policy. American schools now overemphasize achievement tests and ignore the formation and evaluation of the character of their students. Achievement tests—the bedrock of America's educational assessment system—are not designed to measure character. The chapters in this book show why it is important to rediscover and reemphasize character in our national dialogue about creating skills, and why it is feasible to do so.

BIBLIOGRAPHY

Blakemore, Bill, and Jennings, Peter. 1993. "American Agenda (Education: General Education Development Diploma)." ABC Evening News, August 5, 1993. Audiovisual file. http://tvnews.vanderbilt.edu/program.pl?ID=149754.

Cameron, Stephen V., and Heckman, James J. 1993. "The Nonequivalence of High School Equivalents." *Journal of Labor Economics* 11 (1, Part 1):1–47.

Frank, James. 1992. "GED Loses Bit of Respect, But Not Its Faithful." *Chicago Tribune*, January 19:1.

Heckman, James J., and Rubinstein, Yona. 2001. "The Importance of Noncognitive Skills: Lessons from the GED Testing Program." *American Economic Review* 91(2):145–149.

Mann, Horace. 1838. "First Annual Report Covering the Year 1837." Annual Report of the Secretary of the Board of Education, Massachusetts Board of Education.

Marriott, Michel. 1993. "Valuable Diploma or Meaningless Piece of Paper?: Questions Are Raised about Encouraging Dropouts to Pursue G.E.D. Program." *The New York Times*, June 15:B1.

Murphy, Bruce. 2001. "Shortcut to Failure? The GED Is a Growing Force in Education, But Some Critics Say It's Worse Than Useless." *Chicago Tribune*, August 5:10–11.

Pawasarat, John, Reynolds, Peter, and Quinn, Lois M. 1986. "Performance of GED Holders at Milwaukee Area Technical College: 1978–1985." University of Wisconsin-Milwaukee Employment and Training Institute.

Peterson, Iver. 1992a. "As More Earn Equivalency Diploma, Its Value Is Debated." *The New York Times*, October 21:B10.

Peterson, Iver. 1992b. "Less Than Full Equivalency." *The New York Times*, October 25:E16.

Quinn, Lois M. 1986. "Performance of GED Holders at the University of Wisconsin's Thirteen Campuses: 1979–1985." University of Wisconsin-Milwaukee Employment and Training Institute.

Quinn, Lois M. 1990. "GED: The Test that Became an Institution." Ph.D. thesis, University of Wisconsin-Milwaukee.

Quinn, Lois M., and Pawasarat, John. 1986. "Equivalency Certificates Report to the Superintendent: Findings and Recommendations." University of Wisconsin-Milwaukee Employment and Training Institute.

ACKNOWLEDGMENTS

We thank many people over many years for contributing to this project. Stephen Cameron played a central role in the early years of this project and contributed independent work on the GED reviewed in Chapter 5. Yona Rubinstein contributed important ideas in the course of this project that served to focus the analysis on noncognitive (character) traits (Heckman and Rubinstein, 2001). Paul LaFontaine revived work on the GED after a lull and contributed a chapter to this book and to the literature surveyed in Chapter 5. Nicholas Mader provided many helpful insights. Robert Lerman provided valuable research and insight into the programs considered in Chapter 9. John Donohue and Carl Kaestle made helpful suggestions about aspects of this work. We have benefited from helpful comments on this manuscript from Richard Boyle, Tom Coleman, Joe Jackson, David Pervin, Mike Rose, Steve Raudenbush, and two anonymous reviewers. Lynne Heckman gave useful comments on a previous draft. We have benefited from the careful research assistance of Lindsay Atnip, Wenfei Du, Roger Fan, Adam Grealish, Maryclare Griffin, Tal Gross, Jin Soo Han, Alma Heckman, Lisa Kahn, Jacob Katz, Sophia Li, William Ma, Talha Noor Mohammed, Dan Moran, Trey O'Connor, Terrance Oey, Maria Rosales, Ed Sung, Ed Vytlacil, Indra Wechsberg, and Abigail Wagner Wozniak. Linor Kiknadze helped greatly in building and checking the extensive data base used in this monograph. Her careful and consistent analyses help make the empirical work in this book credible. Derek Neal, Lois Quinn, and Chris Taber made helpful comments on the papers presented at an April 2011 workshop, "Studies of the GED Testing Program," sponsored by the Spencer Foundation. Clifton Ingram and Jake Whitaker gave highly competent editorial scrutiny to this work. Paul Tough, author of *How Children Succeed,* visited the GED working group at the University of Chicago in the fall of 2009 and winter of 2010. His best-selling book presents a well-written and accurate summary of some of the main lessons of our analysis for a popular audience. Interactions with personality psychologists, and especially Angela Duckworth and Brent Roberts, both one-on-one and in a series of workshops sponsored by the Spencer Foundation, provided valuable background for the research reported here.

This research was supported, in part, by grants from the Spencer Foundation, the Pritzker Children's Initiative, the Bureau of Labor Statistics, the Donner Foundation, the Andrew W. Mellon Foundation, the Pew Charitable

Trusts, the Buffett Early Childhood Fund, the Joyce Foundation, the Lynde and Harry Bradley Foundation of Milwaukee, Wisconsin, NSF SES 9111455, NSF SBR 9121048, NSF SBR 9709873, NSF SBR 9730657, NSF SES 9321048, NSF SES 0099195, NICHD 5R01HD32058, NICHD 3R01HD34958, NICHD 5R01HD043411, NICHD 5R01HD054702, NICHD 5R37 HD065072, the American Bar Foundation, and anonymous funders. Humphries acknowledges support from a National Science Foundation Graduate Research Fellowship. The views expressed in this book are those of the authors and not necessarily those of the funders or commentators mentioned here.

INTRODUCTION

1

ACHIEVEMENT TESTS AND
THE ROLE OF CHARACTER IN
AMERICAN LIFE

JAMES J. HECKMAN AND TIM KAUTZ

1.1 Introduction

Modern societies rely on written tests. Achievement tests—multiple-choice exams that attempt to measure acquired knowledge—have come to play an especially prominent role. They are used to sift and sort people, to evaluate schools, and to assess the performance of entire nations.[1] The No Child Left Behind Act requires that public schools administer achievement tests and that the test results influence local school policy.

Achievement tests were created in the mid-twentieth century. Their validity in predicting success in outcomes that matter is not well established. Achievement tests were developed as a way to measure *"general knowledge"* that would be useful inside and outside of the classroom. Their developers claimed to have designed pencil-and-paper tests that would predict success in the labor market, in education, and in many other aspects of life. Because achievement tests have been validated by testing experts, most people assume that the tests accomplish these goals. However, achievement tests are typically validated in a circular fashion using IQ tests and grades, and not in terms of their ability to predict important life outcomes. Some have recognized this circularity and have argued that achievement tests miss important skills. There is scant evidence on what skills these tests miss.

This book evaluates the predictive power of achievement tests for life outcomes by examining one widely used achievement test, the General Educational Development test (GED). The GED test is based on the first modern achievement test. The test is a seven-and-a-half hour exam that claims to measure the knowledge acquired in completing high school. It

---

1. The Programme for International Student Assessment (PISA) evaluates student performance in math, science, and reading across countries, and its results attract a lot of media attention and influence policy. Scores from the year 2000 PISA test led Germany to reevaluate its educational system and introduce a variety of reforms (Grek, 2009).

embodies the logic of achievement tests. The GED allows high school dropouts to certify high school equivalency to employers and colleges. Currently, the GED program produces roughly 12% of all high school credentials issued in the United States every year.[2]

On the surface, the GED exam achieves its goal. As measured by scores on a variety of other achievement tests, GED recipients are as smart as high school graduates who do not attend college.[3] But passing a test does not, by itself, prove anything. How do GED recipients compare to high school graduates in terms of meaningful outcomes?

On outcomes that matter, *as a group*, GED recipients are *not* equivalent to high school graduates. High school graduates outperform GED recipients in terms of their earnings, employment, wages, labor market participation, self-reported health, and college completion. Graduates are less likely to use alcohol, commit crime, or go on welfare.

On average, GED recipients perform somewhat better than other dropouts on most outcomes. GED recipients, however, are smarter than other dropouts even before earning their GEDs. After accounting for their greater cognitive ability, as a group, GED recipients are equivalent to other dropouts on almost all outcomes. High school graduates who obtain their credentials through seat time and hard work outperform both GED recipients and uncertified dropouts.[4]

The GED might be a signal that indicates the greater cognitive ability of most recipients compared to dropouts. However, we establish that the GED certificate provides little signaling value in the market. GED recipients earn the same wages before and after they certify.

Our evaluation of the GED provides strong evidence about the predictive power of achievement tests for outcomes that matter. Cognitive ability—as measured by achievement tests—explains the average difference in outcomes between dropouts and GED recipients. Something not captured by achievement tests explains the difference between GED recipients and high school graduates. What is the "dark matter" that the test misses?

We show that achievement tests like the GED do not adequately capture character skills such as conscientiousness, perseverance, sociability, and

2. See GED Testing Service Annual Statistical Reports (Various Years) and National Digest National Center for Education Statistics (Various Years). In the past the figure has been as high as 18%.

3. See the evidence presented in Chapter 4 of this book.

4. These findings are robust. We confirm these general findings using seven different data sets and a variety of statistical methods that account for many potential problems.

curiosity, which are valued in the labor market, in school, and in many other domains. Until recently these skills have largely been ignored. However, in recent research economists and psychologists have constructed measures of these skills and provide evidence that they are stable across situations and predict meaningful life outcomes.[5]

As a group, GED recipients lack character skills compared to high school graduates.[6] In adolescence, these deficits lead to higher rates of drinking, drug use, violent crime, truancy, vandalism, early sexual activity, and smoking.

There are a few apparent exceptions to this rule. For some, the GED appears to offer benefits. As a group, women who drop out of high school due to pregnancy and who later GED certify have levels of character skills much more like those of high school graduates than other GED recipients. This group of GED recipients appears to perform moderately better than other dropouts in the labor market, although the differences come primarily from their greater labor force participation. The evidence of any causal effect of the GED for this group is ambiguous.[7] Many GED recipients earnestly seek to turn their lives around. For most, preparation for the GED exam does not compensate for the skills they lack.

Differences in character skills emerge early between GEDs and high school graduates. Even at age six eventual GED recipients tend to be relatively smart but exhibit behavioral problems. These findings suggest that many young children are destined to drop out of high school, a view shared by many social scientists.

A prime example of a study claiming early life determinism is the influential and inflammatory book by psychologist Richard Herrnstein and political scientist Charles Murray, *The Bell Curve* (1994). Herrnstein and Murray made a major contribution to psychology and social policy by conducting one of the first studies to use meaningful life outcomes in assessing the predictive validity of an achievement test—in their case, the Armed Forces Qualification Test (AFQT). They find that AFQT scores weakly predict success in a variety of life outcomes. However, they do not stop there. They

5. See the studies by Borghans et al. (2008) and Almlund et al. (2011). The modern literature traces back to Bowles and Gintis (1976), and Bowles, Gintis, and Osborne (2001). An important study in sociology is the work of Peter Mueser reported in Jencks (1979). Work in psychology going back to Terman et al. (1925) shows that personality skills predict life outcomes (see also Murray, 1938; Terman et al., 1947; and the analysis in Gensowski, 2012).

6. This evidence is developed in Chapter 4.

7. See Chapter 5.

claim that the AFQT test measures the same dimensions of cognition as IQ and that IQ is highly heritable.[8] In their dystopic vision of American society, public policy cannot influence the skills that affect success in life. Like most people, Herrnstein and Murray overlook character as an important predictor of success and as an avenue for social progress, and also ignore the evidence on the malleability of IQ.

Investment and interventions can foster character. The Perry Preschool program is a telling example. Young (age 3–4) low-IQ African American children were given early stimulation. Participants were taught how to plan, execute, and review tasks. They learned to work with others when problems arose.[9] The program was evaluated by the method of random assignment, and participants and controls have been followed through age 40. The program had no long-term effect on IQ scores. By the Herrnstein and Murray criteria, it failed. Nevertheless, the program improved outcomes for both boys and girls, yielding a rate of return that outperforms the stock market in typical years.[10] Heckman, Pinto, and Savelyev (2013) show that the program worked by improving character.

Because both cognition and character can be shaped, and change over the life cycle, we refer to them as "skills" throughout this book. An older terminology refers to them as "traits," conveying a sense of immutability or permanence, possibly due to their heritable nature. The literature surveyed in Chapter 9 shows how these "traits" can be enhanced. Our distinction between skills and traits is not just a matter of semantics. It suggests new and productive avenues for public policy.[11]

Character training is not a new idea. Aristotle mentions it in the *Nichomachean Ethics*.[12] Prominent American educators since Horace Mann have noted that successful schools produce more than problem-solving skills and factual knowledge. Schools also mold character.

8. In Chapter 9 of this book, we show that IQ tests and achievement tests measure different skills.

9. Sylva (1997) describes the Perry program as a Vygotskian program that fosters personality skills.

10. See Heckman et al. (2010). The return of 7%–10% per annum is on par with the post–World War II, pre–2008 meltdown stock market returns to equity in the United States labor market that are estimated to be 6.9% per annum. See DeLong and Magin (2009).

11. In places in this book, we use "traits" because it represents the term used in the literature we cite.

12. See Aristotle (1956).

Recently, many have come to view character education as the sole province of the family or the church. Families *are* important producers of both cognition and character.[13] However, the American family is under severe challenge.[14] Single-parent families—which provide fewer resources for development of character and necessary life skills—have become pervasive.[15] Even many intact families are stressed because of diminished resources.

This book shows that, as a group, GED recipients lack character skills in part owing to their relatively disadvantaged family backgrounds. Compared to high school graduates, GED recipients are more likely to come from broken families with low incomes and have parents who invest less in their character and cognitive development.

At a time when many families could use more support, character education has been phased out of schools and the ability of schools to enforce discipline has been weakened. In the nineteenth century, character education was prominent in American schools. They had strict disciplinary standards and taught character directly, often through religious texts. A Protestant vision of morality and character was incorporated into public education.

Five primary forces led to the decline of character education in public schools in the last century. First, the rise of cognitive psychology shifted the focus of American education toward cognitive training and measurement (Bruner, 1956). Second, growing support for the separation of church and state removed religious teaching from the classroom and any forms of moral education or character education that smacked of religious training. Third, the "legalization" of schools increased the rights of students but reduced the autonomy of teachers and the use of disciplinary measures that could be used to instill character (Arum, 2005). Fourth, cultural relativism became more widespread in society. The notion of a core set of character skills that was universally agreed upon fell out of favor. Those advocating a core set of values and evaluation of character were accused of seeking to impose their (middle-class) values on others.[16] Fifth, the research of Walter Mischel (1968) appeared to establish that there are no stable personality skills. If character was ephemeral, there was no point in measuring it or trying to foster it. These trends contributed to the demise of character education in schools, which in turn exacerbated the problems created by the emergence of single-parent families in shaping the character of youth.

13. See Cunha et al. (2006) and Ermisch, Jantti, and Smeeding (2012).

14. See McLanahan (2004), Heckman (2008), and Putnam, Frederick, and Snellman (2012).

15. OECD (2011).

16. For a recent example, see the commentary of Lareau (2012).

Character education does not necessarily infringe on the liberties of students or families. Character education has moral components, which some conflate with religious values. Character skills are universally valued regardless of any religious orientation, although churches, temples, and mosques produce character. Removing religion from schools does not require removing character education from the curriculum or preventing evaluation of the character of students. Virtually all parents want their children to be hardworking, honest, persistent, creative, curious, self-controlled, and excited by learning. Curricula that teach these skills in conjunction with cognition are promising ways to foster successful lives while maintaining the sanctity of the family and preserving the separation of church and state.[17]

The curriculum in schools backed off from evaluating and fostering character to focus primarily on producing and measuring cognitive development. Belief in the predictive value of achievement tests became pervasive. It led many to view the GED certificate as equivalent to a high school degree. In some states, the GED is legally mandated to be equivalent to a high school degree for the purposes of employment and admission to post-secondary education.[18]

This book shows that this faith in tests deceives students and policy makers and conceals major social problems. The GED misleads students when they are making educational decisions. High school students as young as sixteen can take the GED. Adolescents are impressionable, and for many the GED seems like an attractive alternative to finishing school.[19] We show that having a GED option available induces students to drop out of high school.[20]

After the GED was introduced in California in 1974, the high school dropout rate increased by three percentage points. More recently, Oregon introduced the GED Option Program in high schools. These programs teach the GED and make it easier for students to GED certify. The Oregon program increased the high school dropout rate in the districts where it was implemented by four percentage points.

The GED deceives its recipients into believing that they are prepared for college. About 40% of GED recipients attend college. About half drop out

17. See the evidence presented in Chapter 9.

18. See, for example, Commonwealth of Pennsylvania (1955). See Web Appendix Section W1.1.15 for a summary of these laws. The Web Appendix mentioned in this note and subsequent notes is found at http://jenni.uchicago.edu/Studies_of_GED.

19. See National Center for Education Statistics (2006) for evidence that many GED recipients certify because it is easier than completing high school.

20. See the studies presented in Chapter 7.

in the first year.[21] Far fewer complete any degree, but pay costly tuition and forego substantial earnings in quest of degrees that they do not obtain.

The deception runs deep. All GED recipients are not alike. Some are hard-working and acquire skills by preparing for the exam. Despite their hard work and high character skills, these GED recipients are lumped into the same category as the relatively smart but unmotivated students who pass the exam. Employers and colleges might overlook the true achievers among the mass of GED test takers because the GED exam does not discriminate between the motivated and the accomplished and those who just pass its minimal standards.

The GED distorts social statistics and masks inequality. Many social statistics classify GED recipients as high school graduates. This misclassification conceals black–white gaps in educational attainment.[22] If GED recipients are counted as high school graduates, the black–white gap in high school graduation rates has closed substantially. If GED recipients are counted as dropouts, there has been no progress in the black–white high school graduation rate in the last 50 years. Many black GED recipients earn their certificate through remediation programs in jail.[23]

Based on the belief that the GED is equivalent to a high school degree, government programs have channeled substantial resources into producing GED certificates. These resources could have been spent on more effective policies.[24,25] The success of many adolescent intervention programs such as the Job Corps is judged by the number of GED recipients they produce. This practice distorts funding choices.[26] Government support also helps to explain why the GED program has become so prevalent even though it offers few benefits to most recipients. The cheap fix has become the byword of American public policy. While the direct costs of the GED program are low, it fixes few problems for most GED recipients and creates a host of new ones.

To address problems with the test, the GED testing service is planning to increase its passing standards. This proposal ignores the fundamental

21. See the evidence in Zhang et al. (2011).
22. Heckman and LaFontaine (2010).
23. See Heckman and LaFontaine (2010).
24. See the evidence in Chapters 2 and 3.
25. In addition, faith in tests and their acceptance as proof of college readiness promoted a boom in GED certification as dropouts perceived the benefits of higher education and used the GED to certify for admission to colleges and technical institutes at a time when the returns to higher education were increasing. See, for example, Autor, Katz, and Kearney (2008) on time trends in the economic returns to education.
26. See, for example, Schochet, Burghardt, and Glazerman (2001) and Bloom, Gardenhire-Crooks, and Mandsager (2009).

problems with the GED, which will not be solved by raising its passing standards. The GED program is a symptom of the deeper problem that American society is failing to produce essential character skills. It is possible to tackle this problem, but not simply by raising standards on achievement tests.

1.2 The Origins of Achievement Testing

The confluence of four cultural and intellectual currents produced the GED testing program and America's heavy reliance on achievement tests. First, technological developments made it cheap to implement multiple choice tests on a large scale. Second, cognitive psychology fostered the belief that cognition is the primary skill required for success in life. Third, for reasons discussed in the previous section, character education and the evaluation of character skills were slowly phased out of schools, partly accelerated by the federal government's entry into public education. Fourth, the accountability movement in government mimicked the logic of private market cost-benefit analysis by using test scores to evaluate and assess a myriad of government programs designed to enhance skills. We now elaborate on these points.

The modern thrust for accountability in schools arose in the nineteenth-century educational reform movements. In the early nineteenth century, Horace Mann introduced the first standardized test used in American schools.[27] The test was an early attempt to evaluate schools by their output—the knowledge they produced—rather than by their inputs. The instrument he devised was very crude. As noted in the Preface to this book, Mann saw the limitations of his primitive achievement test (Mann, 1838). However, Mann's test was not widely implemented because grading it was laborious and time intensive. It would be another century before his ideas for standardized testing became prevalent.[28,29]

In the absence of reliable output-based measures, nineteenth-century educators largely evaluated schools using input-based measures (e.g., standardized curricula). The input-based system was criticized. Teaching was often rote-based. Many critics commented unfavorably on the rigid disciplinary environments in these schools, which were intended, in part, to instill valued character skills in students.[30,31]

---

27. See Cremin (1988).

28. An exception was the New York Regents exam introduced in the 1870s.

29. See Cremin (1988).

30. See Cremin (1988), Reese (1995), and Ravitch (2010).

31. Bowles and Gintis (1976) characterize the American education system as producing docile, compliant, and reliable workers for the capitalist economy; that is, for producing character skills useful for industry.

In the early twentieth century, Progressives like John Dewey sought to free up the curriculum, to engage a wider swath of society than the elites who attended the nineteenth-century high schools,[32] and to produce the whole person—the skills that Mann believed schools should emphasize.[33] The Progressives aimed to make schools the training ground for the life skills of the multitude and to lay the foundations for an informed democracy. They sought to foster a wide array of character skills that gave agency to students to lead flourishing lives.

The Progressives appreciated and fostered individuality among students. They sought a device to filter and track students to tailor programs to individual needs. The recently developed IQ test appeared to serve these purposes well. The tests satisfied the norms of bureaucratic fairness and, at the same time, were perceived to be effective screening tools, although the evidence on their effectiveness was largely anecdotal.[34] The first IQ test was designed to screen out misfits in school (Binet and Simon, 1916). The use of the test was broadened to sort students within schools—the origins of tracking.

Just as Mann was skeptical about the early achievement tests, one of the creators of the modern IQ test, Alfred Binet, realized its limitations:

[Success in school] . . . admits of other things than intelligence; to succeed in his studies, one must have qualities which depend on attention, will, and character; for example a certain docility, a regularity of habits, and especially continuity of effort. A child, even if intelligent, will learn little in class if he never listens, if he spends his time in playing tricks, in giggling, in playing truant. —Binet (1916, 254)

Charles Spearman wrote to similar effect. He is best known for his work on "*g*"—a unitary factor that he claimed captured the structure of intelligence. However, along with his student, Edward Webb, he undertook studies of "character" because of "the urgency of its practical application to all the business of life" (Webb, 1915, 1). Spearman and Webb concluded that many positive aspects of character shared a relation to what modern personality psychologists term "Conscientiousness."[35]

---

32. See Cremin (1988) and Rothstein, Jacobsen, and Wilder (2008).
33. See Cremin (1988).
34. See Resnick (1982), Reed (1987), Ackerman (1988), and Jensen (1998).
35. Chapter 9 defines this and other psychological skills. See also Borghans et al. (2008) and Almlund et al. (2011).

Throughout the century, many scholars expressed concerns about the skills missed by IQ tests. Arthur Jensen, the intellectual heir of Spearman and an ardent proponent of the power of *g*, writing about the determinants of success in life, says:

> What are the chief personality traits which, interacting with *g*, relate to individual differences in achievement and vocational success? The most universal personality trait is conscientiousness, that is, being responsible, dependable, caring, organized and persistent. —Jensen (1998, 575)

The achievement test was developed in the wake of the success of the IQ test. Interest in testing was fueled by American obsession with measurement, accountability, and efficiency. In the late nineteenth century, Frederick Taylor began applying "scientific management" to the workplace. In order to increase efficiency in factories, he created incentive schemes for workers and monitored workflow by measuring the time it took to complete tasks.[36] Chapter 2 discusses the role of Taylorism ("scientific management") in the testing movement.[37]

J. Franklin Bobbitt, a professor of education at the University of Chicago in the early twentieth century, applied Taylor's vision to schools. He thought of schools like Taylor thought of factories:

> Education is a shaping process as much as the manufacture of steel rails; the personality is to be shaped and fashioned into desirable forms. It is a shaping of more delicate matters, more immaterial things, certainly; yet a shaping process none the less. —Bobbitt (1913, 12–13)[38]

While Taylor could readily measure the output of factories, Bobbitt lacked the tools to measure the output of schools. Like Mann, he viewed character as one of the most important products of schooling.[39] The perceived success of IQ testing coupled with a demand for "objective outputs of schools" motivated the creation of the modern achievement test.

---

36. See Lazear (1995) for a recent discussion of incentives in the workplace.
37. See Taylor (1911).
38. See Chapter 2 in this volume.
39. His philosophy of education is summarized in the following quote:
    The social point of view . . . demands that training be as wide as life itself. It looks at the human activities of every type: religious activities; civic activities; the duties of one's calling; one's family duties; one's recreations; one's reading and meditation; and the rest of the things that are done by the complete man or woman. —Bobbitt (1915, 20)

Ralph Tyler at the University of Chicago and Edward Lindquist at the University of Iowa invented the achievement test as a way to measure *"general knowledge."* While IQ tests were created to measure the capacity to learn, achievement tests were designed to measure the capacity to use what is learned—sometimes called *functional knowledge*—not the knowledge taught in any particular course.[40] Functional knowledge was not thought to be a trait like IQ. It was perceived to be an acquired skill.

Tyler was asked to evaluate the performance of the free-form Progressive schools developed under the influence of John Dewey and others.[41] The curricula across schools were not standardized, so input-based measures of evaluation were inappropriate. Instead, he developed output-based measures. Developed in 1942, the Iowa Test of Educational Development (ITED) was the first concrete framework designed to capture general knowledge—what schools "should teach" rather than the specific content of any course. The GED exam is based on this test.

Unlike Mann a century earlier, these pioneers developed the technology to implement the achievement test on a mass scale. Lindquist developed an optical scanner that read punch cards. This innovation made grading the exam fast and efficient, dramatically reducing the costs of evaluation. The modern Iowa tests, ACT, GED, National Assessment of Educational Progress (NAEP), and tests used under the No Child Left Behind Act are all achievement tests that trace their origins back to the ITED (ACT, 2009).[42] The tests gave instant feedback to educational evaluators, who often say they "cannot wait 20 years to learn what is going on in schools."[43]

One developer of the Iowa Test readily admitted the shortcomings of his creation but was pessimistic about measuring the aspects of human performance that the tests missed:

> In general, satisfactory tests have thus far been developed only for objectives concerned with the student's *intellectual* development, or with his purely *rational* behavior. Objectives concerned with his nonrational behavior, or with his emotional behavior, or objectives concerned with such things as artistic abilities, artistic and aesthetic values and tastes, moral values, attitudes toward social institutions and practices, habits relating to personal hygiene and physical fitness, managerial or

40. Lindquist (1951).
41. See Lindquist et al. (1948), Peterson (1983), Tyler (1989), Quinn (2002), and Chapter 2.
42. See Chapter 2, Lindquist et al. (1948), and ACT, Inc. (2009).
43. See, for example, Koretz (2008).

executive ability, etc., have been seriously neglected in educational measurement . . . attainment of these objectives is so difficult to measure, or that so little is known about how to measure them, just as so little is known about how to teach them effectively. —Lindquist (1951, 137–138)

His co-developer, Ralph Tyler, was more optimistic about measuring the important skills that achievement tests missed:

We lean heavily on written examinations, on a few types of objective tests, and on the subjective impressions of teachers. Many other appraisal devices could be used, such as records of activities in which pupils participate, questionnaires, check lists, anecdotal records and observational records, interviews, reports made by parents, products made by the pupils, and records made by instruments (motion pictures, eye-movement records, sound recordings, and the like). —Tyler (1940, 27)

This theme is repeated in his later writings (Tyler, 1949, 1989). We discuss evidence on the predictive value of such criteria in Chapter 9.

Tyler wrote to similar effect about the NAEP, which he created in the 1960s and is still used today to monitor the progress of American students.[44] But time and again the cost effectiveness of the standard achievement test and belief in the primacy of cognitive skills won out, and the apparently more costly evaluation of character was neglected.[45]

As discussed in Chapter 2, the GED originated from a test used to reintegrate World War II veterans back into society. These veterans had the character skills that were required to serve in the military: obedience, self-control, perseverance, and the like. The character skills of veterans were assumed to be substantial by virtue of their successful service in the military. Veterans also acquired knowledge through course work (at armed forces institutes) and through life experiences. The GED test was later applied to civilian populations as a way to solve the dropout problem and give American youth a second chance. The general population to which the GED was applied was far more heterogeneous in its character skills than were the highly disciplined World War II veterans.

Early on, the American Council on Education (ACE) admitted the limitations of its GED test:

44. See Tyler (1989), particularly "The Objectives and Plans for a National Assessment of Educational Progress" (pp. 223–226) and "National Assessment—Some Valuable By-Products for Schools" (pp. 227–237), and Rothstein et al. (2008).

45. The original NAEP was designed to include measures of character skills. See Tyler (1973; 1989, 223–237).

It should be emphasized . . . that the General Educational Development Tests do not measure all the attributes that a high school attempts to develop in its students (character, attitude, interest, etc.). The Fact-Finding Study does not suggest that the high school level General Educational Development Tests are a substitute for a formal high school education. —American Council on Education (1956, 12)

In the 1950s and 1960s, powerful forces propelled the widespread acceptance of achievement tests. A push for egalitarianism and meritocracy created a demand for objective measures of talent. The SAT was designed to identify bright kids and break the old boy networks of Ivy League schools.[46]

During the Kennedy–Johnson administration, the accountability-in-government movement further fueled the proliferation of achievement testing. Robert McNamara and the "Whiz Kids" at the Defense Department applied Taylorism to government. Specifically, they sought to apply the principles of economic cost-benefit analysis to government programs and produce a social version of a profit-loss statement.[47,48]

Lyndon Johnson's Great Society expanded these principles to a wider swath of government activity.[49] It introduced a modern version of Taylorism to monitor a broad array of social policies. Achievement test scores and IQ scores were viewed as valid and objective instruments to evaluate a series of newly launched human capital development programs. Promoting GED certification became part of a broader strategy to alleviate poverty.

Over the past 50 years, the use of tests in American education has changed greatly from serving a low-stakes advisory function to becoming a measuring rod against which schools are evaluated, funds are dispersed, and students are promoted or failed.[50] Figure 1.1 shows the spectacular growth in achievement test sales per student in elementary school or secondary school. By 1974, the U.S. Congress required that a major federal educational program (Title I) be evaluated using scores on achievement tests.[51]

The focus on accountability reached new heights with the publication of *A Nation at Risk: The Imperative for Educational Reform*, which used achieve-

46. See Lemann (1999). The SAT used to be called the Scholastic Aptitude Test, but in its most recent incarnation, the acronym has become the name.

47. See Hitch and McKean (1960) and Aaron (1978).

48. An extreme instance of this mentality was the use of body counts to measure American success in the Vietnam War.

49. See Aaron (1978).

50. See Worner (1973) and Koretz (2008).

51. Koretz (2008). NCLB is a reauthorization and expansion of this program.

Figure 1.1 Standardized Test Industry Sales per Elementary and Secondary School Student

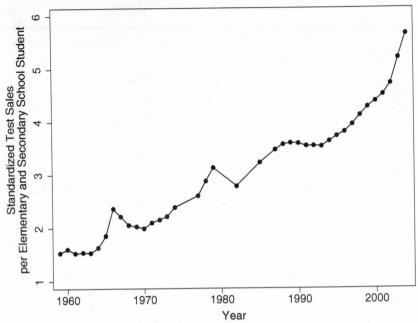

Sources: Digest of Education Statistics (Various Years); *The Bowker Annual: Library and Book Trade Almanac* (Various Years).

ment test scores to document the problems of American education.[52] From that point on, the accountability movement went wild, culminating in the No Child Left Behind (NCLB) Act in the 2000s.[53] As documented by Koretz (2008) and Rothstein, Jacobsen, and Wilder (2008), the narrow focus of the NCLB movement squeezed the curriculum to focus only on the tested domains—reading and mathematics—diminishing the emphasis on many other subjects, never mind character education. Standardized achievement tests are now a major feature of social evaluation and assessment systems. It is possible that test preparation builds certain aspects of character, but the exams fail to measure many character skills.[54] As a result, they divert the focus of the educational system to what achievement tests measure and away from important character skills.

52. National Commission on Excellence in Education (1983).
53. See Koretz (2008).
54. To the best of our knowledge, there are no scholarly studies of the enhancement in character skills arising from preparation for exams.

The secularization of American education also promoted reliance on achievement tests. The Common School Movement in the nineteenth century viewed moral and character education as an integral part of the mission of schools. There was an implicit acceptance of the ethical and moral teachings of Protestant Christianity.[55] As America became religiously and ethnically more diverse, the schools developed a more broad-based moral and ethical curriculum based on a common core of religious belief.[56] A leading historian of American education presents the following summary of Horace Mann's views on the essential nature of moral and character education:

> [I]f common schools were to attract the children of all religious sects, a common religious core of belief had to be identified. On the centrality of moral education, Mann said, "The naked capacity to read and write is no more education than a tool is a workman . . . Moral education is a primal necessity". Indeed, Mann said, "so decisive is the effect of early training upon adult habits and character", that if all children "could be brought within the reformatory and elevating influences of good schools, the dark host of private vices and public crimes, which now embitter domestic peace and stain the civilization of the age, might, in ninety-nine cases in every hundred, be banished from the world." —Kaestle (1984, 102)[57]

As American society became even more diverse in the twentieth century, pressure intensified to secularize education and eliminate any religious overtones of moral education and eventually to deemphasize it in public schools. The U.S. Supreme Court decision in *McCollum v. Board of Education* (1948) mandated the separation of church and state in the schools. Kaestle (1984) discusses how federal government involvement in the schools led to the decline in moral education and assessment of character in the schools:

> One of the key factors is the increased involvement of the federal government. In deciding a series of religious cases, federal jurists have developed a line of thinking about the separation of church and state that underlines a secular definition of public education. Decisions about religious exercises in state schools and financial aid to parochial schools have reinforced the notion that one can distinguish between

55. See, for example, Kaestle (1984) and Cremin (1988).
56. Kaestle (1984, 102).
57. The Kaestle composite is based on Mann (1847, 53) and Mann (1848, 90, 95–96).

secular and religious education and that governments may fund only secular education. —Kaestle (1984, 108)

Since moral education and assessment were perceived to be founded on religious and moral beliefs, any hint of moral education in schools flirted with violation of the boundaries between church and state. Character education was left to the family and the church. During the 1960s when moral education and evaluation were deemphasized, American families were, by and large, functioning entities that could provide adequate instructions in morality and character, even if it was lacking in the schools.

The federal government's intervention in the schools was not limited to separating church and state. In the 1960s and 1970s, the civil rights revolution broadened to guarantee the "rights of students." As documented in Arum (2005), a series of court cases, many initiated by the Legal Services Administration, protected the rights of students and introduced explicit prohibitions on disciplinary practices into the school systems.[58] Traditionally, student discipline was one method for enforcing and instilling character skills.[59] Arum documents how school discipline declined in those regions where litigation was most successful in limiting the rights of teachers to discipline students.

Reinforcing these trends was the emergence of cognitive psychology, which influenced the design and evaluation of school curricula. Jerome Bruner's classic study (1956) appeared to justify a cognitive focus in schools. Reinforcing this trend, an influential book by Mischel (1968) claimed that there were no stable character skills. They were thought too ephemeral in nature and too difficult to measure despite Tyler's concrete suggestions and a rich body of work in personality psychology measuring those skills. Achievement tests and IQ tests were in hand to measure cognition. A cognitive focus appeared to have strong intellectual support, did not infringe on student rights, nor did it bring religion into the schools. It was also viewed as ethically neutral and satisfied the goals of cultural pluralism. Again quoting Kaestle:

But where nineteenth-century educators had asserted that the chief aim of common schooling was moral education—and even their Progressive descendants of the mid-twentieth century had stressed the ethical

58. See also Wise (1979).
59. See Durkheim (1973) and the discussions in Beck, Crittenden, and Sullivan (1971).

socialization of the "whole child"—the emphasis of the 1960s was cognitive: it was on schooling for equal achievement, for pay-off, as well as education of the talented, guided by the new heady curricula of the Bruner generation. While moral education had receded as an educational goal because of pressing cognitive goals, two other developments also affected the schools' approach to moral authority. The potential for a more genuine cultural pluralism flowed from the attention to minority rights. The ideal and the reality of cultural pluralism made educators in the more heterogeneous school settings re-examine some of the comfortable assumptions of an ethnocentric morality. The virtues of manliness, competitive individualism, standard English, future orientation, and Anglo-Saxon superiority could no longer be taken for granted.
—Kaestle (1984, 109)

In sum, numerous cultural, legal, and intellectual factors, as well as technological changes, shifted the emphasis of American education toward cognition. Character education became suspect, and character itself became a "soft skill" deemed as unstable and impossible to adequately measure. The growing diversity in the American population favored a more inclusive curriculum, less oriented toward character education that appeared to have inherently subjective elements associated with it and that appeared to some to introduce middle-class values and religion into the schools and intrude on the prerogatives of the family. The entry of the federal government into the financing and control of education sharpened the separation of church and state and accelerated the decline of character education and character evaluation in schools. At the same time, educational and psychological theories favored cognition over character. Tools had been developed to measure cognition, and they were deemed to be rigorously validated.

The achievement tests developed in the first half of the twentieth century provided grist for the accountability mill, which became increasingly influential as the federal government entered into the arena of public education. Standardized tests promoted uniformity and equality of treatment and satisfied a growing demand for meritocracy. Taylorism, Tylerism, and Brunerism shaped the curriculum of mid-twentieth-century American schools and fostered reliance on achievement tests. The growth of GED testing was part of a broader application of achievement tests throughout American society.

1.3 The Modern GED Test

The GED exam is a seven-and-a-half hour achievement test that covers writing, social studies, science, reading, and mathematics. Most questions on the exam are multiple choice, but the exam also includes a short essay (GED Testing Service, 1959–2008). Scores cumulate across testing occasions. Students who fail sections of the exam can retake them without retaking the portions that they have passed.[60] The math and reading tests attempt to measure the ability to problem-solve, interpret, and synthesize, rather than factual recall. Table 1.1 shows examples of GED test questions.

The GED is a typical achievement test. Table 1.2 shows that GED test scores are highly correlated with scores on other standardized achievement tests. The correlations range from 0.61 with the General Aptitude Test Battery (GATB) to 0.88 with the Iowa Test of Educational Development, the progenitor of the GED.[61] A central issue explored in this book is how well these tests predict important life outcomes.

Since the introduction of the test in 1942, its content and difficulty have changed several times. Table 1.3 shows the key changes to the GED exam. The content has been updated three times with new "series" designed to be relevant for job skills and postsecondary education. The American Council on Education is planning to introduce a new test in 2014.[62]

The passing threshold was originally normed so that 80% of graduation-bound high school seniors could pass (Boesel, Alsalam, and Smith, 1998; Quinn, 2002). An analysis of the 1943 norming study suggests that the 80% pass rate overstates the actual difficulty of the original test (Quinn, 2002). Quinn claims that there was a high probability of passing the original test due to chance, that is, by guessing. Now 60% of current graduation-bound high school seniors are estimated to be able to pass the entire test on their first try (GED Testing Service, 2009). Boesel, Alsalam, and Smith (1998) cite studies claiming that the test certifies knowledge at the eighth- to ninth-grade level.

As the letter reprinted in the Preface to this book vividly describes, for most GED test takers, preparing for the GED does not entail much basic

---

60. See Jepsen, Mueser, and Troske (2011) on the exact rules for retaking the exam; they vary by state. Most pass on the first attempt, but a significant fraction retake the test.

61. See Chapter 2.

62. See GED Testing Service (2012).

Table 1.1 GED Sample Questions

Test Subject	Sample Question
Writing	Sentence 1: **Some people, catch crappie from the shoreline or from a dock.** Which correction should be made to sentence 1? (1) replace Some with Many (2) remove comma after people (3) change catch to caught (4) change from the shoreline to on the shoreline (5) no correction is necessary
Math	If $8x + 16 = 32$, what is x? A) 8 B) 2 C) 4 D) 3 E) 7
Science	Some beach sands in Alaska currently are being worked for gold. Because there are large gold deposits inland, the soils and sediments along the Alaskan coast contain traces of gold. Which of the following **BEST** explains why the gold is concentrated on those beaches? (1) Dense gold particles are left behind as the waves wash away other materials. (2) The gold was floated onto the shore in icebergs, which have completely melted. (3) The large tidal waves from frequent earthquakes wash the gold onto the shore. (4) Low water temperatures prevent the gold from dissolving as it does elsewhere. (5) Many treasure-laden ships have broken up on those dangerous shores.
Social Sciences	[Initiative] Sec. 8. (a) The initiative is the power of the electors to propose statutes and amendments to the Constitution and to adopt or reject them. (b) An initiative measure may be proposed by presenting the Secretary of State a petition that sets forth the text of the proposed statute or amendment to the Constitution and is certified to have been signed by electors equal in number to 5 percent in the case of a statute, and 8 percent in the case of an amendment to the Constitution, of the votes for all candidates for Governor at the last gubernatorial election. To qualify an initiative to amend the state Constitution, how many voters must sign the petition? (1) 52% of the voters in the state (2) 5% of the voters in the state (3) 8% of the voters in the state (4) 5% of the voters who voted for Governor in the last election (5) 8% of the voters who voted for Governor in the last election

Source: Reproduced from Bobrow (2002).
Note: The source is a preparation guide for the most recent 2002 series of the GED test.

Table 1.2 Validities of GED Test (Correlations with Other Measures of Cognition)

Test	Correlation	Source
Armed Forces Qualification Test (AFQT)	0.75–0.79[†]	Means and Laurence (1984)
Iowa Test of Educational Development	0.88[†]	Boesel, Alsalam, and Smith (1998)
American College Test (ACT)	0.80[†]	Boesel, Alsalam, and Smith (1998)
Adult Performance Level (APL) Survey	0.81[†]	Boesel, Alsalam, and Smith (1998)
New York's Degrees of Reading Power (DRP) Test	0.77[†]	Boesel, Alsalam, and Smith (1998)
Test of Adult Basic Education (TABE)	0.66–0.68[†]	Boesel, Alsalam, and Smith (1998)
General Aptitude Test Battery (GATB)	0.61–0.67[†]	Boesel, Alsalam, and Smith (1998)
National Adult Literacy Survey (NALS) factor	0.78[‡]	Baldwin (1995)

Sources: GED Testing Service (1959–2008), Quinn (2002), and GED Testing Service (2009).
[†]Uses mean GED subtest scores.
[‡]Uses a general GED factor.

learning. Figure 1.2 shows the distribution of the amount of time spent studying for the GED exam by test takers in 1980 and 1989. In 1980, the median test taker studied for 20 hours and, in 1989, for 30 hours (GED Testing Service, 1959–2008; Quinn, 2002).[63] More recently, Zhang, Han, and Patterson (2009) found that in 2006 the median study time for those who reported studying for the GED was 32 hours. Earning a high school diploma requires much more effort. An average high school student spends approximately 1,080 hours in class each year, excluding time spent studying and completing homework (Carroll, 1990), and spends 410 hours per year attending core high school courses.[64] It is unlikely that the knowledge acquired while cramming for the GED substitutes for knowledge learned from attending classes.

63. This amount applies only to test takers not qualifying as exceptions to the minimum age requirement.
64. Boesel, Alsalam, and Smith (1998).

Table 1.3 Key Changes to the GED

Year	Changes to the GED Testing Program
1942	GED test introduced for veterans. 80% of graduation-bound high school seniors said to be able to pass all five batteries.
1947	New York offers GED test to civilian high school dropouts.
1959	More civilians taking the GED test than veterans.
1974	California becomes last state to introduce GED test for dropouts.
1978	Second series of the GED test introduced. Test time of 6 hours.
1981	Time limit extended to 6.75 hours. National minimum age for testing abolished.
1982	Standards made more difficult, 75% of graduation-bound high school seniors said to be able to pass the entire test.
1988	Third series of GED test introduced. First series to include a writing sample. Time extended to 7.5 hours for taking the test.
1992	National minimum age for GED test taking of 16 implemented.
1997	Passing standards made more difficult, 67% of graduation-bound high school seniors said to be able to pass the entire test.
2002	Fourth series of the GED test introduced. Calculator allowed for first time on parts of the math test. Passing standards made more difficult; 60% of graduation-bound high school seniors said to be able to pass the entire test. Test time of approximately 7 hours.

Sources: GED Testing Service (1959–2008), Quinn (2002), and GED Testing Service (2009).
Note: Reproduced from Heckman, Humphries, and Mader (2011).

1.3.1 GROWTH OF THE GED TEST

The accountability movement in government created a demand for "performance-driven" policies. Because GED recipients were perceived to be the equivalents of ordinary high school graduates, production of GED certificates was deemed a worthy goal.

Since its introduction in civilian populations, government institutions have promoted the GED certificate and incentivized its use (see Chapter 3). The growth of the welfare state explains a substantial part of the growth of GED certification. To many policy makers, the GED appears to be a valid and cost-effective substitute for high school graduation. As an example, a 2009 report on the GED in New York City claimed that, over a person's lifetime, those without a high school diploma cost the city $135,000 in public services, while those with only a high school diploma benefit the city with $190,000 of taxes, net of costs. Its conclusion was as follows:

Figure 1.2 Hours Spent Studying for the Test by the GED Test Takers

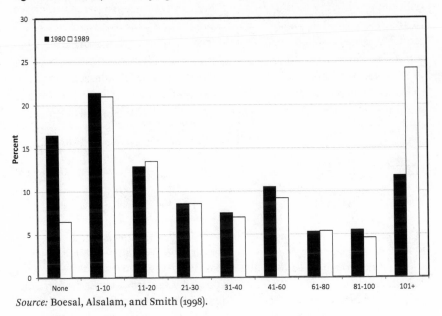

Source: Boesal, Alsalam, and Smith (1998).

Thus, in the aggregate, simply helping one low-skilled New Yorker earn a high school degree or GED is worth more than $325,000 to the city. —Treschan and Fischer (2009, 1)

This sentiment is widespread in many quarters of American society. A number of job training programs promote GED certification.[65] Adult basic education programs prepare students to take the GED test. GED certificates can qualify individuals for welfare. Jails provide incentives for prisoners to obtain GED certificates.[66] The government allocates funds to remedial education programs based on the number of GED certificates issued. Many laws prevent employers from treating GED recipients differently from high school graduates.[67]

65. These job training programs include the Manpower Development and Training Act (MDTA), the Comprehensive Employment and Training Act (CETA), the Job Training Partnership Act (JTPA), and the Work Force Investment (WIA) Act. These are discussed in Chapter 3.

66. See Chapter 3.

67. See Commonwealth of Pennsylvania (1955) and Web Appendix W1.1.15 for a variety of laws that mandate the equivalence between the GED and the high school diploma.

The rise in state-mandated high school exit examinations further contributed to the growth of GED recipiency. In response to perceived crises in American education over the last three decades, states have increasingly required students to pass achievement tests before graduating from high school. Schools are evaluated based on the fraction of students who pass.

Students who are unable to pass high school exit examinations turn to the GED as an alternative. Until recently, it was possible for schools to manipulate state accountability measures by encouraging low-performing students to earn a GED certificate so that those students are not counted in the school's passing rate.[68] This topic is discussed further in Chapters 3 and 8.

1.4 Social and Economic Benefits of the GED Program

1.4.1 ATTRIBUTES OF GED RECIPIENTS

Chapter 4 demonstrates that in multiple samples collected over the past 30-plus years, GED recipients fall short of traditional high school graduates. As a group, GED recipients are as smart as high school graduates who do not attend college, but they lack character. Figure 1.3 shows the distribution of cognitive ability for high school graduates, GED recipients, and other high school dropouts.[69] For both males and females, GED recipients are much more similar to high school graduates than to high school dropouts.

If, as a group, GED recipients are as smart as high school graduates who do not attend college, why do they drop out of high school? GED recipients lack the character skills required to complete high school. Figure 1.4 shows the distribution of character, as measured by risky behaviors during adolescence.[70] GED recipients are almost identical to other dropouts by this measure, whereas high school graduates are much better. In Chapter 4, we show that similar patterns arise across four different data sets for many adolescent behaviors, including sex, drinking, drug use, violent behavior, petty crimes, major crimes, school attendance, grades, and enrollment in remedial classes.

Differences in skills across dropouts, GED recipients, and high school graduates emerge early and are linked in part to family backgrounds. Compared to high school graduates, GED recipients and dropouts are more likely to come from broken families, have mothers with lower levels of education,

68. Starting with the graduating class of 2011–2012, states are required to count GED recipients as high school dropouts in official statistics (Department of Education, 2008).

69. The sample excludes people who attend college.

70. These measures implement Tyler's insight (1940) that adolescent behaviors can provide valid measures of character skills.

Figure 1.3 Distribution of Cognitive Ability by Educational Status (No College Sample, All Ethnic Groups)

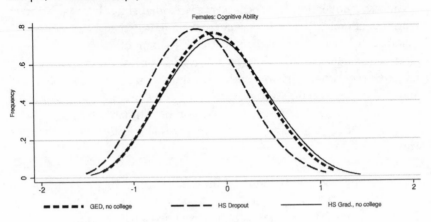

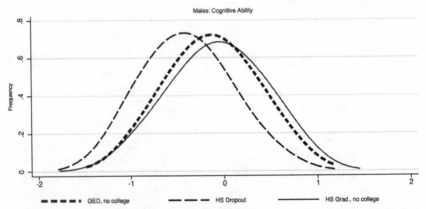

Source: Reproduced from Heckman et al. (2011), which uses data from the National Longitudinal Study of Youth, 1979 (NLSY79).

Notes: The distributions represent cognitive factors, estimated using a subset of the Armed Services Vocational Aptitude Battery (ASVAB). The factors are adjusted for educational attainment, as laid out in Hansen, Heckman, and Mullen (2004). The sample is restricted to the cross-sectional subsample for both males and females. Distributions show only those with no postsecondary educational attainment. The cognitive factors are normalized by gender to be mean zero, standard deviation one.

Figure 1.4 Distribution of Character Skills by Education Group

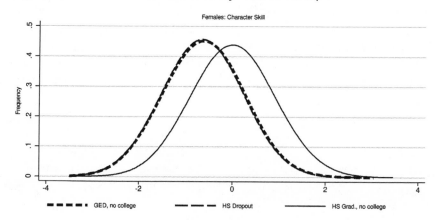

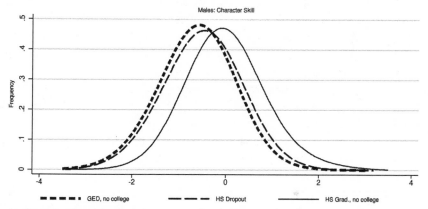

Source: Reproduced from Heckman et al. (2011), which uses data from the National Longitudinal Study of Youth, 1979 (NLSY79).

Notes: The distributions represent noncognitive factors, estimated using measures of early violent crime, minor crime, marijuana use, regular smoking, drinking, and early sexual intercourse. Sample restricted to the cross-sectional subsample for both males and females. Distributions show only those with no postsecondary educational attainment. The noncognitive factors are normalized to be mean zero, standard deviation one.

and receive lower levels of parental investment. The gaps in skills apparent in Figures 1.3 and 1.4 emerge by age 6. These findings suggest that many children are destined to drop out of high school at a very young age unless their character skills are bolstered. Chapter 9 discusses interventions that target children born into disadvantage and effectively combat the school dropout problem. Many of these programs work by improving character skills.

1.4.2 EDUCATIONAL AND LABOR MARKET BENEFITS OF THE GED

The GED is a second-chance program, created with the implicit premise that people may change after making mistakes in adolescence. Adolescence is a time of self-discovery when people push boundaries and experiment with risky activities. Some dropouts might outgrow early problem behaviors and flourish later in life. The GED could be a lifeline for them.

The GED certificate might confer valuable benefits to its recipients. The GED program might promote human capital accumulation by encouraging test takers to enhance their skills to pass the exam. Another benefit might be the signal it sends. It might convey to schools and the market valuable information about the skills of recipients compared to uncertified dropouts even if skills are not acquired in studying for the exam. We investigate these hypotheses and reject them. The wages of GEDs are the same before and after they take the exam.

The GED certificate also provides an option value by allowing recipients to attend college. It opens doors to higher education because many postsecondary institutions accept the GED as equivalent to a high school degree for admitting students. While many GED recipients attempt college, few GED recipients graduate. For most GEDs, the same deficits in character skills that caused them to drop out of high school cause them to drop out of postsecondary education.

Chapter 5 studies the economic and social outcomes of GED recipients through age 40 and finds that most GED recipients continue to lack the skills that caused them to drop out of high school in the first place. Figure 1.5 shows the postsecondary educational attainment of dropouts, GED recipients, and high school graduates. About 40% of GED recipients attend some college. Only half complete more than one year. Only 3%–4% earn bachelor's degrees, although 5%–9% earn associate's degrees. These rates are considerably lower than those for regular high school graduates—27% for bachelor's and 14% for associate's degrees, respectively. Compared to GED recipients, high school graduates who attend college are about twice as likely to earn a degree.[71] In all cases, the differences between high school

Figure 1.5 Postsecondary Educational Attainment across Education Groups through Age 40 (NLSY79)—All Races

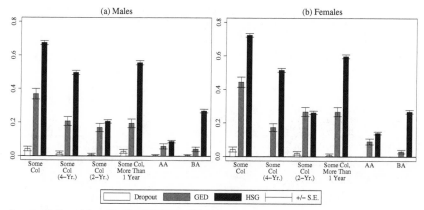

Source: National Longitudinal Survey of Youth, 1979.
Notes: The graph displays the postsecondary educational attainment of dropouts, GED recipients, and high school graduates through age 40. The bars indicate the standard errors, a measure of sampling uncertainty. *Variable Definitions:* "Some Col"—people who entered any postsecondary institution. "Some Col (4-Yr.)"—people who entered a 4-year college. "Some Col (2-Yr.)"—people who entered a 2-year college and never entered a 4-year college. "Some Col, More Than 1 Year"—people who completed at least a year of some postsecondary education. "AA"—people who obtained an associate's degree. "BA"—people who obtained a bachelor's degree. "BA" also includes people with higher education: master's, Ph.D., and professional degrees. Tests of significance are reported in Chapter 5.

graduates and GED recipients are statistically significant, and, for most cases, so are the differences between GED recipients and dropouts.[72]

Figures 1.6 and 1.7 show the performance of GED recipients and high school graduates in the labor market compared to other dropouts. For each outcome, the first pair of bar charts shows the effects of GED certification (the first in the pair) and ordinary high school graduation (the second in the pair) relative to uncertified dropouts after controlling for age, race, and region of residence. The second pair shows GED effects after additionally controlling for the Armed Forces Qualification Test (AFQT), a measure of scholastic ability. In both figures we display standard error bars.

71. Web Appendix tables W1.2.1 and W1.2.2 show education progression and attainment probabilities for GED recipients and high school graduates.
72. See Chapter 5 and Web Appendix 5.

Figure 1.6 Labor Market Differences Compared to Uncertified Dropouts—Ages 20–39 (Males, All Levels of Postsecondary Education)

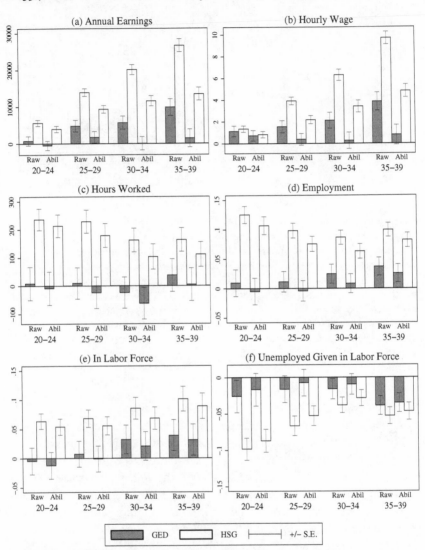

Source: National Longitudinal Survey of Youth, 1979.

Notes: Controls: "Raw"—age and region or state of residence; "Abil"—AFQT adjusted for schooling at time of test. Regressions exclude those reporting earning more than $300,000 or working more than 4,000 hours. The intervals around each bar are standard errors centered around the mean—a measure of sampling variability. All regressions allow for clustered standard errors at the individual level. Tests of significance are presented in Chapter 5.

Figure 1.7 Labor Market Differences Compared to Uncertified Dropouts—Ages 20–39 (Females, All Levels of Postsecondary Education)

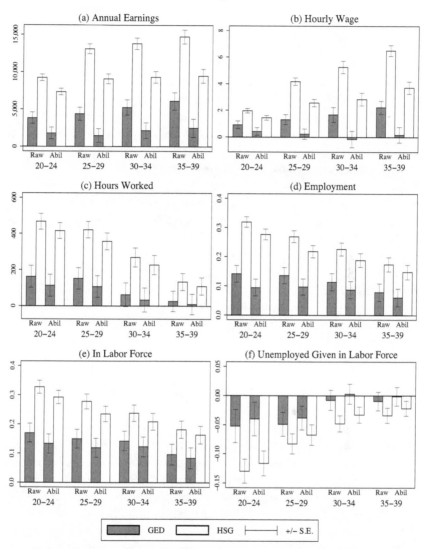

Source: National Longitudinal Survey of Youth, 1979.
Notes: Controls: "Raw"—age and region or state of residence; "Abil"—AFQT adjusted for schooling at time of test. Regressions exclude those reporting earning more than $300,000 or working more than 4,000 hours. The intervals around each bar are standard errors centered around the mean—a measure of sampling variability. All regressions allow for clustered standard errors at the individual level. Tests of significance are presented in Chapter 5.

GED recipients and high school graduates outperform uncertified drop-outs if one only adjusts for age, race, and region of residence. After adjusting for scores on an achievement test (the AFQT), outcomes of male GED recipients are nearly identical to those of other dropouts. Female GED recipients have higher earnings compared to other dropouts, but only because they supply more labor to the market. They do not have higher hourly wages and do not have greater life-cycle wage growth with work experience compared to that of other dropouts. Female GED recipients are more likely than other dropouts to participate in the labor force but are not more likely to be employed, given that they enter the labor force. In virtually all cases, the differences between high school graduates and GED recipients are statistically significant, while the differences between GED recipients and dropouts are not.[73] Controlling for a standard set of background variables does not change this story.[74]

Two groups of women appear to benefit from GED certification. The first group consists of girls who get pregnant and reenter school after their children are old enough to place in child care. Their adolescent character skills are relatively strong compared to those of other dropouts. It is possible that they would have been more attached to the labor force even if they did not earn a GED certification. They have experienced an adverse shock from which they partially recover. The second group is made up of girls who do not get pregnant but have low levels of baseline character skills. They appear to improve their character as they mature. Many go to college.

However, character skills are generally very persistent over time for most groups. Chapter 5 shows that the same skill deficits that cause GED recipients to drop out persist throughout adult life. They divorce and commit crimes at greater rates than high school graduates and are less likely to be employed. Chapter 6 shows that GED recipients drop out of the military at similar, if not higher, rates than other high school dropouts. For this reason, the military now only accepts GED recipients under special circumstances.

Even if earning a GED does not improve skills, the certificate might act as a signal in the labor market. We evaluate this possibility by comparing the labor market performance of GED recipients before and after they receive the certificate. We find little evidence that for most participants the GED is a useful signal of skills present before GED certification.[75] Eventual GED recipients earn the same wages before and after they GED certify.

73. See Chapter 5 and Web Appendix 5 for tests of significance.
74. See Chapter 5 and Web Appendix 5 for analyses that control for other background variables.
75. See Chapter 5 and Cameron and Heckman (1993).

Clark and Jaeger (2006) argue that the GED promotes immigrant assimilation by providing a signal of ability that is more familiar to employers than educational credentials earned outside the United States, or by signaling language skills and cultural assimilation of GED certifiers. The authors analyze earnings data from the Current Population Survey and claim that foreign-born GED recipients with no domestic educational credentials have statistically significantly higher wages than non-GED recipients or native-born dropouts.

Chapter 5 summarizes the evidence in Heckman and LaFontaine (2006) who question the Clark and Jaeger (2006) conclusions. The Clark–Jaeger results are driven by data artifacts and limitations. After accounting for selection, differences in cognitive ability, and cohort effects, there is no earnings premium for any group of immigrant GED recipients.

1.4.3 THE OPTION VALUE OF THE GED

One reason for acquiring a GED is to attain further education (see Figure 1.8). Indeed, the growth in GED certification tracks the rise in the return to postsecondary schooling (see Figure 1.9).

Figure 1.8 Reported Reasons for GED Certification

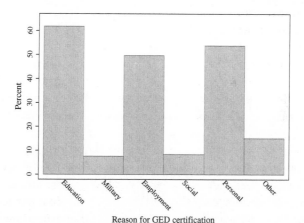

Reason for GED certification

Source: Reproduced from American Council on Education (2009).

Notes: Educational reasons include attending a 4-year college, attending a 2-year college, attending a technical or trade program, and job training. Military reasons include military entrance and military career. Employment reasons include get a first job, keep current job, get better job, and employer required. Social reasons include early release, court order, and public assistance requirement. Personal reasons include positive role model and personal satisfaction. Responses are not necessarily mutually exclusive.

Figure 1.9 College/High-School Log Weekly Wage Ratio, 1963–2008

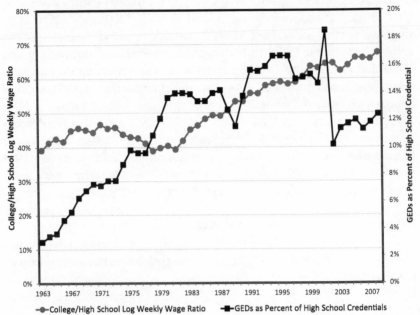

Sources: Reproduced from Acemoglu and Autor (2011); *Digest of Education Statistics* (Various Years); GED Testing Service (Various Years).

Notes: The sharp drop in the proportion taking the GED in 2000 (and the rise just before it) comes from a pre-announced increase in the GED passing standards and a reform in the system that wiped out cumulated scores on past tests. Thus students in the middle of the certification process had to start their GED records from scratch.

The GED benefits a select few who pursue postsecondary education. For these people, the GED has an "option value" because the GED is a pathway to further education, which usually leads to higher earnings. The bulk of any estimated wage or earnings benefit to receiving a GED arises from the option value it confers. The option value for both male and female GEDs tends to be small. For men it is not statistically significantly different from zero at any age. It is larger and statistically significant at most ages for women, but it constitutes much less than half of the total effect of the GED. There is little evidence of any option value benefit for men.

Any benefits from further educational attainment are diminished by the delay in completing schooling associated with dropping out of high school. Even though GEDs who become college graduates have annual earnings comparable to those of other college graduates, the present value of their lifetime earnings is at least 30% lower due to their delay in obtaining their degrees.

1.5 The GED Program Distorts Social Statistics

A one-dimensional focus of public policy on "smarts" conceals major problems by distorting social statistics and by misdirecting the efforts of institutions and individuals. Heckman and LaFontaine (2010) show that counting GED recipients as high school graduates paints a rosy but false picture of the health of the American educational system. If GED recipients are properly counted as high school dropouts, the U.S. high school dropout rate has increased slightly since the early 1960s. This trend is worrying because the return to high school graduation has risen dramatically in the past 30 years.[76]

The rising high school dropout rate helps to explain the recent slowdown in the growth of skills in the American economy and the rise in inequality. At a time when skilled labor has become more valuable and when a high-skill workforce is needed to compete in the world economy and to meet fiscal challenges, America's rate of producing skills has decelerated. Thirty years ago, America had the highest rates of college graduation in the world. Today it is ranked fourteenth (OECD, 2012).

Official statistics suggest that the black–white gap in high school attainment has converged substantially. However, the reported convergence is an illusion manufactured in part by the GED program. Heckman and LaFontaine (2010) show that the apparent educational advance of black males is in large part due to their higher rates of GED certification. Part of the growth in GEDs is attributable to higher black male incarceration rates and the production of GED credentials in prison. Prisoners are not counted in many official statistics on educational attainment. Since most prisoners are high school dropouts, their removal from social statistics inflates the measured high school graduation rate for black males. In addition, many black males obtain GED certificates while incarcerated. If we properly count GED recipients as dropouts, there has been *no* progress in black male high school attainment rates over the past 50 years.

It is revealing that the GED program persists, despite all of the evidence that it is not working. Palliative solutions dominate public policy discussions despite a growing awareness that America has to address long-run

76. See Heckman, Lochner, and Todd (2006).

structural problems.[77] The continued reliance on the GED is part of a broader pattern of self-deception and misrepresentation in American public life.

1.5.1 THE GED INDUCES POTENTIAL HIGH SCHOOL GRADUATES TO DROP OUT

In addition to concealing problems, the GED program creates them by inducing students to drop out of high school. Society recognizes that adolescents are not fully capable of making some important decisions. There are age restrictions on smoking tobacco, drinking, and joining the army. Even though adolescents are not fully mature, they make life-shaping decisions.

Recent evidence from neuroscience suggests that the evolution of the brain with age leads to increased risky behavior among teens. Steinberg (2008) argues that different parts of the brain mature at different rates and that the part that governs the choice of risky activities does not mature until early adulthood. Many adolescents make decisions that yield short-run benefits but have adverse long-run consequences. Choosing to drop out of high school is one such decision. The GED offers a temptation that many cannot resist.

Students report that they obtain a GED because it is easier than finishing high school. A 2002 survey by the National Center for Education Statistics (2006) found that roughly 40% of surveyed high school dropouts listed "would be easier to get the GED" as among their reasons for leaving school.[78] Behind "Missed too many school days," this was the second most frequently cited reason for leaving. Chapter 7 shows that the GED program induces people to drop out. In Oregon, the introduction of programs that facilitate GED preparation and certification in high schools increased the dropout rate in the affected schools by 4%. The analysis of Chapter 8 shows how the growth of high-stakes testing—another manifestation of the push for accountability in government—fosters production of GEDs.

1.6 What Achievement Tests Miss

The poor performance of GED recipients points to a more fundamental problem with the accountability movement in American education. The

---

77. See Rajan (2010) and the National Commission on Fiscal Responsibility and Reform (2010) (commonly referred to as Simpson-Bowles).

78. See Chapter 7, Table 7.1.

GED, a prototypical standardized achievement test, fails to capture character skills that matter in life. Psychologists and economists have studied character skills and have shown that they are predictive of many life outcomes. Chapter 9 summarizes and extends this literature.[79]

Achievement tests are typically validated using other achievement tests, IQ tests, and grades, rather than with tasks or outcomes that matter. Table 1.4 shows correlations among scores on standardized achievement tests, IQ tests, and grades. Standardized achievement tests are correlated with IQ tests, but the correlation depends on the subject area of the standardized achievement test. Hartlage and Steele (1977) report that the arithmetic portions of standardized achievement tests are more highly correlated with IQ than other portions. Grades and scores on IQ tests and standardized achievement tests are far from perfectly correlated, however, suggesting that they measure different aspects of "cognitive functioning."[80]

Psychologists distinguish between fluid intelligence (the rate at which people learn) and crystallized intelligence (acquired knowledge).[81] Achievement tests are heavily weighted toward crystallized intelligence,[82] whereas IQ tests like Raven's progressive matrices (1962) are heavily weighted toward fluid intelligence.[83,84] Many psychologists and economists do not recognize the differences among these measures and use IQ, achievement tests, and grades interchangeably to measure "cognitive ability" or "intelligence."[85]

Validating cognitive ability tests using other measures of cognitive ability is inherently circular. A more relevant measure is how these tests predict outcomes that matter. Table 1.5 shows the extent to which IQ, standardized achievement tests, and grades are correlated with meaningful

79. See also the surveys in Borghans et al. (2008) and Almlund et al. (2011).

80. It is an irony of the testing literature that high school grades are more predictive of first-year college performance than SAT scores (Bowen, Chingos, and McPherson, 2009). The SAT and related tests were once thought to be more objective and more accurate measures of student quality than high school grades (Lemann, 1999).

81. See, for example, Nisbett et al. (2012).

82. Roberts et al. (2000).

83. Raven, Raven, and Court (1988). The high correlation between intelligence and achievement tests is in part due to the fact that both require cognitive ability and knowledge. Common developmental factors may affect both of these skills, and fluid intelligence promotes the acquisition of crystallized intelligence.

84. Carroll (1993) and Ackerman and Heggestad (1997) discuss more disaggregated facets of cognitive ability.

85. See Flynn (2007) and Nisbett et al. (2012). For examples in economics, see Brinch and Galloway (2012) and Benjamin, Brown, and Shapiro (2013).

Table 1.4 Psychometric Validities (Correlations) of Measures of Cognitive Ability with Other Measures

Test	Validation Domain	Estimate(s)	Source(s)
SAT (Achievement)	1st Year College GPA	0.35–0.53	Kobrin et al. (2008)
ACT (Achievement)	Early College GPA	0.42	ACT, Inc. (2007)
GED (Achievement)	HS Senior GPA	0.33–0.49	GED Testing Service (2009)
DAT (Achievement)	College GPA	0.13–0.62[†]	Omizo (1980)
AFQT (Achievement)	9th Grade GPA	0.54	Borghans et al. (2011)
WAIS (IQ)	College GPA	0.38–0.43	Feingold (1982)
WAIS (IQ)	HS GPA	0.62	Feingold (1982)
Various IQ**	9th Grade GPA	0.42	Borghans et al. (2011)
WISC (IQ)	WRAT (Achievement)	0.44–0.75[‡]	Hartlage and Steele (1977)
WISC–R (IQ)	WRAT (Achievement)	0.35–0.76[‡]	Hartlage and Steele (1977)
Various IQ**	AFQT (Achievement)	0.65	Borghans et al. (2011)
Stanford Binet (IQ)	WISC–R (IQ)	0.77–0.87	Rothlisberg (1987); Greene, Sapp, and Chissom (1990)
Raven's (IQ)	WAIS–R (IQ)	0.74–0.84	O'Leary, Rusch, and Guastello (1991)
WIAT (Achievement)	CAT/2 (Achievement)	0.69–0.83*	Michalko and Saklofske (1996)

Definitions: WISC – Wechsler Intelligence Scale for Children, WISC–R – Wechsler Intelligence Scale for Children - Revised, WAIS - Wechsler Adult Intelligence Scale, Raven's IQ – Raven's Standard Progressive Matrices, GED – General Educational Development, DAT – Differential Aptitude Test, WIAT – Wechsler Individual Achievement Test, CAT – California Achievement Test, WRAT – Wide Range Achievement Test.

[†]Large range is due to varying validity of eight subtests of DAT.

[‡]Ranges are given because correlations vary by academic subject.

*Ranges are given because correlations vary by grade level.

**IQ test scores in the NLSY79 are pooled across several IQ tests using IQ percentiles.

life outcomes at age 35 in data from the National Longitudinal Survey of Youth, 1979 (NLSY79). The three groups of columns under each category show estimates for different subsamples that vary depending on the availability of the cognitive measures indicated at the top of the columns. For each category, the first column shows the correlation using only the designated measure of cognitive ability.[86] Achievement tests and grades are more predictive than IQ. But none of these measures explains much of the variation of any outcome, leaving considerable room for the operation of other factors. It is unlikely that measurement error accounts for most of the remaining variance.[87]

Character is an important missing ingredient. The second columns in each category display the explanatory power of measures of character. They show the correlation between the designated outcome and the measures of character.[88] In many cases, the predictive power of our measures of character rivals that of cognitive ability. The relative importance of character depends on the outcome considered.[89] The third columns for each subsample show the multiple correlation coefficient when both the cognitive and character measures are used as predictors. In many cases our measures of character are incrementally predictive, so that including them in a regression with cognitive measures increases explained variance. The correlations between the set of measures of character and the measures of cognition are positive, but not especially strong (see the bottom row of each table). Both character and cognition have independent predictive power.

Measures of character predict many life outcomes beyond those shown in Table 1.5. Of the commonly studied character skills, Conscientiousness— the tendency to be hard-working and persistent—is the most predictive. Conscientiousness rivals IQ in predicting educational attainment, job performance, and health.[90] Table 1.6 shows correlations between SAT

86. See Almlund et al. (2011) for a more complete array of outcomes in the format of Table 1.5.

87. See Bound, Brown, and Mathiowetz (2001). At most 25%–30% of the variance in hourly wages is due to measurement error.

88. They include measures of adolescent risky behavior, self-esteem, and locus of control (the extent to which people feel they have control over their lives). For precise definitions of the measures used, see the notes to Table 1.5.

89. Arguably, the limited measures of personality used to construct the estimates reported in Table 1.5 understate the predictive power of personality. See Heckman and Kautz (2012).

90. See Almlund et al. (2011).

Table 1.5 Predictive Validities of Measures of Cognition and Character in Outcomes that Matter (Adjusted Correlations)

Males	IQ Sample			AFQT Sample			GPA Sample		
	IQ	Non-Cog	Both	AFQT	Non-Cog	Both	GPA	Non-Cog	Both
Earnings at Age 35	0.26	0.22	0.30	0.41	0.26	0.43	0.30	0.25	0.34
Hourly Wage at Age 35	0.27	0.16	0.28	0.36	0.25	0.38	0.26	0.24	0.31
Hours Worked at Age 35	0.10	0.19	0.19	0.17	0.12	0.18	0.12	0.11	0.14
Jail by Age 35	0.17	0.15	0.20	0.25	0.24	0.30	0.17	0.17	0.21
Welfare at Age 35	0.08	0.06	0.09	0.17	0.10	0.17	0.09	0.07	0.10
Married at Age 35	0.09	0.23	0.23	0.20	0.18	0.24	0.17	0.16	0.20
BA Degree by Age 35	0.34	0.28	0.40	0.44	0.31	0.47	0.37	0.31	0.42
Depression in 1992	0.12	0.22	0.23	0.19	0.20	0.24	0.14	0.19	0.21
Adjusted, R Cog, Character	0.26			0.41			0.33		

Females	IQ Sample			AFQT Sample			GPA Sample		
	IQ	Non-Cog	Both	AFQT	Non-Cog	Both	GPA	Non-Cog	Both
Earnings at Age 35	0.12	0.16	0.18	0.29	0.23	0.32	0.22	0.20	0.26
Hourly Wage at Age 35	0.22	0.17	0.25	0.35	0.23	0.37	0.25	0.21	0.29
Hours Worked at Age 35	0.00	0.14	0.14	0.01	0.07	0.07	0.03	0.08	0.08
Jail by Age 35	0.00	0.08	0.07	0.10	0.12	0.14	0.11	0.10	0.13

Welfare at Age 35	0.15	0.19	0.21	0.32	0.23	0.35	0.22	0.22	0.27
Married at Age 35	0.17	0.17	0.21	0.23	0.19	0.27	0.17	0.17	0.22
BA Degree by Age 35	0.31	0.28	0.37	0.41	0.29	0.44	0.31	0.28	0.36
Depression in 1992	0.12	0.21	0.22	0.19	0.23	0.26	0.13	0.22	0.23
Adjusted, R Cog, Character	0.32			0.32		0.39		0.32	

Source: National Longitudinal Survey of Youth, 1979.

Table Description: The table shows the adjusted multiple correlation coefficient (square root of the adjusted R^2) from regressions of later-life outcomes on measures of character and cognition. This is a measure of the variance explained by the predictor variables used. For each cognitive measure, the first column shows the estimate using only the measures of character and cognition. For each cognitive the measure of character (Non-Cog), and the third column shows the estimate from using both the measures of character and cognition (Both). The last row shows the correlation between each cognitive measure and the set of character measures. Measures of Character and Cognition: The measures of character include minor illegal activity in 1979 (vandalism, shoplifting, petty theft, fraud, and fencing), major illegal activity in 1979 (auto theft, breaking/entering private property, and grand theft), participation in violent crime in 1979 (fighting, assault, and aggravated assault), tried marijuana before age 15, daily smoking before age 15, regular drinking before age 15, and any intercourse before age 15. It also includes measures of self-esteem and locus of control. Self-Esteem is measured using the 10-item Rosenberg scale administered in 1980. Locus of control is a measure of how much control an individual believes they have over their life and is measured using the 4-item Rotter scale. IQ and grades are from high school transcripts. IQ is pooled across several IQ tests using IQ percentiles. GPA is the individual's core-subject GPA from ninth grade. Outcomes: Due to the biennial nature of the survey after 1994, some respondents are not interviewed at age 35; for these individuals age 36 is used. Earnings includes zero-earners and excludes observations over $200,000 (2005 dollars). Hourly wage excludes observations less than $3 or over $200 (2005 dollars). Hours worked excludes observations less than 80 or more than 4000. Jail by age 35 indicates whether the respondent had listed residing in a jail or prison at some point before age 35. Welfare at age 35 indicates whether the respondent received any positive amount of welfare at age 35. Married at age 35 indicates whether the respondent was currently married. BA degree by age 35 indicates whether the respondent received a bachelor's degree (or higher) by age 35. Depression in 1992 is based on the 7-item Center for Epidemiologic Studies Depression Scale (CES-D). Sample: The sample excludes the military over sample. The samples differ across the IQ, AFQT, and GPA due to missing measures across the samples.

Table 1.6 The Relative Predictive Power of Conscientiousness and SAT Scores for College GPA

Source	Sample	Timing of Measurement and Outcome	Controls	Metric	Results	Correlation
Conard (2006)	University students in the US (N = 186)	College GPA and SAT were both self-reported during college. Personality was measured in college.	Class attendance	Standardized regression coefficient (β)	SAT Total Conscientiousness	0.27* 0.30*
Noftle and Robins (2007)	University students in the US (N = 10,472)	College GPA and SAT were both self-reported during college. Personality was measured in college.	Gender, other Big Five traits	Standardized regression coefficient (β)	SAT Verbal SAT Math Conscientiousness	0.19 0.16 0.24

				Standardized regression coefficient (β)		
Noftle and Robins (2007)	University students in the US (N = 465)	College GPA and SAT were both self-reported during college. Personality was measured in college.	Gender, other Big Five traits	SAT Verbal		0.28
				SAT Math		0.28
				Conscientiousness		0.18
Noftle and Robins (2007)	University students in the US (N = 444)	College GPA and SAT were both self-reported during college. Personality was measured in college.	Gender, other Big Five traits	SAT Verbal		0.18
				SAT Math		0.25
				Conscientiousness		0.22
Wolfe and Johnson (1995)	University students in the US (N = 201)	GPA and SAT were provided by the college's record office. Personality was measured in college.	High school GPA	SAT Total		0.23
				Conscientiousness		0.31

Notes: Self-reported SAT scores and those obtained from college records were highly correlated ($r = 0.92$). Self-reported GPA and that obtained from college records were highly correlated ($r = 0.89$).

scores and measures of Conscientiousness with grades in college. Even on the measure that the SAT was designed to forecast, Conscientiousness is a (slightly) better predictor. While we have no direct measures of this skill in the data sets that we analyze, the poor performance of GED recipients in school and other outcomes likely reflects a lack of Conscientiousness.

Achievement test scores themselves are explained in part by personality skills. As discussed in Chapter 9, achievement test scores reflect both IQ and personality. The power of "IQ" that Herrnstein and Murray claimed to have established is in truth partly the power of character.[91]

1.7 Character Can Be Fostered

Both character and cognition can be shaped by families, schools, and other social institutions. Chapter 9 summarizes a substantial literature on the effectiveness of various interventions at different stages of the life cycle.

Through heredity and parenting, families play a powerful role in shaping the character of their children.[92] The decline of the two-parent family, and the attendant decline of the parenting resources available to children, lead to adverse child outcomes. While the children of the affluent arguably have richer environments than their predecessors, the children of the disadvantaged do not.[93]

Certain early childhood programs have been successful at supplementing the parenting resources of stressed families. The Perry Preschool Program improved later life outcomes of disadvantaged children primarily by improving their character skills. Chapter 9 discusses other childhood programs that achieve long-term success in part because they shape character. These programs do not intrude on the sanctity of the family.

---

91. While stable skills exist and predict behaviors across a wide array of situations, incentives in situations also matter. Any psychological skill, be it a character skill or a cognitive skill, is measured by performance on tasks. Performance on tasks depends on multiple skills and the efforts applied to the tasks. Effort, in turn, is determined by goals and incentives. Thus, expression of a skill in any situation will depend on what it takes to perform in the situation. Psychologists have been slow to recognize this point, and, accordingly, their measures must be used with caution because they capture many things, not just the designated constructs. See Almlund et al. (2011) and Heckman and Kautz (2012).

92. For evidence, see, for example, Cunha et al. (2006), Moynihan (2006), and Heckman, Pinto, and Savelyev (2013).

93. McLanahan (2004), Heckman (2008), and Putnam, Frederick, and Snellman (2012).

Many work with both the parent and the children to create successful children.

Adolescent programs have been less well studied. A promising strategy is to integrate school and work. The American high school is a recent innovation with certain pathological features. It takes young people out of the larger society and creates an adolescent society with its own values, often detached from those of mainstream society. James Coleman (1961) documented the commonality of anti-intellectual counterculture values in high schools located across broad swaths of the socioeconomic spectrum.

One hundred and fifty years ago most American students stopped their education at grade school. The curriculum in these schools emphasized character education. Post-school apprenticeships integrated adolescents into adult society rather than segregating them from it. Such apprenticeships taught valuable trade skills, including the virtues of working with others, self-control, and showing up on time. The German apprenticeship program is a modern-day paradigm.[94] Chapter 9 discusses several promising American programs that have combined academics with work experience.

As reported in Chapter 9, other adolescent programs have mixed results. Programs that cluster delinquent adolescents appear to run the risk of generating negative peer effects. Programs with individual mentoring and attachment are far more promising.

1.8 The Plan of the Rest of the Book

Chapter 2 (by Lois Quinn) presents a history of the origins and spread of the GED. An achievement test designed to monitor the "general knowledge" of Iowa students was applied to facilitate the integration of disabled veterans into civilian life. It metastasized into a major social institution designed to solve the high school dropout problem that in truth disguised and even fostered it.

Chapter 3 (by John Eric Humphries) investigates why many dropouts decide to earn a GED even though the labor market benefits of certification are low. Changes in demographics, government policies, and the growing emphasis on accountability in public education led to rapid growth in the GED program.

Chapter 4 (by James Heckman, John Eric Humphries, and Tim Kautz) discusses the characteristics of GED recipients. They are smart (relative to high school graduates who do not go on to college) but lack character

94. Evidence on its effectiveness is mixed. See Winkelmann (1996), Clark and Fahr (2002), and Cooke (2003).

skills. They come from more disadvantaged backgrounds than ordinary high school graduates. Their deficits in character emerge early.

Chapter 5 (by James Heckman, John Eric Humphries, and Tim Kautz) surveys the previous literature on the effectiveness of the GED. It also conducts original empirical studies using seven data sets collected in different time periods to evaluate the effectiveness of the GED testing program using a variety of outcome measures. All data show that GED recipients do not perform at the level of high school graduates. After controlling for cognition and background, the vast majority of male GED recipients do no better than uncertified dropouts.

For some women, there is evidence of an apparent benefit, but the interpretation to be placed on these estimates is ambiguous. We argue that it is primarily due to uncontrolled selective factors and is not a causal benefit of GED certification. Any gain appears to come from their greater labor force attachment and not because of higher hourly wages compared to those of other dropouts. Their life-cycle wage growth is the same as that of dropouts. For both men and women, skills present before certification receive the same market wages and earnings before and after GED certification, so the GED does not serve a signaling function.

Chapter 6 (by Janice H. Laurence) studies the performance of GED recipients in the military. GED recipients perform like other high school dropouts. The six-month attrition rates for GED recipients are 45% compared to 50% for other dropouts. It is 28% for traditional high school graduates. The attrition rate for GED recipients is not due to their lack of cognitive ability but because of their lack of character. It is telling that the U.S. military—the originator of the GED program—recognizes that modern GED recipients lack the character skills required to succeed in the military.

Chapter 7 (by James Heckman, John Eric Humphries, Paul LaFontaine, and Pedro Rodríguez) conducts three different empirical studies on how the availability of the GED induces high school students to drop out. All point to the conclusion that GED programs promote dropping out. The estimated effects are substantial.

Chapter 8 (by Andrew Halpern-Manners, John Robert Warren, and Eric Grodsky) investigates how changing the difficulty of completing high school through high-stakes achievement testing changes the incentives for GED certification. Over the last three decades, states have increasingly required students to pass achievement tests before graduating from high school. Currently, three out of four high school students in the United States must take an exam to graduate. Individual schools are evaluated based on the fraction of students who pass. State-mandated high school exit examinations have contributed to the growth of GED recipiency for two distinct reasons. First, students unable to pass a high school exit examination turn to the GED as an alternative. Second, until recently, schools could manipulate state accountability measures by encouraging low-performing students to earn a GED certificate so that they are not counted in the school's passing rate.

Chapter 9 (by James Heckman and Tim Kautz) discusses how character skills can be measured and improved through various interventions. Cognitive and character skills can change and be changed but to different degrees at different ages. The chapter considers the effectiveness of a variety of interventions that improve character, ranging from early childhood programs to workplace-based education and apprenticeship programs.

Chapter 10 (by James Heckman, John Eric Humphries, and Tim Kautz) presents policy recommendations about the GED program and the more general problem of promoting skills in the American economy. It argues that any successful approach going forward should recognize the power of character skills. They can be measured, and effective interventions are available to shape them.

BIBLIOGRAPHY

Aaron, Henry J. 1978. *Politics and The Professors: The Great Society in Perspective.* Washington, DC: Brookings Institution Press.

Acemoglu, Daron, and Autor, David. 2011. "Skills, Tasks and Technologies: Implications for Employment and Earnings." In *Handbook of Labor Economics,* edited by Orley Ashenfelter and David Card, *Handbooks in Economics,* vol. 4, Part B, chap. 12, 1043–1171, Amsterdam, Elsevier.

Ackerman, Phillip L. 1988. "Determinants of Individual Differences during Skill Acquisition: Cognitive Abilities and Information Processing." *Journal of Experimental Psychology* 117(3):288–318.

Ackerman, Phillip L., and Heggestad, Eric D. 1997. "Intelligence, Personality, and Interests: Evidence for Overlapping Traits." *Psychological Bulletin* 121:219–245.

ACT, Inc. 2007. *The ACT Technical Manual.* Iowa City, IA: ACT, Inc.

ACT, Inc. 2009. *ACT: The First Fifty Years, 1959–2009.* Iowa City, IA: ACT, Inc.

Almlund, Mathilde, Duckworth, Angela, Heckman, James J., and Kautz, Tim. 2011. "Personality Psychology and Economics." In *Handbook of the Economics of Education,* edited by E. A. Hanushek, S. Machin, and L. Wößmann, vol. 4, 1–181, Amsterdam: Elsevier.

American Council on Education. 1956. *Conclusions and Recommendations on a Study of the General Educational Development Testing Program: Committee on Evaluation of the Tyler Fact-Finding Study.* Washington, DC: American Council on Education.

American Council on Education. 2009. *Who Took the GED? GED 2008 Statistical Report.* Washington, DC: GED Testing Service, Center for Adult Learning and Educational Credentials, American Council on Education.

Aristotle. 1956. *The Nicomachean Ethics*. Cambridge, MA: Harvard University Press, with an English translation by H. Rackham. New and revised edition. Originally published in 1934. Original text from 350 B.C.

Arum, Richard. 2005. *Judging School Discipline: The Crisis of Moral Authority*. Cambridge, MA: Harvard University Press.

Autor, David H., Katz, Lawrence F., and Kearney, Melissa S. 2008. "Trends in U.S. Wage Inequality: Revising the Revisionists." *Review of Economics and Statistics* 90(2):300–323.

Baldwin, Janet. 1995. *Who Took the GED? GED 1994 Statistical Report*. Washington, DC: American Council on Education, GED Testing Service, Center for Adult Learning.

Beck, Clive, Crittenden, Brian S., and Sullivan, Edmund V. 1971. *Moral Education: Interdisciplinary Approaches*. New York: Newman Press.

Benjamin, Daniel J., Brown, Sebastian A., and Shapiro, Jesse M. 2013. "Who Is 'Behavioral'? Cognitive Ability and Anomalous Preferences." Forthcoming, *Journal of the European Economic Association*.

Binet, Alfred, and Simon, Theodore. 1916. *The Development of Intelligence in Children (The Binet-Simon Scale)*. Psychological Science. Baltimore, MD: Williams & Wilkins Co.

Bloom, Dan, Gardenhire-Crooks, Alissa, and Mandsager, Conrad L. 2009. "Reengaging High School Dropouts: Early Results of the National Guard Youth ChalleNGe Program Evaluation." Report, MDRC, last accessed online February 11, 2013. http://www.mdrc.org/sites/default/files/full_491.pdf.

Bobbitt, J. Franklin. 1913. "Part I: The Supervision of City Schools: Some General Principles of Management Applied to the Problems of City-School Systems." In *Yearbook of the National Society for the Study of Education: Twelfth Yearbook*, 12–13, Bloomington, IL: Public School Publishing Company.

Bobbitt, John Franklin. 1915. *What the Schools Teach and Might Teach*. Cleveland, OH: Survey Committee of the Cleveland Foundation.

Bobrow, Jerry. 2002. *GED (General Educational Development)*. Indianapolis, IN: Cliffs Notes, 1st ed.

Boesel, David, Alsalam, Nabeel, and Smith, Thomas M. 1998. *Educational and Labor Market Performance of GED Recipients*. Washington, DC: U.S. Department of Education, Office of Educational Research and Improvement, National Library of Education.

Borghans, Lex, Duckworth, Angela L., Heckman, James J., and ter Weel, Bas. 2008. "The Economics and Psychology of Personality Traits." *Journal of Human Resources* 43(4):972–1059.

Borghans, Lex, Golsteyn, Bart H. H., Heckman, James J., and Humphries, John Eric. 2011. "Identification Problems in Personality Psychology." *Personality and Individual Differences* 51(3: Special Issue on Personality and Economics):315–320.

Bound, John, Brown, Charles, and Mathiowetz, Nancy. 2001. "Measurement Error in Survey Data." In *Handbook of Econometrics*, edited by James J. Heckman and Edward Leamer, *Handbooks in Economics*, vol. 5, chap. 59, 3705–3843, Amsterdam: Elsevier Science.

Bowen, William G., Chingos, Matthew M., and McPherson, Michael S. 2009. "Test Scores and High School Grades as Predictors." In *Crossing the Finish*

Line: *Completing College at America's Public Universities*, 112–133, Princeton, NJ: Princeton University Press.

Bowles, Samuel, and Gintis, Herbert. 1976. *Schooling in Capitalist America: Educational Reform and the Contradictions of Economic Life.* New York: Basic Books.

Bowles, Samuel, Gintis, Herbert, and Osborne, Melissa. 2001. "The Determinants of Earnings: A Behavioral Approach." *Journal of Economic Literature* 39(4): 1137–1176.

Brinch, Christian N., and Galloway, Taryn Ann. 2012. "Schooling in Adolescence Raises IQ Scores." *Proceedings of the National Academy of Sciences* 109(2):425–430.

Bruner, Jerome. 1956. *A Study of Thinking.* New York: John Wiley and Sons.

Cameron, Stephen V., and Heckman, James J. 1993. "The Nonequivalence of High School Equivalents." *Journal of Labor Economics* 11(1, Part 1):1–47.

Carroll, John B. 1993. *Human Cognitive Abilities: A Survey of Factor-Analytic Studies.* New York: Cambridge University Press.

Carroll, Joseph M. 1990. "The Copernican Plan: Restructuring the American High School." *Phi Delta Kappan* 71(5):358–365.

Clark, Damon, and Fahr, René. 2002. "The Promise of Workplace Training for Non-college Bound Youth: Theory and Evidence from German Apprenticeship." CEP Discussion Paper 518, Centre for Economic Performance, London School of Economics and Political Science, London, UK.

Clark, Melissa A., and Jaeger, David A. 2006. "Natives, the Foreign-Born, and High School Equivalents: New Evidence on the Returns to the GED." *Journal of Population Economics* 19(4):769–793.

Coleman, James S. 1961. *The Adolescent Society: The Social Life of the Teenager and Its Impact on Education.* New York: The Free Press of Glencoe.

Commonwealth of Pennsylvania. 1955. "Pennsylvania Human Relations Act." Act of 1955, P.L. 744, No. 222, as amended in 1980 by Act No. 198, P.L. 1122.

Conard, Maureen A. 2006. "Aptitude Is Not Enough: How Personality and Behavior Predict Academic Performance." *Journal of Research in Personality* 40(3):339–346.

Cooke, L.P. 2003. "A Comparison of Initial and Early Life Course Earnings of the German Secondary Education and Training System." *Economics of Education Review* 22(1):79–88.

Cremin, Lawrence A. 1988. *American Education: The Metropolitan Experience, 1876–1980,* vol. 3. New York: Harper and Row.

Cunha, Flavio, Heckman, James J., Lochner, Lance J., and Masterov, Dimitriy V. 2006. "Interpreting the Evidence on Life Cycle Skill Formation." In *Handbook of the Economics of Education,* edited by Eric A. Hanushek and Frank Welch, chap. 12, 697–812, Amsterdam: North-Holland.

DeLong, J. Bradford, and Magin, Konstantin. 2009. "The U.S. Equity Return Premium: Past, Present and Future." *Journal of Economic Perspectives* 23(1):193–208.

Department of Education. 2008. "A Uniform, Comparable Graduation Rate: How the Final Regulations for Title I Hold Schools, Districts, and States Accountable for Improving Graduation Rates." Tech. rep., Department of Education, No Child Left Behind.

Durkheim, Émile. 1973. *Moral Education: A Study in the Theory and Application of the Sociology of Education.* New York: Free Press.

Ermisch, John, Jantti, Markus, and Smeeding, Tim. 2012. *From Parents to Children: The Intergenerational Transmission of Advantage*. New York: Russell Sage Foundation.

Feingold, Alan. 1982. "The Validity of the Information and Vocabulary Subtests of the WAIS." *Journal of Clinical Psychology* 38(1):169–174.

Flynn, James R. 2007. *What Is Intelligence?: Beyond the Flynn Effect*. New York: Cambridge University Press.

GED Testing Service. 1959–2008. *Who Took the GED?: GED Statistical Report*. Washington, DC: American Council on Higher Education.

GED Testing Service. 2009. *The Technical Manual: 2002 Series GED Tests*. Washington, DC: American Council on Education, http://www.acenet.edu /Content/NavigationMenu/ged/pubs/TechnicalManual_2002SeriesGEDTests.pdf.

GED Testing Service. 2012. *Assessment Guide for Educators: A Guide to the 2014 Assessment Content from GED Testing Service*. Washington, DC: American Council on Education.

Gensowski, Miriam. 2012. "Personality, IQ, and Lifetime Earnings." Unpublished manuscript, University of Chicago, Department of Economics.

Greene, Anthony C., Sapp, Gary L., and Chissom, Brad. 1990. "Validation of the Stanford-Binet Intelligence Scale: Fourth Edition with Exceptional Black Male Students." *Psychology in the Schools* 27(1):35–41.

Grek, Sotiria. 2009. "Governing by Numbers: The PISA 'Effect' in Europe." *Journal of Education Policy* 24(1):23–37.

Hansen, Karsten T., Heckman, James J., and Mullen, Kathleen J. 2004. "The Effect of Schooling and Ability on Achievement Test Scores." *Journal of Econometrics* 121(1–2):39–98.

Hartlage, Lawrence C., and Steele, Carol T. 1977. "WISC and WISC-R Correlates of Academic Achievement." *Psychology in the Schools* 14(1):15–18.

Heckman, James J. 2008. "Schools, Skills and Synapses." *Economic Inquiry* 46(3): 289–324.

Heckman, James J., Humphries, John Eric, and Mader, Nicholas 2011. "The GED." In *Handbook of the Economics of Education*, edited by Eric A. Hanushek, Stephen Machin, and Ludger Wößmann, vol. 3, chap. 9, pp. 423–484. Amsterdam: Elsevier.

Heckman, James J., Humphries, John Eric, Urzúa, Sergio, and Veramendi, Gregory. 2011. "The Effects of Educational Choices on Labor Market, Health, and Social Outcomes." Unpublished manuscript, University of Chicago, Department of Economics.

Heckman, James J., and Kautz, Tim. 2012. "Hard Evidence on Soft Skills." *Labour Economics* 19(4):451–464. Adam Smith Lecture.

Heckman, James J., and LaFontaine, Paul A. 2006. "Bias Corrected Estimates of GED Returns." *Journal of Labor Economics* 24(3):661–700.

Heckman, James J., and LaFontaine, Paul A. 2010. "The American High School Graduation Rate: Trends and Levels." *Review of Economics and Statistics* 92(2):244–262.

Heckman, James J., Lochner, Lance J., and Todd, Petra E. 2006. "Earnings Equations and Rates of Return: The Mincer Equation and Beyond." In *Handbook of the Economics of Education*, edited by Eric A. Hanushek and Frank Welch, vol. 1, chap. 7, 307–458, Amsterdam: Elsevier.

Heckman, James J., Moon, Seong Hyeok, Pinto, Rodrigo, Savelyev, Peter A., and Yavitz, Adam Q. 2010. "The Rate of Return to the HighScope Perry Preschool Program." *Journal of Public Economics* 94(1-2):114–128.

Heckman, James J., Pinto, Rodrigo, and Savelyev, Peter A. 2013. "Understanding the Mechanisms Through Which an Influential Early Childhood Program Boosted Adult Outcomes." Unpublished manuscript, University of Chicago, Department of Economics (first draft, 2008). *American Economic Review* 103(6): 1–35.

Herrnstein, Richard J., and Murray, Charles A. 1994. *The Bell Curve: Intelligence and Class Structure in American Life.* New York: Free Press.

Hitch, Charles J., and McKean, Roland N. 1960. *The Economics of Defense in the Nuclear Age.* Cambridge, MA: Harvard University Press.

Jencks, Christopher. 1979. *Who Gets Ahead? The Determinants of Economic Success in America.* New York: Basic Books.

Jensen, Arthur R. 1998. *The g Factor: The Science of Mental Ability.* Westport, CT: Praeger.

Jepsen, Christopher, Mueser, Peter, and Troske, Kenneth. 2011. "Labor Market Returns to the GED Using Regression Discontinuity Analysis." Working Paper 1014, Department of Economics, University of Missouri.

Kaestle, Carl F. 1984. "Moral Education and Common Schools in America: A Historian's View." *Journal of Moral Education* 13(2):101–111.

Kobrin, Jennifer L., Patterson, Brian F., Shaw, Emily J., Mattern, Krista D., and Barbuti, Sandra M. 2008. "Validity of the SAT for Predicting First-Year College Grade Point Average." Research Report 2008-5, The College Board.

Koretz, Daniel M. 2008. *Measuring Up: What Educational Testing Really Tells Us.* Cambridge, MA: Harvard University Press.

Lareau, Annette. 2012. "Response: The Importance of Social Institutions." *Boston Review* September/October, 28–29.

Lazear, Edward P. 1995. *Personnel Economics.* Cambridge, MA: MIT Press.

Lemann, Nicholas. 1999. *The Big Test: The Secret History of the American Meritocracy.* New York: Farrar, Straus and Giroux.

Lindquist, E. F. 1947. "Goodness of Fit of Trend Curves and Significance of Trend Differences." *Psychometrika* 12(2):65–78.

Lindquist, E. F., Van Dyke, L. A., and Yale, J. R. 1948. *What Good is High School?* Chicago: Science Research Associates.

Lindquist, Everet Franklin. 1951. "Preliminary Considerations in Objective Test Construction." In *Educational Measurement,* edited by E. F. Lindquist, 119–158, Washington, DC: American Council on Education.

Mann, Horace. 1838. "First Annual Report Covering the Year 1837." Annual Report of the Secretary of the Board of Education, Massachusetts Board of Education.

Mann, Horace. 1847. "Eleventh Annual Report of the Secretary of the Board of Education." Massachusetts Board of Education.

Mann, Horace. 1848. "Twelfth Annual Report of the Secretary of the Board of Education." Massachusetts Board of Education.

McLanahan, Sara. 2004. "Diverging Destinies: How Children Are Faring under the Second Demographic Transition." *Demography* 41(4):607–627.

Means, B., and Laurence, Janice H. 1984. "Characteristics and Performance of Recruits Enlisted with General Educational Development (GED) Credentials."

Tech. Rep. FR-PRD-84-6, Human Resources Research Organization, Alexandria, VA.

Michalko, K. T., and Saklofske, D. H. 1996. "A Psychometric Investigation of the Wechsler Individual Achievement Test with a Sample of Saskatchewan Schoolchildren." *Canadian Journal of School Psychology* 12(1):44–54.

Mischel, Walter. 1968. *Personality and Assessment*. New York: Wiley.

Moynihan, Daniel P. 2006. *The Future of the Family*. New York: Russell Sage Foundation Publications.

Murray, Henry Alexander. 1938. *Explorations in Personality: A Clinical and Experimental Study of Fifty Men of College Age*. New York: Oxford University Press.

National Center for Education Statistics. 2006. "Education Longitudinal Study of 2002, First Follow-up, Student Survey." Report ELS:2004/04, National Center for Education Statistics, Washington, DC.

National Commission on Excellence in Education. 1983. *A Nation at Risk: The Imperative for Educational Reform: An Open Letter to the American People. A Report to the Nation and the Secretary of Education*. Washington, DC: National Commission on Excellence in Education.

National Commission on Fiscal Responsibility and Reform. 2010. "The Moment of Truth: Report of the National Commission on Fiscal Responsibility and Reform." Tech. rep., The National Commission on Fiscal Responsibility and Reform, The White House, Washington, DC, available at http://www.fiscalcommission.gov/sites/fiscalcommission.gov/files/documents/TheMomentofTruth12_1_2010.pdf.

Nisbett, Richard E., Aronson, Joshua, Blair, Clancy, Dickens, William, Flynn, James, Halpern, Diane F., and Turkheimer, Eric. 2012. "Intelligence: New Findings and Theoretical Developments." *American Psychologist* 67(2):130–159.

Noftle, Erik E., and Robins, Richard W. 2007. "Personality Predictors of Academic Outcomes: Big Five Correlates of GPA and SAT Scores." *Journal of Personality and Social Psychology* 93(1):116–130.

OECD. 2011. "OECD Family Database." Organization for Economic Cooperation and Development, Paris. Available at http://www.oecd.org/document/4/0,3746, en_2649_37419_37836996_1_1_1_37419,00.html\#TOOLS.

OECD. 2012. "United States, in Education at a Glance 2012: OECD Indicators." Paris: OECD Publishing.

O'Leary, Una-Marie, Rusch, Kathleen M., and Guastello, Stephen J. 1991. "Estimating Age-Stratified WAIS-R IQs from Scores on the Raven's Standard Progressive Matrices." *Journal of Clinical Psychology* 47(2):277–284.

Omizo, Michael M. 1980. "The Differential Aptitude Tests as Predictors of Success in a High School for Engineering Program." *Educational and Psychological Measurement* 40(1):197–203.

Peterson, Julia J. 1983. *The Iowa Testing Programs*. Iowa City: University of Iowa Press.

Putnam, Robert D., Frederick, Carl B., and Snellman, Kaisa. 2012. "Growing Class Gaps in Social Connectedness among American Youth." Harvard Kennedy School of Government, The Saguaro Seminar: Civic Engagement in America.

Quinn, Lois M. 2002. "An Institutional History of the GED." Unpublished manuscript.

Rajan, Raghuram G. 2010. *Fault Lines: How Hidden Fractures Still Threaten the World Economy*. Princeton, NJ: Princeton University Press.

Raven, J., Raven, J. C., and Court, J.H. 1988. *Manual for Raven's Progressive Matrices and Vocabulary Scales*. San Antonio, TX: Harcourt Assessment.

Raven, John C. 1962. *Advanced Progressive Matrices: Sets I and II*. London: H.K. Lewis, revised ed.

Ravitch, Diane. 2010. *The Death and Life of the Great American School System: How Testing and Choice Are Undermining Education*. New York: Basic Books.

Reed, James. 1987. "Robert M. Yerkes and the Mental Testing Movement." In *Psychological Testing and American Society, 1890–1930*, edited by Michael M. Sokal, 75–94. New Brunswick, NJ: Rutgers University Press.

Reese, William J. 1995. *The Origins of the American High School*. New Haven, CT: Yale University Press.

Resnick, Daniel. 1982. "History of Educational Testing." In *Ability Testing: Uses, Consequences, and Controversies*, edited by Alexandra K. Wigdor and Wendell R. Garner, vol. II: Documentation, Washington, DC: National Academy Press.

Roberts, Richard D., Goff, Ginger Nelson, Anjoul, Fadi, Kyllonen, P. C., Pallier, Gerry, and Stankov, Lazar. 2000. "The Armed Services Vocational Aptitude Battery (ASVAB): Little More than Acculturated Learning (Gc)!?" *Learning and Individual Differences* 12(1):81–103.

Rothlisberg, Barbara. 1987. "Comparing the Stanford-Binet, Fourth Edition to the WISC-R: A Concurrent Validity Study." *Journal of School Psychology* 25(2):193–196.

Rothstein, Richard, Jacobsen, Rebecca, and Wilder, Tamara. 2008. *Grading Education: Getting Accountability Right*. New York: Economic Policy Institute and Teachers College Press.

Schochet, Peter Z., Burghardt, John, and Glazerman, Steven. 2001. *National Job Corps Study: The Impacts of Job Corps on Participants' Employment and Related Outcomes*. Princeton, NJ: Mathematica Policy Research.

Steinberg, Laurence. 2008. "A Social Neuroscience Perspective on Adolescent Risk-taking." *Developmental Review* 28(1):78–106.

Sylva, Kathy. 1997. "The Quest for Quality in Curriculum." In *Lasting Differences: The High/Scope Preschool Curriculum Comparison Study through Age 23*, edited by L. J. Schweinhart and D. P. Weikart, 89–93. Ypsilanti, MI: High/Scope Press.

Taylor, Frederick Winslow. 1911. *Principles of Scientific Management*. New York: Harper and Brothers.

Terman, Lewis M., Baldwin, Bird T., Bronson, Edith, DeVoss, James C., Fuller, Florence, Lee Kelley, Truman, Lima, Margaret, Marshall, Helen, Moore, Albert H., Raubenheimer, A. S., Ruch, G. M., Willoughby, Raymond L., Benson Wyman, Jennie, and Hazeltine Yates, Dorothy. 1925. *Genetic Studies of Genius: Mental and Physical Traits of a Thousand Gifted Children*, vol. 1. Stanford University, CA: Stanford University Press.

Terman, Lewis M., Oden, Melita H., Bayley, Nancy, Marshall, Helen, McNemar, Quinn, and Sullivan, Ellen B. 1947. *Genetic Studies of Genius: The Gifted Child Grows Up: Twenty-Five Years' Follow-Up of a Superior Group*, vol. 4. Stanford University, CA: Stanford University Press.

Treschan, Lazar, and Fischer, David J. 2009. "From Basic Skills to Better Futures: Generating Economic Dividends for New York City." Tech. rep., The Community Service Society Reports, New York.

Tyler, Ralph. 1949. *Basic Principles of Curriculum and Instruction*. Chicago: University of Chicago Press.

Tyler, Ralph. 1989. *Educational Evaluation: Classic Works of Ralph Tyler*. Boston: Kluwer.

Tyler, Ralph W. 1940. "The Place of Evaluation in Modern Education." *The Elementary School Journal* 41(1):19–27.

Tyler, Ralph W. 1973. Assessing Educational Achievement in the Affective Domain. *National Council on Measurement in Education* 4(3).

U.S. Supreme Court. 1948. *McCollum v. Board of Education*. Illinois ex rel. McCollum v. Board of Education of School District, No. 71, Champaign County, Illinois, No. 90, Argued December 8, 1947, Decided March 8, 1948, 333 U.S. 203.

Webb, Edward. 1915. "Character and Intelligence." *British Journal of Psychology* Supplement 1(3):1–99.

Winkelmann, Rainer. 1996. "Employment Prospects and Skill Acquisition of Apprenticeship-Trained Workers in Germany." *Industrial and Labor Relations Review* 49(4):658–672.

Wise, Arthur E. 1979. *Legislated Learning: The Bureaucratization of the American Classroom*. Berkeley: University of California Press.

Wolfe, Raymond N., and Johnson, Scott D. 1995. "Personality as a Predictor of College Performance." *Educational and Psychological Measurement* 55(2):177–185.

Worner, Roger B. 1973. "PPBS and the Derivation of Cost/Effectiveness." Paper presented at the Association of Educational Data Systems Annual Convention (New Orleans, Louisiana, April 16 through 19, 1973).

Zhang, Jizhi, Guison-Dowdy, Anne, Patterson, Margaret Becker, and Song, Wei. 2011. "Crossing the Bridge: GED Credentials and Postsecondary Educational Outcomes." Year two report, GED Testing Services.

Zhang, Jizhi, Han, Mee Young, and Patterson, Margaret Becker. 2009. "Young GED Examinees and Their Performance on the GED Tests." GED Testing Service Research Studies 2009-1, GED Testing Service, Center for Adult Learning and Educational Credentials, American Council on Education, Washington, DC.

II

THE HISTORY OF THE GED

2

AN INSTITUTIONAL HISTORY OF THE GED

LOIS M. QUINN[1]

2.1 Introduction

This history of the General Educational Development (GED) credential was originally requested as one of a series of studies conducted by the University of Wisconsin-Milwaukee Employment and Training Institute in the late 1980s for then Wisconsin Superintendent of Public Instruction Herbert J. Grover. As part of his statewide initiatives to improve students' preparation for the world of work and to expand educational programming for teens identified as "at risk" of dropping out of high school, Grover sought data on the experience of teen and adult high school noncompleters who had secured GED credentials in the state. He asked the Institute researchers to analyze the growing use of the GED by 16- and 17-year-old dropouts and in-school youth, the low success rates of Wisconsin GED recipients (of all ages) in postsecondary education, and the issuance of GED credentials to candidates with grade school reading levels. The history was requested to help explain why a program requiring minimal educational coursework should be targeted toward those teens and adults who had unsuccessful school records, often resided in low-income neighborhoods, and showed serious behavioral problems.

The story of the GED's founding was not what the Institute researchers had expected, and this history is far more critical of the GED test publisher than a "house history" typically provides (Stewart, 1992, 6). It does help explain the role of the American Council on Education (ACE) and its GED

1. The author is indebted to the members of her 1990 dissertation committee, who provided critical insights throughout her research on the history of the GED: Margo Anderson, Ann Lennarson Greer, the late Scott Greer, Michael Barndt, and Frank Cassell. The work of John Pawasarat, the late Philip E. Lerman, and former Wisconsin State Superintendent of Public Instruction Herbert Grover in assessing the use of the GED credential in Wisconsin and recommending reforms was invaluable. Kathy Van Hecke provided very helpful editing suggestions. The history draws on original source materials from the National Archives (NAB), the University of Iowa Blommers Measurement Resources Laboratory (Blommers Library), the American Council on Education archives (now at the Hoover Institute at Stanford University), and the University of Chicago Presidents' Papers and Ralph W. Tyler Collection.

Testing Service in promoting the GED as "equivalent" to four years of high school and state department of education awards of high school diplomas to GED recipients who have not met their state-mandated course and competency test requirements (see Chapter 8). At the same time, the research studies in this book document the many negative aspects of the GED: the low payoff for the GED in the workplace (Chapter 5), the poor performance of GED recipients in the military (Chapter 6), the negative impact of GED policies on high school completion rates (Chapter 7), and the need for improved noncognitive skills among lower-achieving youth (Chapter 9).

This history of the GED explores how a multiple-choice test (along with a short general topic essay) became recognized as "equivalent" to high school completion by federal and state education officials. The GED was first introduced in 1942 during World War II as a college entrance exam for wounded servicemen, and then at the war's end it was promoted as a substitute for states' previously issued "wartime diplomas" for veterans returning to the states (Hess, 1946b). The test's emphasis on reading, writing, and arithmetic derived in large part from the minimalist general education life-adjustment curriculum advocated by the American Council on Education in the 1930s and 1940s and the evolution of the Iowa Tests of Educational Development, the first GED test. This chapter explores the early years when the GED was presented as a vehicle for awarding high school degrees to returning war heroes and then was encouraged for use by high school dropouts who lacked military service but were able to pass the tests at the minimal standards set. At key periods in the 1960s and 1970s, decisions were made to lower the test's reading requirements for use with younger teens, to market the test to school-age youth, and to distance the test's subject matter away from Carnegie unit requirements, which were being imposed by legislators on the states' traditional high school graduates. Finally, this history examines the responses of the ACE test publisher to state and national educational initiatives to improve high school instruction since the 1980s.

2.2 Origins of the "General Education" Curriculum: From Taylorism to "Tylerism"

Debates over appropriate curricula and standards for secondary education (whether college preparatory, vocational, or "general education") have a relatively short history. At the end of the nineteenth century elite colleges interested in enrolling students with classical education backgrounds developed a common college-preparatory high school curriculum. In 1892, the National Educational Association convened a Committee of Ten, headed by Charles W. Eliot, president of Harvard University, that endorsed four alternative tracks of college-preparatory study. All tracks included four years of foreign languages (Latin, Greek, German, French, or Spanish), four years of English literature and composition, three years of mathematics (algebra, geometry, and trigonometry), three years of science (including physics and chemistry), three years of history, and a limited number of electives. The committee recommended that all students, whether or not college bound, meet the same coursework expectations; the rationale was that this would give them "four years of strong and effective mental training" (Tyack, 1967, 385).

Initially, adoption of Eliot's high school "unit" measurement—defined as a course offered five periods weekly for one academic year—was vigorously promoted by the Carnegie Foundation for the Advancement of Teaching, whose board of trustees was also headed by Eliot. The Carnegie Foundation used the clout of its pension fund to promote this system of recording school credits by mandating that college teachers would be eligible for Carnegie pensions only if their institution adopted freshman admissions standards requiring 14 high school "units" (Lagemann, 1983). Although the foundation soon embraced the development of college admissions tests as a more efficient technique for holding secondary schools accountable to college-determined standards, high school units continue to carry the Carnegie name. Meanwhile, rather than leading to a standardized curriculum, the "Carnegie unit" measure has allowed local school districts to offer a broad range of high school courses, including vocational training, while imposing a uniform amount of "seat-time" per course as necessary for high school graduation. The coursework measure persisted even after the National Education Association formally abandoned its support for the Committee of Ten's college-preparatory curriculum and advocated that high schools offer both academic coursework and "practical" subjects, including business education, household arts, agriculture, art education, industrial arts, music, and physical education (National Education Association of the United States, 1918).

The so-called general education curriculum, which formed the underpinning philosophy of the GED test, was developed by progressive educators as a reaction against the college-preparatory track. Its minimalist approach was explained in large part by its origins in the scientific movement of the 1910s. Franklin Bobbitt, an education professor at the University of Chicago, advocated that the scientific management principles and time motion studies used by Frederick W. Taylor and his colleagues to increase worker productivity in manufacturing should also be applied to decisions about what to teach students in high school (Callahan, 1962). Rather than relying on past traditions to determine the high school curricula, Bobbitt (1924) urged curriculum planners to conduct task analyses to identify the knowledge and competencies needed for specific work activities and to then measure attainment of the skills identified. Using the model of the factory, Bobbitt (1913) envisioned the student as the raw material, the teacher as the worker, and the ideal adult as the finished product. The curriculum expert would determine the skills a student needed, while the teacher's job would be to meet the expert's prescribed outcomes as quickly and efficiently as possible. Bobbitt expected all high school students to acquire only "general education," which he defined as "that portion of the training, both foundational and functional, which is of general need, whatever be one's occupation or station in life." Subjects not needed in daily life would be taken only by students pursuing specific occupational training (Bobbitt, 1924, 66). He argued, for example, that "activity-analysis" indicated that trigonometry was needed by engineers, but not by "typists, physicians or milliners," and therefore should not be prescribed as a course for general education (Bobbitt, 1924, 67).

In the 1930s and 1940s, two men responsible for creating the GED testing program held particular prominence in the general education movement: Ralph W. Tyler, a dominant force in the field of curriculum evaluation, and E. F. Lindquist, who became the foremost authority on multiple-choice testing. Tyler's applications of "activity analysis" for his doctoral dissertation at the University of Chicago led him into the field of educational evaluation and helped shape his thinking on appropriate methods for determining the high school curriculum. Tyler's views on secondary education were likely also influenced by the short time that he had spent in high school. Tyler entered ninth grade at age 12 and was soon expelled for a school prank: adding skunk secretions to the paint used to coat the school radiators. Tyler's father, seeking to occupy the highly energetic and intelligent youth upon his reinstatement in school, arranged for him to attend high school in the mornings and to work afternoons and evenings in a local creamery. Although Tyler was employed nine hours a day seven days a week, he managed to graduate from high school at age 15. He went on to earn his undergraduate degree at age 19 while working 56 hours a week as a telegraph operator (Tyler, 1987).

In 1934 Tyler attained national prominence as a spokesman on high school reform when he was made research director for the evaluation staff of the Eight Year Study, a Progressive Education Association project supporting curriculum changes at 30 mainly affluent schools (Krug, 1964; Tyler, 1935). The initiative was supported with over one million dollars—a staggering sum during the Great Depression—in grants from the Rockefeller General Education Board, which was committed to applying business management principles to schools and moving high schools away from the traditional college-preparatory curriculum. (Midway through the project, Tyler and most of his staff moved from Ohio State University to the University of Chicago, where Tyler was named university examiner and chairman of the Education Department.)

While Tyler collaborated with classroom teachers on development of course objectives, he and his staff prepared their own quantitative instruments to measure the students' outcomes. As Tyler and his group explained, they distrusted the ability of the classroom teachers to be objective in scoring essay tests. They criticized teachers' usage of short-answer questions as limiting "the number of principles which could be sampled because of the time required by the student to write out the answers" (Smith, Tyler, and the Evaluation Staff, 1942, 85). The multiple-choice tests designed by Tyler and colleagues—the experts—were heralded as providing objective assessments of student progress. Writing skills and creative thinking were not concerns since students would not be expected to share their own ideas on the new-style tests. The Eight Year Study's quantitative measures also helped attract media attention and continued financial support. A *Time* Magazine cover story in October 1938 reported that one school's pupils "came through with flying colors" on "the most searching [tests] of their kinds ever made" and included examples of the quantitative "test results":

> From Lincoln School in Manhattan, perhaps the top-ranking Progressive school in the U.S., which is subsidized by Rockefeller money and had two Rockefeller boys as students, groups of pupils last year went to visit coal mines, steel mills, farms, TVA. This experiment was financed by the Alfred P. Sloan Foundation. Last week, after careful tests, Ohio State's Dr. Louis Rath, an evaluator for P.E.A., reported that in a ten-day trip and six weeks of related classroom study, high-school juniors gained 15% in consistency of their thinking, became markedly more liberal, [and] matured two years in thinking power. (*Time*, Editorial, October 31, 1938, 33–34)

The Eight Year Study brought Tyler support from the American Council on Education, one of the national groups championing the general education curriculum and a publisher of new-style tests. The council had been organized during World War I to involve the national associations of higher education in the war effort. One of its first objectives was to prevent college-educated men from being used on the battle lines in order to avoid "destroying the reservoirs for the production of experts" and "the reckless waste of irreplaceable talent" (Capen, 1940, 42). Toward that end, ACE had developed tests for use in selecting, training, and assigning World War I military personnel. ACE continued its testing work after the war and maintained a membership of national education organizations, colleges and universities, state departments of education, city school systems, and private schools (Dobbins, 1968; Tyler, 1987). After World War I, ACE experimented with psychological examinations for college freshmen (supported by a grant from the Commonwealth Fund) and sponsored a Cooperative College Study in General Education (financed with Rockefeller and Carnegie money) to encourage colleges to develop new-style tests for appraising student outcomes in general education studies (Dobbins, 1968; Fosdick, 1962). By 1939, ACE was drawing income from annual sales of over two million copies of its new-style measurement tests. ACE used these financial resources and its national position to advocate for educational policies related to testing and curricula (American Council on Education, 1939).

To advance fundamental changes in high school curricula, in 1940 ACE published a report, *What the High Schools Ought to Teach*, authored by an ACE committee that included Tyler (Graham, 1940). The book recommended that schools prepare youth for the daily activities they would encounter in adult life through "general education" coursework in subjects such as personal problems, physical and mental health, family life, and social studies, along with paid and unpaid work experience programs. The book attacked the college-preparatory curriculum of English composition, algebra, science, history, and foreign language as "the vicious aspects of ninth grade" (Graham, 1940, 31). It went on to recommend that youth be taught to persist at work largely through part-time volunteer or paid work experience rather than vocational classes, arguing that a large portion of American workers held jobs requiring little skill or training.

2.3 The Basis for the GED Test Battery: Testing What Iowa High Schools "Ought" to Teach

E. F. Lindquist, a faculty member at the University of Iowa and one of Tyler's fellow test writers for ACE projects, was the author of the first statewide tests written to measure "general educational development." It was the need for speed in grading tests that had first led Lindquist to develop expertise in the new-style tests approach used for the Iowa testing program and adopted for the GED test—speed and the popularity of a statewide academic contest. Lindquist's work in standardized test development began in 1929 when the University of Iowa initiated a contest, the "Iowa Academic Meet," to provide an incentive for academic achievement in high school. University faculty explained the need for the testing competition:

> Accounts of dinners given to reward heroes of the gridiron, the track, the basketball floor, constitute a large feature in our high school papers, together with extended accounts of such games portraying in graphic detail the fine teaching or coaching because of which the contestants vied so fiercely. However, we look over these high school papers in vain for accounts of dinners in honor of pupils of outstanding achievements in English, mathematics, science or other activities that are presumed to furnish the basic activities by which high school pupils are educated. (Kirby, 1928, 1)

The first tests for the meet focused on Carnegie unit subjects taught in the Iowa high schools and drew upon state "courses of study," commonly used textbooks, and classroom materials. In addition, Lindquist and his staff published "subject matter circulars" to guide teachers in preparing for the contests. Under Lindquist's direction, the University of Iowa developed tests in 12 high school subjects: first-year algebra, plane geometry, English mechanics for grades nine and ten, English and American literature for grades eleven and twelve, general science for grade nine, physics, American history, world history, fourth-semester typewriting, and stenography. The tests were 45 minutes in length in order to fit into the normal class period and were later lengthened to 60 minutes (Peterson, 1953).

The academic contests were an immediate success, and within three years over half of the high school students in Iowa were participating. Local school winners competed at district contests, with a thousand students progressing to a state contest in Iowa City, dubbed the "Brain Derby." The top two winners in each subject were announced at an awards banquet (Lindquist, 1930, 1970).

The first Iowa tests included a variety of matching, fill-in-the-blank, true-false, and multiple-choice questions. The English mechanics test required students to mark grammar corrections directly in their test booklets; some algebra and geometry items were computational and required open-ended responses. The typewriting test featured an actual typing demonstration, and the stenography exam included dictation exercises, but these two vocational tests were soon dropped. Given the popularity of the contest and the number of participants, the speed of scoring became increasingly important to question design. Consequently, during the early years of the competition, Lindquist converted many of the questions to multiple-choice items that could be marked on separate answer sheets and graded quickly by staff and volunteers. Julia Peterson, one of Lindquist's colleagues, described the advantages of the testing format in her 1953 history of the Iowa testing program:

> Local school staffs administered and scored the first set of tests, computed local averages, and reported their results to Iowa City in nine days. Administration and scoring of the district tests were also done locally under supervision by the superintendent of the host school and assistants from nearby schools, duly approved by the central office. With up to 24 pupils qualifying from each school, 2,000 "whiz kids" might assemble in a single district—quite an invasion for the smaller towns to handle. The tests had to be scored the same day—or night—so that results could be announced promptly to anxious contestants. In the final contest in Iowa City, test scoring was done by the chairman's colleagues and staff; again, scoring was virtually curbside, to permit announcement of all winners at the banquet on the second evening. (Peterson, 1953, 5)

The university provided staff time for development of the tests and supervision of their use, with schools paying for the test booklets and administration at the local level. This modest beginning provided the University of Iowa with test scores from thousands of students in the state and laid the basis for what would become a national testing industry. After Lindquist was named program director in 1931, he discontinued the district contests, renamed the event the State Scholarship Contest, and relabeled the test battery the Iowa Every-Pupil Achievement Tests. Lindquist required school districts entering the competition to test their entire student bodies so that he could develop statewide norms for each course area, conduct "postmortem" test item analysis, and experiment with improvements in test questions and format. In 1935, Lindquist began reporting school rankings to each school in confidential summary reports (Lindquist, 1970; Peterson, 1953).

Lindquist and his staff constantly strove to improve the scoring of the tests at the lowest possible cost. Over the years they invented everything from a device for normalizing the moisture content of answer sheet paper to a high-speed electronic scoring and recording machine. After developing the separate answer sheet, Lindquist introduced a scoring procedure to discourage students from guessing on their test answers (Peterson, 1953). Lindquist also worked to change the type of test questions used, efforts spurred by his association with Tyler and others in the general education movement.

During his collaboration with Tyler on test development for ACE, Lindquist came to view the Iowa contest tests as extremely limited in their approach to knowledge, placing too much emphasis on memorization and the competitive nature of the "Brain Derby." He resolved to revise the Iowa testing program by experimenting with test items used by his ACE colleagues in order to advance those educational objectives he viewed as most important. In 1938, Lindquist sought university funding to develop a new high school testing program "that would very significantly improve the quality of educational guidance in Iowa schools, [and] that would counteract the 'subject matter consciousness' which now permeates high school teaching." Echoing the themes of the Eight Year Study, Lindquist argued to his dean that the Iowa high schools' ninth- and tenth-grade instruction in mathematics was "futile, if not worse" (Lindquist, 1935). Lindquist also tried to eliminate the academic contest. Campus administrators, however, refused to drop the event, given its great popularity throughout the state and its importance in recruiting academically talented high school graduates to the state university (Lindquist, 1970).

In an October 1941 address to school administrators, Lindquist openly voiced his concern about the limitations of the Iowa Every-Pupil Tests and other course-oriented examinations: "The selection of content of the tests used has been based on an analysis of the things now being taught in the school subjects, not on our or anyone else's notion of what *ought* to be taught in these subjects" (Lindquist, 1941, 14). What were needed, Lindquist (1942a) contended, were tests of general educational development that would force teachers to redirect their focus to skills not emphasized in their current classes.

America's entry into World War II provided the climate in which Lindquist could permanently discontinue the spring testing contest and introduce his new test battery, the Iowa Tests of Educational Development (ITED). "We had spent five years developing the materials and planning procedures for a new high school program," Lindquist later explained, "and thus were all set to go when the time seemed opportune" (Lindquist, 1970, 11).

The ITED had nine subtests in the battery and required about seven and one-half hours to complete. The ITED test questions were unrelated to specific high school coursework, and Lindquist (1942b) initiated new practices of administering the *same* test battery to students in all four grade levels and at the *beginning*, rather than the end, of the school year. Consistent with the progressive educators' emphasis on teaching reading in high school, three ITED reading tests equated high school performance with the ability to understand reading passages in the social sciences, natural sciences, and literature. These tests, which Lindquist viewed as the heart of his ITED battery, provided paragraphs for students to read and interpret through a series of multiple-choice questions. The approach was considered avant-garde since it had not been used previously in published standardized tests (Peterson, 1953). As Lindquist explained, "There are many different kinds of situations in which a person has occasion to use his education, but *that which lends itself most readily to testing is the reading situation*—that in which he interprets, evaluates critically, and employs in his own thinking, information and ideas which are presented to him in print [emphasis added]" (Lindquist, 1944, 367). The math test focused on practical problems in arithmetic, the only math Lindquist thought the majority of students needed. Accordingly, the ITED did not test knowledge of high school algebra, plane geometry, solid geometry, or trigonometry, but instead measured "the ability to deal with numbers, and . . . problems on such things as estimating expenses on home repairs, handling simple business transactions, figuring out costs on your own insurance, taxes, investments, installment purchases, and so on" (Lindquist, Van Dyke, and Yale, 1948, 34–35). Consistent with the ACE's tract *What the High Schools Ought to Teach*, the test excluded composition exercises, questions on foreign languages, and measures of outcomes from vocational education and other elective courses.

2.4 Advocating Educational Changes during the War Years

Like Lindquist, other educational reformers seized upon America's entry into World War II as an opportune time to promote their new-style multiple-choice tests, general education curriculum, and testing-for-credit alternatives to the Carnegie unit system. Within two weeks after the bombing of Pearl Harbor, the College Entrance Examination Board announced suspension of its College Board essay examinations in favor of the Scholastic Aptitude Test (SAT), which the board had been trying to promote since 1926 (Lemann, 1999). Six months after the Pearl Harbor attack, Robert Maynard Hutchins (1942) announced that the University of Chicago would begin awarding Bachelor of Arts college degrees in general education to students completing only two rather than four years of college. In an article in the *Educational Record* defending his position, Hutchins rationalized that

> the [bachelor's] degree is universally recognized as something everybody ought to have if he can scrape up the time and money to get it. It is time-honored in the sense that people have wanted it for a long time. It is not universally recognized as meaning anything except graduation from some kind of college. (Hutchins, 1942, 570–571)

The credential, Hutchins maintained, had served to "thwart the national reorganization of American education." Hutchins therefore proposed "to give it meaning and function and to use the recognition and honor in which it is held for good educational ends" (Hutchins, 1942, 571–572).[2] Similarly, the American Council on Education began using foundation funds to prepare a one-year high school general education program to introduce as a response to the federal government's reduction in the military draft age (American Council on Education, 1943a; Zook, 1943).

The vehicle Tyler, Lindquist, and the ACE staff used to further their general education curriculum and tests was a civilian panel appointed to help the military plan for the off-duty entertainment of U.S. troops as America prepared for war. In early 1941, the military established a Joint Army and Navy Committee on Welfare and Recreation to address soldier morale by focusing on entertainment programs, motion picture schedules, Red Cross services, and control of prostitution and venereal disease. Its Subcommittee on Music coordinated musical entertainment at the military camps. Its Subcommittee on Education, for which ACE offered to provide staff, was charged with arranging discussion groups, library services, correspondence course programs, visual education, and pamphlet materials for use by military personnel in their leisure hours (Advisory Council of the Joint Army Navy Committee on Welfare Education, 1943; Aiken, 1942; Subcommittee on Education, Welfare, and Recreation, 1942).

When the War Department established the Army Institute of Correspondence Study (later renamed the United States Armed Force Institute, USAFI) at the University of Wisconsin in Madison in April 1941, ACE used the center as a focal point for promoting both its new-style testing and its curriculum changes (Aiken, 1942; Keppel, 1943; Zook, 1943). ACE successfully lobbied the Army Institute to pay for creation of new-style tests for military courses as well as for correspondence courses being offered to service personnel—even though the correspondence courses that the University

2. Reaction to Hutchins's announcement was almost universally negative. The president of Allegheny College criticized the so-called reform as short-changing students and denounced Hutchins's excuse of the war to promote his changes. The plan was prepared, he charged, "as a coldly calculated, cleverly timed, permanent change" (Trolley, 1942, 596). The president of the University of Texas disagreed with Hutchins's claim that the contemporary bachelor's degree lacked a clear definition. College, he maintained, "required fifteen good Carnegie units to enter, and it took four years and 120 semester hours of good solid content to get out with its degree" (Rainey, 1942, 586). He urged other schools to ignore the University of Chicago's action, observing that any school willing to drop intercollegiate football, as Hutchins had recently done, had nothing left to fear from public criticism. In 1950, the University of Chicago, finding that its "bachelor's degrees" were not generally accepted, returned to the traditional four-year college degree program (Wechsler, 1977).

of Wisconsin was collecting from around the country already had final exams (Aiken, 1942).

Accordingly, in May of 1942, the military contracted with the University of Chicago, whose examination staff was headed by Tyler, to develop subject matter exams in specific fields of study. They rewrote 700 end-of-the-course tests for existing correspondence courses, replacing the colleges' essay examinations with new multiple-choice questions promising "greater comparability and less danger of error" (Detchen, 1947, 467). In short order, a three-man team of testing experts—Tyler, Lindquist, and E. G. Williamson (a psychology professor from the University of Minnesota)—gained authority through the Army Institute/USAFI to review the teaching materials for all correspondence courses, to broker with colleges and universities for recognition of college credits for military courses, and to "appraise the comprehensive examinations developed to measure the competence of the soldier" (American Council on Education, 1943b; Subcommittee on Education, Welfare, and Recreation, 1942, 8–9).

Throughout the war, the testing experts pressed for civilian educational reforms, including greater emphasis on general education, an end to Carnegie unit coursework standards, and adoption of tests alone to measure the educational advancement of military personnel. The singlemindedness with which Tyler and his colleagues promoted multiple-choice testing to the exclusion of other measures of achievement is evidenced in the minutes of their meetings with the military, which are now stored at the National Archives. The experts objected strenuously in the summer of 1942 when they learned of the Navy Department's proposals to give credits for specialists' courses and for "character and leadership shown by ratings and promotions" (Advisory Committee to the Army Institute, 1942a, 1). They charged that such credits violated ACE's positions that credit recommendations should be made only by civilian educators and that only norm-referenced tests be used for credit determinations. The experts even objected to the issuance of certificates for completing military courses, warning that the service personnel might later present these certificates to colleges for credit. When a military officer proposed issuing certificates that would report competence demonstrated in major course objectives, Lindquist protested that the military could distribute coursework certificates only if his evaluation team had first developed civilian norms for each objective. A countersuggestion was to issue soldiers papers upon their completion of military training programs, which would state that they were "ready" to take examination. The military rejected the idea as insulting to the service personnel (Advisory Committee to the Army Institute, 1943b).

The testing experts spurned job performance as a measure of course competence. They turned down a proposal to develop tests to allow college credit for foreign language skills that service personnel were acquiring in Turkish, Dutch, Moroccan, Arabic, Japanese, Russian, and other languages not typically offered in American colleges. The experts dismissed these skills as "scarcely of the quality that merits consideration for credit" (Advisory Committee to the Army Institute, 1943a, 2). They opposed recommending credits for Army training in radio maintenance, for one example, unless end-of-course tests were developed and first given to samples of high school and college students, ignoring the obvious alternative measure of successful performance on the job (Aiken, 1942). In another case, the experts described tests that might be considered appropriate for a military course in contemporary European history. Here, the ACE experts, with their life-adjustment curricular emphasis, advised the military that they could test the student's knowledge of events along with true-false attitudinal questions, calculating "the degree to which the student accepts current prejudice and the degree to which he is open minded" (Aiken, 1942, 6).

2.5 Testing General Educational Development in the Military

Going well beyond the Subcommittee on Education's original purpose of encouraging off-duty educational programming, the testing experts recommended that for-credit exams be made available to all service personnel. They thought that even those who had not enrolled in military courses, taken correspondence courses, or used self-instructional materials should be included. They urged USAFI to finance this new testing work to appraise the level of "general competence" reached by personnel through any type of experience while in the armed forces. To spur this work, Tyler, Lindquist, and Williamson began searching for what they described as "a battery of tests of general educational competence; to enable the school or college to effect an appropriate educational placement of the applicant in terms of his indicated educational maturity and the extent to which he has met the general educational requirements of the school or college" (American Council on Education, 1943b, 13). The meeting minutes of the testing advisers acknowledged that "there might be some search made for a body of common experiences which would be typical for the men who will have undergone the Army 'culture'" (Army Institute Project Staff, 1942, 3), but this approach was never pursued. Instead, the group moved quickly to identify an existing test battery that met their list of criteria: immediate availability, ease of administration, availability of existing norms, usefulness for counseling, minimum overlapping of tests, and the extent to which the tests recognized skills and knowledge resulting from "maturity" rather than mastery of traditional high school content. Two intelligence tests, the Army's General Classification Test and the American Council on Education Psychological Examination, were considered and rejected. Tyler's comprehensive exams used by University of Chicago students were deemed too "indigenous" to that school except for use as subject matter tests. The Eight Year Study tests on logical reasoning, interpretation of data, and social sensitivity were recommended for use in granting college credit rather than for admissions purposes. (The group suggested that colleges could grant a year's work, 32 semester hours of credit, based on measures of "social maturity.") The experts agreed that the best tests for reading, general information, and English were the Iowa Tests of Educational Development (ITED).

The Iowa tests had features that were of critical importance to Tyler and Lindquist. The ITED reflected the progressive educators' agenda for practical coursework that downplayed both the classical and vocational high school curricula and emphasized what the progressives believed high school *ought* to teach rather than current course offerings. The multiple-choice test battery appeared to be "objective," thus avoiding subject matter debates that would inevitably arise from essay exams, the commonly used tests of the day. The ITED tests had the added advantage that staff with little or no education in test taking (or knowledge of high school subjects) could grade them. They had already been normed on high school students in Iowa (Lindquist, 1944, 1970). Lindquist proposed that USAFI use his Iowa test battery for the first GED test battery in order to implement the testing program as quickly as possible (Lindquist, 1970; Peterson, 1953). While the Iowa tests were totally unrelated to military life or to the war experience, they would allow the testing experts to compare veterans on the same scales used to rank high school students in Iowa.

At its October 1942 meeting, the three-man advisory team selected five of the nine Iowa tests to use for their test battery (Special Committee of the Army Institute, 1942). Williamson, in particular, wanted the Iowa tests shortened so that time would be available to counsel each veteran. For his part Lindquist supported shorter tests to simplify the scoring and to encourage more service personnel to take the exams. The group concluded that the three Iowa reading tests, the general mathematics test, and the grammar ("Correctness and Effectiveness of Expression") test, altogether requiring 265 minutes, would constitute a suitable time frame for their proposed "general educational development" (GED) test battery. Lindquist opposed the addition of essay exams, regardless of whether the essays were evaluated by military personnel or forwarded to the colleges for review. He urged that he be allowed to keep the high school GED test battery as nearly correlated as possible with the current ITED so that his staff could concentrate on writing questions for a college-edition GED test battery (Feister and Whitney, 1968).[3]

Tyler suggested that the new testing program be introduced during the war, and that the first to be tested should be injured service personnel who were being discharged or transferred into veteran rehabilitation programs. The advantages of using early war casualties were laid out in the minutes of his meeting with the Army Institute Project staff:

1. The way will be led by certain prestige institutions. 2. It will be considered a patriotic duty to help in the situation. 3. With high school and college enrollments depleted as they are, and with the great possibility that the government will subsidize the education of these men, institutions will be happy to cooperate for economic reasons. (Army Institute Project Staff, 1942, 1–2)

At this stage, the GED test was offered as one of several tools for guiding school administrators in student placement (American Council on Education, 1943b), and ACE held meetings around the country to lobby for its acceptance. ACE distributed a civilian version of the high school-level GED test, which it encouraged colleges to use with their current students and civilian applicants. The idea behind this test was to develop local campus norms for admission of veterans who had not completed high school or who had poor high school records (Zook, 1944). ACE assembled representatives of the regional college accrediting associations, all of whom subsequently endorsed the concept of using the GED test for college admissions and credit. ACE held meetings for college administrators where it warned that some colleges might repeat the post–World War I

---

3. Other civilian consultants to the military recommended using the Iowa Tests of Educational Development on a *temporary basis* and expressed concern that colleges would be dissatisfied if the battery were continued indefinitely (Advisory Committee to the Army Institute, 1942–1943; Special Committee of the Army Institute, 1942). They recommended that the mathematics test be "stepped up in difficulty and include a bit more of formal high school mathematics"; that the literature section include more references to significant "classics"; that the social sciences reading test include more environmental concepts; and that the natural sciences reading test provide more evaluation of data used to support conclusions (Advisory Committee to the Army Institute, 1942–1943, 3). These changes were not made, however, even though Lindquist worked with Tyler's USAFI examination staff at the University of Chicago for two years constructing additional forms of the high school and college-level GED test (Lindquist, 1970).

"indefensible practice of liberal blanket credit for military experience" (Zook, 1944, 206), tempting students to "shop around" for the school or college where they could obtain the largest number of credits. Ralph Tyler (1954) later explained that his opposition to "blanket credit" stemmed from concerns that many veterans admitted into college after World War I and granted college credits based on their wartime records were unprepared for college-level work or were enrolled directly in advanced coursework that they could not handle, causing them to drop out of college altogether.

By mid-1943, ACE reported that over 400 colleges and universities had officially endorsed its recommendations for the GED entrance test and awarding of end-of-the-course test credits (American Council on Education, 1943b; Zook, 1943). Using funds from the military, ACE distributed 50,000 booklets describing its course credit recommendations and hired staff to stump the country arguing for accepting the testing programs. At first, the ITED/GED test battery was presented *not* as a credentialing device but solely as a tool for placing returning war veterans in school and for determining how these men and women compared to the student populations traditionally enrolled at each institution. Thus, Lindquist and Tyler offered the fruits of the Iowa "Brain Derby" to save veterans from wasting time back in high school and to allow those with sufficient "general educational development" to advance directly to college.

2.6 Using the ITED/GED Test as an Alternative to High School "Wartime Diplomas"

While the colleges were debating policies to use for injured war veterans and future GI enrollees, local school districts were faced with the immediate problem of high school students enlisting or facing the draft into military service. Within months after the United States entered World War II, the U.S. Office of Education War-Time Commission (U.S. Office of Education War-Time Commission, 1942) urged high schools to provide accelerated education for teenagers desiring to enlist. The Commission recommended summer school, longer school days, and special scheduling to allow part-time attendance by students who farmed or secured jobs in wartime industries. Schools also were encouraged to permit students to graduate early so that they could enter the military or college in the spring. When the draft age was lowered from 20 to 18 in November 1942, local educators debated whether to encourage their students to seek deferments or to grant them diplomas before they left high school. In December of 1942,

Wisconsin passed a law requiring high schools and teachers colleges to grant diplomas to all seniors who went into the armed services (Advisory Committee to the Army Institute, 1942b). By October 1943, at least 11 states were providing diplomas for youth who had enlisted during their junior or senior year of high school (Elicker, 1943). Delaware "war diplomas," for example, were given to veterans who had completed their junior year and entered the service before graduation, and read, "Serving with the colors; diploma on completion of eleven (or eleven and one-half, as appropriate) years" (Hess, 1946b, 102). Iowa allowed local high schools to issue a "Special Veteran's Diploma" for two years of high school, provided that the veteran had taken American history and civics. One high school principal who favored this approach for enlistees with satisfactory high school records wrote in the National Association of Secondary-School Principals (NASSP) *Bulletin*, "If your conscience balks, your conscience needs education. . . . No harm can possibly come from the issuance of a diploma under such conditions. The candidate will have the equivalent before he is through, so that the spirit will be satisfied, though the letter may be lacking" (Hill, 1943, 40).

ACE cited the argument it had used against "blanket" college credits for war veterans' military service as its primary reason for opposing state and high school issuances of "wartime diplomas" to teens leaving for war and to GIs returning to the states from the battlefield (regardless of whether they were interested in college). The numbers involved were considerable. According to later military estimates, nearly 10 million World War II veterans had not completed high school, although half had some high school education (Lynde, 1945). Since neither the military nor the federal government could grant high school credentials, ACE staff worked to convince the various state departments of education of the value of using their GED test as the basis for awarding high school degrees. ACE actively lobbied to discourage states from awarding high school "wartime diplomas" to returning veterans. It also successfully thwarted a wartime attempt by the Marine Corps Institute to provide high school accreditation through the New York State Board of Regents; this would have allowed development of an alternative high school credential that more closely mirrored traditional high school requirements (Advisory Committee to the Army Institute, 1943b).

In early 1943, Lindquist prevailed upon the War Department to ask over 1,000 high schools to participate in a GED norming study, announcing: "In the near future these tests will be given primarily to men being discharged because of wounds or illness—at the time of general demobilization the tests will be given to a much larger group."[4] In all, 35,000 high school seniors from around the country were given one of the GED subtests for the norming study—thus providing Lindquist with a national database for his testing work.

Given ACE's aversion to granting high school "wartime diplomas" to young recruits who entered the military before completing their senior year, one might have expected that the standard set for passing the GED test at a score deemed "equivalent" to high school would be quite high. On the contrary, ACE's Committee on Accrediting Procedures selected the *seventh percentile* as the recommended cut score for passing each GED subtest— that is, the score higher than only 7% of high school seniors tested for the norming study but lower than the other 93% of the high school population tested (United States Armed Forces Institute, 1944). Lindquist also decided not to penalize test takers for guessing, a procedure he had introduced in the ITED. As a result, for most of the GED subtests the seventh percentile required answering only one or two questions above that which could be achieved by random guessing (Spaulding, 1943).[5] Only on the grammar test were candidates required to answer well above chance (i.e., to answer 15 questions above chance out of 100) to pass (United States Armed Forces Institute, 1944).

Because the Iowa test's content served as the basis for the GED test, the questions were geared toward the interests and knowledge base of traditional Iowa school students rather than veterans. According to a contemporary reviewer, *none* of the reading passages on the social studies test related to war, geography, or military strategy, and nearly 40% of the items on the

4. Lindquist did not sample those schools most likely to enroll the largest number of adults—evening, technical, vocational, or continuation schools. Nor did he sample two-year high schools or Negro schools.

5. The "Tables for Converting Raw Scores to Standard Scores" indicate that the raw score required to pass the GED mathematics test at the seventh percentile (a standard score of 35 on the GED's 20-to 80-point scale) was 11 questions correct out of 50. Since each question on the mathematics test had five multiple-choice stems, a student guessing on all 50 questions would on average answer 10 correctly, and the ACE-recommended score required only one question correct above chance. In fact, the seventh percentile on the mathematics tests marked the lowest possible score above the chance score that could be achieved by random guessing on all test items. In the GED test of reading in social studies, the candidate again was required to answer only one question above chance—out of 73 questions. In the GED test of reading in the natural sciences, the candidate was required to answer only 2 questions above chance out of 65. In the test of reading in literature, the candidate was required to answer only 3 questions above chance out of 85.

grammar test related to punctuation, "with a heavy concentration on the use of quotation marks for indicating conversation" (Conrad, 1949, 41). Later, Lindquist would begin describing the GED test as measuring the "lasting outcomes" of a high school education, even though he had designed the ITED to help teachers measure academic progress *during* not *after* high school. Ignoring the GED's origins as a test for Iowa high schoolers, Lindquist (1944) also began citing a whole series of wartime experiences (i.e., international travel, exposure to foreign languages and social customs, technical training) that presumably were being quantified through the ITED/GED test. These wartime concerns were notably missing from the Iowa test questions and subsequent test batteries based on the ITED. Given the ITED/GED test's emphasis on the three R's rather than on knowledge more likely acquired through military experiences or in the current high school-level courses, many *elementary* school completers could pass the test, as evidenced by the Iowa test scores for students entering their freshman year. Test score data from the Iowa Tests of Educational Development indicate that the cut scores recommended for passing each GED subtest were achieved by a majority of Iowa students at the *beginning* of high school.[6] Since the GED test did not reduce test scores for wrong answers, the percentages of Iowa freshmen passing would have been, if anything, even higher.

While Lindquist had provided percentile ranking scores to Iowa students for the ITED, none of the early GED test manual materials identified the seventh percentile as the recommended cut score. Nor did they discuss why such a low norm was selected as the appropriate passing score. Instead, three years into the program the ACE staff (Detchen, 1947) announced that only 80% of the seniors tested could pass all five tests, even though *none* of the high school seniors in the 1943 norming group actually took more than one subtest (Bloom and Statler, 1957; United States Armed Forces Institute, undated). Early high pass rates for the GED test among veterans tested also appear to refute this claim (as discussed below).

6. Lindquist (1946) provided ITED test scores comparable to the norms recommended for passing the GED test battery to the coordinator of the Veterans School in Dubuque. See also the norming tables in College of Education, "Grade Percentile Norms for the Iowa Tests of Educational Development" (1943). Published grade-percentile norms for the ITED at levels comparable to the GED pass scores showed that even when penalized for wrong answers 81% of freshmen *entering* Iowa high schools could pass the mathematics test, 70% could pass the reading test in the natural sciences, 60% could pass the reading test in literature, 57% could pass the correctness and effectiveness of expression test, and 55% could pass the reading test in social studies.

2.7 Promoting the General Education Curriculum

A less successful initiative of ACE and its testing experts during the war was their promotion of the general education curricula. The primacy of the experts' interest in general education was seen in an argument at a December 1942 advisory committee meeting with the military. Even with Russia under siege and most of the European continent under Axis control, Lindquist expressed regret that the testing staff had to devote its major attention to technical courses. He was anxious to develop general education programs. In reaction, a school superintendent from Michigan observed that he "thought the primary job of the committee was to promote the work of the Army Institute in winning the war and not to promote any particular type of education" (Advisory Committee to the Army Institute, 1942b, 3). In spite of pressure from the ACE advocates, the Army Institute refused to finance coursework planning for general education; the Institute's position was that such courses should be developed at university, rather than military, expense (Advisory Committee to the Army Institute, 1943a). At one Advisory Committee meeting, the principal of the Milwaukee Vocational School questioned whether the testing experts' own colleges would accept the general education curriculum they were promoting for the military. He was told that "acceptance of the accreditation principle based on tests was a powerful first step" (Advisory Committee to the Army Institute, 1943b, 3).

In June 1944, the month of the Allied invasion of Normandy, the American Council on Education (1944) issued a detailed outline for a general education curriculum for the last two years of high school and first two years of college. Vocational education was downplayed, and the only math recommended was high school algebra. A single, nondiversified curriculum was proposed that would lead the graduates to a "common set of ideals" and "common outlook on life." Among the life-adjustment courses recommended were personal and community health, problems in social adjustment, marriage and family adjustment, and development of American thought and institutions. ACE claimed that this curriculum would address the "war emergency" and was also necessary to guide colleges in redesigning higher education after the war (Zook, 1943). This curriculum and the "general education" test supporting it garnered little interest, however, at the college level (as seen below).

2.8 Institutional Support for GED Testing at the War's End

The American Council on Education's success in furthering its testing-for-credit program at the war's end was due in no small part to the considerable financial support it received from the Rockefeller General Education

Board and the Carnegie Corporation. Both of them were eager to champion the expanded use of the new-style multiple-choice testing (Zook, 1946). In addition, ACE had secured copyrights for the GED, subject matter, and end-of-the-course tests prepared for USAFI by the Examination Staff at the University of Chicago. ACE sold its test booklets at cost to the military and at competitive prices to educational institutions and signed a contract with the University of Chicago to serve as its publishing agent for the tests.

The accrediting associations and several other national agencies provided financial support for developing a 900-page ACE guide (Tuttle, 1944), listing courses provided in the military along with credit recommendations. The Veterans Administration purchased 25,000 copies for free distribution to high schools and colleges (Zook, 1946, 1947). USAFI carried on a voluminous correspondence with educational institutions answering their specific concerns and clarifying the content of coursework and also provided transcripts to service personnel summarizing the extent of their military training. At the same time, USAFI guidelines emphasized the military's "hands-off" policy toward determining which military activities were deserving of college or high school credits (Sims, 1974).

To facilitate GED testing outside the military, in 1945 ACE established the Veterans Testing Service (VTS) at the University of Chicago to distribute GED tests for use in credentialing war veterans as high school graduate equivalents. In January 1946, Tyler reported that the VTS had contracted with 58 civilian institutions, including high schools and colleges, to handle GED testing for discharged personnel (Advisory Committee to the United States Armed Forces Institute, 1946). Three years later, ACE President Zook was able to announce, "Notwithstanding the many questions which may properly be raised with respect to the GED tests, it seems to me clear that we shall not again return to a system which requires actual attendance in class as an indispensable element in receiving academic credit" (Zook, 1948, 241).

2.9 Acceptance of the ITED/GED as a College Entrance Exam for Veterans

The task of selling the GED as a college entrance exam was greatly facilitated by the enthusiastic reception war veterans received upon their return to the states and by federal legislation that supported their enrollment in colleges and universities. The Servicemen's Readjustment Act, nicknamed the GI Bill of Rights by an American Legion ex-newspaperman, was unanimously passed by Congress in the summer of 1944. In all, over two million World War II veterans would attend college under the GI Bill (Olson, 1974).

Given postwar patriotic sentiments, the maturity of veteran college applicants, and the GI Bill funding, it is not surprising that whenever possible, campuses sought to accept veterans who had dropped out of high school to fight in the war, but who possessed sufficient academic skills to handle college-level work. Procedures for admitting high school noncompleters varied widely; most surveyed colleges accepted the GED test as a basis for admitting veterans, and about half indicated no restrictions other than a passing score on the tests (National Association of Secondary-School Principals, 1948). Most schools gave veterans preference over nonveterans for admission and praised their seriousness in college, noting their maturity and stronger motivation (Atkinson, 1949) as well as their determination in spite of having fewer high school prerequisites (Roeber, 1950). Several studies, however, raised questions about the long-term efficacy of using the GED testing route for college. A study at Indiana University attributed veterans' higher grade point averages to their age rather than their military service. The study warned that the quality of veteran students was declining because "the present entering veterans are simply younger, and, therefore, more like the non-veteran students" (Shaffer, 1948, 205). A second Indiana study reported that GED-certified veterans earned poorer grades and had higher attrition rates, and recommended raising the total GED test score required for college admission and limiting GED testing to persons over age 20 (D'Amico, 1953). Another study of 16 colleges found that veterans who never left the States generally earned better grades than those who served overseas, with or without combat duty (Olson, 1974).

2.10 States Adopt GED Credentials: Giving Veterans "the Benefit of the Doubt"

Most state departments of education supporting the GED test as the basis for veterans' high school diplomas preferred passing scores set low enough to ensure credentials for nearly all veterans tested. After all, these applicants were soldiers, sailors, marines, and airmen who would have been offered state high school "wartime diplomas" had it not been for ACE's opposition. In 1946, ACE staff held conferences for state departments of education staff around the country to promote the GED test, and the NASSP published two surveys of the policies evolving in each state to grant equivalency certificates (Hess, 1946a, 1946b). Several states awarded credits for military activities using Carnegie unit course-completion standards, and a few still gave "wartime diplomas." Minnesota recognized credit for courses in special military service schools, considering 160 hours of class work equivalent to one high school credit, whereas Mississippi recognized military coursework as one high school unit for each 180 clock hours or five weeks of attendance.

But such "seat-time" requirements were the exception. A total of 25 states granted high school credentials using the GED test, and 30 states allowed their local high schools to grant diplomas to veterans on the basis of the GED test.[7] Commonly, the state credential was called a High-School Equivalent Certificate. Local schools were often allowed to award high school *diplomas*, usually based solely on the GED test scores. Some states, however, also required specified courses (typically, American history and civics) and a minimum number of Carnegie units (usually equaling one or two years of high school). Most states followed ACE's recommendations for setting low passing scores. By the fall of 1946, all but four states were issuing high school certificates or diplomas to veterans based on the GED test (Hess, 1946b). The importance of the candidates' veteran status to the public's acceptance of the GED high school equivalency testing program was acknowledged by a test reviewer, who in an article for the *Third Mental Measurements Yearbook* identified the critical limitations of the GED test:

There are . . . fundamental questions regarding accreditation by examination which the authors of the *Tests of General Educational Development* have apparently failed to face. First, written examinations fail to cover adequately the laboratory or field experiences, which practically all good courses provide. Second, written examinations fail to cover such intangibles as the social and other benefits from class discussion, the favorable emotional orientation toward a subject-matter field created by an alert, stimulating instructor, and the moral and ethical values flowing from a qualified teacher successfully leading an interested classroom of students. To deny such intangibles is to deny most of the usefulness of face-to-face teaching. Finally, there is the question whether it is desirable to permit an A-student to "get by" with a barely passing performance on an academic examination, when he might well have done distinguished work, had he taken the course. (Conrad, 1949, 36)

The reviewer went on to expose the generally unspoken rationale for acceptance of the GED credential: "However, the war has created special circumstances; and we may be entitled to give the veterans 'the benefit of the doubt'" (Conrad, 1949, 36).

7. Four states had high school equivalency certificates based on comprehensive exams predating the GED: New Jersey since 1914, Connecticut since 1935, New Hampshire since 1937, and Maryland since 1941 (Hess, 1946a).

Data were not published on the number of GED credentials issued in the early years, but the director of USAFI later estimated that 586,000 military personnel were tested. The Veterans' Testing Service (VTS) staff estimated that from the war's end to the summer of 1947 about one million tests were administered to persons who had been released from the services (Dressel and Schmid, 1951). The number of VTS agencies established throughout the United States by state departments of education and educational institutions to conduct testing totaled over 560 by 1948.

Not surprisingly, given the low cut scores established and the levels of reading, grammar, and math skills tested, the rate of veterans passing the GED test was exceedingly high. In the first years of the program, VTS reported that 92% of veterans taking the GED test met the recommended standard for a high school diploma. At the Chicago Public Schools testing center, where 6,600 veterans were tested from June 1945 to November 1946, the pass rate on the GED test was 86%. The three reading tests proved the easiest for veterans, with a staggering 98% passing each of these subtests; 95% passed the general mathematics test. Pass rates were lowest (87%) on the grammar test (with its heavy emphasis on use of commas and quotation marks), the only subtest that required a passing score well above chance.[8]

In Los Angeles a breakdown of 3,000 veterans tested failed to reveal any relationship between the percent passing the tests and their years of schooling. ACE argued that the lack of correlation between GED scores and high school units completed was to be expected since the GED test was designed to measure long-term educational outcomes gained through war experience as well as schooling (Dressel and Schmid, 1951). Another study, however, of soldiers tested upon entry to the service *before* they had received any training or military experience found only a gradual increase in mean GED scores for each year of high school completed, with the standard deviation of such size that scores could not discriminate among years of schooling. After citing high correlations between GED test scores and the Army General Classification Test, the study concluded that "there is very little evidence for the validity of the GED, High School Level, as a measure of educational development apart from general mental ability" (Mosel, 1954, 133).

In 1947, the American Council on Education scored a major marketing advance by securing the support of the New York Education Department to issue GED credentials to high school dropouts who had not gone to war

8. Nearly all of the veterans tested were former students at Chicago public high schools, although a few had only completed elementary school (Engelhart, 1946).

or served in the military. New York was the last state in the union to issue GED credentials for veterans and the first to issue credentials to nonveterans (Zook, 1948). Within a year 22 states were using the GED as the basis for offering high school credentials to civilians. In an apparent move to prevent current high school students from taking the GED test, most states established minimum ages for testing of nonveterans, ranging from 18 to 22 (Hess, 1948).

2.11 ACE and USAFI Studies of the GED in the 1950s

In the 1950s, ACE commissioned two studies of its GED test program. A report by Paul Dressel and John Schmid (1951) summarized existing research on the GED and analyzed data on university students admitted through the GED exam. The authors reported that applicants admitted to college with GED scores above 275 were able to successfully complete their first years of college, but that students with lower GED scores often showed heavy course failures and dropout rates. They reasoned that completion of high school in itself demonstrated a measure of persistence and drive needed for success in college. The authors recommended that the GED test be improved by including writing exercises; broadening the exams in techniques used and in content to cover other educational objectives; restricting testing dates to specific times of the year; and raising the standard for passing to the fiftieth percentile, the average score of high school seniors in the norming group. These changes, they contended,

> would insure more all-around performance and would obtain greater prestige and security for the recognition program. The person who truly merits the recognition would be able to qualify, but the higher standards would rule out some who reflect discredit on the award of diplomas or the granting of college admission by examination. The result should be that the recognition would be much more meaningful and much more respected. (Dressel and Schmid, 1951, 50)

Finally, while supporting continued use of the high school-level GED test, the authors called for studies of the relative performance of students at the ninth-, tenth-, eleventh-, and twelfth-grade levels, as well as norms comparing student performance on the GED test *before* entering high school to scores of seniors at the time of graduation.

In a second GED study, this one authored by Ralph Tyler himself, the test publisher rebutted the need for higher standards for the GED credential and test improvements. Tyler dismissed the call for higher passing scores for the GED, arguing, "Many persons have expressed concern over the 'low scores' recommended as 'passing'. . . . If the scores are low it is because students actually graduating from high school or actually completing successfully a general college course make low scores" (Tyler, 1954, 28). In fact, Tyler's review of data on a thousand GED applicants tested by USAFI showed that 62% of examinees who had never attended high school could pass the GED test, as could 70% of examinees with only one year of high school (Committee on Evaluation of the Tyler Fact-Finding Study, 1956). Tyler acknowledged that military staff considered the GED test as requiring academic achievement at approximately the eighth- or ninth-grade level rather than 12 years of school. As he observed in his report, "[A]t one Air Force base if the individual passes the USAFI Achievement III Test at the 8th grade level, or if he has finished the 9th grade and has had varied training and work experience, he will be advised to take the high-school level GED Tests immediately" (Tyler, 1954, 56–57). Further, Tyler catalogued a whole series of current high school objectives for English, social studies, and science that were "broader than the abilities, skills and knowledge which are appraised" by the GED (Tyler, 1954, 12, 14, 15). In spite of these limitations, Tyler asserted that the GED test satisfactorily measured the equivalence of high school and could be applied to civilians as well as veterans.

To gain greater acceptance of Tyler's study, ACE assembled a committee to actually release Tyler's report. The committee chairman, a former dean at the University of Chicago, explained that "it was . . . felt that the conclusions derived from the study would be regarded as more impartial and would, therefore, carry more weight with the educational public if they were drawn by educators who had no part in the Fact-Finding Study" (Committee on Evaluation of the Tyler Fact-Finding Study, 1956, ix). The committee chose not to include Tyler's lists of the contemporary objectives for English, social studies, and science, which would have called attention to the many limitations of the GED test in measuring expected academic outcomes of high school. One committee member recommended that the final report exclude Tyler's data showing that GED recipients performed less well in college than high school graduates (American Council on Education, 1955). In the end, the group decided to reference the data and to emphasize that young people should be encouraged to complete high school. They wrote,

> First, the committee was in general agreement that passing of the Tests of General Educational Development should not be interpreted as an adequate substitute for the completion of a formal high school education. The demonstration of educational achievement by means of the GED tests constitutes an alternative avenue into college or into positions

in business, industry, or government, but should not be interpreted or portrayed as the full equivalent of a high school education. (American Council on Education, 1955, x)

The group then introduced a theme that would be echoed for years to come by the American Council on Education:

[T]he committee recognized that the GED tests do not measure all characteristics essential for success in college or employment. At the same time the committee recognized that the completion of high school, as evidenced by the granting of a high school diploma, does not reflect all the qualifications and characteristics essential to success in college or employment. Both constitute significant data that colleges or employers may use in combination with other pertinent items of information. (American Council on Education, 1955, x)

The GED proponents began to argue that while the GED was not equivalent to high school, high school graduation was not necessarily all that it had been purported to be either. And even though the Tyler study evaluated the performance of *war veterans* with GED credentials, his conclusions were extended to civilians with no similar training or experience.

While the high school-level GED test continued to gain acceptance, ACE had little success promoting Lindquist's college-level GED test. ACE had recommended that colleges grant 24 semester college credits in social studies, English, science, and literature based on passage of four GED college-level subtests using cutoff scores appropriate to their institution. Most schools, however, appeared unwilling to grant "general education" college credits on this basis. Dressel and Schmid found little use for the college-level GED test. "College officials," they observed, "do not think in terms of the generalized outcomes measured by the [college-level] GED tests, but rather in terms of specific course content. Judged on this basis, the tests are naturally considered unsatisfactory" (Dressel and Schmid, 1951, 12–13). According to Tyler's report, less than 1,600 college-level GED test batteries were administered in 1953, compared to 40,000 high school-level tests used in civilian testing centers. In 1961, ACE discontinued distribution of the college-level batteries of the GED test (American Council on Education, 1981).

In the later 1950s, the staff at the United States Armed Forces Institute began to express reservations about continuing the GED testing program, particularly after 45 faculty members from Ohio State University conducted a comprehensive review of the USAFI exams. The faculty encouraged USAFI to consider replacing the GED test with subject matter tests (thus enabling the Institute to introduce coursework instruction for persons needing to complete high school) and recommended that USAFI "reserve the right to appraise the adequacy of the [GED] test norms and to adjust them, if needed, without the expressed consent of the original test maker(s)" (American Council on Education, 1958c).

In 1956, USAFI had also entered into a contract with the University of Chicago for Benjamin Bloom to develop and field-test an alternative format to the GED test battery. Bloom, who had studied under Ralph Tyler at Chicago, was experimenting with a taxonomy of educational objectives and wanted to prepare new GED exams in English grammar and mathematics based on his experimental sequential item test forms. In addition, Bloom offered two extra studies for USAFI:

(1) An analysis of the present GED Tests in relation to current educational objectives of the secondary schools which are relevant to the areas in general education, to determine specific gaps, particular objectives which are adequately sampled and objectives which are only partially sampled and to arrive at a set of recommendations for the further development of the GED Tests.

(2) An analysis of the relationship between performance on GED Tests and such variables as over-all school grades, level of scholastic aptitude, interest in particular subjects, curriculums followed, plans for future education, and extent to which they have studied in particular areas relative to the GED Tests to obtain further evidence of validity for the GED Tests.[9]

Bloom (1956a) had conducted the 1955 renorming study of the GED test for ACE and shared the concerns of other researchers that the tests were normed exceedingly low and failed to measure many aspects of high school. In his proposal to USAFI, he wrote,

The Tests of General Educational Development were first constructed in 1942. Since that time parallel tests have been developed along the lines of this initial form with only changes in content being permitted. . . . It would be possible to rest content with these tests in their present form and hope that few critics will arise in the future to question the value and use of these instruments. (Bloom, 1956b, 1)

9. Extracted from "DD Negotiated Contract, Order No. IE-47-043-389-57, to the Bursar, The University of Chicago, 6 December 1956," attachment to the Minutes of Twenty-Second Meeting of Commission on the Accreditation of Service Experiences, 19 May (1958c, ACE Archive).

Improvements were necessary, Bloom argued, because of changes in curricula and new developments in the field of testing and because of deficiencies in the GED testing instrument that he had already observed:

> There have been a number of critics who have raised serious questions about the appropriateness of these tests for accreditation purposes and additional critics are likely to further attack this program if the tests are to continue to be used in their present form. Furthermore, we ourselves are aware of a number of limitations in these tests. For example, the passing score on one form of the Mathematics test is below the chance level, the reliability of some of the tests is not as high as we would desire, the relationships between the test scores and measures of scholastic aptitude are higher than we believe desirable, the number of items used to sample an individual's level of achievement in certain aspects of mathematics and science are lower than appears defensible, whole areas of the humanities, such as art and music, are not sampled, etc. (Bloom, 1956b, 1)

When the American Council on Education learned about the Bloom study nearly a year after the contract was signed, ACE staff and commissioners expressed concerns that USAFI might deem the GED test inadequate and consider using another testing instrument or approach. Cornelius Turner of the ACE staff expressed his fears that publicity on the Bloom study research would jeopardize public confidence in the GED testing program. Turner noted that several states did not wholeheartedly support the GED test and that Bloom had published articles on the 1955 norming study that ACE had not approved prior to publication (American Council on Education, 1957).[10] After ACE representatives met with several top military officers, the military terminated the Bloom study and notified the director of USAFI that any subsequent USAFI proposals "concerning modification of the GED testing program" would need to be submitted to the president of the American Council on Education (American Council on Education, 1957, 1958a, 1958b).

Meanwhile, the GED testing program enjoyed a steady growth, and Bloom's criticisms had little apparent impact. The eruption of the Korean conflict (1950–1955) brought several states that had dropped out during the postwar period back into the GED veteran testing program. California,

10. In 1957, Bloom had written in the *School Review* that "the GED tests measure only a small portion of the educational objectives of the schools, and other indices of the merits of a school are needed before one has a completely valid indicator of the educational outcomes of twelve years of public school attendance" (Bloom and Statler, 1957, 215).

Kansas, Ohio, Oklahoma, South Dakota, and Washington all began allowing the new Korean War veterans to obtain GED certificates, although as of 1954 none of these states were granting GED credentials to nonmilitary civilians. The expansion of the GED testing program to the general population continued slowly, with 24 states allowing the testing of nonmilitary civilians and 24 states still restricting the GED certificate to veterans and military personnel in 1954 (Commission on Accreditation of Service Experiences, 1954). Reaching a milestone in 1959, the American Council on Education reported that the number of civilians taking the GED test had surpassed the number of veterans tested. In 1963, to emphasize the civilian nature of the program, ACE changed the name of its Veterans Testing Service to the General Educational Development Testing Service (GEDTS) (Stewart, 1992).

2.12 "Teaching to the Test"

In spite of the availability of the GED test, over three million World War II veterans used the GI Bill (which included living allowances for veterans and their dependents as well as support for tuition and books) to return to high school after their discharge from the service. As of 1949, more than half of the public school systems in urban areas were operating continuation or evening schools (Elicker, 1944; Kempfer and Wright, 1949; U.S. Senate Committee on Veterans' Affairs, 1973). Some institutions, however, embraced *teaching to the GED test* as an alternative that could allow veterans to bypass the time required for completing high school. An Ohio State University educator reported, "All around us we hear of men who started back to high school and 'dropped out' after a few weeks or a month" (Ramseyer, 1945, 83). His solution was to set up 12 weeks of individualized instruction in math, reading and discussion, and science, after which his adult students took the GED test in order to earn a high school credential. In his 1954 review of military uses of the GED, Tyler acknowledged evidence of the GED "teaching-to-the-test" mentality that is common today. Tyler's report included the example of a military center that offered "a GED preparatory course of two months' duration in which a systematic covering of the five areas is attempted" (Tyler, 1954, 58). The low level of academic skills required to pass the GED test facilitated this approach, as Tyler reported: "Oftentimes the applicant will be advised to brush up on elementary mathematics at the eighth or ninth grade level and to study an English grammar text at about the same level" (Tyler, 1954, 70–71). Tyler noted that several agencies offered "special refresher courses" for persons planning to take the GED test and that these "courses" required only 10 to 15 hours of instruction. Tyler also described agencies that advised unsuccessful GED test-takers to enroll in evening or part-time classes—not to earn high school credits, but to gain the knowledge needed to pass the GED test—suggesting that examinees were already permitted to retake sections of the GED to raise their scores.

During the 1960s, with the baby boomers approaching adulthood and new federal funding available for GED test instruction, the number of people taking the GED test increased nearly fivefold, from 61,093 in 1960 to 293,451 in 1969. The number of GED testing sites increased from 658 to 1,566 (GED Testing Service, 1978). The development of GED instructional programs in which students are coached in test taking and offered coursework loosely modeled on the GED test item groupings emerged during the War on Poverty in the 1960s under the Johnson administration. (See Chapter 3.) The Economic Opportunity Act of 1964 provided federal funds for basic education for adults who had not completed eighth grade, and the 1970 Adult Education Act reauthorization expanded the program to include secondary education, although its priority remained persons with lower grade skills. Adult educators championed GED test instruction, which was far less costly than full-fledged high school completion programs and still capitalized on students' motivation to secure high school credentials. In 1978, the U.S. House of Representatives Committee on Education and Labor estimated that over 900,000 adults had achieved a high school equivalency credential under the Adult Basic Education Act, even though state plans were required to place special emphasis on adult basic education, that is, instruction in skills below eighth grade. The committee criticized adult education programs for failing to give priority to the least educated adults. At the same time, it noted the appeal of the high school credentialing program, quoting the testimony of the director of the U.S. Office of Education Division of Adult Education that "the failure to attract the least educated adults is attributable in part to local adult education directors' inclination to serve adults who are striving to earn their high school diploma and are demanding services. This goal is not often part of the motivation of those functioning at the fourth grade level and below" (United States House Committee on Education and Labor, 1978, 129).

One federal antipoverty program, the Job Corps, established in 1964, developed a curriculum for teaching youth how to pass the GED test. Moving completely away from the GED's purported objective of measuring the "lasting outcomes" of high school that *adults* had already acquired through their life experiences, the Job Corps developed a set of self-paced units of instruction based on the GED test items for use with school-age youth. According to Sar Levitan and Benjamin Johnston's 10-year history of the Job Corps, the GED credential offered "the high school 'education' demanded by a credentials-conscious society" (Levitan and Johnston, 1975, 62). The GED's appeal rested in no small part on the Job Corps experience that even youth testing below the sixth-grade level on the Stanford Achievement Test could be taught to pass the GED through a 200-hour preparatory course. The authors concluded: "An expanded GED program promised great rewards for all concerned: the goal was achievable by many in a reasonable period of time and obviously valuable in the outside world" (Levitan and Johnston, 1975, 62).

The time required to prepare high school dropouts (whether unemployed workers, mothers receiving welfare, or Job Corps teens) to pass the GED was substantially reduced in 1978 when the American Council on Education released officially sanctioned "GED practice tests." Prior to 1978, many adult educators offering GED classes had focused instruction on reading comprehension, vocabulary skills, grammar, and math, often using a variety of textbooks designed for the GED "student" or even the "pre-GED student." It was difficult to predict, however, when students were ready to pass the test battery, although many adult education programs would only begin GED test-taking drills after students had reached a seventh- or eighth-grade reading level on other standardized tests available. With the publication of the GED practice tests, adult educators could use the practice tests to help predict the level of skill required to pass the GED. Then they could limit their instruction to the exact types of questions on the exam in order to shorten the time students needed for their GED test instruction (Musgrove, 1981; Pawasarat and Quinn, 1986).

2.13 GED Testing of School-Age Youth

Starting in the 1970s, ACE initiated a series of policy changes to accommodate the federal government's interest in financing GED testing for disadvantaged teenagers. Each year since 1955 ACE had required a minimum age of 20 or 21 for obtaining a GED credential. The Council later explained this policy, stating, "While this seems rather conservative by today's standards, it clearly represented a concern that the program *not* be seen by young people as an attractive alternative to a regular high school program of study" (Whitney, 1985b). A request by the Job Corps to provide educational credentials for school-age high school dropouts led to exceptions to the age requirements. In the mid-1970s, the American Council on Education lowered the age allowed for taking the GED test and commissioned the Educational Testing Service (ETS) to revise the 1978 GED test questions to ensure that they could be used for youth as young as 14 years of age. The ETS outlined the rationale for the requests in a project paper:

> In one state the minimum age for compulsory education had been already lowered to 14 years. It was therefore decided to conduct test administrations of the new forms at grade 9 (the grade during which most youngsters attain the age of 14 years), and also at grades 10 and 11, in addition to the grade 12 reference group. . . . In fact, the *new GED tests were found to be only slightly difficult for grade 9 students,* with the middle difficulty for all five tests in the battery occurring at about grade 10, or a little higher [emphasis added]. (Educational Testing Service, 1978, 12–13)

ACE requested that the difficulty level of the GED test be reduced in a number of specific areas. ACE instructed ETS to shorten the test reading passages, simplify the language of the math questions, and reduce the total time required for GED testing. According to the ETS, the GED program had "received complaints that too much higher level mathematics was being required" (Educational Testing Service, 1978, 3) and so the ETS agreed to develop math problems with practical applications and to adapt the reading level of math problems "to the GED population" (Educational Testing Service, 1974, 16). The test writers indicated that they would continue to include a small number of higher level math items, while acknowledging that "many of the concepts . . . which were classified as algebra and/ or geometry were concepts that most pupils were exposed to during or prior to 9th grade" (Educational Testing Service, 1978, 3). They also noted that these test items were not significant in determining whether candidates passed or failed the math subtest.

Citing criticisms that too much emphasis was placed on reading in the science and social studies subtests, ACE recommended use of "concept" test items that would be "noncourse oriented, with the emphasis placed on information that the GED candidate may have acquired through mass media or general reading" (Educational Testing Service, 1974, 12). The reading passages preceding science questions were expected to minimize the actual knowledge of science required of the GED candidate. As the ETS explained,

> Graphs, charts, and diagrams will be used to supplement the written material where appropriate. Although the majority of the test items will deal with the interpretation of information and ideas presented in the passages, *some outside knowledge* of basic principles of science *may be required* in order to answer *some* of the items [emphasis added]. (Educational Testing Service, 1974, 13)

ACE specified other changes as well: "Short, simple sentences free of unnecessarily abstract, difficult, or technical vocabulary should predominate. Pictures, graphs, or charts should also be used to help reduce the reading load" (GED Testing Service, 1974, 8). Similarly, ACE directed that the social science test include "reading comprehension items at a reduced reading level and pitched to issues of greater relevancy to the everyday life of GED candidates" (Educational Testing Service, 1974, 14). Finally, acknowledging the close proximity of the recommended GED passing requirements to scores that could be achieved purely by guessing, ACE asked the ETS to increase the number of multiple-choice stems to five for all questions. Upon completion of the new tests, ETS reported: "While the need to equate new tests with older forms through the use of common items has held this process back somewhat, the objective has essentially been realized, with ETS research showing that for *virtually* all the tests the cut score is *now* above the chance score [emphasis added]" (Educational Testing Service, 1974, 18).

Even with the reduced odds for guessing correct answers, a majority of the ninth-grade students tested in the spring of 1977 for the ETS equating study reached the standard score of 35, which ACE recommended as the minimum passing score on each subtest (Swineford, 1978). All but 9% of ninth graders (and all but 4% of twelfth graders) passed the science subtest with a standard score of 35 or better. Although U.S. history courses typically are not offered until the tenth or eleventh grade, the ETS found that all but 17% of freshmen in the high school equating study could pass the social studies subtest, as could all but 6% of high school seniors. In fact, the ETS equating study estimated that 73% of ninth graders could pass all five GED subtests at the passing scores recommended by ACE, as could 77% of tenth graders (Creech, 1978). The ETS paper on standardizing the 1978 GED test explained,

> Ordinarily, questions considering the usefulness of a test with pupils at a particular grade/age level would also include a comparison of the content of the tests being investigated with the accepted curricula for the grade/age level of the pupils being tested. . . . The extremely broad range of performance of grade 12 pupils on survey tests such as the GED virtually requires that many items in such tests are closely related to educational concepts that are first learned at grade 9, or even earlier. The effort to develop tests that contain a large number of lower than average difficulty items for grade 12 students also results in the inclusion of a large number of items that reflect educational topics for levels

substantially lower than the grade 12 level. (Educational Testing Service, 1978, 14)

The extent to which marketing considerations rather than the standards for high school coursework influenced test construction can be seen in other ACE specifications that had directed the 1978 ETS test writers to avoid questions on the social studies test related to U.S. history and government—or even to an English-speaking heritage—so that it could broaden its market into Canada:

> Since the GED testing program has achieved an international stature, it is imperative that the tests be developed with no intentional English speaking cultural, economic, or political bias. Particular efforts should be directed towards development of the social studies and reading tests to ensure no alienation of examinees of other countries, especially Canada. This concern may be alleviated by de-emphasizing concepts unique to the United States, and inclusion of some reading passages and problems commonly encountered in Canada and the U.S. (GED Testing Service, 1974, 9)

When Canadian administrators reviewed the 1978 "generic" social studies subtest, they declared it unacceptable and demanded a separate social studies subtest for Canada. Meanwhile, the "generic" social studies exam was used in the United States as well as for Canadian candidates requiring Braille, large-print, and audiotaped exams. A French version of the five GED subtests was prepared by the Canadian province of New Brunswick, using the Canadian social studies questions, and was promoted for use in Quebec. After the provinces of Quebec and Ontario declined to enter the GED testing program, extra copies of the printed "French-Canadian" test were used in Haiti and with Haitian immigrants to New York (Quigley, 1987). A Spanish-language GED test was introduced based on the high school curriculum in Puerto Rico and normed with Puerto Rican high school students, and yet used primarily in the continental United States (Baldwin, 1995; GED Testing Service, 1995).

After the GED tests were renormed in 1980, ACE reported that it was increasing its minimum passing score to 40 for each subtest (reportedly, to the sixteenth percentile for the high school norming group) because the standard score of 35 had fallen so close to chance (Spille, 1981a). Meanwhile, ACE encouraged increased use of the GED test among high school–age youth in 1981 when it eliminated its minimum age requirement for taking the test, leaving the establishment of age restrictions entirely in the hands of state departments of education. By 1985, five states had lowered the minimum age for GED testing to 16, ten states to 17, and eight more states allowed exceptions for younger persons under particular conditions (Whitney, 1985a).

2.14 ACE Reacts to the Call for Higher Standards in High School

In the 1980s, while ACE was reducing the academic skills required to pass the GED test, national studies were calling for higher educational standards, more instructional time in school, more homework, and an increase in the number of Carnegie units required for high school graduation. In 1983, the National Commission on Excellence in Education released *A Nation at Risk*, which called for a tougher core high school curriculum, higher standards for high school graduation, and longer school days and years.

In response, Henry Spille, director of the GED Testing Service, issued a memorandum to state GED administrators and state directors of adult education regarding the study. He candidly explained: "You will probably be receiving questions from your superiors, legislators, and others regarding the GED tests and how well they address, or do not address, the recommendations made in the report *A Nation at Risk*. I will try to give you some assistance by responding, from our perspective, to each of the report's recommendations" (Spille, 1984, 1). Several of Spille's examples are illuminating. Spille noted that the *Nation at Risk* study recommended that significantly more time be devoted to higher level math and science either through more effective use of the present school day, longer school days, or a lengthened school year. His response:

> Because of prior learning that adults have acquired and bring to the teaching/learning process and setting, they often need less time, not more time, to learn the basics of reading, writing and computation. Availability of other than time-based assessment methods should allow adults to progress at their own pace. (Spille, 1984, 5)

Just how much time adults needed was explained in Spille's reaction to the *Nation at Risk* recommendation that students in high school be assigned far more homework:

> The typical GED examinee spends 20 hours preparing to take the GED Test. Many of the examinees do not prepare by enrolling in classes; they study independently. Additional homework for them is probably not important; focused learning time is probably the key. (Spille, 1984, 5)

The heart of the *Nation at Risk* report was a recommendation that all high school students be required to complete four years of English, three years of mathematics, three years of science, three years of social studies, and one-half year of computer science. Additionally, college-bound students were encouraged to take two years of foreign language. Spille responded, "The five tests of the current battery measure the lasting outcomes of a high school program of study in all of the areas (English—Reading Skills and Writing Skills—Mathematics, Science, and Social Studies) except computer science" (Spille, 1984, 1). In fact, this response directly contradicted an earlier Spille Memorandum (Spille, 1981b) indicating that the entire GED test battery might equate to only four units of introductory high school subjects and not to the 13 units of English, math, science, and social studies recommended by *Nation at Risk*. In a September 1980 memo on "Awarding Carnegie units on the basis of GED test results," Spille had informed state GED administrators that one credit ("or more") in English might be awarded for candidates who passed the GED writing skills subtest and the reading subtest "except of course, that no composition exercises are included" and that three high school credits might be awarded for passing the other three GED subtests:

> The award of a unit in general science, general mathematics and general social studies on the basis of scores of the Science Test, the Mathematics Test and the Social Studies Test respectively also may be appropriate, if the concepts and developed abilities measured on these tests are comparable to those normally acquired through successful completion of a high school's or local school district's "general" courses. (Spille, 1980, 3)

Spille warned against granting Carnegie unit credits for specific high school courses such as U.S. history, algebra, or chemistry on the basis of GED test scores. For example, he noted that an examinee could answer every U.S. history question incorrectly and still achieve a passing score on the social studies test.

During this period, the federal government's Job Training Partnership Act (JTPA), passed in 1982, provided financial support for the GED shortcut to high school graduation. Under the JTPA, youth were considered successfully served (a "positive termination") if they returned to school (which included enrollment in a GED class) or completed a level of schooling (which included graduation from a four-year high school—or earning a GED credential). Since the JTPA provided an average of only 18 weeks of instruction, the GED was an attainable goal for youth who had been unsuccessful in school, and the instruction could be provided by minimally trained staff, particularly if the youth already had reading and math skills at the sixth- to eighth-grade level.

Meanwhile, in the wake of the *Nation at Risk* recommendations, state governments were increasing standards for the four-year high school graduates. Between 1980 and 1985, 38 states raised their minimum Carnegie unit course requirements for high school graduation, and 18 states established new minimum-competency testing programs (National Center for Education Statistics, 1987). When ACE developed its specifications for the 1988 GED test battery, the nationwide emphasis on increased Carnegie units and more math and science coursework was largely ignored. ACE, in an article entitled "Don't Hurry to Take the GED Tests!" reassured its client base that pass rates for the test were expected to remain about the same. ACE explained:

> While it is true that the revised tests will require a *slightly* higher level of problem solving and critical thinking skills than do the current tests, as well as the ability to write coherently, most of the changes represent only small adjustments to the levels of content mastery required to pass the tests. For example, the percentage of questions on the mathematics test that require the use of concepts from algebra will increase from 25% to 30%—but this is a difference of only 2–3 questions per test [emphasis in original]. (GED Testing Service, 1985, 8)

The *Nation at Risk* call for high school instruction in computer technology was addressed in the GED test, not by requiring students to be able to use computers or even to understand their use, but superficially by references to "computers" in questions. For example, a math item might ask the test taker to calculate how long it would take to print several pages of a computer document (GED Testing Service, 1995).

For the first time, in 1988 the GED test battery added a short essay test as part of the writing subtest. While continuing to maintain that its multiple-choice writing skills subtest provided an adequate indirect measure of writing, ACE was receiving pressure to include an actual writing requirement. The Council had noted that as of October 1985, 71% of candidates taking the GED test in the United States were in states requiring writing assessments of high school graduates, and in July 1986, New York State had begun requiring GED candidates to present a 200-word composition (Baum, 1986; Swartz, Patience, and Whitney, 1985; Swartz and Whitney, 1985). Accordingly, in 1988 ACE began requiring GED candidates to complete an essay, which was holistically scored and combined with the multiple-choice test score on the writing subtest in order to provide an overall writing test score. The essay question was designed to measure the student's ability to write coherently on a topic of general knowledge and did not require a demonstration of competence in a high school subject area. As outlined in the GED technical manual,

> The topic must be based upon information or a situation that is general enough to be familiar to most examinees. For example, a topic calling for a writer's views regarding the effect of automobiles on American life might well be appropriate, while one calling for an opinion of the space shuttle's value to the American economy would fail to meet this specification because it would require specialized knowledge. (GED Testing Service, 1995, 111)

By 1989, after all of its GED test changes had been implemented, ACE reported that GED candidates had increased their average study time preparing for the GED test to 30 and ½ hours. This was only 10 hours above the average preparation time reported in 1980 (Baldwin, 1990; Malizio and Whitney, 1981).

Most GED candidates are no longer war veterans, and neither the GED test preparation time nor the GED "curriculum" is persuasive evidence for considering the credential equal to high school completion. The American Council on Education uses its internal norming program with high school seniors as justification that this test measures the outcomes of four years of high school. ACE argues that if GED candidates can score as well on a norm-referenced test as many high school seniors, they must have acquired an education equivalent to that of high school graduates. Unlike the ACT, SAT, and the Armed Forces Qualification Test that attract test takers with strong motivation for entering college or the military, the GED test has no apparent value to high school students in the norming group. Nor are they typically offered coaching instructions on how (or why) to improve their scores or opportunities to retake tests after additional study as are actual GED test candidates. Two GED norming studies conducted by ACE in Wisconsin suggested serious problems with student motivation and quality control (Quinn and Pawasarat, 2011). Of the 1,112 high school seniors who began the testing process for the first study, only 38% finished their tests. In the second study, 85 schools were asked to participate, but only 39 agreed to do the testing and no replacement schools were drawn. ACE first reported in 1988 that for the passing score selected by Wisconsin (i.e., minimum subtest scores of 40 and a total score of 250) 81% of Wisconsin seniors could pass the test. Later ACE notified the state that it had "made systematic errors in developing the conversion tables" and claimed that only 67% of Wisconsin seniors could pass. Six years later, based on its second norming study, ACE reported that barely half (52%) of Wisconsin seniors could pass the same test (GED Testing Service, 1993; Quinn and Pawasarat, 2011). The wide differences in the Wisconsin results raised further questions about the integrity of the GED norming procedures.

2.15 Blurring the Distinction between High School Graduation and the GED

With government funding for GED instruction firmly in place through adult basic education, public assistance, and job training programs, much of the GED marketing in the 1970s and 1980s focused on labeling the GED credential as a "diploma" and blurring the distinction between high school graduation and attainment of a GED credential. At the 1989 GED administrators' conference, Douglas Whitney, director of the GED Testing Service, urged the participants to promote measures that would label the GED credential as equal to high school graduation. Whitney advocated several measures to "build the credibility of the GED program" at the state level: "use the term 'diploma' to help GED achieve parity with other traditional diploma programs; seek legislation to recognize the GED diplomas as the legal equivalent of a traditional diploma . . . ; stop the GED Test from being used as part of a credit-based diploma program; refer to the GED program as a 'dropout recovery program' " (GED Testing Service, 1989, 6). Through its college loan requirements, the federal government also has encouraged the notion that skills necessary to pass the GED test are adequate for college work. A 1991 study for the U.S. Department of Education (Dynarski, 1991) reported default rates on Guaranteed Student Loans for postsecondary education of 56% for high school dropouts and 44% for GED recipients, compared to 14% for high school graduates. The response of the Department of Education was to tighten the "ability to benefit" provisions for high school dropouts, effectively encouraging more high school noncompleters to utilize GED testing as a means of securing federal funding for their education.

In 1994, a new National Education Goals Panel issued demands that U.S. students "be first in the world in mathematics and science achievement" and that all students leave grade twelve "having demonstrated competency over challenging subject matter including English, mathematics, science, foreign languages, civics and government, economics, arts, history and geography" (National Education Goals Panel, 1994, 14). Even though most GED test takers have completed two years or fewer of high school, the 13-member National Education Panel on High School Completion (which included the policy research director for the GED Testing Service) inserted a provision in the National Education Goals that high school completion could be achieved either by completing four years in the newly improved American high schools or by passing the GED test.

The American Council on Education's contradictory roles in representing colleges and universities while aggressively marketing a testing instrument for dropouts who rarely succeed in college may be explained in part by ACE's heavy reliance on GED testing revenues. Bruce Murphy (2001) found that 27 of ACE's 100 staff members were funded by and working on the GED program and that over 40% of its annual revenues appeared to come from the GED tests.

In 2002, when ACE released its latest version of the GED, it claimed that only 68% of graduating seniors nationally could pass the test at the recommended passing score levels. The testing manual noted, however, that the norming tests are "administered to high school seniors in a low-stakes setting" (GED Testing Service, 2009c, 67) and acknowledged concerns with lack of motivation among the norming population:

> The low stakes associated with the administration of these tests may have affected the quality and integrity of the reported data. No measure of motivation or effort was obtained directly from the student during these studies. However, data records in which more than one third of the item responses were missing were excluded from analyses. (GED Testing Service, 2009c, 40)

The high school senior norming claims are further challenged by the "gaming" allowed under the GED test-taking policies whereby candidates can repeatedly retake any or all sections of the GED test to bring up their total and subtest scores. Data from Missouri (Jepsen, Mueser, and Troske, 2012) found that 70% of test takers near the pass–fail score levels retook portions or all of the GED test.[11]

As to test construction, like its predecessors, the 2002 GED testing series included five subtests with multiple-choice items from which the examinee must select the correct answer. (Eight of fifty math questions asked the test takers to supply their own numerical answer.) Half of the math

11. A presentation at the 2009 annual GED administrators' conference offered tips on how to help students raise their math scores, observing that many examinees only needed to answer one or two more questions correctly to pass. The presentation reported that an analysis of missed questions showed that too many examinees were checking the item answer "not enough information is given." It was suggested that another response should be chosen when guessing (GED Testing Service, 2009b).

test could be completed using a calculator, although the math questions in that section did not appear to require computation skills beyond grade school arithmetic.[12] The writing exercise remained a single simple general essay, which the ACE graders spend an average time of only two minutes reading and scoring (Martz and Pearson, 2010). Students were not expected to prepare research papers, distinguish between reliable and unreliable Internet sources, develop a job resume, or demonstrate any of the other myriad writing skills expected in high school. In social studies, students were tested on their reading comprehension skills and comfort level deciphering (but not preparing) graphs. The distance between the 2002 GED test and the demands of high school coursework has been suggested by the popular GED test preparation guides available in book stores and libraries. In *Cracking the GED*, the authors observed that the math test "does not cover most of the normal high school algebra curriculum" (Martz and Pearson, 2010, 378) and that the social studies test "does not require any specific knowledge of history, economics, or geography" (Martz and Pearson, 2010, 208).[13]

The low standards in place for passing the 2002 GED test series are evident from reports of the minimal time low-achieving in-school teens spent opting out of their regular high school coursework under a program that ACE calls the "GED Option." In Wisconsin, GED testing has come full circle away from the reforms initiated by State Superintendent Grover in the 1980s. As a result of studies of the GED in the state, Grover had barred school-age teens from receiving GED credentials, promoted alternative education programs for adult dropouts, and raised passing standards for GED credentials. Under the current state superintendent's "GED Option" program, Wisconsin in-school teens at least two years behind their classmates in credit attainment now spend an average of 50 hours preparing for the GED test, yet the state counts them as "graduates" for No Child Left Behind and directs their high schools to award them regular diplomas at the same graduation ceremony given their classmates who have completed

12. Most of the problems in the portion of the test using a calculator require simple arithmetic calculation that is easily completed without a calculator. The calculator does appear to make decimal and percentage problems easier to solve for persons who have trouble determining placement of decimal points. See the "Official GED Practice Tests" for the 2002 Series, developed by the GED Testing Service and distributed by Steck-Vaughn Company.

13. Martz and Pearson (2010) noted that the geometry-type questions are particularly easy to answer since the figures are drawn roughly to scale and lengths can be easily estimated using a scrap of paper.

four years of high school (Evers, 2011; GED Testing Service, 2009a). The national record is little better. Students one to three years behind in their high school coursework and enrolled in the "GED Option" programs spend an average of 80 hours studying for their GED exams (GED Testing Service, 2009a; Chapter 6). At the school district level, New York City has spent nine years preparing thousands of school-age teens to receive high school credentials based on the 2002 series of the GED test, even though the mayor and chancellor of schools describe the GED passing scores as "only equivalent to an 8th grade proficiency level in reading and math," and note that "students can pass the writing section with only a 6th grade level proficiency" (City of New York, 2010). With evidence mounting as to the low standards required by the 2002 GED test series, predictably the American Council on Education (along with Pearson, its new for-profit testing partner) is once again promising that the *next* GED test will be harder (American Council on Education, 2011).[14]

2.16 Conclusion

In 1999, a half century after the conclusion of World War II, media coverage of a graduation ceremony held at Gardner (Massachusetts) High School for surviving World War II veterans sparked legislation in three dozen states authorizing the awarding of high school diplomas to veterans (living and deceased), including GED recipients, based on their wartime service. The organizer of the ceremony called it "a small, overdue gesture of our society's gratitude for the sacrifice these individuals made in the name of freedom."[15] States and local school districts would have issued high school "wartime diplomas" in the 1940s had such an option not been aggressively opposed by a small group of educational reformers promoting their multiple-choice test of "general educational development" and an end to the Carnegie unit high school. Not surprisingly, their attempts to dismantle the Carnegie unit approach to traditional high school failed, with nearly every state legislature now requiring specific Carnegie units for high school graduation.

The ACE group did have success in promoting its GED test, first as a college entrance exam for wounded veterans and then at the war's end as a requirement for GIs to meet before they could be issued a state high school

14. ACE announced that it is partnering with Pearson in establishing a GED business that will market the GED tests and GED test-preparation programs.

15. "Honoring Veterans of World War II," Massachusetts Department of Veterans Services, at www.state.ma.us/veterans/operationrecognition.htm, and "Operation Recognition," at www.wwiimemorial.com/Education/operation_recognition.htm, accessed July 25, 2002.

diploma. The tests focused on reading, grade school math, and grammar rules, and pass rates among the early veterans tested were very high. The popularity of the GED was cemented during the postwar period when thousands of war veterans were given the test to gain admission to college under the GI Bill. During the 1950s, at a time when the Soviet launching of Sputnik led to new emphasis in American high schools on rigorous math and science coursework, the GED test was requiring students to answer only a few multiple-choice questions above the chance level and was available to civilians without military service or comparable life experiences. In spite of concerns raised by the United States Armed Forces Institute, ACE's own studies, and Benjamin Bloom's norming studies, the American Council on Education locked the GED test into its original Iowa Tests of Educational Development multiple-choice format for measuring basic reading, math, and grammar skills.

As the baby boom population came of age in the 1960s and 1970s, GED testing began a rapid increase. During the same period, the federal government provided substantial funding for GED test instruction classes under the Adult Basic Education Act and employment training initiatives, funding that still continues today. In the 1980s, reformers of public high schools demanded more rigorous course content, advanced studies in science and math, increased foreign language requirements, longer school days and school years, more homework, and minimum competency testing. Yet, these high school reform initiatives did not acknowledge the surge of GED credentials that was threatening to undermine their reform efforts. Instead, states began adopting credentialing policies that allowed GED testing for in-school teens. Furthermore, during this period the GED test was downgraded, requiring even lower levels of reading and math skills than for the earlier test versions, and the ability to use a computer remained untested as late as 2013.

Politicians continue to call for high-stakes graduation testing for four-year high school students, more challenging coursework, and longer time spent in school, while school districts are allowed to meet federal No Child Left Behind standards by counting GED recipients as high school "completers" and in some states as high school "graduates" (GED Testing Service, 2009a). With the GED test frozen in its World War II design, only high school dropouts are offered a non-Carnegie unit approach to education, encouraged to avoid both academic and vocational education courses, and asked to spend *less* rather than *more* time studying in school. Today, as they have for the last three decades, dropouts who have failed or skipped two or more years of high school coursework are enrolled in short-term

GED test-prep classes where they "study" the GED test, practice answering questions from the "Official GED Practice Tests," and then test and re-test to raise their GED scores to the state passing levels. The evidence in this book and elsewhere finds that this GED testing program is not just producing teens and adults underprepared for college and the workplace, but also enticing other teens to leave school to seek the GED shortcut to a high school education. World War II is over. It is time to close the door on America's GED "high school."

BIBLIOGRAPHY

Advisory Committee to the Army Institute. (1942a). "Minutes of the Advisory Committee to the Army Institute, 21 June 1942." p. 1, in Box 30, Record Group 225. (National Archives).

Advisory Committee to the Army Institute. (1942b). "Minutes of the Advisory Committee to the Army Institute, 12–13 December 1942." USAFI Papers, Folder VI-3-1. (Blommers Measurement Resources Laboratory, University of Iowa).

Advisory Committee to the Army Institute. (1942–1943). "Minutes." Box 30, RG225, National Archives Building (NAB) and USAFI Papers. (Blommers Measurement Resources Laboratory, University of Iowa, Iowa City).

Advisory Committee to the Army Institute. (1943a). "Minutes of the Advisory Committee to the Army Institute, 27 January 1943." p. 2 in USAFI Papers, Folder VI-3-1. (Blommers Measurement Resources Laboratory, University of Iowa).

Advisory Committee to the Army Institute. (1943b). "Minutes of the Advisory Committee to the Army Institute, 27–28 February 1943." p. 3 in USAFI Papers, Folder VI-3-1. (Blommers Measurement Resources Laboratory, University of Iowa).

Advisory Committee to the United States Armed Forces Institute. (1946). "Minutes of the Advisory Committee to the United States Armed Forces Institute, 12–13 January 1946." USAFI Papers, Folder VI-3-1. (Blommers Measurement Resources Laboratory, University of Iowa).

Advisory Council of the Joint Army Navy Committee on Welfare Education. (1943). "History of the Joint Army and Navy Committee on Welfare and Recreation." Box 52, Record Group 225. (National Archives).

Aiken, W. M. (1942). "Memorandum to the Joint Army and Navy Committee on Welfare and Recreation, Subcommitee on Education, 6 April 1942." (American Council on Education (ACE) Archives).

American Council on Education. (1939). "A Proposal for the Future Support of the American Council on Education." Memorandum. (Problems and Plans Committee Folder, ACE Archives).

American Council on Education. (1943a). "Cooperative Study in General Education." (ACE Archives, Staff Newsletter).

American Council on Education. (1943b). *Sound Educational Credit for Military Experience: A Recommended Program.* (Washington, DC: American Council on Education).

American Council on Education. (1944). "A Design for General Education for Members of the Armed Forces." (ACE Archives).

American Council on Education. (1955). "Second Meeting of the Committee on Evaluation of the Tyler Fact Finding Study." (ACE Archives).

American Council on Education. (1957). "Memorandum of Cornelius P. Turner to Dr. Arthur S. Adams." (ACE Archives).

American Council on Education. (1958a). "Memorandum from Lt. Col. H. U. Bookhart to Director of the U. S. Armed Forces Institute." (ACE Archives).

American Council on Education. (1958b). "Memorandum on Actions on Motions Passed by the Commission on Accreditation of Service Experiences." (ACE Archives).

American Council on Education. (1958c). "Minutes of the Twenty-Second Meeting of the Commission on the Accreditation of Service Experiences, 19 May 1958." Folder 2, Box 104, Entry 14. (ACE Archives).

American Council on Education. (1981). *Guide to Credit by Examination*. (Washington, DC: American Council on Education).

American Council on Education. (2009). "GED Administrator's Conference." Accessed from www.acenet.edu on June 7, 2011. (American Council on Education).

American Council on Education. (2011). "ACE and Pearson Collaborate to Transform GED Test, Aligned with Common Core State Standards, Based on GED 21st Century Initiative." (ACE Press Release).

Army Institute Project Staff. (1942). "Minutes of the Army Institute Project Staff."

Atkinson, Byron H. (1949). "Veteran Vs. Non-Veteran Performance at U.C.L.A.: The G.I. Bill as an Academic Experiment." *Journal of Educational Research* 43:302.

Baldwin, Janet. (1990). *GED Candidates: A Decade of Change*. (Washington, DC: American Council on Education).

Baldwin, Janet. (1995). *Who Took the GED? GED 1994 Statistical Report*. (Washington, DC: American Council on Education, GED Testing Service, Center for Adult Learning).

Baum, Myra. (1986). *The Cambridge Program for the New York State GED Writing Sample*. (New York: Cambridge University Press).

Bloom, B. S. (1956a). "The 1955 Normative Study of the Tests of General Educational Development." *The School Review* 64(3):110–124.

Bloom, Benjamin Samuel. (1956b). "Proposal to the United States Armed Forces Institute for Research on the Application of Sequential Item Forms to the Tests of General Educational Development." Attachment to the "Minutes of Twenty-Second Meeting of Commission on the Accreditation of Service Experiences."

Bloom, Benjamin Samuel, and Statler, Charles R. (1957). "Changes in the States on the Tests of General Educational Development from 1943 to 1955." *The School Review* 65(2):204–221.

Bobbitt, J. Franklin. (1913). "The Supervision of City Schools: Some General Principles of Management Applied to the Problems of City-School Systems." in *Twelfth Yearbook of the National Society for the Study of Education*. J. F. Bobbitt and S. C. Parker, eds. I. (Bloomington, IL: Public School Publishing Company), 12–13.

Bobbitt, J. Franklin. (1924). *How to Make a Curriculum*. (New York: Houghton Mifflin Company).

Callahan, Raymond E. (1962). *Education and the Cult of Efficiency: A Study of the Social Forces That Have Shaped the Administration of the Public Schools*. (Chicago: University of Chicago Press).

Capen, Samuel P. (1940). "The Effect of the World War 1914–18 on American Colleges and Universities." *Educational Record* 21:42.

City of New York. (2010). "Mayor Bloomberg, Chancellor Klein, and Education Secretary Arne Duncan Announce Pilot Program to Modernize the General Educational Development Test to Better Prepare Students for College and Careers." Press Release PR-503-10. (Office of the Mayor).

College of Education. (1943). "Grade-Percentile Norms for the Iowa Tests of Educational Development." Iowa Tests of Educational Development Papers, Folder ITED-1943-3B. (Blommers Measurement Resources Laboratory, University of Iowa).

Commission on Accreditation of Service Experiences. (1954). *Accreditation Policies of State Departments of Education for the Evaluation of Educational Experiences of Military Personnel.* (Washington, DC: American Council on Education).

Committee on Evaluation of the Tyler Fact-Finding Study. (1956). *Recommendations on a Study of the General Educational Development Testing Program.* (Washington, DC: American Council on Education).

Conrad, Herbert S. (1949). "Tests of General Educational Development," in *The Third Mental Measurement Yearbook.* O. K. Buros, ed. (Highland Park, NJ: Gryphon Press).

Creech, F. Reid. (1978). *The Spring 1977 Norming of the Tests of General Educational Development (GED).* (Princeton, NJ: Educational Testing Service).

D'Amico, Louis A. (1953). "The Comparative Achievement of Veterans Admitted to Indiana University on the Basis of General Educational Development Tests and a Selected Group of Other Indiana University Students." (Ph.D. Thesis, Department of Psychology, Indiana University).

Detchen, Lily. (1947). "The U.S. Armed Forces Institute Examinations." *Educational Record* 28:467.

Dobbins, Charles G. (1968). *American Council on Education: Leadership and Chronology, 1918–1968.* (Washington, DC: American Council on Education).

Dressel, Paul Leroy, and Schmid, John. (1951). *An Evaluation of the Tests of General Educational Development.* (Washington, DC: American Council on Education).

Dynarski, Mark. (1991). *Analysis of Factors Related to Default.* (Washington, DC: U.S. Department of Education, Office of Planning, Budget and Evaluation).

Editorial. (1938). "Education: Progressives' Progress." *Time Magazine,* **October** **31:**33–34.

Educational Testing Service. (1974). *GED Research Project.* (Princeton, NJ: Educational Testing Service).

Educational Testing Service. (1978). *The Final Report for a Project to Develop Twelve New Forms of the Tests of General Educational Development and to Standardize the Tests Nationally in the United States.* (Princeton, NJ: Educational Testing Service).

Elicker, Paul E. (1943). "Secondary-School Credit for Military Experience: An Abstract of a Committee Recommendation for Secondary Schools." *NASSP Bulletin* 27(116):7–14.

Elicker, Paul E. (1944). "Education for the War Veteran." *NASSP Bulletin* 28(125):37–40.

Engelhart, Max D. (1946). "A Report on GED Testing." (USAFI Papers, Folder VI-3-4, Blommers Measurement Resources Laboratory, University of Iowa).

Evers, Tony. (2011). *The GED Option #2: Frequently Asked Questions and Answers.* (Madison: Wisconsin Department of Public Instruction).

Feister, W. J., and Whitney, D. R. (1968). "An Interview with Dr. E. F. Lindquist." *Epsilon Bulletin* 42:17–28.

Fosdick, Raymond Blaine. (1962). *Adventure in Giving: The Story of the General Education Board, a Foundation Established by John D. Rockefeller.* (New York: Harper and Row).

GED Testing Service. (1974). *Specifications for the Development of Tests of General Educational Development (GED).* (Washington, DC: American Council on Education).

GED Testing Service. (1978). *The GED Statistical Report, 1977.* (Washington, DC: American Council on Education.)

GED Testing Service. (1985). "Don't Hurry to Take the GED Tests!" American Council on Education (ACE), GED Items, 2.

GED Testing Service. (1989). "The 18th Annual GED Conference." *GED Items: The Newsletter of the GED Testing Service* 6:6.

GED Testing Service. (1993). *Wisconsin 1993 GED Norming Study Final Report.* (Washington, DC: American Council on Education).

GED Testing Service. (1995). *The Tests of General Educational Development, Technical Manual.* (Washington, DC: American Council on Education).

GED Testing Service. (2009a). *2008–09 GED Option Statistical Report.* (Washington, DC: American Council on Education).

GED Testing Service. (2009b). "Administrators' Conference." July 9, 2009. (Accessed from www.acenet.edu on June 7, 2011).

GED Testing Service. (2009c). *Technical Manual: 2002 Series GED Tests.* (Washington, DC: American Council on Education).

Graham, Ben George. (1940). *What the High Schools Ought to Teach: The Report of a Special Committee on the Secondary School Curriculum.* (Washington, DC: American Council on Education).

Hess, Walter E. (1946a). "State Requirements for a High School Diploma for the Veteran." *NASSP Bulletin* 30(137):55–108.

Hess, Walter E. (1946b). "State Requirements for a High School Diploma for the Veteran." *NASSP Bulletin* 30(140):92–144.

Hess, Walter E. (1948). "How Veterans and Nonveterans May Obtain High School Certification." *NASSP Bulletin* 32(156):23–41.

Hill, William C. (1943). "Should Secondary Schools Accelerate Their Programs?" *NASSP Bulletin* 27(113):37–42.

Hutchins, Robert Maynard. (1942). "The University of Chicago and the Bachelor's Degree." *Educational Record* 23:570–571.

Jepsen, Christopher, Mueser, Peter R., and Troske, Kenneth. (2012). "Labor-Market Returns to the GED Using Regression Discontinuity Analysis." Institute for the Study of Labor (IZA), Discussion Paper, 6758.

Kempfer, Homer, and Wright, Grace S. (1949). *100 Evening Schools.* (Washington, DC: Federal Security Agency, Office of Education).

Keppel, Francis. (1943). "Civilian Aid in the Armed Forces' Educational Program." *Journal of Educational Sociology* 16:534–590.

Kirby, Thomas J. (1928). "Iowa Academic Meet." *Epsilon Bulletin* 9:1.

Krug, Edward A. (1964). *The Shaping of the American High School.* (Madison: University of Wisconsin Press).

Lagemann, Ellen Condliffe. (1983). *Private Power for the Public Good: A History of the Carnegie Foundation for the Advancement of Teaching.* (Middletown, CT: Wesleyan University Press).

Lemann, Nicholas. (1999). *The Big Test: The Secret History of the American Meritocracy.* (New York: Farrar, Straus, and Giroux).

Levitan, Sar A., and Johnston, Benjamin H. (1975). *The Job Corps: A Social Experiment That Works.* (Baltimore, MD: Johns Hopkins University Press).

Lindquist, Everet Franklin. (1930). "The Iowa Academic Contest: Its Purposes and Possibilities." in *Bulletin of the State University of Iowa. New Series 577.* (Iowa City, IA: Blommers Measurement Resources Laboratory, University of Iowa).

Lindquist, Everet Franklin. (1935). "Personal Communication to Dean P.C. Parker, January 8, 1935." Lindquist File. (Special Collections, University of Iowa).

Lindquist, Everet Franklin. (1941). "New Program of Testing for Guidance and Evaluation in Iowa High Schools." *Epsilon Bulletin* 21:14.

Lindquist, Everet Franklin. (1942a). "Fall Testing Program for Iowa High Schools." *University of Iowa Bulletin* 1242:9–12.

Lindquist, Everet Franklin. (1942b). "The Iowa Tests of Educational Development. Use and Interpretation of the Test Results by the Classroom Teacher." Lindquist Papers, University of Iowa.

Lindquist, Everet Franklin. (1944). "The Use of Tests in the Accreditation of Military Experience and in the Educational Placement of War Veterans." *Educational Record* 25:367.

Lindquist, Everet Franklin. (1946). "E. F. Lindquist to Max V. Warner, 18 May 1946." USAFI Papers, Folder VI-3-4. (Blommers Measurement Resources Laboratory, University of Iowa).

Lindquist, Everet Franklin. (1970). "The Iowa Testing Programs—a Retrospective View." Unpublished manuscript, University of Iowa.

Lindquist, Everet Franklin, Van Dyke, Lauren Andrew, and Yale, John R. (1948). *What Good Is High School?* (Chicago, IL: Science Research Associates).

Lynde, Samuel A. (1945). "Schooling for the Under-Educated Veteran." *NASSP Bulletin* 29(129):14–17.

Malizio, Andrew G., and Whitney, Douglas R. (1981). *Who Takes the GED Tests?: A National Survey of Spring 1980 Examinees.* (Washington, DC: American Council on Education).

Martz, Geoff, and Pearson, Laurice. (2010). *Cracking the GED.* (New York: Random House).

Mosel, James N. (1954). "The General Educational Development Tests (High School Level) as a Predictor of Educational Level and Mental Ability." *Journal of Educational Research* 48(2):129–134.

Murphy, Bruce. (2001). "Shortcut to Failure? The GED Is a Growing Force in Education, but Some Critics Say It's Worse Than Useless." *Chicago Tribune*, August 5, 2011:10.

Musgrove, Walter J. (1981). "How Useful Are the Official Practice GED Tests and General Educational Performance Index for Predicting Performance on the GED Tests?" GED Testing Service, Research Brief, 3.

National Association of Secondary-School Principals. (1948). "The GED Test and College Entrance Requirements." *NASSP Bulletin* 32(156):42–44.

National Center for Education Statistics. (1987). *Digest of Education Statistics.* (Washington, DC: U.S. Government Printing Office).

National Commission on Excellence in Education. (1983). *A Nation at Risk: The Imperative for Educational Reform: An Open Letter to the American People. A Report to the Nation and the Secretary of Education.* (Washington, DC: National Commission on Excellence in Education).

National Education Association of the United States, Commission on the Reorganization of Secondary Education. (1918). *Cardinal Principles of Secondary Education: A Report of the Commission on the Reorganization of Secondary Education.* (Washington, DC: U.S. Government Printing Office).

National Education Goals Panel. (1994). *Data for the National Education Goals Report. Volume One: National Data.* (Washington, DC: U.S. Government Printing Office).

Olson, Keith W. (1974). *The G.I. Bill, the Veterans, and the Colleges.* (Lexington: University Press of Kentucky).

Pawasarat, John, and Quinn, Lois M. (1986). *Research on the GED Credential and Its Use in Wisconsin.* (Milwaukee: University of Wisconsin-Milwaukee, Employment and Training Institute, Division of Outreach and Continuing Education).

Peterson, Julia J. (1953). *The Iowa Testing Program: The First Fifty Years.* (Iowa City: University of Iowa Press).

Quigley, Benjamin Allan. (1987). *The Canadianization of the GED: The History and Development of the General Educational Development Testing Program in Canada.* (Washington, DC: American Council on Education).

Quinn, Lois M., and Pawasarat, John. (2011). "Attempted Reform of the GED Credential in Wisconsin." Unpublished manuscript. (University of Wisconsin—Milwaukee, Employment and Training Institute).

Rainey, Homer P. (1942). "The Devaluation of the Educational Currency." *Educational Record* 23:586.

Ramseyer, John A. (1945). "Ex-GI's Will Continue High School Education." *NASSP Bulletin* 29(134):83–90.

Roeber, Edward C. (1950). "The G.E.D. Tests as a Measure of College Aptitude." *Educational Research Bulletin* 29(2):40–53.

Shaffer, R. H. (1948). "A Note on the Alleged Scholastic Superiority of Veterans." *School and Society* 67:205.

Sims, R. S. (1974). "A Chronology of Selected Events in the History of the United States Armed Forces Institute." Unpublished Manuscript. (United States Armed Forces Institute).

Smith, Eugene R., Tyler, Ralph W., and the Evaluation Staff. (1942). *Appraising and Recording Student Progress: Adventures in Education.* (New York: Harper and Brothers).

Spaulding, Francis T. (1943). "Letter of Colonel Francis T. Spaulding to High School Principals." USAFI Papers, Folder VI-2-C. (Blommers Measurement Resources Laboratory, University of Iowa).

Special Committee of the Army Institute. (1942). "Minutes." Box 31, RG225, NAB. (Army Institute).

Spille, Henry A. (1980). "Awarding Carnegie Units on the Basis of GED Test Results." American Council on Education, GED Testing Service Memorandum, 9.

Spille, Henry A. (1981a). "The 1980 Norming of the GED Tests." American Council on Education, GED Testing Service Memorandum, 15.

Spille, Henry A. (1981b). "Interpreting GED Test Results." American Council on Education, GED Testing Service Memorandum, 21.

Spille, Henry A. (1984). "GED Testing Service (GEDTS) Response to the Recommendations and Implementing Recommendations Made in the Report 'A Nation at Risk'." American Council on Education, GED Testing Service Memorandum, 32.

Stewart, David W. (1992). "GED: 50 Years at a Glance." in *GED Testing Program: The First Fifty Years*. C. A. Allen and E. V. Jones, eds. (Washington, DC: American Council on Education).

Subcommittee on Education, Joint Army, and Navy Committee on Welfare, and Recreation. (1942). "Minutes."

Swartz, Richard, Patience, W., and Whitney, Douglas R. (1985). "Adding an Essay to the GED Writing Skills Test: Reliability and Validity Issues." GED Testing Service, GEDTS Research Studies, 7.

Swartz, Richard, and Whitney, Douglas R. (1985). *The Relationship between Scores on the GED Writing Skills Test and on Direct Measures of Writing.* (Washington, DC: General Education Development Testing Service).

Swineford, Frances. (1978). *Test Analysis, Tests of General Educational Development, ZGE1.* (Princeton, NJ: Educational Testing Service).

Trolley, William Pearson. (1942). "A Counterfeit Bachelor's Degree." *Educational Record* 23:596–597.

Tuttle, George P. (1944). *A Guide to the Evaluation of Educational Experiences in the Armed Services.* (Washington, DC: American Council on Education).

Tyack, David B. (1967). *Turning Points in American Educational History.* (Waltham, MA: Blaisdell Publishing Company).

Tyler, Ralph W. (1935). "Evaluation: A Challenge to Progressive Education." *Educational Research Bulletin* 14:9–16.

Tyler, Ralph W. (1954). *A Summary of the Findings of the Fact-Finding Study of the Testing Program of the United States Armed Forces Institute.* (Chicago: University of Chicago Press).

Tyler, Ralph W. (1987). "Interview by M. Chall." (Regional Oral History Office, Bancraft Library, University of California).

United States Armed Forces Institute. (1944). *Examiner's Manual: Nature and Purpose of the Tests, Norms for Interpretation of Test Results, Directions for Administering and Scoring the Tests.* (Washington, DC: American Council on Education).

United States Armed Forces Institute. ([Undated]). "Tests of General Educational Development Norms and Equivalence Tables." Box 31, Record Group 225. (National Archives).

United States House Committee on Education and Labor. (1978). "A Report on Education Amendments of 1978, Together with Additional Supplemental Views." U.S. House, 95, 2, H. R. 15. Washington, DC: U.S. Government Printing Office.

U.S. Office of Education War-Time Commission. (1942). "War-Time Acceleration of Secondary-School Pupils." *NASSP Bulletin* 26(104):29–32.

U.S. Senate Committee on Veterans' Affairs. (1973). "Final Report on Educational Assistance to Veterans: A Comparative Study of Three G. I. Bills; Prepared by the

Educational Testing Service." U.S. Senate, 93, 1, Washington, DC: U.S. Goverment Printing Office.

Wechsler, Harold S. (1977). *The Qualified Student: A History of Selective College Admission in America*. (New York: John Wiley and Sons).

Whitney, Douglas R. (1985a). *The 1988 Tests of General Education Development: A Preview*. (Washington, DC: GED Testing Service).

Whitney, Douglas R. (1985b). "Correspondence with Beret Harmon." On file with author.

Zook, George F. (1943). "The President's Annual Report." *Educational Record* 24:213–250.

Zook, George F. (1944). "The President's Annual Report." *Educational Record* 25:205.

Zook, George F. (1946). "The President's Annual Report." *Educational Record* 27:235–237.

Zook, George F. (1948). "The President's Annual Report." *Educational Record* 29:241.

Zook, George Frederick. (1947). "The President's Annual Report." *Educational Record* 28:235–361.

3

GROWTH IN GED TESTING

JOHN ERIC HUMPHRIES

3.1 Introduction

The GED testing program grew from 37,000 takers in 1950 to over one million in 2001. In 2010, GED certificates accounted for over 12% of high school credentials issued in the United States. For minorities, GED certificates account for a larger share of high school credentials issued: 20.7% of new high school credentials for blacks and 17.4% for Hispanics in 2008.[1]

Figure 3.1 shows substantial growth in GED test taking between 1960 and 1980, with little growth between 1980 and 2000. The pattern is similar whether one looks at the total number of test takers, the proportion of the population taking the GED, or the percentage of high school credentials accounted for by GEDs. The sharp rise in test taking in 2001 and the fall in 2002 were caused by the introduction of a new, more difficult, exam.[2] After 2002, growth in GED test taking resumed but at a lower level.

The analysis presented in this book shows that the GED credential provides little or no economic benefit for most.[3] How do we reconcile the large number of dropouts who take the GED test with this evidence? Heckman and LaFontaine (2010) show that from 1960 to 2000, high school graduation rates remained stagnant or decreased slightly. Growth in the dropout rate is not the cause of the growth in GED test taking.

Government policies founded on the premise that achievement tests adequately measure the skills that matter in life are the major causes of

---

1. Calculated from data from the GED Testing Services Annual Statistical Reports (2008) and National Center for Educational Statistics (NCES), Common Core Data. NCES Common Core Data does not include private schools. Percentages are calculated by dividing the number of GED recipients by the number of high school diplomas and GED recipients that year.

2. Another factor has to do with the way scores are aggregated across testing occasions. The GED has multiple subtests. A test taker can fail one component and pass others. Passing scores accumulate across testing occasions. With the introduction of the new test, the slate was wiped clean. This gave further incentives for persons with partial credit to fulfill their requirements using the old exam.

3. Chapter 5 demonstrates that the economic benefit of the GED does not arise from the signalling of hidden traits, nor from skills acquired in studying for the GED.

Figure 3.1 Growth in GED Test Taking

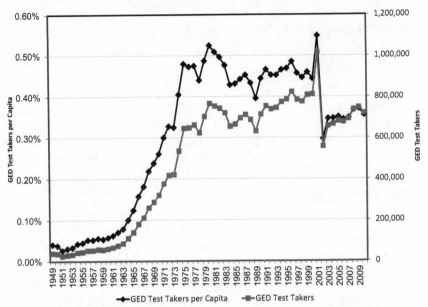

Source: GED Testing Service Annual Statistical Reports (Various Years), U.S. Census Bureau National Population Estimates.

the growth in GED certification. A variety of federal programs promote GED certification as a cheap way to produce high school graduates.

Prisons encourage GED certification. Dropouts qualify for welfare or other state transfers by earning a GED certificate. Remedial education programs measure their success by the number of GED certificates issued. Students seek out the GED in efforts to avoid high-stakes high school graduation exams and increasing graduation standards.

The rise of single-parent families promotes dropping out. Single-parent families invest less in their children, with consequent diminution of cognitive and character skills. Many smart but struggling students attain GEDs rather than traditional high school diplomas. The composition of GED recipients has shifted toward younger ages. Many recipients are only 16 or 17 years old.

3.2 Early History

As discussed in the previous chapter, the precursor to the GED test was introduced to integrate World War II veterans back into civilian life. The program rapidly expanded to include civilians. In 1947, New York became

Figure 3.2 Veterans as a Percent of GED Test Takers

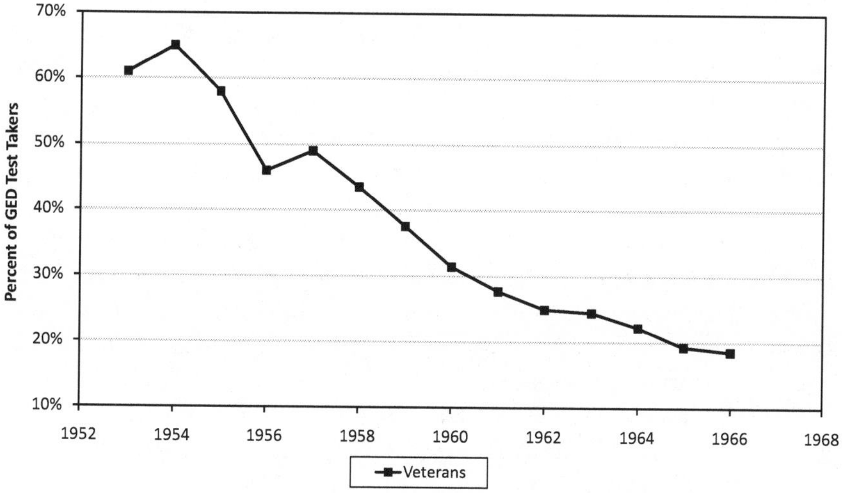

Source: GED Testing Service Annual Statistical Reports (Various Years).

the first state to offer the credential to civilians. By 1948, 20 more states followed.[4] In 1974, California became the last state to issue civilians GED certificates.[5]

By 1960, most civilian dropouts were eligible to take the GED test and earn a state-issued certificate stating that they were equivalent to traditional high school graduates. As indicated in Figure 3.2, from 1953 to 1966, the percentage of veteran GED test takers fell from 60% to 20%. Offering GED certificates to civilians set the stage for its inclusion in government programs.

3.3 The Role of Government Skill Programs

In the 1960s, the federal government introduced a variety of programs to help disadvantaged, unemployed, and displaced people acquire skills.[6] Many of these programs offered GED test preparation. Preparation was offered on the premise that achievement test scores were valid measures of the relevant life skills of high school graduates.

Chapter 4 shows that GEDs are smarter than other dropouts. Smarter people generally earn more. Comparing GEDs to uncertified dropouts, one

4. Hess (1948) and Chapter 2 of this volume.
5. Allen and Jones (1992).
6. See the insightful history of the War on Poverty in Aaron (1978).

might conclude that substantial benefits are to be gained from exam certification. Yet, as shown in Chapter 5, the GED certificate yields few benefits after controlling for characteristics present before GED certification. Simple comparisons of earnings between GEDs and uncertified dropouts can be misleading.

To demonstrate this point, consider a recent Congressional hearing on the Workforce Investment Act (WIA). One witness at the hearing presented evidence that people who enroll in GED preparation earn $8,500 more than other dropouts, while GED preparation only costs $3,000, substantially less than other training programs.[7] The GED looks like a good bargain. This testimony incorrectly assumes that the apparent earnings difference is caused by GED certification rather than by preexisting differences between dropouts who attain a GED and dropouts who do not. On the basis of such arguments, GED certification became a part of workforce investment programs, adult education, and other government programs.

3.3.1 WORKFORCE INVESTMENT PROGRAMS

Since the 1960s, GED certification has been promoted by a succession of federal training programs. This began with the Manpower Development and Training Act (MDTA) of 1962—the first major federal legislation that aimed to promote workforce investment.[8] MDTA was replaced by the Comprehensive Employment and Training Act (CETA) of 1973, followed by the Job Training Partnership Act (JTPA) of 1982 and the Workforce Investment Act (WIA) of 1998.[9] The Job Corps is part of the panoply of these programs.

The Job Corps: To understand the type of programs funded through workforce investment legislation, consider the Job Corps as a case study. The Job Corps is well known, and many of its participants earn GED certificates.[10]

---

7. U.S. Congress, *Workforce Investment Act: Recommendations to Improve the Effectiveness of Job Training*, 2007.

8. Earlier manpower utilization legislation from the 1930s and early 1940s such as the Employment Act of 1942 may have served as a precursor to the MDTA, but it focused on government employment and job subsidies. See http://www.dol.gov/oasam/programs/history/mono-mdtatext.htm for details on earlier workforce investment by the federal government.

9. For a comprehensive overview of these programs, see Lalonde (2003).

10. The Job Corps provides participants room, board, intensive training, and a small stipend. For an overview of the program and its history, see Lalonde (2003), Jablonsky (1970), and Purcell (1966).

The Job Corps was established under the Economic Opportunity Act of 1964 and has been a fixture of job training in America ever since. Early evaluations of the Job Corps claimed substantial benefits for participants, but later evaluations found that the benefits of the program do not outweigh the costs.[11,12]

The Job Corps produces far more GED certificates than high school diplomas. The program appears to have focused on GED certification because the students preferred the quicker and easier certificate. One study notes that

> Although education program staff try to encourage students to obtain their diploma by describing the additional value of a high school diploma over a GED, they reported that it is often difficult to persuade students to commit the additional time and effort. (Johnson et al., 1999, 138)

MDTA: One of the first government programs designed to enhance workforce skills was the MDTA. This program attempted to train workers who were displaced by technological progress. It served as a precursor to later workforce investment programs managed by the U.S. Department of Labor. The MDTA initially focused on development of adult skills and provided stipends for up to 52 weeks while participants received training. In 1966, an amendment shifted its focus from investing in displaced workers to solving skills shortages in the general population.[13]

GED certification was adopted into MDTA training programs.[14] Use of the GED in these programs set the stage for its more prominent role in later workforce investment legislation.

CETA: In 1973, the Comprehensive Employment and Training Act replaced the MDTA. The Act consolidated many workforce investment programs and introduced "revenue sharing," where states chose how to allocate blocks of federal funding. States used this funding to increase their focus on the GED.[15] Leading manpower authorities of the era, Sar Levitan and Garth Mangum, describe the goals of the program:

> The expansion of nonoccupational training is one of the most intriguing developments among CETA training activities. . . . The steady increase

11. Levitan and Mangum (1981); Taggart (1981).

12. Schochet, Burghardt, and McConnell (2008). For further discussion of the Job Corps, see Chapter 9.

13. Lalonde (2003).

14. Zuckerman (2001); Welker and Ginn (1974).

15. Lalonde (2003); Levitan and Mangum (1981); Rashkow (1981).

in the educational attainment of the workforce and the decline of jobs that do not require at least some reading, writing, and simple arithmetic skills make lack of basic education an increasingly serious handicap. General education development (GED) certification as a substitute for a high school diploma is, therefore, a component of growing importance. (Levitan and Mangum, 1981, 28–29)

In 1977, the CETA was supplemented by the Youth Employment and Demonstration Projects Act, which prioritized youth employment.[16] By 1978, one-third of youth participants and 12.6% of adult CETA participants had received GED preparation.[17] The CETA offered shorter training periods than the MDTA.

Under CETA, policy evaluators viewed the GED as a way to measure success. Another manpower expert, Robert Taggart, observed that

the evidence on remedial education is somewhat more dependable [than other job training] because changes can be measured using refined and relatively accepted standardized academic credit for work experience, the GED, and the diploma. (Taggart, 1981, 140)

A sizable portion of trainees received GED test preparation. The number of GED credentials produced became a measure of program success.

JTPA: In 1982, the Job Training Partnership Act (JTPA) replaced CETA. The transition to this program further reduced workforce investment funding and shortened training periods. The JTPA eliminated stipends altogether and promoted quicker, less expensive training strategies.[18] States were given more control of workforce investment programs to tailor programs to fit perceived community needs.

To monitor the effectiveness of training, the JTPA required programs to report performance indicators. Programs were awarded bonuses for surpassing performance standards and could lose funding if they did not meet requirements.[19] They were evaluated on the basis of employment statistics six months after training and the number of high school credentials *or equivalents* produced.[20] Since producing GED credentials helped meet performance standards, JTPA centers had incentives to certify any uncredentialed dropout, regardless of whether the GED provided meaningful

16. Zuckerman (2001).
17. Taggart (1981).
18. Lalonde (2003); Zuckerman (2001); Levitan and Mangum (1994).
19. Heckman, Heinrich, and Smith (2011).
20. Courty, Heinrich, and Marschke (2005).

economic benefits. In addition, JTPA programs had incentives to *cream skim* highly able trainees who could pass the GED with minimal effort.[21] The JTPA made GED certification a benchmark for judging its success.

WIA: The Workforce Investment Act of 1998 is the most recent legislation to fund and regulate workforce training programs. The WIA further limits the time and budgets for training, making GED preparation an even more attractive option. Unlike the JTPA program, the WIA program requires states to design "one-stop shops" where participants can receive help with job placement through intensive classroom training. The Act has a dual focus of employing out-of-work adults and equipping low-ability youth with the skills needed for employment.[22] For both groups, the program's success is judged by the number of state-recognized or industry-recognized credentials produced, including GED certificates.[23]

The Scale of Support for Job Training Programs: Figure 3.3 plots both federal outlays for workforce investment programs and enrollment in workforce investment programs funded by the U.S. Department of Labor. Total training and employment outlays are shown in the top panel, while new enrollment in the department's administered work, employment, and training programs is shown in the bottom panel. Outlays for training and employment programs grew substantially from the 1960s to the early 1980s but have slowly declined since. The inclusion of the GED in workforce investment programs, followed by the reductions in financial support evident in Figure 3.3, promoted GED certification.

3.3.2 ADULT EDUCATION FUNDING

Coincident with the development of workforce investment programs, the Department of Education created educational training programs for adults. The Economic Opportunity Act of 1964 established the Adult Basic Education program, which was designed to teach basic numeracy and literacy to adults.[24] In 1966, the program was revised in an attempt to help people develop the skills necessary for employment and for responsible and productive citizenship.[25] In 1970, an additional amendment established the Adult

---

21. See Heckman, Heinrich, and Smith (2011) for an overview.

22. Lalonde (2003).

23. Courty, Heinrich, and Marschke (2005); Fernandes-Alcantara (2011).

24. See Ulin (1976).

25. National Advisory Council on Adult Education (1980); Public Law 88-452, Part B—Adult Basic Education Programs, Sec. 212, page 520 (1964).

Figure 3.3 Workforce Investment (Outlays and Enrollment)

New Enrollment to Work/Employment and Training Programs Administrated by Department of Labor

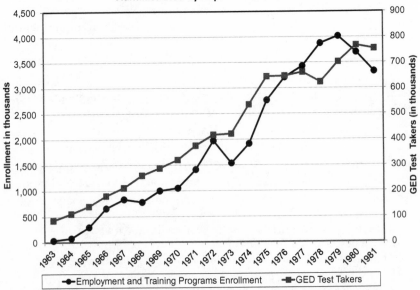

Sources: U.S. Office of Management and Budget (2011); Employment and Training Report of the President (Various Years); GED Testing Service Annual Statistical Reports (Various Years); Manpower Report of the President (Various Years).

Note: Data on new enrollment in training programs administered by the U.S. Department of Labor are only available from 1963 to 1981.

Figure 3.4 GED Credentials Obtained through Adult Education

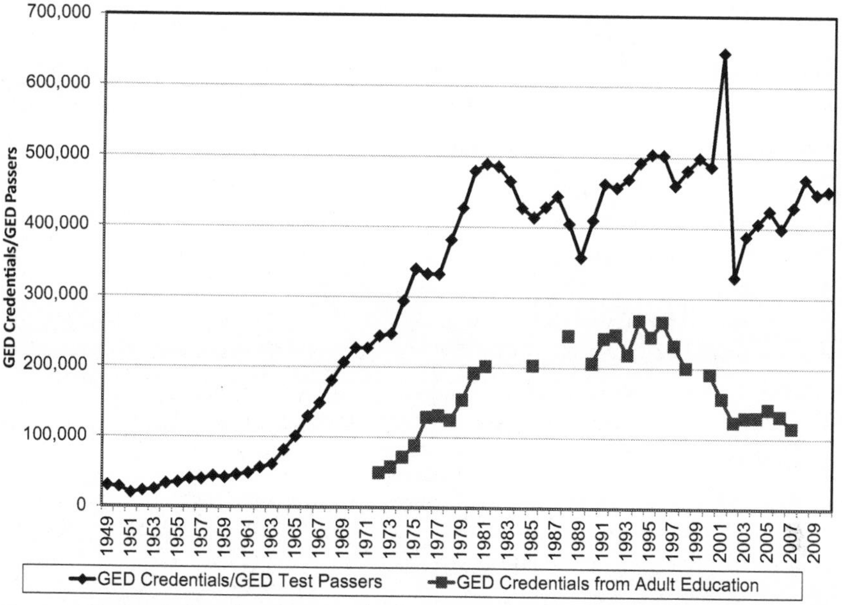

Sources: Digest of Education Statistics (Various Years); The National Advisory Council on Adult Education Annual Report (Various Years); NCES, Adult Basic Education Program Statistics (Various Years); unpublished data.

Notes: In the early years, the number of GED credentials issued is reported, which later switches to the number of people passing the GED test. For later years, the number of GED credentials and high school diplomas produced are pooled. For these years, the ratio of GEDs to high school diplomas from the previous five years is used to estimate what percentage of the pooled GEDs and diplomas are GEDs.

Secondary Education (ASE) program to provide secondary-level training and promote the acquisition of high school diplomas or their equivalents.[26,27]

Adult Education programs produce nearly half of new GED credentials. As is evident from Figure 3.4, Adult Education produced 26% of the stock of all new GED credentials in 1975, which increased to 40% in 1980 and 50% in 1990.[28] In the National Longitudinal Survey of Youth 1997,

26. National Advisory Council on Adult Education (1980).

27. For more details on the history of adult education, see Sticht (2002), Leahy (1991), Rose (1991), and National Advisory Council on Adult Education (1980).

28. Alternative sources report similar numbers. The GED Testing Service reports that 46% of GED test takers prepared through Adult Education programs (McLaughlin, Skaggs, and Becker Patterson, 2009).

40% of GED recipients prepared for the GED test through Adult Education programs.

3.3.3 EDUCATION IN PRISONS

Since 1970, the incarceration rate in the United States has more than quadrupled. As shown in Figure 3.5, minority groups account for most of this growth. In response, prison education programs have been promoted in the hope of decreasing recidivism.[29] Federal and state prisons have implemented a number of mandates and incentives that encourage prisoners to earn GEDs.

Several federal laws provide funding for GED preparation in correctional institutions.[30] This legislation promotes earning "high school equivalency degrees" or "a high school diploma or an equivalent degree." Furthermore, the Violent Crime and Control and Law Enforcement Act of 1994 mandates that prisons offer GED programs for inmates:

> The Attorney General shall ensure that the Bureau of Prisons has in effect an optional General Educational Development program for inmates who have not earned a high school diploma or its equivalent.[31]

Additional legislation introduced incentives to encourage prisoners to GED certify. In addition, the Violent Crime Control and Law Enforcement Act of 1994 requires federal prisoners to obtain a GED before receiving any credit toward reduction of their sentence. The legislation stipulates that

> credit toward a prisoner's service of sentence shall not be vested unless the prisoner has earned or is making satisfactory progress toward a high school diploma or an equivalent degree.

The Federal Bureau of Prisons also requires inmates without a diploma or GED certificate to participate in literacy programs for a minimum of 240 hours or until earning a GED.[32] Furthermore, inmates are required to

---

29. Research has found little or no reduction in recidivism or increase in postincarceration earnings from GED certification. See the evidence reported in Chapter 5.

30. Such laws include the Violent Crime Control and Law Enforcement Act of 1994, Neglected and Delinquent Youth State Grants of 1994, Workplace and Community Transition Training for Incarcerated Youth Offenders State Grants of 1998, Workplace and Community Transition Training for Incarcerated Individuals 2008, and funding through Adult Education legislation.

31. The Violent Crime Control and Law Enforcement Act of 1994, Title 2, Subtitle D, Section 20412.

32. Lappin (2009).

Figure 3.5 Growth in the Prison Population

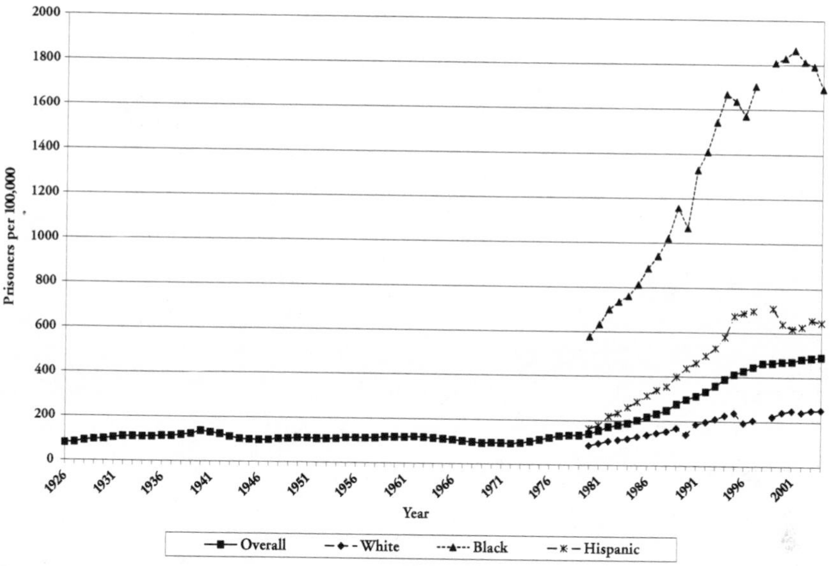

Source: Reproduced from Heckman and LaFontaine (2010).

have a GED credential or high school diploma to work above the minimum pay.[33]

These incentives have increased GED certification among prisoners. A Bureau of Justice Statistics report finds that, in 1997, 26% of all inmates earned a GED in prison.[34] Moreover, as shown in Figure 3.6, the estimated percentage of GED credentials issued to the incarcerated has grown substantially over the last two decades. The figure uses two different data sources, but both sources find that the incarcerated account for a growing proportion of new GEDs. The percent of GED credentials earned in correctional education programs grew from 8% in 1994 to nearly 14% in 2005 according to the first source, and from 5% in 2002 to almost 11% in 2010 according to the second source.

3.3.4 DEMAND FOR SCHOOLING AND
THE SUPPLY OF EDUCATIONAL FINANCE

The returns to education have increased since 1980. As shown in Figure 3.7, highly educated people have experienced rapid wage growth, while male dropouts have experienced wage declines. This increasing wage differential

33. Code of Federal Regulations part 544.
34. Harlow (2003).

Figure 3.6 Percent of GEDs Credentials Earned by the Incarcerated

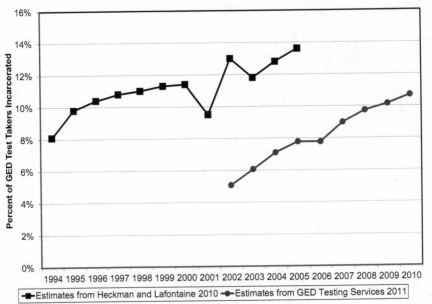

Sources: GED Testing Service (2011); Heckman and LaFontaine (2010).

Notes: The estimates from Heckman and LaFontaine (2010) are the estimated percentage of GED credentials issued to the incarcerated in federal or state prisons. Numbers were calculated using estimates from each state for which data were available. The estimates from GED Testing Services (2011) are the percentage of GED passers taking the test at state or federal correctional facilities. As discussed in GED Testing Service (2011), the use of GED tests passed in correctional facilities underestimates the total number of GED credentials issued to the incarcerated, as it excludes tests taken at any facility testing both the incarcerated and nonincarcerated.

encourages some dropouts to seek postsecondary education.[35] Most postsecondary programs do not accept applicants without a high school diploma or equivalent. GED certification gives dropouts the option of pursuing further education.[36]

The costs of attending college have been subsidized by federal funding for college such as the GI Bill, Educational Opportunity Grants, Pell Grants, and Perkins Loans. As shown in Figure 3.8, such funding has increased over

35. Figure 1.9 in Chapter 1 displays the strong temporal relationship between the rise in the college–high school wage differential and the proportion of GED test takers who report they are taking the exam to qualify for higher education.

36. Chapter 5 shows that few GED recipients earn postsecondary degrees, though many try.

Figure 3.7 Growth in Log Wages by Education

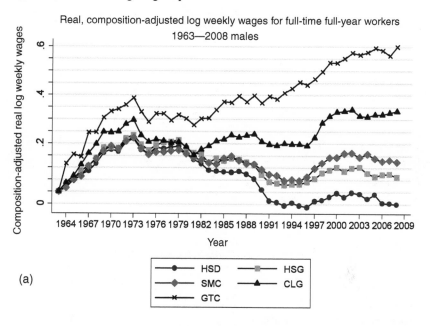

(a)

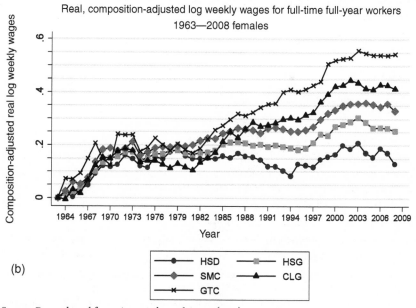

(b)

Source: Reproduced from Acemoglu and Autor (2011).

Notes: "HSD" stands for high school dropout, "HSG" stands for high school graduate, "SMC" stands for some college, "CLG" stands for college, and "GTC" stands for greater than college. Data from March CPS data for earnings years 1963–2008. The real log weekly wage for each education group is the weighted average of the relevant composition adjusted cells using a fixed set of weights equal to the average employment share of each group. Nominal wage values are deflated using the Personal Consumption Expenditure (PCE) deflator.

Figure 3.8 Pell Grants and Educational Opportunity Grants

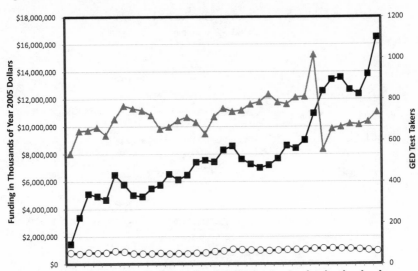

Sources: "2000 Status Report on the Pell Grant Program," Federal Campus-Based Programs Data Book (Various Years), U.S. Census Bureau; GED Testing Service Annual Statistical Reports (Various Years).

time. Until recently, dropouts seeking these funds were eligible only if they first earned a GED or passed an alternative "ability to benefit" test. The GED has indirect value to dropouts through the option it creates to access postsecondary education.[37]

3.3.5 OTHER NATIONAL LEGISLATION

Other national legislation supports GED certification by promoting the production of high school diplomas and *state-recognized equivalents*. Legislation promotes GED certification in two ways: (1) it provides dropouts incentives to certify, and (2) it uses the number of credentials issued to evaluate the performance of social programs.

Federal laws incentivize groups previously outside the purview of the GED program to pursue GED certification. Programs such as the Work Incentive (WIN) Program of 1967 and the Job Opportunities and Basic Skills

37. Data shows that many older dropouts certified when Pell Grants were introduced. In 1972, the average age of GED recipients jumped by nearly two years as older dropouts certified to qualify for newly introduced Pell Grants.

Figure 3.10 Percent of GED Test Takers by Age

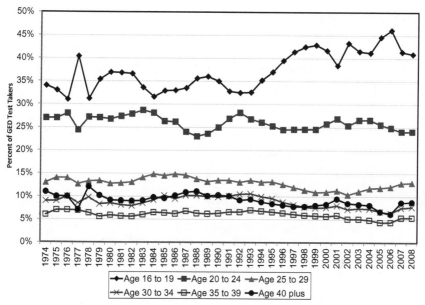

Source: GED Testing Service Annual Statistical Reports (Various Years).
Notes: New York did not report GEDs by age until 1984. Missouri did not report GEDs by age until 1977.

response, in 1955, the American Council of Education implemented 20 as the national minimum age threshold for taking the GED test. As shown in Table 3.1, federal age requirements have been steadily relaxed since 1955.

Many states set minimum age requirements for taking the GED test above the national minimum, but these requirements have been steadily relaxed. Figure 3.12 shows the population-weighted average national age requirement for taking the GED and the average age of GED test takers over time. Falling minimum age requirements for GED certification were followed by a rapid decrease in the average age of test takers.

Many states also permit exceptions to their age requirements. Originally, states granted exceptions in special cases, such as teenage pregnancy; over time the number of exceptions has increased. Some GED test takers are also exceptions to the minimum age at which students can drop out of high school in their states.

Figure 3.13 plots both the percentage of GED test takers qualifying as exceptions to the age requirement to take the test and the percentage of GED

Figure 3.11 Growth in Young GED Test Takers

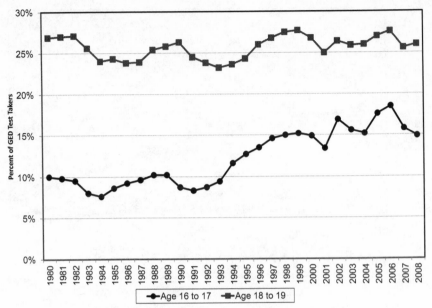

Source: GED Testing Service Annual Statistical Reports (Various Years).

Table 3.1 Federal Minimum Age Requirement to Take the GED Test

Years	Age
1955	20 years of age
1970	18 years of age
1981	No federal age requirement
1992	16 years of age

Note: See Chapter 2 for additional details on age changes over time.

test takers qualifying as exceptions to *both* requirements. The percentage of GED test takers qualifying as exceptions to the minimum age for GED testing has more than doubled since 1980. The percentage of GED test takers qualifying as exceptions to both the minimum age for testing and the minimum age for compulsory schooling grew from 1% in 1990 to over 6% in 2007.

Figure 3.12 Average Age and Minimum Testing Age of GED Test Takers

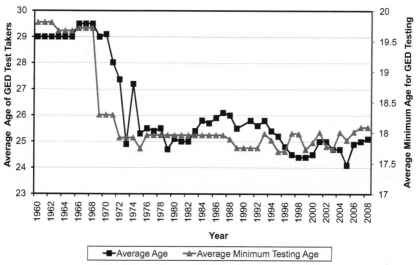

Source: GED Testing Service Annual Statistical Reports (Various Years).
Note: State mandatory test age (or the federal mandatory age if higher than state requirements) is weighted by the state's population.

Figure 3.13 Age Exceptions to GED Testing Age and Dropout Age

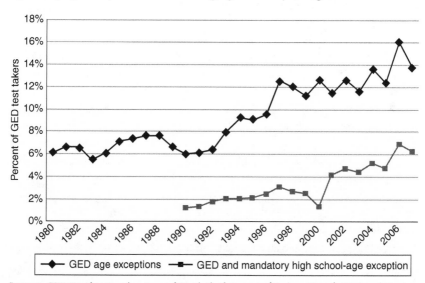

Sources: GED Testing Service Annual Statistical Reports (Various Years); National Center for Educational Statistics data.
Notes: "GED age exceptions" are individuals taking the GED at ages below the minimum GED testing age. "GED and mandatory high school-age exceptions" are individuals from GED age exceptions who are also below the compulsory schooling age in their state, making them double exceptions.

Figure 3.14 Number of States with GED Option Programs

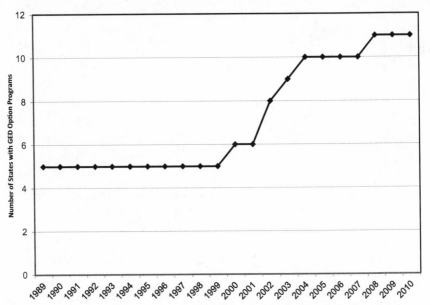

Source: GED Statistical Report on the GED Option Program (2009a, 2010).

3.4.1.2 *The GED Option Program and Promotion of the GED to High School Students*

The GED is now offered in high schools through an American Council of Education–sponsored program called the GED Option program. Introduced in 1989, Option programs target students who are at risk of dropping out and help them acquire GED certificates in place of traditional high school diplomas.[43] States have discretion in implementing it. There is substantial variation across states. Figure 3.14 shows that the number of states implementing GED Option programs has grown substantially. Evidence presented in Chapter 7 shows that the GED Option programs induce students who would have otherwise graduated to drop out and pursue a GED certificate.

In combination with the GED Option program, teenagers may receive information that leads them to mistakenly assume that a GED certificate provides the same opportunities as a high school diploma. Many GED certificates have names such as Kansas High School Diploma or Maryland High

---

43. The definition of "at risk" varies by state. To be eligible, students must typically be at risk of not graduating with his or her class or be more than a year behind in credits.

Figure 3.15 Children in Single Parent Households by Marital Status—All Education Levels, All Races

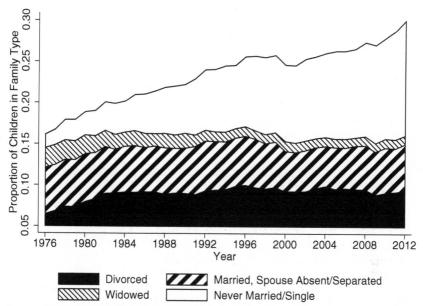

Source: IPUMS CPS March data, 1968–2010.

Notes: Only households with children under 18 are included in the calculations. Household responses are averaged with weights equal to the household weight multiplied by the number of children under 18 in the household. The "Married, Spouse Absent" category includes parents who are separated.

School Diploma.[44] These names likely mislead students about the value of the GED degree.

3.4.2 CHANGING FAMILY CHARACTERISTICS

Since the 1980s, the number of teenagers coming from single-parent homes has increased. As demonstrated in Chapter 4, children from single-parent families are less likely to graduate from high school. GED recipients are as likely to come from single-parent homes as other dropouts.

Figure 3.15 shows the proportion of children in single-parent homes by marital status. Since 1976, the percent of children growing up in single-parent families has doubled.[45] In 2012, approximately 30% of all children were being

44. All GED certificates or credentials are issued by the state.

45. Single-parent homes are more common among blacks than Hispanics and more common among Hispanics than whites.

Figure 3.16 Population-weighted Average Number of Carnegie Units Needed to Graduate

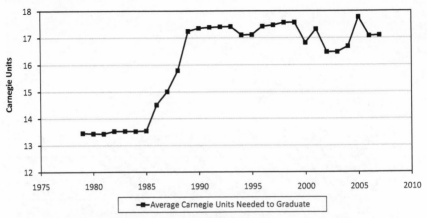

Source: National Center for Educational Statistics.
Notes: Carnegie units are standardized class-hour measurements roughly equivalent to taking one class for one academic year. The increase in the 1980s corresponds to the publication of the National Commission on Excellence in Education's report *Nation at Risk* in 1983. The reports specifically called for increases in graduation requirements. Variation in requirements come from state laws and regulations. National averages were constructed by population-weighting state requirements for the states and years for which data were available.

raised in single-parent homes. Children from single-parent homes receive less cognitive and emotional stimulation than children from traditional two-parent families (Moon, 2012) and as a consequence have diminished cognitive and character skills (Cunha and Heckman, 2008; Cunha, Heckman, and Schennach, 2010).

3.4.3 CHANGES IN HIGH SCHOOL GRADUATION STANDARDS

In 1983, the *Nation at Risk* reported that American schools were failing students. In response, states increased graduation requirements, such as the required number of class hours, the number of classes in core subjects, and the number of days in the school year.[46] As shown in Figure 3.16, states increased the average number of Carnegie units required for graduation by nearly four units in the half decade following publication of the *Nation at Risk* report. Graduating from high school became more difficult as the amount of time, effort, and knowledge expected from students increased.

46. Patall, Cooper, and Allen (2010).

Figure 3.17 Number of States with High School Exit Exams

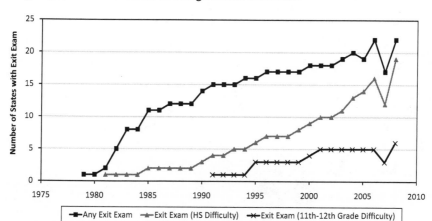

Source: Minnesota Population Center, State High School Exit Examinations for Graduation Classes Since 1977.

Notes: The data series are not defined exclusively. "Any Exit Exam" includes all states with exit exams, including those not reporting difficulty. "Exit Exam (HS Difficulty)" includes those states reporting a passing difficulty of ninth grade or higher. "Exit Exam (11th-12th Grade Difficulty)" includes only those states reporting test difficulties in the eleventh- or twelfth-grade level.

As discussed in Chapter 8, a growing number of states require students to pass high school exit exams in order to earn high school diplomas. Figure 3.17 plots the number of states with mandatory high school exit examinations over time. Since 1977, the number of states requiring exit exams has grown from 1 to 22. The exams have also become more difficult. Warren, Jenkins, and Kulick (2006) and the analysis in Chapter 8 show that introducing high school exit exams leads to increased GED certification.

3.5 New Trends in GED Certification

Policies regarding the use of GED certification are continuously evolving. States have reintroduced additional GED certification requirements. In addition, No Child Left Behind (NCLB) legislation prohibits states from counting GED recipients as high school graduates.

Many states have reintroduced additional requirements for GED certification, reversing a long pattern of expanding eligibility and reducing requirements. Some states now require potential recipients to take courses or pass civics tests. Other states require additional courses or tests for test takers who fail the GED on their first try.[47]

47. See the 2008 GED Statistical Report (2009a).

Figure 3.18 Number of States That Require Passing the Official Practice Test

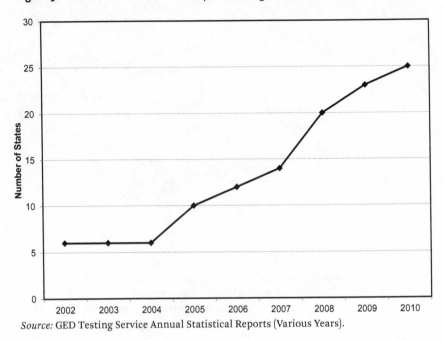

Source: GED Testing Service Annual Statistical Reports (Various Years).

The largest change in GED preparation has been the introduction and expansion of the Official Practice Test (OPT). As shown in Figure 3.18, many states now require GED candidates to take the OPT before taking the actual GED test. Since 2004, the number of states requiring the OPT has increased substantially. Oddly, some states use the OPT to increase the difficulty of earning a GED certificate. Iowa, for example, requires potential recipients to earn a score on the OPT that exceeds the score necessary to pass the actual test. In Iowa, the OPT is so difficult that 99% of people who pass the OPT pass the actual GED exam.[48]

The No Child Left Behind Act of 2001 limits the use, and potential abuse, of GED certification by states and school districts.[49] NCLB defines graduation rates as "the percentage of students who graduate from secondary school with a regular diploma in the standard number of years."[50]

48. Some have misinterpreted the 99% passing rate to mean that Iowa's GED program is more successful than others.

49. Prior to NCLB, schools were able to count students who obtained GED certifications as high school graduates, thereby inflating high school graduation rates.

50. Department of Education (2008a).

Figure 3.19 Major Events in GED Growth

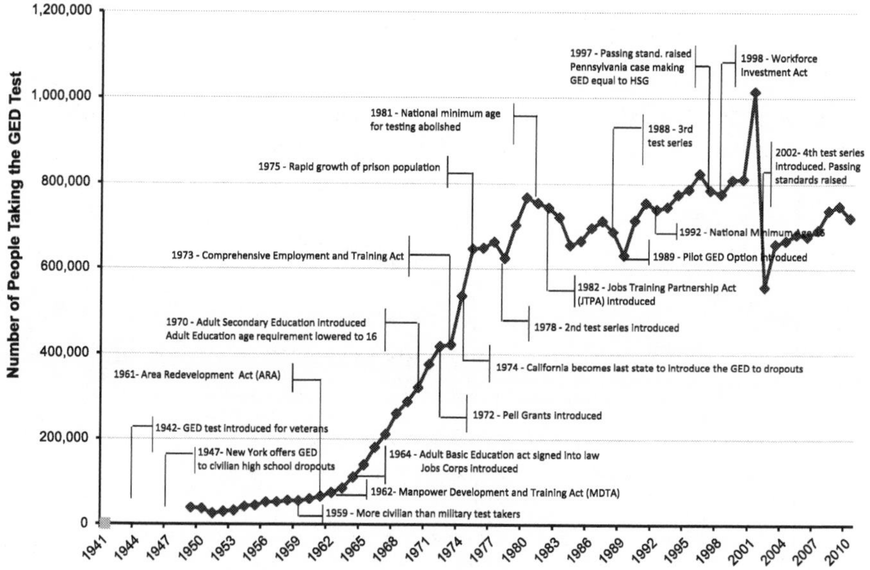

Sources: GED Testing Service Annual Statistical Reports (Various Years), Lalonde (2003), and Chapter 2 of this volume.

In addition, NCLB requirements stipulate that

to remove a student from a graduation cohort the school must confirm in writing that the student transferred, left the country, or is deceased. For students who transfer, schools must demonstrate that they transferred to a program that culminates in a traditional high school diploma.[51]

These two changes prevent states and high schools from counting GED recipients as high school graduates and from removing GED recipients from their books.

After the NCLB legislation was passed in 2001, the Department of Education began constructing new universal standards for high school graduation. A committee was assembled to determine a national guideline for calculating high school graduation rates.[52] The committee released a standardized guideline in 2008, but some states were granted short-term exemptions from the new standards. All states are required to comply with the new regulations for the freshman cohort of the 2008–2009 school year.

51. Department of Education (2008a).
52. Department of Education (2008b).

Once the uniform guidelines are in place, schools will no longer be able to use GED certification to shunt students from their books.

3.6 Summary

This chapter presents reasons for the growth and continued use of GED certification despite the strong evidence against benefits for most certifiers. The GED is promoted by many government education and training programs. Dropouts are encouraged to GED certify. Teenagers are taking the GED at higher rates, and the GED is promoted in high schools. Figure 3.19 summarizes the lessons of this chapter and the previous one. It plots the number of GED test takers over time, and it highlights the key developments that promoted the adoption and expansion of GED certification.

BIBLIOGRAPHY

Aaron, H. J. (1978). *Politics and The Professors: The Great Society in Perspective.* Washington, DC: Brookings Institution Press.

Acemoglu, D., and D. Autor (2011). Skills, tasks and technologies: Implications for employment and earnings. In O. Ashenfelter and D. Card (Eds.), *Handbook of Labor Economics,* Volume 4, Part B of *Handbooks in Economics*, Chapter 12, pp. 1043–1171. Amsterdam: Elsevier.

Allen, C. A., and E. V. Jones (1992). *GED Testing Program: The First Fifty Years.* Washington, DC: American Council on Education.

American Council on Education (2011). GED testing in correctional centers. Research Studies 2011-3, GED Testing Service, Washington, DC.

Courty, P., C. Heinrich, and G. Marschke (2005). Setting the standard in performance measurement systems. *International Public Management Journal 8*(3), 321–347.

Cunha, F., and J. J. Heckman (2008, Fall). Formulating, identifying and estimating the technology of cognitive and noncognitive skill formation. *Journal of Human Resources 43*(4), 738–782.

Cunha, F., J. J. Heckman, and S. M. Schennach (2010, May). Estimating the technology of cognitive and noncognitive skill formation. *Econometrica 78*(3), 883–931.

Department of Education (2008a, October). A uniform, comparable graduation rate: How the final regulations for Title I hold schools, districts, and states accountable for improving graduation rates. Technical report, Department of Education, No Child Left Behind.

Department of Education (2008b, December). High school graduation rate: Non-regulatory guidance. Technical report, Department of Education, No Child Left Behind.

Fernandes-Alcantara, A. L. (2011). Vulnerable youth: Employment and job training programs. CRS Report for Congress 7-5700, Congressional Research Service.

GED Testing Service (2009a, July). *2008 GED Testing Program Statistical Report.* Washington, DC: American Council on Education. http://www.acenet.edu/Content /NavigationMenu/ged/pubs/GED_ASR_2008.pdf.

GED Testing Service (2009b, December). *2008–2009 GED Option Statistical Report.* Washington, DC: American Council on Education.

GED Testing Service (2010). *2009–10 GED Option Statistical Report*. Washington, DC: American Council on Education.

GED Testing Service (Various Years). *The GED Annual Statistical Report*. Washington, DC: American Council on Education.

Harlow, C. W. (2003). Education and correctional populations. Bureau of Justice Statistics Special Report NCJ 195670, Bureau of Justice Statistics.

Heckman, J. J., C. Heinrich, and J. Smith (2011). Performance standards and the potential to improve government performance. In J. J. Heckman, C. J. Heinrich, P. Courty, G. Marschke, and J. Smith (Eds.), *The Performance of Performance Standards*, Chapter 1, pp. 1–4. Kalamazoo, MI: W. E. Upjohn Institute for Employment Research.

Heckman, J. J., and P. A. LaFontaine (2010, May). The American high school graduation rate: Trends and levels. *Review of Economics and Statistics* 92(2), 244–262.

Hess, W. E. (1948). How veterans and nonveterans may obtain high school certification. *NASSP Bulletin* 32(156), 23–41.

Jablonsky, A. (1970). The Job Corps: A review of the ERIC literature. ERIC-IRCD Urban Disadvantaged Series Number 13, ERIC Clearinghouse on Urban Education.

Johnson, T., M. Gritz, R. Jackson, J. Burghardt, C. Boussy, J. Leonard, and C. Orians (1999). National Job Corps Study: Report on the process analysis. Technical Report 8140-510, Mathematica Policy Research.

Lalonde, R. J. (2003). Employment and training programs. In R. A. Moffitt (Ed.), *Means-Tested Transfer Programs in the United States*, Chapter 8, pp. 517–585. Chicago, IL: University of Chicago Press.

Lappin, H. G. (2009). Statement of Harley G. Lappin, director of the Federal Bureau of Prisons before the United States sentencing commission. Regional Hearing on the State of Federal Sentencing, Western District of Texas, November 20, 2009.

Leahy, M. A. (1991). The adult education act: A guide to the literature and funded projects. Guide ED341876, Eric Clearinghouse on Adult, Career, and Vocational Education.

Levitan, S. A., and G. L. Mangum (1981). *The T in CETA: Local and National Perspectives*. Kalamazoo, MI: W. E. Upjohn Institute for Employment Research.

Levitan, S. A., and G. L. Mangum (1994). *Federal Human Resource Policy: From Kennedy to Clinton*. Arlington, VA: Public Interest Publications.

McLaughlin, J. W., G. Skaggs, and M. Becker Patterson (2009). Preparation for the performance on the GED test. Research Studies 2009-2, GED Testing Service.

Moon, S. H. (2012, July). Time to invest in disadvanted young children. *Samsung Economic Research Institute Quarterly* 5(3), 50–59.

National Advisory Council on Adult Education (1980). *A History of the Adult Education Act*. Washington, DC: National Advisory Council on Adult Education.

Patall, E. A., H. Cooper, and A. B. Allen (2010). Extending the school day or school year: A systematic review of research (1985–009). *Review of Educational Research* 80(3), 401–436.

Purcell, F. (1966). *Low Income Youth, Unemployment, Vocational Training and the Job Corps*. New York: New York University, Center for the Study of Unemployed Youth.

Rashkow, I. (1981). *Comprehensive Employment and Training Act (CETA)*. Washington, DC: Congressional Research Service.

Rose, A. D. (1991). Ends or means: An overview of the history of the adult education act. Information Series 346, Center on Education and Training for Employment, The Ohio State University.

Schochet, P. Z., J. Burghardt, and S. McConnell (2008, December). Does Job Corps work? Impact findings from the National Job Corps Study. *American Economic Review 98*(5), 1864–1886.

Sticht, T. G. (2002). The rise of the adult education and literacy system in the United States: 1600–2000. In *Annual Review of Adult Learning and Literacy*, Volume 3, Chapter 2. New York: John Wiley and Sons.

Taggart, R. (1981). A fisherman's guide: An assessment of training and remediation strategies. Technical report, W. E. Upjohn Institute for Employment and Research, Kalamazoo, MI.

Tolbert, M. (2002). State correctional education programs: State policy update. Technical report, National Institute for Literacy.

Ulin, J. K. (1976). *An Historical Perspective: The Adult Education Act 1964–1974*. Washington, DC: National Advisory Council on Adult Education.

U.S. Congress, House of Representatives (2007). Workforce Investment Act: Recommendations to improve the effectiveness of job training. Hearing before the Subcommittee on Higher Education, Lifelong Learning, and Competitiveness. Committee on Education and Labor, U.S. House of Representatives, One Hundred Tenth Congress. June 28, 2007.

U.S. Department of Labor, Employment and Training Administration (Various Years). *Employment and Training Report of the President*. Washington, DC: U.S. Government Printing Office.

U.S. Department of Labor, Manpower Administration (Various Years). *Manpower Report of the President*. Washington, DC: U.S. Government Printing Office. A Report on Manpower, Requirements, Resources, Utilization, and Training.

U.S. Office of Management and Budget (2011). *Fiscal Year 2012: Historical Tables, Budget of the United States Government*. Washington, DC: Executive Office of the President, Office of Management and Budget. Available from: http://www.whitehouse.gov/sites/default/ files/omb/budget/fy2012 / assets/hist.pdf.

Warren, J. R., K. N. Jenkins, and R. B. Kulick (2006, Summer). High school exit examinations and state-level completion and GED rates: 1975 through 2002. *Educational Evaluation and Policy Analysis 28*(2), 131–152.

Welker, C., and C. Ginn (1974). The impact of institutional manpower development and training act programs on vocational and technical education in the state of Mississippi. Technical Report 26, University of Southern Mississippi, Hattiesburg, Bureau of Educational Research.

Zuckerman, A. (2001). The more things change, the more they stay the same: The evolution and devolution of youth employment programs. In P. L. Benson and K. J. Pittman (Eds.), *Trends in Youth Development*, Volume 6 of *Outreach Scholarship*, pp. 269–289. New York: Springer.

EVALUATING THE BENEFITS

4

WHO ARE THE GEDS?

JAMES J. HECKMAN, JOHN ERIC HUMPHRIES, AND TIM KAUTZ

4.1 A New Breed of GED

The first cohort of exam-certified high school equivalents were World War II veterans who had been trained and disciplined in the armed forces. After the war, they were welcomed home as heroes. Many had left high school to serve their country, and the early high school equivalency program helped reintegrate them into society. Given their training and discipline, it is not surprising that the veterans who were able to pass the exam were relatively successful later in life, often performing as well in college as high school graduates.[1]

The modern GED program does not target war heroes; modern GED recipients leave high school for very different reasons. Figure 4.1 displays self-reported reasons for dropping out of high school for GED recipients and other dropouts based on evidence from two longitudinal data sets.[2] For each demographic group, it shows the proportion reporting the indicated reason for dropping out of school for both dropouts and GED recipients. Responses are mutually exclusive in the top panel but are not mutually exclusive in the bottom panel. A black dot indicates whether the means are statistically significantly different from each other, comparing GEDs and other dropouts. The "⊢─┤" represents standard error bars for each mean.

Today, GED recipients leave school for reasons similar to other dropouts: Figure 4.1 shows that many GED recipients leave school because they

---

1. See the discussion in Chapter 2 about the performance of exam-certified veterans in college. Atkinson (1949) reports that veterans outperformed nonveterans due to their higher levels of maturity and motivation. Gowan (1949) reports that exam-certified veterans performed better than nonveterans, despite having lower grades in high school. For a contrasting view, see D'Amico (1953), who found that the exam-certified veterans had lower grades and higher attrition rates from college.

2. The National Longitudinal Survey of Youth 1979 (NLSY79) and the National Education Longitudinal Study (NELS). For a detailed description of these data sets, see Web Appendix Sections W5.1.1.1 and W5.1.1.8. The Web Appendix mentioned in this note and subsequent notes is found at http://jenni.uchicago.edu/Studies_of _GED.

Figure 4.1 Reasons for Leaving School

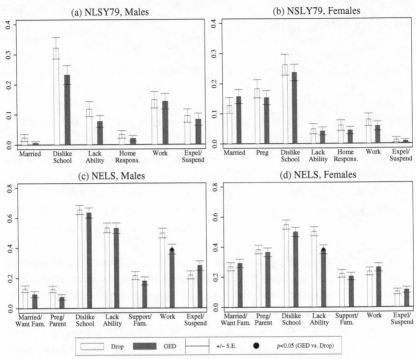

Sources: National Longitudinal Survey of Youth 1979 (NLSY79); National Education Longitudinal Study (NELS).

NLSY79 Notes: The reasons for leaving are mutually exclusive. Their education status (GED recipient vs. dropout) is measured at age 35. The reason for leaving school is defined as the reason they reported for leaving school before dropping out permanently. Responses giving an unspecified reason are omitted from the calculations. The responses "Entered Military," "School Too Dangerous," and "Moved Away from School" are not displayed due to low response rates. They represent 1%, 1%, and 3% of the sample respectively. *NELS Notes:* The reasons for leaving school are not mutually exclusive. *Variable Definitions:* The unspecified "Other Problems" category is omitted. "Married/ Want Fam." includes people who listed married or wanted a family. "Preg/Parent" includes people who listed that they were pregnant or became a parent. "Dislike School" includes people who listed that they disliked their school, their teachers, other students, or a new school. "Lack Ability" includes people who listed that they were unable to do the work or were failing. "Support/Fam." includes people who reported they left to care for a family member or to support their family. "Work" includes people who reported finding a job or that school conflicted with a current job. The categories "Unsafe," "Travel," "Friends Left," and "Drug/Drinking" are not displayed due to low response rates. Less than 10% of respondents reported one of these omitted reasons.

are expelled, lack ability, or dislike school. Many female GEDs drop out due to pregnancy.[3,4] GEDs tend to dislike school less than dropouts. Male GEDs are more likely to report the desire to work as their reason for leaving school, and female GEDs are less likely to report that they lack ability compared to other female dropouts.

This chapter shows that the GED recipients of today are as smart as high school graduates who do not attend college but lack a variety of character skills. During adolescence, GED recipients are as likely as, or even more likely than, other dropouts to take drugs, exhibit violent behavior, participate in criminal activities, and have sex at a young age. Their behavioral problems start at early ages. As a group, they have disadvantaged backgrounds. These patterns are found in four major data sets that span different cohorts.

People and their circumstances can change. Measures of adolescent behaviors and skills might miss important changes in skills or circumstances that occur after people drop out of school. We do not have direct measures of skills over the life cycle. As a partial substitute, we explore which life events coincide with GED certification. Male GED recipients often certify during spells of recent joblessness.[5] Females who do not work after dropping out are much less likely to certify. As Figure 4.1 shows, about half of female dropouts leave high school due to pregnancy or marriage. These women tend to have better adolescent behaviors and to complete more grades of school than noncertifying dropouts. It is likely that some of them would have graduated from high school had they not become pregnant. They tend to earn their GED certificate at the age where their youngest child is between 2 and 3, typically when their children enter day care or school.

Our study of GED recipients shows that graduation from high school depends on skills not captured by standardized achievement tests.[6] In many aspects of character, GED recipients are not equivalent to high school

3. See Chapter 3 for a discussion of trends in average age at which recipients take the test.

4. The reasons for dropping out from the NELS data have been aggregated to similar categories in the NLSY79 data. Figures A4.1–A4.8 in the Web Appendix show similar figures by race and final levels of postsecondary education.

5. This is reminiscent of the "Ashenfelter's dip" associated with participation in job training programs. See, for example, Ashenfelter (1978), Heckman and Robb (1985), and Heckman et al. (1999) for discussions of this empirical regularity.

6. See Heckman and Rubinstein (2001) for an early discussion of this finding.

graduates. The main message from this chapter, and indeed this book, is that achievement tests fail to capture important character skills. Chapters 5 and 9, and an entire recent literature, show how important these skills are for success in life.[7]

4.2 GEDs Have Greater Cognitive Ability Than Other Dropouts

The GED exam is an achievement test. Thus, it is not surprising that GED recipients perform better than other dropouts on a variety of other achievement tests.[8] Figure 4.2 shows mean test scores on other achievement tests besides the GED for the achievement tests noted at the bottom of each figure.[9] The top panels show scores for the entire population of GEDs, including those who eventually attend college. The bottom panels show scores for the population that never attends college.[10]

Figure 4.2 presents results from a series of pairwise tests of differences in means using a 5% significance level. As before, a black dot represents a statistically significant difference in the means between GEDs and dropouts. White diamonds represent a statistically significant difference between high school graduates and dropouts. A white circle repre-

7. See the surveys in Borghans et al. (2008a) and Almlund et al. (2011).

8. See Table 1.2 in Chapter 1. See the data description section in the Web Appendix for more details on these tests. Table A4.1 describes these tests. Figures A4.9–A4.12 show similar figures by race. We use the Armed Forces Qualification Test (AFQT) from the National Longitudinal Survey of Youth 1979 (NLSY79) and National Longitudinal Survey of Youth 1997 (NLSY97), the Peabody Individual Achievement Test (PIAT) from the NLSY97, and the eighth-grade subject tests from the National Education Longitudinal Study (NELS). For more details on these data sets, see Section W5.1.1 of the Web Appendix.

9. Scores are reported in terms of units of population standard errors.

10. Test scores for the NLSY79 and NLSY97 are adjusted to a common baseline level of schooling, accounting for the effects of schooling at the time the test is taken. When the AFQT was administered, the surveyed individuals were of different ages and had acquired different levels of schooling. These differences affect their measured performance. In order to make valid comparisons of academic ability, we adjust individual scores to account for the level of schooling at the time the test is taken. This adjustment controls for final educational attainment using procedures developed in Hansen et al. (2004), Carneiro et al. (2005), and Heckman et al. (2011) that account for selection into schooling based on unobserved ability. This adjustment enables us to make comparisons of latent cognitive ability between dropouts, GED recipients, and high school graduates at a common baseline level of schooling. See Section A4.2.2 in the Web Appendix for a detailed description of the method. The adjustments do not change any conclusions of our analyses.

Figure 4.2 Cognitive Ability Tests

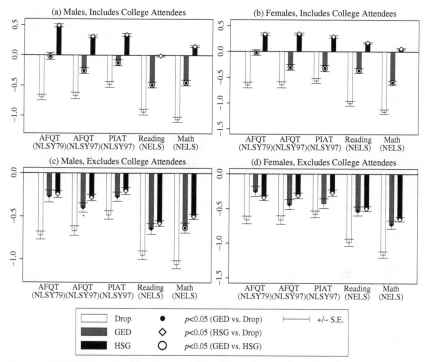

Sources: National Longitudinal Survey of Youth 1979 (NLSY79); National Longitudinal Survey of Youth 1997 (NLSY97); National Education Longitudinal Study (NELS).
Notes: The AFQT test was administered to the NLSY79 in 1980 when individuals were age 15 to 22. The AFQT was administered to the NLSY97 when individuals were age 12 to 16. The NELS subject tests were administered in eighth grade. NLSY79 and NLSY97 AFQT scores are adjusted for years of schooling at the time of test as described in the Web Appendix Section A4.2.2. The "Excludes College Attendees" sample consists of individuals who never attended a two- or four-year college.

sents a statistically significant difference between GEDs and high school graduates.

In the top panels of Figure 4.2 (which include people who attend college), both male and female GED recipients have higher test scores than other dropouts but lower scores than high school graduates. The GED allows recipients to enroll in college. Those who enroll differ from those who do not. However, as noted in Chapter 1 and as discussed further in Chapter 5, only 40% of GED recipients pursue any postsecondary education. Most GED recipients who attend some college stay for less than one

Figure 4.3 Distribution of Cognitive Skill by Education Group

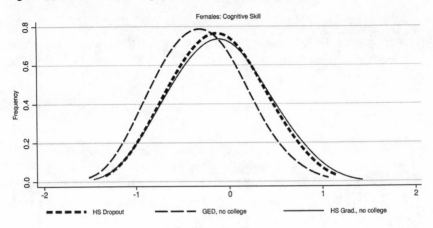

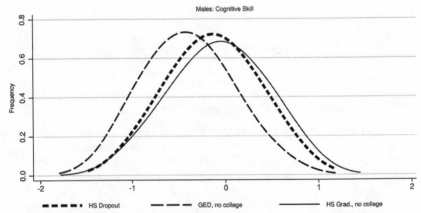

Source: Reproduced from Heckman et al. (2011), which uses data from the National Longitudinal Survey of Youth 1979 (NLSY79).
Notes: The distributions above represent cognitive factors, estimated using a subset of the Armed Services Vocational Aptitude Battery (ASVAB), and educational attainment, as laid out in Hansen et al. (2004). The sample is restricted to the cross-sectional subsample for both males and females. Distributions show only those with no postsecondary educational attainment. The cognitive factors are normalized by gender to be mean zero, standard deviation one.

year.[11,12] The bottom panels of Figure 4.2 show that GED recipients and high school graduates who do not attend postsecondary education have very similar test scores.[13] We cannot reject the hypothesis of equality of mean test scores for GEDs and high school graduates who do not attend any postsecondary education. Passing the GED exam is a good predictor of the cognitive ability measured by achievement tests.

Figure 4.2 presents mean achievement test scores by educational level. A focus on means can be misleading. It is possible that the distributions are skewed so that only a select group of GED recipients have higher cognitive ability than dropouts. Figure 4.3, taken from the analysis of Heckman et al. (2011), shows that GED recipients and high school graduates who do not go on to postsecondary education have almost identical distributions of cognitive ability.[14,15]

4.3 GEDs Lack Character Skills

If GED recipients have the same cognitive ability as high school graduates who do not attend college, what explains their lower educational attainment? Standardized achievement scores capture only some of the skills required for success in school. Completing high school requires other skills such as self-control, persistence, focus, and determination.

Personality psychologists have long studied character skills. Almlund et al. (2011) and Borghans et al. (2008b) discuss the evidence on the predictive power of "noncognitive" skills, sometimes called character or personality skills. For many outcomes, personality measures are as predictive or more predictive than cognitive measures.[16] GED recipients manifest behaviors indicating their lack of basic character skills.

11. A few dropouts attain some postsecondary education. Some postsecondary institutions do not require a high school diploma or GED certificate to attend. Chapter 5 presents a detailed analysis of educational attainment for each of these groups.

12. Despite their lack of success in college, GED recipients who attempt college might be more able or ambitious than dropouts who do not.

13. An exception is the NELS math test for males, where high school graduates have higher scores.

14. See Heckman et al. (2006) for a similar analysis.

15. The patterns are similar across all races in both the NLSY79 and National Adult Literacy Survey (NALS) data. An exception is that black female GED recipients have cognitive ability more similar to dropouts in the NLSY79. See Figures A4.13–A4.14 in the Web Appendix.

16. See Borghans et al. (2008b) and Almlund et al. (2011) for histories of personality psychology and a review of some trait taxonomies and their predictive power.

Figure 4.4 Personality

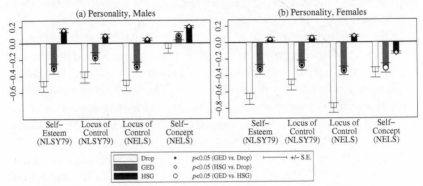

Sources: National Longitudinal Survey of Youth 1979 (NLSY79); National Education Longitudinal Study (NELS).

Figure 4.4 shows standardized personality measures, including self-esteem (a degree of approval or disapproval toward oneself),[17] locus of control (the extent to which people feel that they have control of their lives),[18] and self-concept (a person's self-perceptions or how a person feels about himself)[19] for dropouts, GED recipients, and high school graduates.[20] On these measures, GED recipients are intermediate between high school graduates and dropouts. These differences are statistically significant.

Personality is multifaceted. The measures used in Figure 4.4 represent only a portion of the full array of measures discussed in personality psychology.[21] Another source of information on character uses behaviors to capture the character skills of adolescents.[22] We examine a host of risky and school-related behaviors measured in the adolescent years as a way to capture differences in personality skills among GED recipients, other dropouts, and high school graduates. As noted in Almlund et al. (2011), all psychological measures are assessments on some task. Some tasks are

17. See Rosenberg (1965) for a detailed description of this test.
18. See Rotter (1966) for a detailed description.
19. See Weinberg and Abramowitz (2002) for a detailed description.
20. Tables A4.2–A4.5 in the Web Appendix provide the survey questions used to construct the measures. Figures A4.15–A4.22 show similar figures by race and levels of postsecondary education.
21. See Almlund et al. (2011).
22. See Almlund et al. (2011), Heckman et al. (2011), and Heckman and Kautz (2012).

tests; other tasks are behaviors. The distinction between test-based measures of skills and measured behaviors is arbitrary.[23]

Figures 4.5 and 4.6 show measures of early adolescent risky behavior across education categories, including drug use, smoking, criminal activity, and violent behavior.[24] GED recipients engage in risky behaviors as much as, or, in many cases, more than, other dropouts. As an exception, female GED recipients are less likely to have been in a fight or committed a violent crime. In all cases, high school graduates are less likely to engage in these behaviors compared to both GED recipients and high school dropouts.

There are substantial differences among the different attainment groups. Figure 4.7 shows a number of school-related behaviors for dropouts, GED recipients, and high school graduates.[25] Across many measures of performance in school, GED recipients tend to do worse than high school graduates and are much more similar to dropouts. GED recipients and dropouts are very similar in terms of GPA, days absent, credits earned by ninth grade, and remedial class placement. The primary difference between GED recipients and other dropouts is that GEDs, on average, complete more grades of high school. It is not surprising that GED recipients have grades similar to those of other dropouts because grades depend on character skills more strongly than achievement tests.[26]

Figure 4.8 shows differences in the distributions of character skills for dropouts, GEDs, and high school graduates who never attend college. This is the character counterpart of the distributions of cognitive ability displayed in Figure 4.3. GED recipients have the same level of cognitive ability as high school graduates who do not go on to college, but they have the same low levels of character skills as dropouts. Inadvertently, the GED test developed by the American Council of Education (ACE) is a powerful instrument for identifying relatively smart people who, on average, have the same character deficits as dropouts.

In Chapter 5, we show that GEDs have higher rates of turnover from jobs, college, and marriages than high school graduates. On some tasks, they

---

23. See our discussion in Chapter 9, in Almlund et al. (2011), and in Heckman et al. (2011).

24. Figures A4.23–A4.38 in the Web Appendix show similar graphs across race and postsecondary education.

25. Figures A4.39–A4.46 in the Web Appendix show similar graphs across race and postsecondary education.

26. See, for example, Duckworth and Seligman (2005), Almlund et al. (2011), and Borghans et al. (2011).

Figure 4.5 Risky Behaviors (Males)

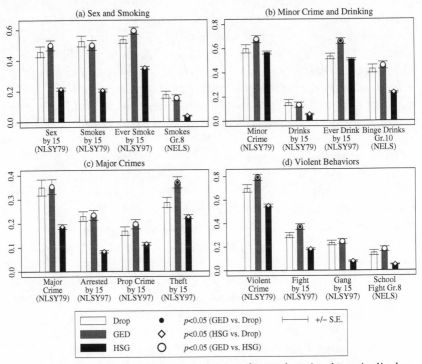

Sources: National Longitudinal Survey of Youth 1979 (NLSY79); National Longitudinal Survey of Youth 1997 (NLSY97); National Education Longitudinal Study (NELS). Variable Definitions: Drinks by 15—Whether the respondent used to drink on a regular basis—at least once or twice per month by age 15; Ever Drink by 15—Whether the respondent ever drank alcohol by age 15; Binge Drinks Gr. 10—Whether the respondent had at least 5 drinks in a row within the past two weeks in 10th grade; Sex by 15—Whether the respondent had sexual intercourse by age 15; Smokes by 15—Whether the respondent smoked more than 100 cigarettes in his life and smoked daily by age 15; Ever Smoke by 15—Whether the respondent smoked an entire cigarette by age 15; Smokes Gr. 8—Whether the respondent smoked daily in 8th grade; Minor Crime—Whether the respondent was involved at least once in one of the following: vandalism, shoplifting, petty theft, fraud, and holding or selling stolen goods; Major Crime—Whether the respondent was involved at least once in one of the following: auto theft, breaking/entering private property, and grand theft; Violent Crime—Whether the respondent was involved at least once in one of the following: fighting at work or school, assault and battery, and aggravated assault.

Figure 4.6 Risky Behaviors (Females)

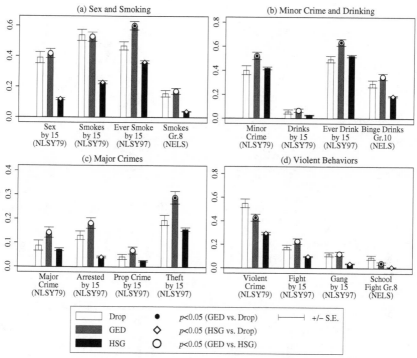

Sources: National Longitudinal Survey of Youth 1979 (NLSY79); National Longitudinal Survey of Youth 1997 (NLSY97); National Education Longitudinal Study (NELS).
Variable Definitions: Drinks by 15—Whether the respondent used to drink on a regular basis—at least once or twice per month by age 15; Ever Drink by 15—Whether the respondent ever drank alcohol by age 15; Binge Drinks Gr. 10—Whether the respondent had at least 5 drinks in a row within the past two weeks in 10th grade; Sex by 15—Whether the respondent had sexual intercourse by age 15; Smokes by 15—Whether the respondent smoked more than 100 cigarettes in her life and smoked daily by age 15; Ever Smoke by 15—Whether the respondent smoked an entire cigarette by age 15; Smokes Gr. 8—Whether the respondent smoked daily in 8th grade; Minor Crime—Whether the respondent was involved at least once in one of the following: vandalism, shoplifting, petty theft, fraud, and holding or selling stolen goods; Major Crime—Whether the respondent was involved at least once in one of the following: auto theft, breaking/entering private property, and grand theft; Violent Crime—Whether the respondent was involved at least once in one of the following: fighting at work or school, assault and battery, and aggravated assault.

Figure 4.7 School-Related Behaviors

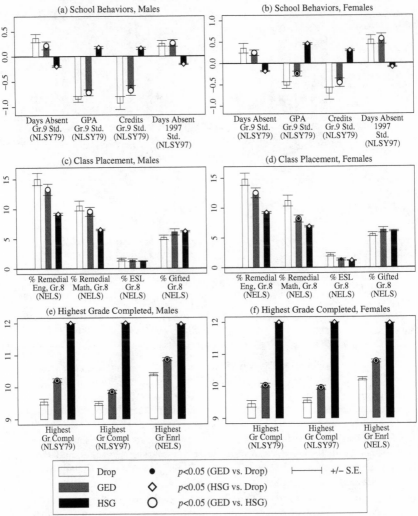

Sources: National Longitudinal Survey of Youth 1979 (NLSY79); National Longitudinal Survey of Youth 1997 (NLSY97); National Education Longitudinal Study (NELS).

Variable Definitions: Days of Absence—The number of days that the student was absent during 9th grade in the NLSY79 and the number of days that the student was absent during fall semester of 1997 in the NLSY97; GPA was calculated based on credits and grades earned in 9th grade; Credits Gr. 9—Cumulative number of credits obtained in 9th grade; Remedial English, Gr. 8—Percent of students in the remedial reading program in 8th grade; Remedial Math, Gr. 8—Percent of students in the remedial math program in 8th grade; ESL Gr. 8—Percent of students in English as Second Language (ESL) training in 8th grade; Gifted Gr. 8—Percent of students in gifted and talented education in grade 8; Highest Grade Completed—Highest grade the respondent completed in elementary and secondary school.

Note: Days absent, GPA, and Credits have been normalized to have a mean of zero and a standard deviation of one.

Figure 4.8 Distribution of Character Skills by Education Group

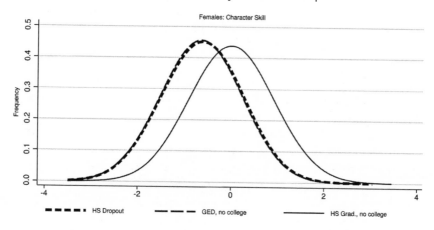

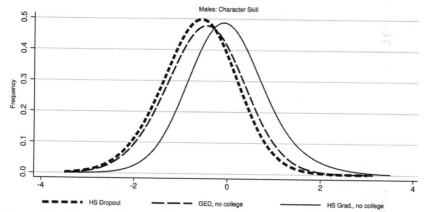

Source: Reproduced from Heckman et al. (2011), which uses data from the National Longitudinal Survey of Youth 1979 (NLSY79).

Notes: The distributions represent noncognitive factors, estimated using measures of early violent crime, minor crime, marijuana use, regular smoking, drinking, and early sexual intercourse. Sample restricted to the cross-sectional subsample for both males and females. Distributions show only those with no postsecondary educational attainment. The noncognitive factors are normalized to be mean zero, standard deviation one.

perform worse than dropouts. GED recipients also drop out of the military at much greater rates than high school graduates.[27] For most GEDs, the skill deficits that cause them to drop out of school persist throughout their lives.

4.4 Differences in Skills Emerge Early across Educational Groups

Differences in cognitive ability across education groups emerge in elementary school, long before the decision is made to drop out of high school. The top panels of Figure 4.9 show standardized PIAT scores by educational group between ages 6 and 12.[28] Even at age 6, there are sharp differences among future dropouts who never certify, GEDs, and high school graduates. As in Figure 4.2, GED recipients are intermediate between other dropouts and high school graduates. Relative levels of cognitive ability among dropouts, GED recipients, and high school graduates are stable across ages. The shortfalls for female GED recipients compared to high school graduates are much less than the shortfalls for male GED recipients. This presages an important conclusion of the analysis of Chapter 5. On many dimensions, female GED recipients compare more favorably to dropouts who never GED certify than male recipients. This pattern persists through life.

Differences in behavioral problems also emerge early. The bottom panels of Figure 4.9 show how differences in the Behavioral Problems Index (BPI) evolve between ages 6 and 12. The BPI is based on a 28-question survey given to parents about their child.[29] Higher values of the index indicate worse behaviors. Even at these early ages, eventual GED recipients are similar to high school dropouts, while eventual high school graduates are much better.

4.5 Differences in Background between Educational Certification Groups

Behavioral problems are linked to poor family backgrounds.[30] A substantial body of recent evidence suggests that investment in early childhood

---

27. See Chapter 6.

28. The data are from the Children of the National Longitudinal Survey of Youth (CNLSY). Unlike the measures in the NLSY79 and NLSY97, these tests require no adjustment for age of schooling at the date of the test because the participants took the tests at the same ages.

29. Table A4.2 in the Web Appendix defines the BPI index.

30. See Carneiro, Cunha, and Heckman (2003), McLanahan (2004), and Francesconi (2007).

Figure 4.9 Early Cognitive and Noncognitive Tests

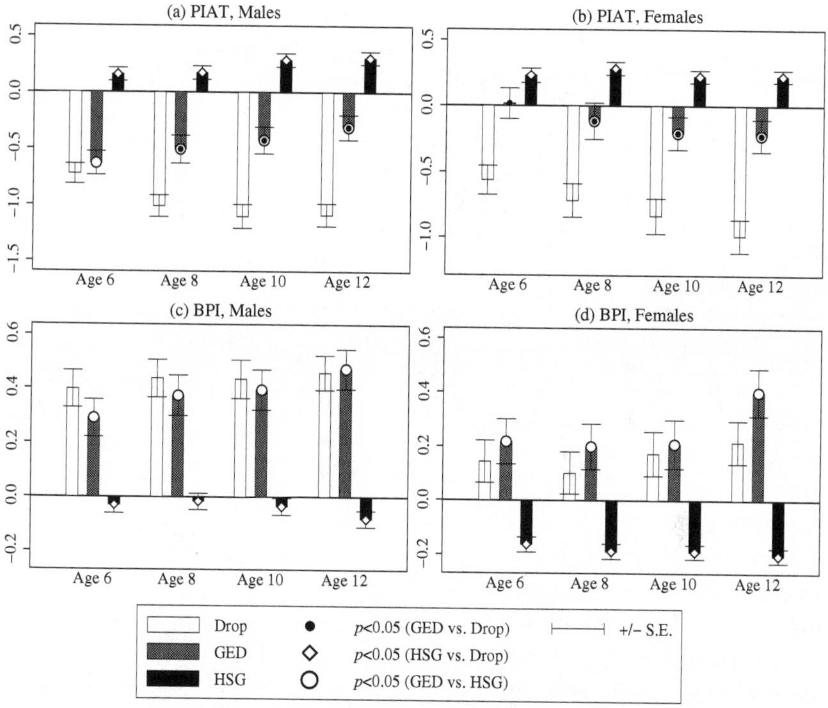

Sources: Children of the National Longitudinal Survey of Youth 1979 (CNLSY); Moon (2012).
Notes: The Peabody Individual Achievement Test (PIAT) is a widely used childhood achievement test. The PIAT score is normalized to have mean zero and variance one across the entire population. The Behavioral Problems Index (BPI) is based on a 28-question survey given to parents about their child. The BPI is normalized to have mean zero and variance one across the entire population.

is an important determinant of later-life outcomes.[31] High school completion is no exception.

Figure 4.10 shows background variables for dropouts, GED recipients, and high school graduates.[32] In general, high school graduates come from better backgrounds. Both dropouts and GED recipients are more likely to come from poorer families and broken homes with mothers who have lower levels of education. Compared to other dropouts, GED recipients

31. See, for example, Knudsen et al. (2006), Heckman (2008), Cunha, Heckman, and Schennach (2010), Heckman et al. (2010), and Moon (2012).
32. The sources are NLSY79, NLSY97, NELS, and CNLSY.

Figure 4.10 Background

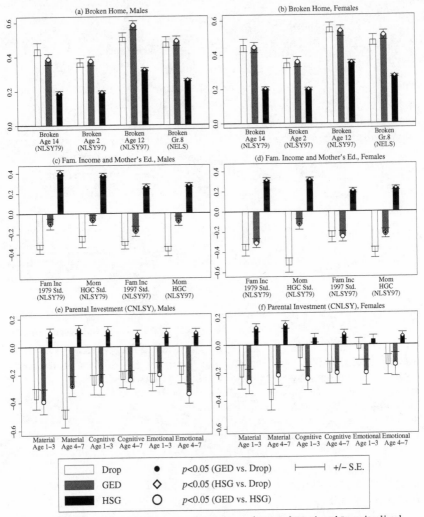

Sources: National Longitudinal Survey of Youth 1979 (NLSY79); National Longitudinal Survey of Youth 1997 (NLSY97); National Education Longitudinal Study (NELS); Children of the National Longitudinal Survey of Youth (CNLSY).

Variable Definitions: Parental Investment is measured by material resources (child's access to books, toys, CD or tape player, musical instruments, and books or magazines at home), cognitive stimulation investments (how often the children are read to, taught lessons, and brought to cultural events, and characteristics of the home environment) and emotional support investments (verbal and physical interactions with child, disciplinary behavior, and responsibility of child for household chores). Broken Home rates are defined as percent of children who don't live with their two biological parents. Mother's Highest Grade Completed represents years of schooling completed by mother.

are more likely to come from wealthier families and have more educated mothers.[33] The bottom panels show measures of material, cognitive, and emotional parental investment for ages 1–3 and 4–7.[34] Poor parenting might contribute to the behavioral problems of the GED recipients.[35,36]

4.6 Life Events Surrounding GED Certification

The previous sections establish that, as a group, GED recipients are relatively smart but lack character skills. People and their circumstances can change. Considerable evidence from economics and psychology shows that skills can change and be changed throughout the life cycle.[37] Given that many GED recipients earn their degrees long after dropping out of high school, it is possible that some change. Figure 4.11 shows the distribution of the ages when people GED certify. About half certify after the age of 20.

Our data lack repeated measures on character and cognitive skills. As a partial substitute, we investigate whether GED certification coincides with other life events that could be indicative of a change in people or their circumstances. We consider fertility patterns, incarceration, and employment histories.

As previously noted, many young women drop out of high school due to pregnancy. These women differ from other female GED recipients in important ways. Figure 4.12 compares women who drop out due to pregnancy with other GED recipients. Panel (a) shows that the women who drop out due to pregnancy have similar cognitive abilities, self-esteem, locus of control, grades, and credits earned. On a variety of other measures they are better than other female recipients. They miss fewer days of school, complete more grades of high school, and are less likely to engage in other risky behaviors, with the exception of adolescent sex. Most of these differences are statistically significant. If they had not become pregnant, these women likely would have graduated from high school.

---

33. These findings are consistent across all data sets.

34. The measures of investment are based on home environment and parental interactions and are represented by factor scores that have been standardized to have mean zero and variance one across the entire population. GED recipients and dropouts receive much less parental investment compared to high school graduates.

35. See the literature surveyed in McLanahan (2004) and Cunha et al. (2006).

36. See the discussion in Chapter 3 about the possible role of changes in family structure in contributing to the increase in rates of GED test taking and the stagnation of high school graduation rates.

37. See Borghans et al. (2008b) and Almlund et al. (2011) for reviews of the evidence.

Figure 4.11 The Fraction of Eventual GEDs Who Certify at Each Age

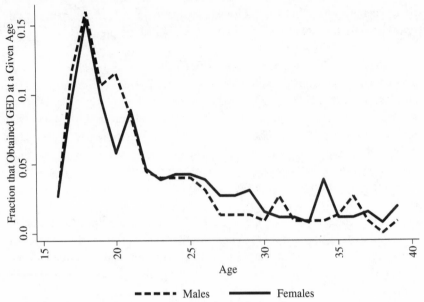

Source: National Longitudinal Survey of Youth 1979 (NLSY79).

Most of the women who drop out due to pregnancy GED certify either shortly after the birth of their child or when the child is old enough to attend school. Figure 4.13 shows whether women have children at the time of certification, and if so, the age of the youngest child. The bars on the left show estimates for women who drop out due to pregnancy, and the bars on the right show the estimates for other GED recipients. Over 40% of the women who drop out due to pregnancy earn their GED when their youngest child is 2 or 3, the age when many children enter day care or preschool. As their children grow up, they are less constrained and have more opportunities to seek employment or a GED certificate. The majority of female certifiers who do not drop out due to pregnancy earn their certificates before they have children. Chapter 5 shows that the women who drop out due to pregnancy and later earn a GED are relatively more successful in the labor market compared to other female GED recipients and dropouts. Their better character skills pay off.

As discussed in Chapter 3, prison has become a major source of GED certification because prisoners are given incentives to certify. GED certification is encouraged in many prisons and often helps qualify a prisoner for early parole. Figure 4.14 shows the fraction of GED certificates issued

Figure 4.12 Attributes of Female GED Recipients Who Drop Out Due to Pregnancy Compared to Other Female GED Recipients

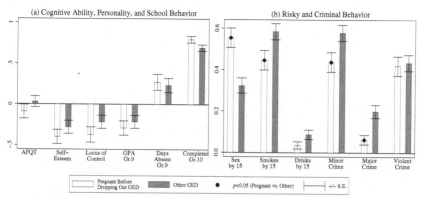

Source: National Longitudinal Survey of Youth 1979 (NLSY79).
Variable Definitions: AFQT scores are adjusted for years of schooling at the time of test as described in Web Appendix Section A4.2.2. Days of Absence—The number of days that the student was absent during 9th grade in the NLSY79 and the number of days that the student was absent during fall semester of 1997 in the NLSY97. GPA was calculated based on credits and grades earned in 9th grade. Drinks by 15—Whether the respondent used to drink on a regular basis—at least once or twice per month by age 15. Sex by 15—Whether the respondent had sexual intercourse by age 15. Smokes by 15—Whether the respondent smoked more than 100 cigarettes in her life and smoked daily by age 15. Minor Crime—Whether the respondent was involved at least once in one of the following: vandalism, shoplifting, petty theft, fraud, and holding or selling stolen goods. Major Crime—Whether the respondent was involved at least once in one of the following: auto theft, breaking/entering private property, and grand theft. Violent Crime—Whether the respondent was involved at least once in one of the following: fighting at work or school, assault and battery, and aggravated assault.

in prison out of the total number of GED certificates for black, Hispanic, and white males. Almost 20% of black male GED recipients earn their GED in prison. Fewer than 1% of females of any race obtain their GED while incarcerated.

A number of studies have noted that employment or earnings decline before people enter job training programs. This phenomenon is called Ashenfelter's dip in the literature in labor economics.[38] We find a similar pattern for male GED recipients. Figure 4.15 shows the annual hours worked surrounding certification for males and females. We restrict the

---

38. See, for example, Ashenfelter (1978), Heckman and Robb (1985), and Heckman, LaLonde, and Smith (1999).

Figure 4.13 Age of Youngest Child at Time of GED Receipt for Female GED Recipients Who Drop Out Due to Pregnancy Compared to Other Female GED Recipients

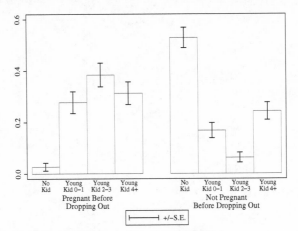

Source: National Longitudinal Survey of Youth 1979 (NLSY79).

Figure 4.14 Fraction of the Eventual Male Certificate Holders Earning a GED While in Jail

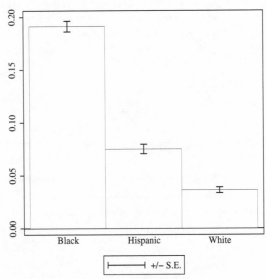

Source: National Longitudinal Survey of Youth 1979 (NLSY79).
Sample: The sample includes those who attend college.

Figure 4.15 Proportion Employed Before and After Certification

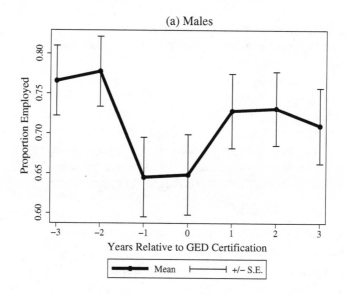

(a) Males

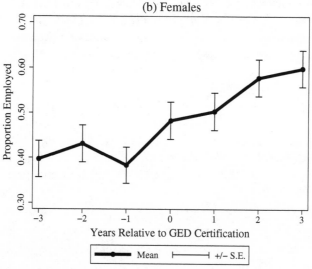

(b) Females

Source: National Longitudinal Survey of Youth 1979 (NLSY79).
Sample: The sample includes only GED recipients who have at least three years of potential labor market experience before and after GED receipt. The sample excludes people who are incarcerated at any point in the 7-year period.

sample used to create the figure to people who have at least three years of potential labor market experience before and after certification and those who have not been incarcerated during that period.[39]

The employment profiles surrounding GED certification are strikingly different between men and women. The number of hours worked for males dips at the time of certification and rebounds within three years. This dip is consistent with the explanation that men who lose their jobs obtain a GED with the hope that it will help them become reemployed. For females, the number of hours worked is roughly stable until the time of certification and then rises. GED certification is followed by an increase in their labor supply. It seems that female dropouts planning to work in the future are more likely to attain a GED certificate. We further investigate the labor supply of female GEDs in Chapter 5.

4.7 The Relative Importance of Skills and Background in Determining Educational Outcomes

The previous sections describe the characteristics of GED recipients but do not address the relative importance of different characteristics in determining educational outcomes. The descriptive analyses presented earlier suggest a number of potential determinants of dropping out of high school and GED certification. Studying one cause at a time may present a misleading picture of the important determinants taken together.

This section presents multivariate models of the determinants of high school graduation and GED receipt. We estimate a model of the determinants of high school graduation, using measures of background and ability.[40] Variables are normalized so that a higher value represents a "better" value; for example, a higher value for the crime variable indicates lower levels of criminal behavior.[41]

Figure 4.16 presents estimates of how a standardized change in a variable changes the probability of graduating from high school. All continuous variables are standardized, and for them we report one standard deviation

39. Potential labor market experience is measured from the last year of attendance in secondary school.

40. Among the variables are mother's highest grade completed, family income, intact family status, AFQT, and factors based on adolescent risky behavior, criminal behavior, and personality measures (self-esteem and locus of control). For females, we also include teen pregnancy.

41. We additionally control for race, region of residence, whether the respondent lived in the South at age 14, and whether the respondent lived in an urban area at age 14.

Figure 4.16 Estimated Marginal Effects of Predictors of High School Graduation for Males and Females

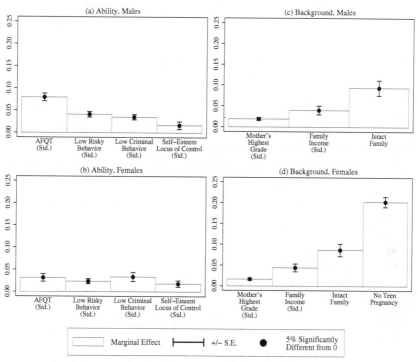

Source: National Longitudinal Survey of Youth 1979 (NLSY79).

Other Controls: The model also includes controls for race, region of residence, whether the respondent lived in the South at age 14, and whether the respondent lived in an urban residence at age 14. AFQT scores are adjusted for years of schooling at the time of test as described in the Web Appendix Section A4.2.2. Risky Behavior—A factor based on drinking (on a regular basis at least once or twice per month), hard drug use, daily smoking (among people who already smoked at least 100 cigarettes), and sexual intercourse by 15. Criminal Behavior—A factor based on participation in minor crime (vandalism, shoplifting, petty theft, fraud, holding or selling stolen goods), major crime (auto theft, breaking/entering private property, and grand theft), and violent crimes (fighting at work or school, assault and battery, and aggravated assault). Self-Esteem and Locus of Control—A factor based on self-esteem (Rosenberg) and locus of control (Rotter). Mother's Highest Grade Completed represents years of schooling completed by mother. Intact Family—Child lived with his two biological parents at age 14. Teen Pregnancy is defined as being pregnant before 18. (Std.) means the measure was presented in standard deviation units. For more information, see Table A4.6 in the Web Appendix.

changes. For discrete variables we report the effects of binary changes.[42] The marginal effects are estimated for each individual and then averaged across individuals. All continuous variables have been standardized to have mean 0 and variance 1.

The results from the multivariate model are consistent with the general patterns observed in the univariate tabulations. For both males and females, cognitive skills, character skills, and background all predict graduation from high school. For females, teen pregnancy is a major determinant of dropping out. These measures of character skills have incremental validity above and beyond the measures of cognitive ability. Graduating from high school requires skills besides cognitive ability.

We also investigate the determinants of GED certification. We estimate the probability of GED certification at different ages for dropouts. We restrict the estimation sample to persons who drop out of high school and estimate a discrete hazard model for whether an individual earns a GED in any time period.[43,44] To examine the effect of joblessness on certification that is evident in Figure 4.15, we include a measure for whether the

---

42. Let $\Phi(X_i\beta)$ be the probability of high school graduation given variables X_i for individual i, where $\Phi()$ is the normal cumulative distribution function (cdf). For any continuous covariate, say the kth, the marginal effect of X_{ki} is $MFX_i = \beta_k\phi(X_i\beta)$, where ϕ is the normal probability distribution function (pdf) where continuous variables are normalized to have a unit variance. The marginal effect of the kth discrete variable is $MFX_i = \Phi(\beta_k + X_{qi}\beta_q) - \Phi(X_{qi}\beta_q)$, where X_{qi} are the other covariates. We average across individuals to obtain the average marginal effect: $\overline{MFX} = \frac{1}{N}\sum_{i=1}^{N} MFX_i$.

43. We construct the following likelihood function: Let δ_{ij} be receipt of the GED in period j by person i, measured on an annual scale starting after person i drops out of high school.

$$\text{Define } m_i = \begin{cases} j & \text{associated with } \delta_{ij} = 1, j \in \{1,...,T\} \text{ if such a } j \text{ exists,} \\ T & \text{if there is no } j \text{ such that } \delta_{ij} = 1, j \in \{1,...,T\}, \end{cases}$$

where T is the longest possible available panel observation and m_i is the length of time the GED recipient spends in the dropout state before GED certifying. m_i is T if a person never GED certifies. For a sample of size N, the likelihood is

$$\mathcal{L} = \prod_{i=1}^{N}\prod_{j=1}^{m_i} \Phi((\alpha_j + x_{ij}\beta)(2\delta_{ij} - 1)),$$

where Φ is the CDF of a normal random variable.

44. We use the same set of background and ability measures as used to predict high school graduation (except for teen pregnancy), but also include variables describing sets of life events. For males, we include whether the respondent is currently incarcerated, married, or divorced.

respondent is currently not working but was recently employed in the past two years (No Work, Recently Employed) and whether the respondent is currently not working but was not recently employed within the past two years (No Work, Not Recently Employed). For females, we also include a measure of whether the respondent was pregnant before dropping out of high school and include interaction with dummy variables indicating the age of the youngest child.[45]

Figure 4.17 graphs the effects of the indicated variables on the discrete hazards averaged over the sample realizations for males. The estimated effect for those not working is graphed relative to the effect for those who are working. The effects for marriage and divorce are measured relative to people who have never been married. Consistent with the univariate tabulations, cognitive ability predicts GED certification, but the measures of character skills and background have little incremental effect. Not working but having been recently employed predicts certification. Being married or divorced has a positive but statistically insignificant effect on certification. Being incarcerated has a substantial positive effect on certification. Figure 4.18 displays the corresponding estimated average effects on the hazards for females. Panels (a)–(c) are analogous to the male results. As for males, cognitive ability predicts earning a GED, while the measures of character skills are less powerful predictors of GED certification.

Panel (d) shows the marginal effect of the age of children at home on GED recipiency separately for women who drop out of high school due to pregnancy and women who do not. The first three bars show the average effects of the age of the youngest child given for women who dropped out due to pregnancy.[46] The second set of bars shows the effects for females who

45. For both genders, we also control for the years since dropping out of high school, race, region of residence, whether the respondent lived in the South at age 14, and whether the respondent lived in an urban residence at age 14.

46. We calculate these "conditional" marginal effects for the discrete hazards in the following way. Let $\Phi(\beta X_{ij})$ be the probability of earning a GED given covariates X_{ij} for individual i at time j, where $\Phi()$ is the normal CDF. Let β_k be the coefficient associated with one of the dummy variables for having a youngest child of a given age, β_l be the coefficient associated with being a woman who drops out due to pregnancy, and β_m be a coefficient associated with the interaction term between the dummy variables for having a youngest child of a given age and being a woman who drops out due to pregnancy. Let X_{nij} be a vector of other covariates. The "conditional" marginal effect of having a child of a given age for person i at time j is given by $MFX_{ij} = \Phi(\beta_k + \beta_l D + \beta_m D + \beta_n X_{nij}) - \Phi(\beta_l D + \beta_n X_{nij})$, where D is set to 1 when calculating the effect for women who drop out due to pregnancy and 0 when calculating the effect for other GED recipients.

Figure 4.17 Average Marginal Effects on the Hazard Rate for GED Certification for Males

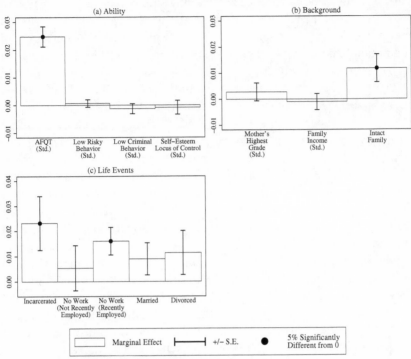

Source: National Longitudinal Survey of Youth 1979 (NLSY79).

Controls: The model also includes controls for years since dropping out of high school, race, region of residence, whether the respondent lived in the South at age 14, and whether the respondent lived in an urban residence at age 14. AFQT scores are adjusted for years of schooling at the time of test as described in the Web Appendix Section A4.2.2. Risky Behavior—A factor based on drinking (on a regular basis at least once or twice per month), hard drug use, daily smoking (among people who already smoked at least 100 cigarettes), and sexual intercourse by 15. Criminal Behavior—A factor based on participation in minor crime (vandalism, shoplifting, petty theft, fraud, and holding or selling stolen goods), major crime (auto theft, breaking/entering private property, and grand theft), and violent crimes (fighting at work or school, assault and battery, and aggravated assault). Self-Esteem and Locus of Control—A factor based on self-esteem (Rosenberg) and locus of control (Rotter). Mother's Highest Grade Completed represents years of schooling completed by mother. Intact Family—Child lived with his two biological parents at age 14. No Work (Not Recently Employed)—Currently not working and was not employed during the previous two years. No Work (Recently Employed)— Currently not working and has been employed during at least one of the previous two years. (Std.) means the measure was presented in standard deviation units. For more information, see Table A4.7 in the Web Appendix.

Figure 4.18 Average Marginal Effects on the Hazard Rate for GED Certification for Females

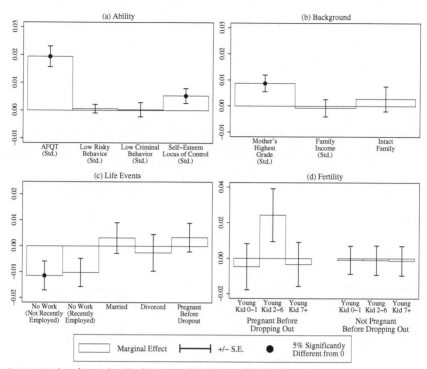

Source: National Longitudinal Survey of Youth 1979 (NLSY79).
Controls: The model also includes controls for years since dropping out of high school, race, region of residence, whether the respondent lived in the South at age 14, and whether the respondent lived in an urban residence at age 14. AFQT scores are adjusted for years of schooling at the time of test as described in the Web Appendix Section A4.2.2. Risky Behavior—A factor based on drinking (on a regular basis at least once or twice per month), hard drug use, daily smoking (among people who already smoked at least 100 cigarettes), and sexual intercourse by 15. Criminal Behavior—A factor based on participation in minor crime (vandalism, shoplifting, petty theft, fraud, and holding or selling stolen goods), major crime (auto theft, breaking/entering private property, and grand theft), and violent crimes (fighting at work or school, assault and battery, and aggravated assault). Self-Esteem and Locus of Control—A factor based on self-esteem (Rosenberg) and locus of control (Rotter). Mother's Highest Grade Completed represents years of schooling completed by mother. Intact Family—Child lived with her two biological parents at age 14. No Work (Not Recently Employed)—Currently not working and was not employed during the previous two years. No Work (Recently Employed)— Currently not working and has been employed during at least one of the previous two years. (Std.) means the measure was presented in standard deviation units. Pregnant/ Not Pregnant Before Dropout means the respondent was pregnant/not pregnant before dropping out of school. For more information, see Table A4.7 in the Web Appendix.

do not drop out due to pregnancy. The estimates are graphed relative to those for women who have no children in the household. As suggested by Figure 4.13, women who drop out due to pregnancy and have a child 2 to 3 years old are likely to certify.

Evidence from Heckman et al. (2011) is consistent with the finding in this chapter that both cognitive and character skills predict high school graduation, whereas only cognitive skill predicts receipt of a GED. Heckman et al. (2011) estimate a sequential model of education to study the effects of education on a variety of outcomes, controlling for cognitive and character skills and the endogeneity of education. As part of their model, they estimate the effect of cognitive skills and character skills on

Figure 4.19 Probability of Graduating from High School, by Cognitive and Noncognitive Skill Decile

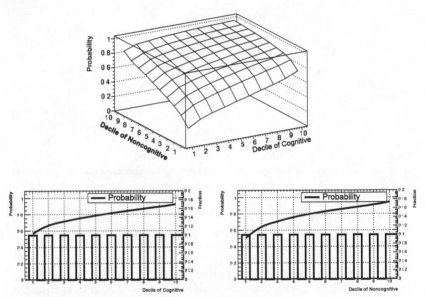

Source: Reproduced from Heckman et al. (2011), which uses data from the National Longitudinal Survey of Youth 1979 (NLSY79).

Notes: This figure reports the average probability of graduating from high school from a multistate dynamic model of schooling attainment. The 2D plots show the marginal effect of increasing cognition (left) or noncognitive skills (right) on probability of finishing high school (i.e., where noncognitive and cognitive skills, respectively, have been integrated out). The bars in the 2D plots display, for a given decile of the endowment, the fraction of individuals who reach the state where they make the decision of whether or not to complete high school. The fact that these decile bars are uniform indicates the fact that all individuals in the analysis face this decision.

Figure 4.20 Probability of GED Certification, Conditional on Having Dropped Out, by Cognitive and Noncognitive Skill Decile

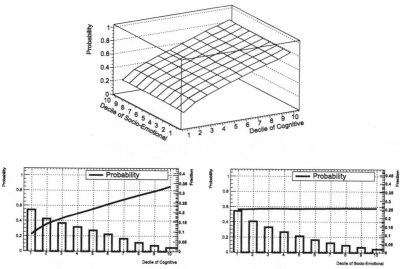

Source: Reproduced from Heckman et al. (2011), which uses data from the National Longitudinal Survey of Youth 1979 (NLSY79).

Notes: This figure reports the average probability of getting a GED, given that an individual has chosen to drop out. The 2D plots show the marginal effect of increasing cognition (left) or noncognitive skills (right) on probability of obtaining a GED (i.e., where noncognitive and cognitive skills, respectively, have been integrated out).
The bars in the 2D plots display, for a given decile of the endowment, the fraction of individuals who reach the state where they make the decision of whether or not to certify as a GED.

the probability of obtaining different educational choices, allowing for nonlinear relationships between skills and choices. Figure 4.19, taken from their paper, shows how changes across deciles of cognitive ability and noncognitive skills affect the probability of graduating from high school.[47] Both cognitive and noncognitive skills affect the probability of graduating from high school across all deciles of the skill distributions. People can compensate for deficits in cognitive skills with noncognitive skills. Even people with low cognitive skills are still likely to graduate from high school if they have high levels of noncognitive skills. Figure 4.20

47. This analysis also controls for the economic incentives that might affect these choices.

shows how character and cognitive skills affect the probability of obtaining a GED conditional on having dropped out of high school. Consistent with the findings in this chapter, only cognitive skills affect the probability of receiving a GED.

4.8 Summary and Conclusions

The pool of exam-certified high school equivalents has changed greatly over the past 60 years. At the outset, exam-certified equivalents were World War II veterans. The early equivalency tests were successful because they targeted these veterans who had abundant character skills. The test certified their cognitive skills, and their military experience certified their character skills.

Nowadays, GED exam certification sends a mixed signal. In this chapter we show that across four different data sets, GED recipients have higher cognitive ability than other dropouts, but come from similar backgrounds and exhibit similar behaviors. The GED exam certifies cognitive skills, but dropping out of high school reflects a shortfall of character skills.

It is telling that the military—the organization that first promoted exam-certified equivalency—generally does not accept applicants with only a GED certificate.[48] Chapter 5 investigates how GED recipients perform in the labor market and other aspects of life.

BIBLIOGRAPHY

Almlund, M., A. Duckworth, J. J. Heckman, and T. Kautz (2011). Personality psychology and economics. In E. A. Hanushek, S. Machin, and L. Wößmann (Eds.), *Handbook of the Economics of Education*, Volume 4, pp. 1–181. Amsterdam: Elsevier.

Ashenfelter, O. (1978, February). Estimating the effect of training programs on earnings. *Review of Economics and Statistics 60*(1), 47–57.

Atkinson, B. H. (1949, December). Veteran vs. non-veteran performance at U.C.L.A.: The G.I. Bill as an academic experiment. *Journal of Educational Research 43*(4), 299–302.

Borghans, L., A. L. Duckworth, J. J. Heckman, and B. ter Weel (2008a, Feburary). The economics and psychology of personality traits. *IZA Discussion Paper* (3333). http://ftp.iza.org/dp3333.pdf.

Borghans, L., A. L. Duckworth, J. J. Heckman, and B. ter Weel (2008b, Fall). The economics and psychology of personality traits. *Journal of Human Resources 43*(4), 972–1059.

Borghans, L., B. H. H. Golsteyn, J. J. Heckman, and J. E. Humphries (2011). Identification problems in personality psychology. *Personality and Individual Differences 51*(3: Special Issue on Personality and Economics), 315–320.

48. Chapter 6 presents an analysis of the performance of GEDs in the military.

Carneiro, P., F. Cunha, and J. J. Heckman (2003, October 17). Interpreting the evidence of family influence on child development. Paper presented at the conference The Economics of Early Childhood Development: Lessons for Economic Policy, Federal Reserve Bank of Minneapolis, Minneapolis, MN, October 17, 2003.

Carneiro, P., J. J. Heckman, and D. V. Masterov (2005, April). Labor market discrimination and racial differences in pre-market factors. *Journal of Law and Economics 48*(1), 1–39.

Cunha, F., J. J. Heckman, L. J. Lochner, and D. V. Masterov (2006). Interpreting the evidence on life cycle skill formation. In E. A. Hanushek and F. Welch (Eds.), *Handbook of the Economics of Education*, Chapter 12, pp. 697–812. Amsterdam: North-Holland.

Cunha, F., J. J. Heckman, and S. M. Schennach (2010, May). Estimating the technology of cognitive and noncognitive skill formation. *Econometrica 78*(3), 883–931.

D'Amico, L. A. (1953). *The Comparative Achievement of Veterans Admitted to Indiana University on the Basis of General Educational Development Tests and a Selected Group of Other Indiana University Students*. Ph.D. thesis, Indiana University.

Duckworth, A. L., and M. E. P. Seligman (2005, November). Self-discipline outdoes IQ in predicting academic performance of adolescents. *Psychological Science 16*(12), 939–944.

Francesconi, M. (2007, May). Adult outcomes for children of teenage mothers. Discussion Paper 2778, IZA.

Gowan, A. M. (1949, April). Characteristics of freshman veterans. *Journal of Higher Education 20*, 205–206.

Hansen, K. T., J. J. Heckman, and K. J. Mullen (2004, July–August). The effect of schooling and ability on achievement test scores. *Journal of Econometrics 121*(1–2), 39–98.

Heckman, J. J. (2008, July). Schools, skills and synapses. *Economic Inquiry 46*(3), 289–324.

Heckman, J. J., J. E. Humphries, S. Urzúa, and G. Veramendi (2011). The effects of educational choices on labor market, health, and social outcomes. Unpublished manuscript, University of Chicago, Department of Economics.

Heckman, J. J., and T. Kautz (2012, August). Hard evidence on soft skills. *Labour Economics 19*(4), 451–464.

Heckman, J. J., R. J. LaLonde, and J. A. Smith (1999). The economics and econometrics of active labor market programs. In O. Ashenfelter and D. Card (Eds.), *Handbook of Labor Economics*, Volume 3A, Chapter 31, pp. 1865–2097. New York: North-Holland.

Heckman, J. J., S. H. Moon, R. Pinto, P. A. Savelyev, and A. Q. Yavitz (2010, August). Analyzing social experiments as implemented: A reexamination of the evidence from the HighScope Perry Preschool Program. *Quantitative Economics 1*(1), 1–46.

Heckman, J. J., and R. Robb (1985, October–November). Alternative methods for evaluating the impact of interventions: An overview. *Journal of Econometrics 30*(1–2), 239–267.

Heckman, J. J., and Y. Rubinstein (2001, May). The importance of noncognitive skills: Lessons from the GED testing program. *American Economic Review 91*(2), 145–149.

Heckman, J. J., J. Stixrud, and S. Urzúa (2006, July). The effects of cognitive and noncognitive abilities on labor market outcomes and social behavior. *Journal of Labor Economics 24*(3), 411–482.

Knudsen, E. I., J. J. Heckman, J. Cameron, and J. P. Shonkoff (2006, July). Economic, neurobiological, and behavioral perspectives on building America's future workforce. *Proceedings of the National Academy of Sciences 103*(27), 10155–10162.

McLanahan, S. (2004, November). Diverging destinies: How children are faring under the second demographic transition. *Demography 41*(4), 607–627.

Moon, S. H. (2012). Decomposing racial skill gaps in the U.S. Unpublished manuscript, University of Chicago, Department of Economics.

Rosenberg, M. (1965). *Society and the Adolescent Self-Image*. Princeton, NJ: Princeton University Press.

Rotter, J. B. (1966). Generalized expectancies for internal versus external control of reinforcement. *Psychological Monographs: General and Applied 80*(1), 1–28.

Weinberg, S., and S. Abramowitz (2002). *Data Analysis for the Behavioral Sciences Using SPSS*. New York: Cambridge University Press.

5

THE ECONOMIC AND SOCIAL BENEFITS
OF GED CERTIFICATION

JAMES J. HECKMAN, JOHN ERIC HUMPHRIES, AND TIM KAUTZ

5.1 Introduction

This chapter evaluates the benefits of GED certification in the labor market and in postsecondary education. On the surface, GED recipients appear to perform better in the labor market than other high school dropouts. Figure 5.1 presents data for males and females from the 2009 American Community Survey, a large national sample.[1] The bars show mean annual earnings (including nonworkers), employment, and hours worked (excluding nonworkers) for high school dropouts, GED recipients, and high school graduates. The sample excludes people who attend college.

The data show a clear pattern. GED recipients perform better than other dropouts but substantially worse than high school graduates who do not enroll in postsecondary education. Compared to male GED recipients, female recipients supply more labor than other dropouts. This chapter examines whether GED certification causes the relatively successful performance of GED recipients apparent in Figure 5.1, or whether it simply signals the greater cognitive ability of GED recipients present before they take the GED exam and if the signal is known by the market before certification.

Figure 5.1 may be very misleading because it does not account for differences in background, ability, and character skills present in early adolescence before dropping out is possible. As documented in Chapter 4, GED recipients are smarter, complete more grades of school, and come from better backgrounds than other dropouts but have the same or higher rates of adolescent criminal and risky behavior before they drop out. Although GED recipients are as smart as high school graduates who do not enroll in postsecondary education, they have much higher rates of adolescent criminal and risky behavior and come from more disadvantaged family backgrounds.

---

1. See Section W5.1.1 of the Web Appendix for more detail on the data sets used in this analysis. The Web Appendix mentioned in this note and subsequent notes is found at http://jenni.uchicago.edu/Studies_of_GED.

Figure 5.1 Unadjusted Differences in Economic Outcomes—Males and Females, Age 25 to 55

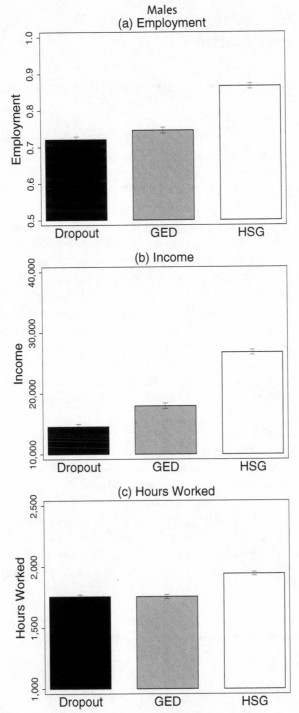

Figure 5.1 (Continued)

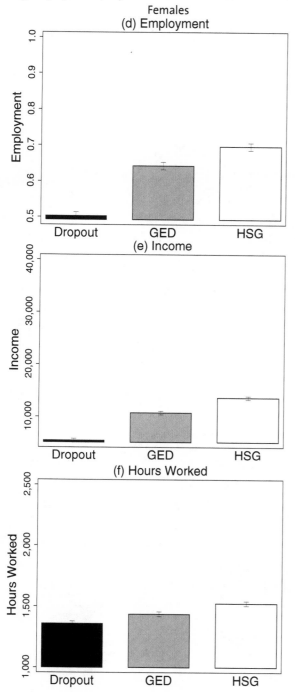

Females
(d) Employment

(e) Income

(f) Hours Worked

Source: American Community Survey, 2009. *Notes:* Sample restricted to people age 25 to 55. Income includes nonworkers. Hours worked excludes nonworkers. Employment includes people both in and out of the labor force. Outcomes are adjusted by age, region, and race dummies. Error bars show one standard error. Tests of equality across groups strongly reject the hypothesis for all means (except those for the hours worked of male dropouts and GED recipients) at *p*-values below the 1% level. See Tables W5.1.3 and W5.1.4 in Web Appendix W5.1.2.

A substantial body of research establishes that the labor market values the skills that differ among GED recipients, other dropouts, and high school graduates.[2] Differences in skills that exist before GED certification might explain the evidence in Figure 5.1.

To address this issue, we analyze six data sets that span different time periods and have different measures of background and skills. Analyzing multiple data sets minimizes the danger of generalizing from quirks of any particular data set. Table 5.1 summarizes important features of each survey we use.[3]

The data sets differ in their information about GED certification and measures of background, ability, and personality.[4] Three of the data sets that we use—the American Community Survey (ACS), National Adult Literacy Survey (NALS), and National Assessment of Adult Literacy (NAAL)—report only the final education attained, and in these surveys we can only identify GED recipients who do not attend college. We cannot identify whether a college attendee had previously earned a GED. The ACS, NALS, and NAAL data contain few measures of background or ability.[5] The National Education Longitudinal Study (NELS), National Longitudinal Survey of Youth 1997 (NLSY97), and National Longitudinal Survey of Youth 1979 (NLSY79) contain information about the complete educational histories, backgrounds, and abilities of respondents. Of the three longitudinal sets, only the NLSY79 follows individuals through age 40.[6]

Using the NELS, NLSY97, and NLSY79 data, we can determine whether differences in background and ability account for the apparent benefits of GED certification visible in Figure 5.1. Figure 5.2 shows annual earnings by reported level of final education for people who do not attend college. The top panels show unadjusted income from all six data sources. The bottom panels show adjusted income for the data sets with measures of pre-GED ability and background (NLSY79, NLSY97, and NELS). We restrict the age range to be comparable across data sets.

---

2. See Borghans et al. (2008) and Almlund et al. (2011).

3. For a complete description of each data set, see Section W5.1.1 in the Web Appendix.

4. Some major data sources like the U.S. Census do not report GED status.

5. The NALS and NAAL contain measures of ability but do not release them for public use. The ACS contains only rudimentary measures of background.

6. NLSY79 data past age 40 are subject to severe attrition problems. See Table W5.1.7 in Web Appendix W5.1.3.

Table 5.1 The Data Sets Analyzed in This Chapter

Data Set	Birth Cohorts	Age Ranges across All Survey Years	Survey Years	Measures of Cognitive Ability?	Measures of Early Adolescent Behavior?	Information on Family Background?	Information on GEDs Who Get Higher Levels of Schooling	Longitudinal	Sample Size
American Community Survey (ACS)	all ages	0–95	2009	no	no	no	no**	no	N = 3,030,728 GEDs = 94,262
National Adult Literacy Survey (NALS)	all ages	16–99	1992	yes*	no	no	no**	no	N = 9,620 GEDs = 868
National Assessment of Adult Literacy (NAAL)	all ages	16–65+	2003	no***	no	no	no**	no	N = 8,363 GEDs = 811
National Education Longitudinal Study of 1988 (NELS88)	1973–1975	12–30	1988, 1990 1994, 2000	yes	yes	yes	yes	yes	N = 12,144 GEDs = 826
National Longitudinal Survey of Youth 1979 (NLSY79)	1957–1964	14–52	annually 1979–1993, biannually 1994–2008	yes	yes	yes	yes	yes	N = 9,763 GEDs = 1,155
National Longitudinal Survey of Youth 1997 (NLSY97)	1980–1984	12–27	annually 1997–2008	yes	yes	yes	yes	yes	N = 8,984 GEDs = 967

Notes: All data sets are nationally representative. The two National Longitudinal Survey of Youth data sets include minority oversamples, which we use when analyzing races separately. NAAL reports age ranges rather than individual ages. Thus, the highest age specified is "65+". For full descriptions of the data sets used, see Web Appendix W5.1.1. *Cognitive ability is measured. **Only education at time of survey is measured. ***Cognitive ability is available at group but not individual level.

Figure 5.2 Raw and Ability-Adjusted Income—Males and Females, Age 23 to 27

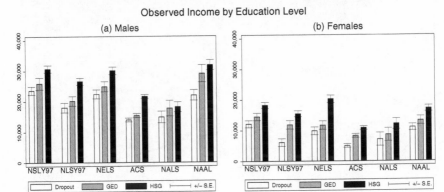

Observed Income by Education Level

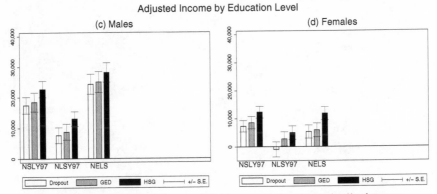

Adjusted Income by Education Level

Sources: National Longitudinal Survey of Youth, 1979; National Longitudinal Survey of Youth, 1997; National Education Longitudinal Study, 1988; National Adult Literacy Survey, 1992; National Assessment of Adult Literacy, 2003; American Community Survey, 2009.

Notes: Raw income is adjusted for region or state of residence and age and includes nonworkers. Adjusted income adjusts for schooling-adjusted AFQT scores, mother's education, and family income in 1979 or 1997 in the NLSY79 and NLSY97 and 8th grade reading and math scores, mother's education, and family income in 8th grade in NELS. Error bars show one standard error. All regressions allow for heteroskedastic errors and, when appropriate, clustering at the individual level. All individuals are between the ages of 23 and 27. In NELS individuals are age 24 to 27, and in NAAL individuals are age 24 to 39 due to data limitations. Tests of equality between means for the unadjusted income levels are reported in Web Appendix W5.1.2. High school graduates tend to be statistically significantly different from GED recipients in the raw and adjusted regressions. We fail to reject equality of GED recipients and dropouts for males, and after adjusting for ability and background fail to reject equality even more strongly. For females, the difference between GED recipients and dropouts is statistically significant, but becomes insignificant after adjusting for ability and background. Adjustments are made for ability, mother's education, and family income before dropping out.

The top panels of Figure 5.2 show that for all six data sets, GED recipients have annual earnings that are intermediate between those of other dropouts and high school graduates, consistent with the pattern shown in Figure 5.1. The data sets that contain measures of background and ability show patterns that are qualitatively similar to the patterns found in the other data sets. The bottom panels show that differences in ability and background account for the differences in income between male GED recipients and other dropouts for all three data sets. Even after adjustment, female GED recipients perform slightly better than other dropouts, but the difference is no longer statistically significant. Even after adjusting for background and ability, both male and female high school graduates still have statistically significantly higher earnings than dropouts and GED recipients.

For several reasons, Figures 5.1 and 5.2 might be misleading. First, Figures 5.1 and 5.2 show outcomes for people who do not attend college. Using only these samples biases downward the estimated economic benefits of the GED because, as we show below, about 40% of the GED recipients—and among them relatively more women than men—enroll in some form of postsecondary education.

Three of the data sets displayed in Table 5.1 have information on educational histories. Using these data, we evaluate the benefits of GED certification for samples that include those who attend college. GED recipients who complete degrees benefit substantially. We find that at the same level of ability, GED recipients who complete college appear to have the same earnings as high school graduates who complete college. However, a body of literature starting with Cameron and Heckman (1993, 1994) and Cameron (1996) shows that very few GED recipients (3%–4%) complete bachelor's degrees. The analysis of this chapter confirms and extends these early findings.

The same traits that cause GED recipients to drop out of high school cause them to drop out of college as well as the military, marriage, and jobs.[7] After accounting for preexisting traits, *on average*, GED recipients do no better than other dropouts. This finding holds even when GED recipients who complete degrees are included, because so few do.

The few GED recipients who earn degrees have lower discounted lifetime earnings than high school graduates who earn degrees because GED recipients earn their degrees later. On average, among those who earn degrees, male GED recipients earn associate's degrees three years later

7. Chapter 6 discusses the performance of the GED recipients in the military.

and bachelor's degrees seven years later than high school graduates. Female GED recipients earn associate's and bachelor's degrees six years later. This delay results in a roughly 30% reduction in the present value of lifetime earnings when compared to high school graduates who earn the same degrees in a more timely fashion.

Figures 5.1 and 5.2 combine all racial and ethnic groups. We find that when we disaggregate our analyses by race and ethnicity and condition on pre-GED traits for males and females, the GED provides few benefits for most demographic groups. A few groups benefit moderately. The primary beneficiaries are female GED recipients, who are more likely to participate in the labor force than other female dropouts. However, as we note below, female GED recipients do not earn higher hourly wages.

One potential criticism of the analysis summarized in Figure 5.2 is that it only captures early segments of the life cycle. The GED certificate might open doors to new opportunities that pay off later. To study this possibility, we follow recipients through age 40.

The literature summarized in the next section shows that the GED offers few benefits over the life cycle.[8] However, this conclusion is not universally accepted. Richard Murnane and a group of scholars affiliated with him claim that low-ability GED recipients benefit from exam certification and that the benefits increase with age.[9]

The evidence reported in this chapter shows few life-cycle benefits, if any, after adjusting for traits present before receipt of the GED. A few groups of GED recipients exhibit life-cycle growth in earnings; most do not. Any evidence for life-cycle earnings growth is found for women, and even for them the evidence is quite weak.

Benefits are confined to increased labor supply. The GED does not impact their hourly wage rates.[10] The rate of increase of the earnings of GED recipients with age is well below that of high school graduates. For persons who do not attend college, GED recipients and dropouts have similar wage profiles. Even these apparent benefits for women might not be a direct causal effect of the GED. Any estimated labor supply benefits come primarily through increased labor force participation. The evidence is consistent with the hypothesis that women who choose to take the GED do so in anticipation of

8. See Web Appendix Section W5.2.
9. See Murnane, Willett, and Boudett (1999), Murnane, Willett, and Tyler (2000), and Tyler, Murnane, and Willett (2003).
10. This finding accords with the analysis of Boudett, Murnane, and Willett (2000).

entering the workforce. The measured benefit might be a result of greater taste for work that was present before the GED was attempted.[11]

For those who benefit, what produces the benefits? Is it through the acquisition of skills in preparing for the GED? As discussed in Chapter 1, few GED recipients study more than 20 or 30 hours—far less than the thousand or so hours of time spent in school (never mind homework).[12] For most GED recipients, it is unlikely that they acquire much knowledge by studying for the exam.

Another mechanism of benefits, featured in a widely cited paper by Tyler, Murnane, and Willett (2000), is *signalling*.[13] As first noted by Heckman and Rubinstein (2001) and as supported by the analysis of Chapter 4, GED certification sends a mixed signal. GED recipients are smarter than other dropouts, but their character skills are as bad or worse than those of other dropouts. Both cognitive and character skills are valued in the market and in schools. Hence, the net signal sent by a GED certificate is inherently ambiguous.

We identify various groups that benefit from GED certification. The GED may also signal *changes* in skills, goals, and motivation. Figures 5.1 and 5.2 present average outcomes. We show that the primary beneficiaries are a group of women. They include high-ability women who become pregnant, drop out of high school, and later GED certify. They also include bright young girls who do not become pregnant and have low levels of character skills but appear to mature after they drop out of high school. As noted in Chapter 4, female GED recipients who drop out due to pregnancy have higher levels of pre-dropout character skills than other female GED recipients. For these groups, the GED may be a lifeline. Attaining a GED may also signal changes in their attitudes and traits. The birth of a child may change the motivations of a young woman, and the constraints she faces.

Even if traits do not change, exam certification might signal abilities that are not otherwise revealed in the labor market. We address this issue by using panel data to compare the wages of GED recipients before and after certification. On average, accounting for life-cycle wage growth that would occur in the absence of exam certification, we find little

11. Under this interpretation, such women would work whether or not the GED had a true causal effect.

12. See Carroll (1990).

13. See Spence (1974).

evidence of a signalling effect of GED certification. For most groups, what is signalled after certification is signalled before. The finding of no signalling effect is confirmed in a recent study by Jepsen, Mueser, and Troske (2011).

The rest of this chapter proceeds as follows. Section 5.2 reviews the previous literature on the GED. Section 5.3 presents cross-sectional comparisons by age for a variety of labor market and educational comparisons for dropouts, GED recipients, and high school graduates. We present results for all groups, including those who go on to achieve further levels of education, as well as for those who terminate their education with GED certification. On average, those who pursue higher education do better than those who do not, but there are few who attain postsecondary degrees. Section 5.4 presents a longitudinal analysis. Section 5.5 shows how the differences in skills between male and female GEDs explain the relatively superior performance of female GEDs over male GEDs in comparison with uncertified dropouts of the same gender. Section 5.6 summarizes our results. Finally, Appendix Section 5.7 presents a brief sketch of our methodology.

5.2 The Previous Literature

In order to place the analysis of this chapter in context, we briefly review the previous literature.[14] The Web Appendix presents a more extensive literature review.[15]

5.2.1 OVERVIEW

The literature is unanimous in establishing that GED recipients perform substantially below the level of high school graduates in the labor market, in higher education, and in the military. This conclusion survives a variety of adjustments for personal and family background characteristics that are present before the GED certificate is acquired. We affirm this finding in multiple data sets.

Adjusting for their pre-GED traits, we find that male GED recipients perform no better in the labor market than other dropouts. In this chapter, we present new evidence for women. We discover that the labor supply of female GED recipients is an apparent exception to the general rule that the GED has no benefits. Female GED recipients are more likely to be employed and work more hours than female dropouts who do not certify.

---

14. See Boesel, Alsalam, and Smith (1998) for a survey of the evidence through 1998.
15. See Web Appendix Table W5.2.1.

They are more likely to participate in the labor force and actively seek work when they are not employed. However, their hourly wages are no higher than those of other female dropouts. They earn more than uncertified dropouts because they work more. Despite their greater work experience, female GED recipients do not have higher hourly wage rates than dropouts, suggesting that female GED recipients take dead-end jobs, possibly in response to the exigencies of supporting their families. Consistent with the previous literature, even under the most favorable interpretation of the benefits of GED certification, few female GED recipients escape the poverty associated with being a high school dropout.[16]

The first analytical papers on the effectiveness of GED certification are those of Cameron and Heckman (1993, 1994) and Cameron (1996). These papers frame much of the discussion in the academic and policy literatures. The subsequent literature builds on and sometimes contests the major conclusions of these authors.

For a sample of young males from the NLSY79 (age 25–28 in the late 1980s), Cameron and Heckman (CH) study the determinants of GED certification, as well as the post-GED training and educational choices of GED recipients. They examine the political economy behind the growth of GED certification over the post–World War II period.

Consistent with the analysis reported in Chapter 4, Cameron and Heckman show that male GED recipients are smarter (as measured by an achievement test) than other dropouts but are not as smart as the average high school graduate. They are, however, as smart as the average high school graduate who does not attempt any postsecondary schooling. GED recipients come from more advantaged backgrounds than other dropouts but have less advantaged backgrounds than high school graduates—even graduates who do not attend college. CH show that the mean preparation time is low for GED recipients. GED recipients drop out with more years of schooling attained than other dropouts.

Compared to dropouts, the authors show that male GED recipients are more likely to attempt further education and training, including (a) formal schooling, (b) vocational certificates, (c) company training, (d) off-the-job training (which for this group is largely government-sponsored job training), and (e) participation in the military. They are less likely to participate in all of these activities than are high school graduates except for off-the-job training programs and programs that offer vocational certificates.

16. See Boudett, Murnane, and Willett (2000).

Although many male recipients (around 40%) try some form of higher education, the vast majority drop out before they finish.[17] The same traits that cause GED recipients to drop out of high school explain their performance in further levels of education. Cameron and Heckman show that very few (2%) GED recipients get bachelor's degrees, compared to 35% of high school graduates. However, they show that the few GED recipients who attempt college at any level complete associate's degrees at about the same, or slightly higher, rate as high school graduates. Most male GED recipients complete less than two years of college, and many do not last a semester. GED recipients who graduate from college with a bachelor's degree or an associate's degree have the same annual earnings and labor supply as ordinary high school graduates with the same ability. However, there are few of them. These findings are substantiated both in the subsequent literature and in this chapter. Here we show that because GED recipients earn postsecondary degrees later than high school graduates, their discounted lifetime benefits are substantially lower. The delay induced by dropping out of high school is costly.

CH show that, on average, the GED certificate offers few benefits unless recipients complete further education. Controlling for their greater ability, the authors find that GED recipients earn at the same rate as other dropouts.[18] GED recipients earn substantially less than high school graduates, even compared to those who do not attempt college. The economic benefit of an additional hour of work experience is the same for a dropout as it is for a GED recipient. It is somewhat below that of a high school graduate, but the difference is not precisely determined. The analysis in this chapter is consistent with the previous literature and finds the same rate of wage growth with work experience for GED recipients and other dropouts, but it is lower than that of high school graduates. CH state that any wage or labor supply benefits to the GED are present in the market before the GED certificate is obtained. They show that adjusting for greater work experience and job tenure closes the gap between GED recipients and high school graduates but does not eliminate the gap. Cameron and Heckman (1993) report before–after differences in GED certification and show that any traits present after certification were pres-

17. About 60% of high school graduates attempt college. See the discussion in Section 5.3.5.

18. CH report similar findings controlling for years of schooling attained at the time they drop out. We are unable to replicate this finding.

ent before and were already signalled to the market. They find no signalling effect of GED certification.

Differences in cognitive ability and years of schooling attained explain the differences in the labor market experiences of GED recipients and other dropouts. For CH's sample of males, a substantial portion (60%–100%) of any economic return to the GED is indirect, coming through the return to postsecondary schooling, training, and work experience. The estimates reported in this chapter are consistent with these findings.

In a companion paper, Cameron and Heckman (1994) study the schooling and training choices of young males, using a sequential life-cycle framework. They find substantial differences in educational attainment and training paths among racial and ethnic groups. Their evidence is in agreement with the analysis of Chapter 4 that GED recipients are more likely to come from broken homes and that labor market opportunities in unskilled labor markets encourage students to drop out and acquire GED certificates.

They also examine the determinants of postsecondary schooling and training, which are the principal contributors to any effect found for GED certification. They show that, controlling for ability, GED recipients enroll in a variety of postsecondary, nonacademic training programs at about the same rate as high school graduates.

In an unpublished Ph.D. thesis, Cameron (1996) extends Cameron and Heckman's analysis of males in the NLSY79 to study females. In addition, he analyzes (in a cursory fashion) two other longitudinal data sets on the performance of females age 34–44 in 1988 and age 52–65 in 1989. His findings for women generally support the conclusions for men presented in CH.

Cameron (1996) reports some interesting differences from CH, however, that resonate with the findings of this book. (1) Consistent with the evidence reported in Chapter 4, female GEDs, unlike male GEDs, come from better backgrounds than other dropouts. Female GEDs also perform less badly in school and drop out with more years of schooling than male GEDs. (2) Both Cameron (1996) and we find that female GED recipients are more likely to have dropped out of school due to pregnancy than other female dropouts and are more likely to have been married and divorced. (3) Both studies show that unlike male GED recipients, even after adjusting for differences in background traits, female GED recipients are more likely to be employed than other dropouts.

(4) In this chapter we show that the indirect effects of GED certification on wages and earnings through post-GED work experience and schooling are a substantial component of any estimated GED effect. CH and Cameron use data for a limited segment of the life cycle. Their estimates for both men and women might not apply to longer segments of the life cycle. In this book, we find substantial direct and indirect effects of GED certification for women arising from (a) the greater labor supply of GED recipients (direct effect) and (b) post-GED educational attainment (indirect effect). (5) The evidence on the determinants and consequences of the GED for women age 34–44 reported by Cameron is consistent with our evidence for younger women. Unlike the analysis for men reported in CH, for younger women, conditioning on tenure and work experience does not equate the wages of GED recipients with those of high school dropouts. (6) Cameron shows that there is some evidence that the GED has a marginally statistically significant effect on hourly wages for older women (age 52–65), but only after controlling for their greater tenure on the job and for work experience.

5.2.2 OPEN QUESTIONS FROM THE RESEARCH OF CAMERON AND HECKMAN

While the research of Cameron and Heckman (1993) and Cameron (1996) opened the door to understanding the GED, it left open many questions:

1. Cameron and Heckman (1993, 1994) and Cameron (1996) study the wages, earnings, and labor supply of young people. Do their results hold over the life cycle for certifiers who acquire work experience with the GED? The human capital investment model of Becker (1964) and Mincer (1962) suggests that initial payoffs to certification might be negative if GED recipients invest in further schooling, job training, and work experience and take lower starting wages to pay for their training. Payoffs would come later. The analysis of Cameron (1996) hints that, for older women, returns to the GED may be more substantial and suggests that the early training of GED recipients might pay off later in life.

2. Cameron and Heckman (1993) and Cameron (1996) show that a substantial part of the return to the GED comes from investments made after GED certification. Does this result hold up in longer run analyses?

3. Is the GED an effective signal? Even if preparing for the GED does not produce human capital, the credential may be an effective signal to the market about information that employers and academic institutions do not possess. Cameron and Heckman (1993) and Cameron (1996) show that the hourly wages earned by GED recipients before they certify are

the same as their hourly wages after certification. This finding suggests that the information conveyed by the GED signal is known in the market before the signal was obtained. But their result is for young persons and for wages shortly after GED certification. The GED may have long-run signalling value that is not detected in the short stretches of the life cycle that they study.

4. Do immigrants who enter the United States having completed their education benefit from GED certification? The GED might be a more informative signal for this group, given the uncertainty surrounding the quality of schooling in many origin countries.

Many of these issues were addressed in the subsequent literature, which is reviewed in depth in the Web Appendix.[19] We summarize the major studies in the text.

5.2.3 THE ANALYSES OF THE MURNANE GROUP

Papers by Richard Murnane and various coauthors address many of the open questions surrounding the research of Cameron and Heckman, using a variety of data sources.[20] A tabular summary of this work appears in the Web Appendix.[21]

The cumulative body of work by the Murnane group supports many of the conclusions of Cameron and Heckman (1993, 1994) and Cameron (1996) but contradicts or supplements others. Their main conclusions are as follows.

1. GED recipients are intermediate between dropouts and high school graduates in terms of ability, years of secondary schooling attained, and family background.

2. For both men and women, GED recipients perform below the level of high school graduates in the labor market. *On average*, adjusting for differences in pre-GED traits, GED recipients earn the same wages as dropouts.

3. GED recipients do not attain postsecondary educational credentials at the same rate as high school graduates. At the same level of educational

---

19. See Web Appendix Table W5.2.1.

20. See Murnane, Willett, and Boudett (1995, 1997, 1999), Boudett, Murnane, and Willett (2000), Murnane, Willett, and Tyler (2000), and Tyler, Murnane, and Willett (2000, 2003).

21. See Web Appendix Table W5.2.1, which provides a comprehensive summary of the literature and which has a separate block on their work (see "Murnane et al. Studies").

attainment and ability, GED recipients earn at the same level of annual earnings as ordinary high school graduates.

4. Building on the work of Cameron and Heckman, but substantially extending it by using longer panels that sample later ages, Murnane, Willett, and Boudett (1995, 1997, 1999), Murnane, Willett, and Tyler (2000), and Tyler, Murnane, and Willett (2000, 2003) present evidence that shows wage and earnings growth due to GED certification that appears three to five years after receipt of the certificate. This evidence is consistent with an investment interpretation of the benefits of the GED. This effect was not found by CH, who studied shorter stretches of the life cycle. Growth effects appear to be stronger for women than for men but are present for both. Consistent with an investment story, one of their papers finds depressed earnings in the early periods following receipt of the GED with enhanced earnings at later ages as investments pay off (see Boudett, Murnane, and Willett, 2000).

5. In a series of papers beginning in 1999, the Murnane group reported that the benefits of the GED for both men and women are localized to *low-ability* recipients, although the definition of what constitutes low ability varies across studies. Different papers use different tests, and test scores are not equated across studies. In Murnane, Willett, and Boudett (1999), low ability is defined as being in the bottom quartile of the distribution of scores on an achievement test (the AFQT) for males. In Tyler, Murnane, and Willett (2000), it is those at the margin of passing the GED.[22] In Tyler, Murnane, and Willett (2003), lower ability is the bottom half of a distribution of AFQT test scores for males. Estimated GED effects for low-ability groups range from 19% to 36%.[23] The authors interpret this finding as arising from the greater noncognitive skills of the low-ability GED certifiers who persist and pass the GED exam. This claim is contradicted by the analysis of Heckman et al. (2011), which shows that the benefits of the GED are greatest for those with the greatest cognitive and noncognitive endowments.

6. A widely cited paper by Tyler, Murnane, and Willett (2000) claims that the GED is a successful signal of traits that were unknown to the market before receipt of the credential.

7. Many GEDs are obtained in prison. There is no payoff to prison-issued GEDs in terms of either wages or recidivism (Tyler and Kling, 2006).

22. Scores on GED tests are highly correlated with scores on AFQT tests (see Means and Laurence, 1984; Boesel, Alsalam, and Smith, 1998; Heckman and Kautz, 2012).
23. See Table W5.2.1.

8. The benefits of the GED are quite modest, and few recipients escape poverty. The exception occurs when GED recipients attain postsecondary credentials (Boudett, Murnane, and Willett, 2000).

9. Cameron and Heckman report that the wage and earnings returns to post-GED work experience for males are the same as the returns to the work experience of dropouts. Using a different measure of experience, Murnane, Willett, and Boudett (1999) and Tyler, Murnane, and Willett (2003) contest this conclusion. In Section 5.4, we confirm the analysis of Cameron and Heckman.

The models estimated, the variables used, and the samples analyzed differ greatly across papers from the Murnane group and those used by Cameron and Heckman and Cameron. For example, in studies based on the NLSY, the Murnane group uses an oversample of poor families instead of the random sample. This practice runs the danger of making inferences from censored samples, and they do not correct for the biasing effects of censoring.[24] Measures of work experience vary across and within their studies. The Web Appendix highlights the variety of different assumptions made in their work.[25] This variety makes it difficult to summarize their research succinctly.

The most influential paper of the Murnane group is Tyler, Murnane, and Willett (2000), who use a modified version of a regression discontinuity estimator to identify the benefit of GED certification. Passing standards vary across states. Comparing the outcomes of GED recipients in low-standard states with the outcomes of GED exam failures in high-standard states, and adjusting for differences in labor market conditions across states, they report a 10%–19% earnings benefit *for whites only* to GED certification at the margin of passing.[26] They argue that these estimates are consistent with earlier studies by Cameron and Heckman (1993) and Cao,

---

24. See, for example, the analysis of Heckman (1987) for the danger of using censored samples without correcting for censoring.

25. See Web Appendix Table W5.2.1.

26. They suggest that their lack of a significant GED effect for nonwhites may be due to an institutional effect where both disproportionate representation of minorities in prison and the growth of GED programs for the incarcerated lead to negative associations with the test, thus decreasing its signalling value. See Chapter 3 for evidence of demographic trends in prison-based GED receipt. The separate estimation of the GED effect by race is rare in the literature, which typically includes regression controls for race but does not treat it as a separate conditioning variable. See Section W5.2.1 of the Web Appendix for a full account of study samples, treatment of race, and separate estimates by race. Other papers by this group report effects for blacks, and they do not discuss the discrepancy among the studies.

Stromsdorfer, and Weeks (1996), who find no effect of certification for the average test taker. They claim that for the margin they investigate—that of low-skilled exam takers—there are substantial "signalling" benefits to certification that are absent for the general population of test takers (i.e., the causal effect is positive for low-ability test takers). Averaging over all quartiles of ability, the white GED certifiers earn a 4% greater return.[27]

Jepsen, Mueser, and Troske (2011) explicitly address the issue of whether low-ability (marginal) GED test takers benefit from exam certification. They use a large sample of 86,345 persons who first attempted the GED in Missouri in the period 1995–2005. Their sample also contains GED test scores for all attempts to pass the test. These scores are matched to unemployment insurance earnings data. They analyze earnings and employment outcomes for males and females of all demographic groups over the time period 1995–2005, using individual data on quarterly earnings up to 7.5 years after receipt of the GED and four quarters before the first attempt. For samples with long earnings histories pre- and postcertification, they compare GED passers with GED failers at the margin of passing on their first attempt of the GED exam.[28]

In contrast to the claims of Tyler, Murnane, and Willett (2000), Jepsen, Mueser, and Troske find that GED certification has *no* causal effect on the earnings of any demographic group, even 7.5 years after a person's first attempt. Certification increases the probability of *attempting* further education by 4 percentage points for males and by 8 percentage points for females. Earnings gaps between GED recipients and dropouts are the same before and after certification. Their analysis shows no evidence that GED recipients at the margin of passing (i.e., the "low-ability" GED recipients) receive any benefit from certification.

Jepsen, Mueser, and Troske note a fundamental flaw in the identification strategy of Tyler, Murnane, and Willett. The GED exam has multiple component tests. Persons may attempt the GED on repeated occasions, and scores cumulate across the components that have been passed. Tyler, Murnane, and Willett do not account for this feature of GED certification, which Jepsen, Mueser, and Troske show produces violations of the identifying assumptions of their version of a regression discontinuity estimator. The research by Jepsen, Mueser, and Troske shows that careful treatment of this issue critically affects the estimated effects of the GED.

27. For a more extensive discussion of their paper, see Web Appendix Section W5.2.
28. They develop and apply an innovative econometric extension of the regression discontinuity design estimator that accounts for the multiple thresholds and requirements that constitute the core standards for the GED.

The simplicity of their procedures, the cleanliness of their data, and the large sample sizes (which make it more likely to find GED effects using conventional significance levels) speak powerfully against claims that low-ability GED recipients experience substantial wage growth as a consequence of GED certification.

Both the Tyler, Murnane, and Willett and Jepsen, Mueser, and Troske studies are for persons who *attempt* the GED. Arguably, those who attempt the test are more motivated individuals.[29] Before–after comparisons might eliminate this effect but only under strong assumptions.[30]

5.2.4 STUDIES OF THE EFFECT OF THE GED ON IMMIGRANT
ASSIMILATION AND THE EFFECTS OF THE PRISON–ISSUED GED

Clark and Jaeger (2006) use Current Population Survey (CPS) data to examine the life-cycle consequences of GED certification and to investigate whether GED certification promotes immigrant assimilation by establishing that GED recipients have skills required to pass the GED test. The advantage of the CPS is that it provides large samples—typically, an order of magnitude larger than the samples used in much of the literature. They estimate GED effects across a wide array of age groups. They also provide information on the earnings of foreign-schooled immigrants who GED certify. The Web Appendix reviews their study and its central claims.[31]

One disadvantage of the CPS is that it only records terminal degrees. It is not possible to use CPS data to investigate the benefits of the GED for those who complete additional postsecondary schooling. Another disadvantage is that the CPS has no measures of ability or family background, which the previous literature shows to be important in explaining the performance of GED recipients compared to that of dropouts.

Clark and Jaeger (2006) report substantial effects on wages and earnings from receiving a terminal GED compared to not having the GED credential. They have data on outcomes at much later ages than are examined in most of the literature.[32] They report substantial growth in the returns to

---

29. Thus, taking the GED exam may distinguish GED test takers from those who do not try. Passing or failing may be irrelevant to any estimated effect of the GED. With their data, they cannot directly test this hypothesis.

30. Sufficient assumptions are that skills are stable over time and age and, in particular, before and after GED certification, and that they enter outcome models in an additively separable fashion. Any combination of these assumptions that produces a fixed effect will also reduce bias.

31. See Web Appendix Table W5.2.1.

32. An exception is Cameron (1996).

the GED credential with age, evidence that is in apparent agreement with the claims of the Murnane group. Like previous studies, they find little evidence that GED recipients are the equivalents of high school graduates who do not attain further education.

Heckman and LaFontaine (2006) use the CPS data to check the claims of Clark and Jaeger. They also study a sample of immigrants and natives using the National Adult Literacy Survey (NALS) data. They find that CPS imputation procedures produce an upward biased estimate of the GED effect.[33] When the bias is properly accounted for, estimated GED effects substantially weaken.

Heckman and LaFontaine (2006) also show that the life-cycle wage growth of GED recipients compared to dropouts that is reported by Clark and Jaeger is due to a cohort effect. The average years of schooling of high school dropouts has increased over time, while that of GED recipients has not.[34] This trend produces the statistical illusion of GED life-cycle wage growth in any cross section. Older cohorts of GED recipients are relatively better educated—and hence have higher earnings—than younger cohorts. Due to this cohort effect, older GED recipients (compared to dropouts) are more able and learn more than younger GED recipients, producing the appearance of life-cycle growth in cross-sectional analyses when none is present.

Heckman and LaFontaine (2006) also challenge the claim that the GED benefits immigrants. Using NALS data, Heckman and LaFontaine show that foreign-born dropouts have substantially lower ability than foreign-born GED recipients. After adjusting for these differences, immigrant GED recipients have the same earnings as immigrant dropouts.[35]

As noted in Chapter 1 and discussed further in Chapter 3, the GED testing program has been introduced into prisons. Prison-issued GEDs account for a substantial portion of the growth of GED receipt among black males. Recent studies by Tyler and Kling (2006) and Zgoba, Haugebrook, and Jenkins (2008), reviewed in the Web Appendix, show no effect of prison-issued GEDs on either post-incarceration wages or recidivism.[36]

33. Many GED recipients have missing data and are imputed to have the wages of high school graduates. See the discussion in Appendix Section W5.2.

34. See Web Appendix Figure W5.2.1.

35. For further discussion, see Appendix W5.2.

36. See Table W5.2.1.

While all studies agree that GED certification is not the same as high school graduation, they disagree as to whether dropouts benefit from earning a GED certificate. After accounting for preexisting ability and background, some studies find that GED recipients earn no more than other dropouts. Other studies find that the average GED recipient earns slightly more than the average dropout, while others claim that GED recipients in some groups earn much more.

This chapter reconciles the differences in the findings by providing comprehensive cross-sectional and panel analyses of the benefits to GED certification. We test a wide range of models across a variety of data sets for many subpopulations. In general, differences in ability and background account for many of the cross-sectional differences in labor market outcomes between GED recipients and other dropouts. For some groups, GED recipients are more likely to work and to work longer hours than other dropouts.

Differences in the estimated returns to the GED across studies stem from four primary methodological sources. First, studies account for preexisting ability in very different ways. The evidence in Chapter 4 shows that GED recipients are more able than other high school dropouts before they receive the GED. This finding suggests that it is important to account for differences in preexisting ability. Not all studies that use the NLSY79 treat or control for cognitive ability in the same way. Some control for cognitive ability and find that after doing so the GED has little benefit for dropouts (Heckman and LaFontaine, 2006). Some argue that it is inappropriate to control for cognitive ability in the NLSY79 (Murnane, Willett, and Boudett, 1995; Murnane, Willett, and Tyler, 2000). Others allow for statistical interactions between the returns to the GED and cognitive ability in the NSLY79, and find that the GED benefits low-skilled recipients (Murnane, Willett, and Boudett, 1999).

This chapter considers a wide range of specifications. We report robust patterns and interpret the differences across specifications. We conduct statistical tests using over 100,000 different empirical models to avoid the arbitrariness of relying on one model—especially one arrived at through a battery of "specification tests." Our approach avoids the problem of "pretesting"—that the standard errors reported in the literature do not account for sifting and sorting across alternative models that is part of the standard practice of selecting a "final" empirical model.

A second source of differences across studies in estimated returns to the GED lies in the different measures of labor market outcomes used. For example, Murnane, Willett, and Boudett (1995) only study log wages, log earnings, or log hours worked, implicitly conditioning on employment. They compare the outcomes of *working* GED recipients with the outcomes of *working* dropouts. Since the GED might increase the probability of obtaining a job, this research does not address a potential source of selection bias.

Different labor market outcomes reflect conceptually different types of returns. Some studies only examine broad measures such as annual earnings. In this chapter, we consider six important economic outcomes: annual income, hourly wages conditional on employment, hours worked conditional on employment, the probability of employment, labor force participation, and unemployment conditional on labor force participation.

Annual income is an overall measure of economic success but obscures the source of any estimated success story. People could earn more because they have higher wages, because they work more hours when they are employed, or because they are more likely to be employed. We show that accounting for labor supply makes a difference in interpreting estimated GED effects.

Third, much of the literature focuses on male GED recipients or combines males and females in the same analysis. A large body of research in labor economics shows that female labor supply behavior is fundamentally different from male behavior.[37] We separate males and females for all analyses and show that estimated GED effects differ across genders. Some studies only analyze particular ethnic groups or control for ethnicity by including a dummy variable in regression analyses. We report pooled and separate analyses for each ethnic group and discuss differences across groups when they are found.

Fourth, different studies measure work experience in different ways. We systematically investigate a variety of measures of work experience. We study life-cycle wage growth attributable to GED certification. There is no evidence that the life-cycle wage growth of GEDs with work experience is greater than that of other dropouts. We now turn to our primary data analysis.

5.3 Cross-Sectional Analyses

In this section of the chapter, we present cross-sectional analyses. In Section 5.4 we exploit the panel features of our data.

37. See, for example, the essays in Smith and Cogan (1980) and Killingsworth (1983).

5.3.1 BENEFITS ACROSS DATA SETS

In an appendix to this chapter (Section 5.7), we discuss the methodology used to control for unobserved differences in precertification characteristics between GED recipients and others. We control for unobservables using the rich set of measured variables at our disposal.

Figures 5.3 and 5.4 present the average benefits of GED certification between ages 23 and 27 compared to those of other dropouts. We remove observations on people currently enrolled in school.[38] At each age, the raw estimates adjust only for age (within the reported category) and region or state of residence (to adjust for variations in market conditions). The ability-adjusted estimates also adjust for ability as measured by an achievement test with the effect of years of schooling removed from the adjusting test score using a procedure applied in Heckman, Humphries, and Mader (2011) that is discussed in detail in the Web Appendix.[39]

The background-adjusted estimates adjust for both ability and standard measures of family background at young ages that are used in the literature.[40] We use the same format introduced in Chapter 4. The bars attached to each column represent one-standard-deviation ranges of statistical variability in the estimates. The black dots on the tops of the bars indicate whether the estimate for GED recipients is statistically different from that of other high school dropouts at the 5% level; the white dots indicate whether the estimates for GED recipients and high school graduates are statistically different from each other; and the diamonds indicate whether the estimates for high school graduates are different from those of dropouts.

Two conclusions emerge from these figures. (1) GED recipients perform much worse than high school graduates. (2) With the exception of employment and annual earnings for females in the NLSY surveys, on average, GED recipients perform at the level of dropouts. This pattern is found repeatedly throughout this chapter.

---

38. When analyzing annual income, this restriction excludes 10.1% of males and 9.1% of females in the NLSY79 data, 8.5% of the male observations and 10.2% of the female observations in the NLSY97 data, and 22.5% of males and 23.0% of females in the NELS data. The figures in the NELS data are higher because the variable indicates whether the person was enrolled in postsecondary education at any point in the year, whereas the NLSY79 and NLSY97 variables are at the time of interview.

39. See Web Appendix Sections W5.3.1 and W5.3.2. The estimates that adjust ability for schooling attained are very similar to the effects without adjusting for schooling attained.

40. See, for example, Taubman (1977) or Cameron and Heckman (2001).

Figure 5.3 Labor Market Differences, Ages 23 to 27, across Data Sets (Males, All Levels of Postsecondary Education)

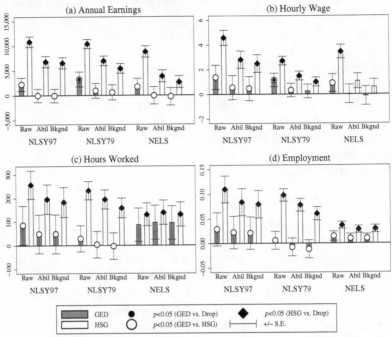

Sources: National Longitudinal Survey of Youth, 1979; National Education Longitudinal Study, 1988; National Longitudinal Survey of Youth, 1997.

Notes: All NLSY79 and NLSY97 results are for individuals age 23 to 27. In NELS, individuals are age 24 to 27. All regressions allow for heteroskedastic errors and, when appropriate, clustering at the individual level. "Raw" Controls: NLSY97—age, region of residence, year, and race; NELS—age, region of residence, and race; NLSY79—age, region of residence, year, and race. "Abil" Controls: NLSY97—raw controls and AFQT adjusted for schooling at time of test; NLSY79—raw controls and AFQT adjusted for schooling at time of test; NELS—raw controls and 8th grade subject test scores in reading, history, math, and science. "Bkgnd" Controls: NLSY97—ability controls, broken home status at age 6, family income in 1997, mother's highest grade completed, and urban residence; NLSY79—ability controls, broken home status at age 14, family income in 1979, mother's highest grade completed, urban residence at age 14, residence in the South at age 14, and factors based on adolescent risky behavior and criminal behavior; NELS—ability controls, 8th grade family socioeconomic status, urban residence in 8th grade, broken home in 8th grade, hybrid home in 8th grade, if the mother had a high school diploma, and if the mother had a college degree. Regressions exclude those who report earning more than $300,000 (2005$), working more than 4,000 hours, or earning hourly wages less than $3 (2005$) or more than $200 (2005$). For more information, please see Table W5.1.9 of the Web Appendix.

Figure 5.4 Labor Market Differences, Age 23 to 27, across Data Sets (Females, All Levels of Postsecondary Education)

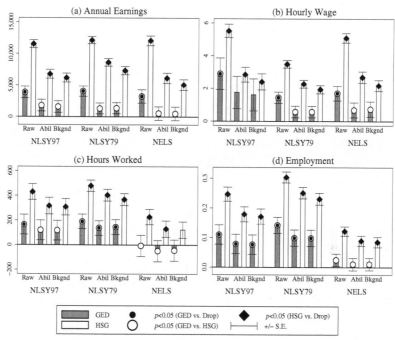

Sources: National Longitudinal Survey of Youth, 1979; National Education Longitudinal Study, 1988; National Longitudinal Survey of Youth, 1997.

Notes: All NLSY79 and NLSY97 results are for individuals age 23 to 27. In NELS, individuals are age 24 to 27. All regressions allow for heteroskedastic errors and, when appropriate, clustering at the individual level. "Raw" Controls: NLSY97—age, region of residence, year, and race; NELS—age, region of residence, and race; NLSY79—age, region of residence, year, and race. "Abil" Controls: NLSY97—raw controls and AFQT adjusted for schooling at time of test; NLSY79—raw controls and AFQT adjusted for schooling at time of test; NELS—raw controls and 8th grade subject test scores in reading, history, math, and science. "Bkgnd" Controls: NLSY97—ability controls, broken home status at age 6, family income in 1997, mother's highest grade completed, and urban residence; NLSY79—ability controls, broken home status at age 14, family income in 1979, mother's highest grade completed, urban residence at age 14, residence in the South at age 14, and factors based on adolescent risky behavior and criminal behavior; NELS—ability controls, 8th grade family socioeconomic status, urban residence in 8th grade, broken home in 8th grade, hybrid home in 8th grade, if the mother had a high school diploma, and if the mother had a college degree. Regressions exclude those who report earning more than $300,000 (2005$), working more than 4,000 hours, or earning hourly wages less than $3 (2005$) or more than $200 (2005$). For more information, please see Table W5.1.10 of the Web Appendix.

The estimates just presented are for young people. How do these conclusions change if we follow GED recipients to later ages? It is possible that GED certification pays off with age, as some papers claim. The NLSY79 data is the only data set with information past age 27 that contains rich detail on ability, background, and educational histories. As noted in our review of the literature, the NLSY79 has been the principal data set for examining the effects of GED certification. Relying solely on the NLSY79 for our life-cycle analysis could be problematic if the GED recipients in the NLSY are atypical. We now establish that they are not.

As noted in Table 5.1, other data besides the NLSY79 have information by age on the earnings of GED recipients who attain no postsecondary education. Figure 5.5 shows the annual income for GED recipients and high school graduates who do not attain any postsecondary education relative to dropouts for the NLSY79, ACS, and NALS. The estimates are comparable across data sets for each age, suggesting that the NLSY79 is not an anomalous sample of GED recipients. Heckman and LaFontaine (2006) establish the comparability of NLSY79 estimates of GED effects with CPS-based estimates after adjusting for imputation bias in the CPS. These comparisons give greater confidence in using the NLSY79 to study the effects of the GED over the life cycle.

Figures 5.6 and 5.7 report the average estimated effects of GED certification and high school graduation across four age groups from the NLSY79 data.[41] Persons enrolled in school or in formal job training programs are not included because they are likely to work less and have lower wages when they work owing to competing demands on their time.

Across all age groups, the pattern for labor market outcomes present in Figures 5.3–5.4 generally continues to hold. On average, GED recipients perform worse than high school graduates, usually statistically significantly so. Female GED recipients are more likely to be employed than other dropouts (see Figure 5.8). At some ages, the estimated effect is statistically significant. Their greater employment is not associated with greater hourly wages or hours worked even at later ages when their work experience cumulates and might be thought to produce higher hourly wages. Female GED recipients earn more than other dropouts, but the effect arises in large part from their greater employment.

---

41. See Web Appendix Section W5.3.6 for similar figures for race and postsecondary educational attainment groups.

Figure 5.5 Annual Income Differences, across Data Sets, No College

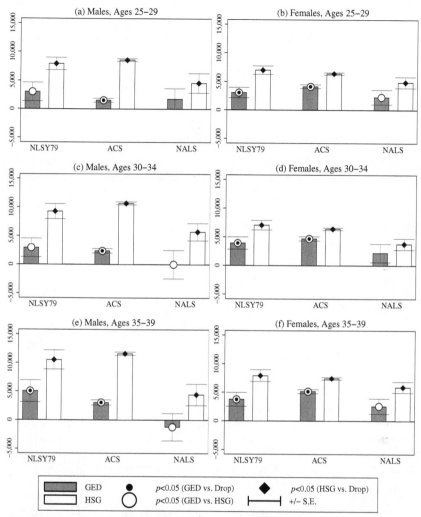

Sources: National Longitudinal Survey of Youth, 1979; National Adult Literacy Survey, 1992; American Community Survey Data, 2009.

Sample: Sample is restricted to those with no college. *Controls:* Estimates are adjusted for the age, race, and region or state of residence. Regressions exclude those reporting earning more than $300,000. For more information, please see Table W5.3.1 of the Web Appendix.

Figure 5.6 Labor Market Differences, Age 20–39 (Males, All Levels of Postsecondary Education)

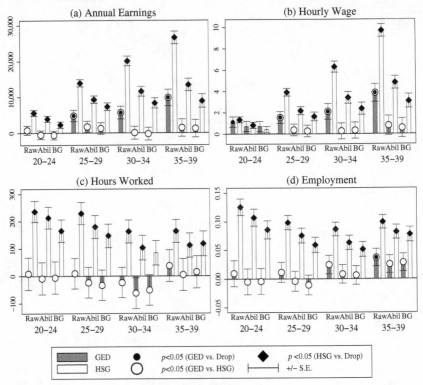

Source: National Longitudinal Survey of Youth, 1979.
Controls: "Raw"—age, region of residence, year, and race; "Abil"—raw controls and AFQT adjusted for schooling at time of test; "BG"—ability controls, broken home status at age 14, family income in 1979, mother's highest grade completed, urban residence at age 14, residence in the South at age 14, and factors based on adolescent risky behavior and criminal behavior. Regressions exclude those who report earning more than $300,000 (2005$), working more than 4,000 hours, or earning hourly wages less than $3 (2005$) or more than $200 (2005$). Notes: All regressions allow for clustered standard errors at the individual level. For more information, please see Table W5.3.2 of the Web Appendix.

Employment of male GED certifiers increases with age. At ages 35–39, it is borderline statistically significantly greater than that of dropouts. There is no corresponding GED effect on income, wages, and hours worked. In Section 5.3.7 we show that the employment effect is partly due to a decrease in the employment rate for a group of black high school dropouts starting around age 30. It is not found for any other male demographic groups.

Figure 5.7 Labor Market Differences, Age 20–39 (Females, All Levels of Postsecondary Education)

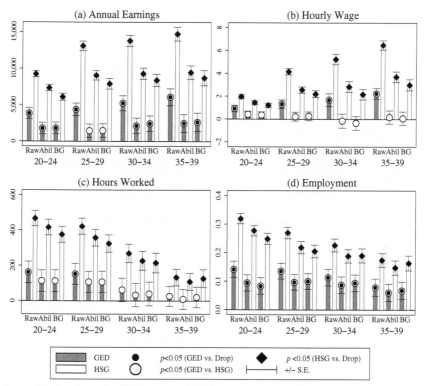

(a) Annual Earnings   (b) Hourly Wage

(c) Hours Worked   (d) Employment

GED	●	p<0.05 (GED vs. Drop)	◆	p <0.05 (HSG vs. Drop)
HSG	○	p<0.05 (GED vs. HSG)	├───┤	+/– S.E.

Source: National Longitudinal Survey of Youth, 1979.

Controls: "Raw"—age, region of residence, year, and race; "Abil"—raw controls and AFQT adjusted for schooling at time of test; "BG"—ability controls, broken home status at age 14, family income in 1979, mother's highest grade completed, urban residence at age 14, residence in the South at age 14, and factors based on adolescent risky behavior and criminal behavior. Regressions exclude those who report earning more than $300,000 (2005$), working more than 4,000 hours, or earning hourly wages less than $3 (2005$) or more than $200 (2005$). *Notes:* All regressions allow for clustered standard errors at the individual level. For more information, please see Table W5.3.3 of the Web Appendix.

5.3.3 OTHER DIMENSIONS OF LABOR SUPPLY

Thus far we have only considered labor supply in terms of whether or not someone is working and in terms of hours worked conditional on working. We have not considered labor force participation—whether people are employed or are actively searching for a job.

Figure 5.8 decomposes employment by separating labor force participation and unemployment, given labor force participation. At each

Figure 5.8 Ability- and Background-Adjusted Employment and Labor Force Participation (All Races, All Levels of Postsecondary Education)

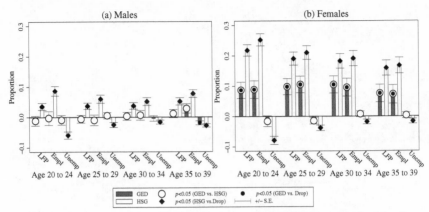

Source: National Longitudinal Survey of Youth, 1979 Nationally Representative Sample.
Controls: Age, region of residence, year, race, AFQT adjusted for schooling at time of test, broken home status at age 14, family income in 1979, mother's highest grade completed, urban residence at age 14, residence in the South at age 14, and factors based on adolescent risky behavior and criminal behavior.
Notes: Respondents are classified as GED recipients if they earn a GED before the age of 40. LFP, Empl, and Unemp signify the labor force participation rate, employment, and unemployment (conditional on labor force participation). All regressions allow for heteroskedastic errors and, when appropriate, clustering at the individual level. For more information, please see Table W5.3.4 of the Web Appendix.

age, from left to right, the pairs of bars show ability- and background-adjusted labor force participation (LFP), employment (Empl), and unemployment (conditional on labor force participation) (Unemp) for GED recipients and high school graduates relative to dropouts. The figure shows that most of the labor supply differences between GED recipients and dropouts arise because of their greater labor force participation. Among those actively seeking jobs, GED recipients and dropouts have similar levels of unemployment.

This finding sheds light on the observed labor supply differences between GED recipients and dropouts. As discussed in Chapter 1, the GED certificate opens doors to employment. Motivated persons may work more and enter the labor force to obtain jobs. Women who are not planning to enter the labor force may never attempt to earn a GED certificate. The evidence in Figure 5.8 is consistent with these conjectures and with the results from Jepsen, Mueser, and Troske (2011), who find no labor market differences between GED recipients and dropouts who *attempt* to earn a GED certificate. Those who attempt the GED are more motivated than those who do not, but the motivation is signalled before the exam is taken, and it is also present for the dropouts who do not pass the exam.

5.3.4 BENEFITS IN TERMS OF POST-GED SCHOOLING AND TRAINING

One possible objection to the preceding analysis is that it is too highly aggregated. It combines the outcomes of terminal GED recipients with those of more aspiring GED recipients who attain further education and training. How many GED recipients attempt further education? How many are successful in these attempts?

The GED Testing Service provides a partial answer to this question. A recent document by Zhang et al. (2011) studies the educational attainment of a large cohort of GED recipients six years after they certify. The study does not disaggregate by age, race, or gender. Figures 5.9–5.10 present estimates from that study.

Six years after certification, the study shows that 57% of GED recipients did not participate in any form of postsecondary education. It also shows

Figure 5.9 Postgraduate Status of GED Passers in 2004, as of October 2010

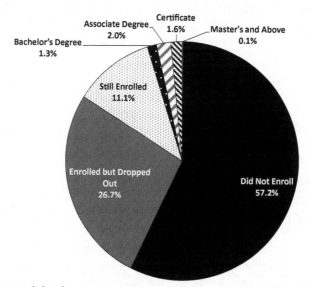

Source: Zhang et al. (2011).
Notes: Total number of 2004 cohort of GED passers who enrolled in postsecondary education between 2004 and 2010 was 175,382. The results presented in the graph exclude the type of degree earned for 5,146 individuals due to missing information.

Figure 5.10 Survival Rates of Enrollment in Postsecondary Education by Total Number of Semesters, 2004 Cohort of GED Test Passers, as of October 2010

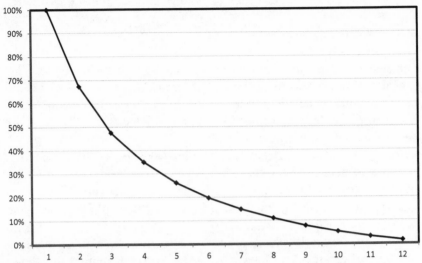

Source: Zhang et al. (2011).
Notes: Total number of 2004 cohort of GED passers who enrolled in postsecondary education between 2004 and 2010 was 175,382. 13,646 individuals were excluded from the graph due to missing data. The survival rate represents the proportion of GED test passers who enrolled into postsecondary education for a given number of semesters. The survival rate changes with changes in both graduation and dropout rates.

that 37% have enrolled but have dropped out or have not yet earned a credential; 1.3% receive bachelor's degrees, 2% receive associate's degrees, and 1.6% receive vocational certificates; and less than 0.1% receive a master's degree. Figure 5.10 shows that few GED recipients enroll for more than two semesters of postsecondary education.

We find comparable rates of educational attainment in the NLSY79, NLSY97, and NELS data. These data sets allow us to analyze follow-up periods longer than six years. Figures 5.11 and 5.12 show final schooling for GED recipients and high school graduates through age 27—the last age available for the NLSY97 and NELS data for males and females. We consider five categories of postsecondary attainment: any enrollment in college ("some college"), completion of at least a year of college ("some college, more than a year"), and earning a certificate, an associate's degree, or a bachelor's degree. The three data sets differ in their information on these categories. NELS does not allow us to identify the duration of time that people spend

Figure 5.11 Postsecondary Educational Attainment across Education Groups through Age 27, All Races

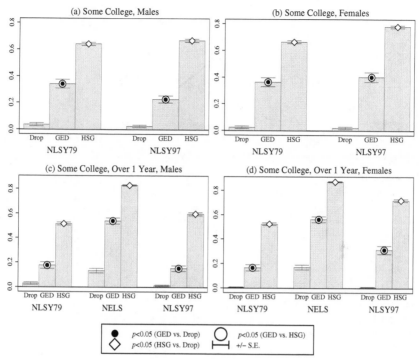

Sources: National Longitudinal Survey of Youth, 1979; National Longitudinal Survey of Youth, 1997; National Education Longitudinal Study.

Notes: The graph represents postsecondary educational attainment of dropouts, GED recipients, and high school graduates. *Variable Definitions:* "Some College" represents people who entered any postsecondary institution ever. "Some College, Over 1 Year" represents people who completed at least a year of some postsecondary education ever. For more information, please see Table W5.3.5 of the Web Appendix.

in college. We have limited information on vocational certificate-holders in the NLSY79.

Some features are common across all three data sets. More than half of GED recipients who enroll in college complete less than one year. GED recipients obtain certificates at higher or similar rates as high school graduates. However, they earn associate's degrees and bachelor's degrees at much lower rates. Less than 3% of all GED recipients earn a bachelor's degree by age 27, compared to over 20% for high school graduates.

Figure 5.12 Postsecondary Educational Attainment across Education Groups through Age 27, All Races

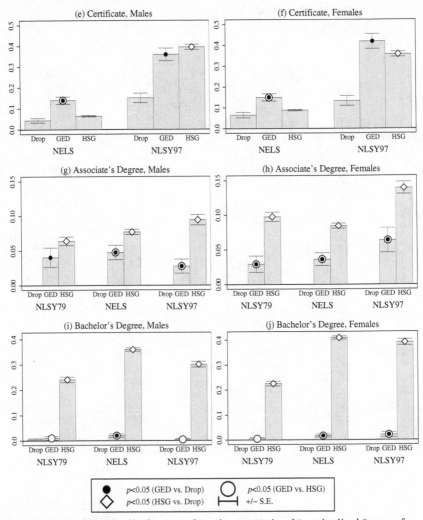

Sources: National Longitudinal Survey of Youth, 1979; National Longitudinal Survey of Youth, 1997; National Education Longitudinal Study.

Notes: The graph represents postsecondary educational attainment of dropouts, GED recipients, and high school graduates. *Variable Definitions:* "Certificate" represents people who obtained any certificate or license ever. "Associate's Degree" represents people who obtained associate's degrees ever. "Bachelor's Degree" represents people who obtained bachelor's degrees ever. "Bachelor's Degree" also includes people with higher education: master's, Ph.D., and professional degrees. For more information, please see Table W5.3.6 of the Web Appendix.

Figure 5.13 Postsecondary Educational Attainment across Education Groups through Age 40 (NLSY79), All Races

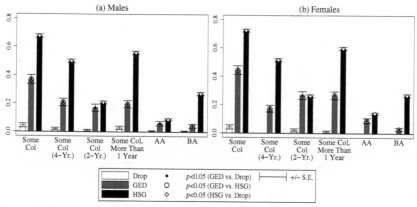

Source: National Longitudinal Survey of Youth, 1979.
Notes: The graph displays the postsecondary educational attainment of dropouts, GED recipients, and high school graduates through age 40. The bars indicate the standard errors, a measure of sampling uncertainty. *Variable Definitions:* "Some Col"—people who entered any postsecondary institution. "Some Col (4-Yr.)"—people who entered a 4-year college. "Some Col (2-Yr.)"—people who entered a 2-year college and never entered a 4-year college. "Some Col, More Than 1 Year"—people who completed at least a year of some postsecondary education. "AA"—people who obtained an associate's degree. "BA"—people who obtained a bachelor's degree. "BA" also includes people with higher education: master's, Ph.D., and professional degrees.

GED recipients might not have had a chance to return to school by age 27. The NLSY79 data allow us to study their educational attainment through age 40. Figure 5.13 shows educational attainment through age 40 in the NLSY79. Although more GED recipients earn degrees by age 40, the general patterns are very similar to those found in other data sets. In terms of educational attainment, GED recipients do not catch up with high school graduates.

We also consider enrollment in other forms of training. Figure 5.14 shows the rates of government training, on-the-job training, and technical/vocational training for high school dropouts, GED recipients, and high school graduates in the NLSY79 data. The data on government training are only available between 1979 and 1987, so the estimates do not reflect all enrollment in training through age 40. As with other forms of educational attainment, male GED recipients are intermediate between dropouts who do not GED certify and high school graduates in their attainment of job training and vocational/technical training. Female GED recipients are as likely to obtain vocational/technical training as female high school graduates.

Figure 5.14 Rates of Government-Sponsored Training, On-the-Job Training, and Vocational/Technical Training by Educational Status

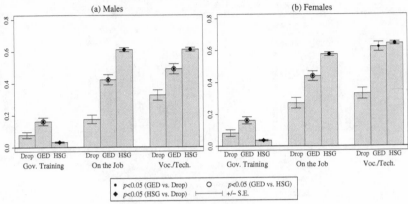

Source: National Longitudinal Survey of Youth, 1979, Nationally Representative Sample.
Notes: The government training category includes skills training from a government-sponsored program such as CETA, Job Corps, or other programs targeted to young individuals who are not attending regular school. Company training is training received directly from one's employer. Vocational and technical training includes apprenticeship, barber/beauty, business college, correspondence, company training, flight school, nursing program, vocational or technical institute. The government training variable is only available between 1979 and 1987, so the estimates do not reflect averages through age 40. For more information, please see Table W5.3.8 of the Web Appendix.

Both male and female GED recipients are more likely than dropouts or high school graduates to obtain government training. This finding is consistent with the observation in Chapter 3 that many government training programs encourage participants to earn GED certificates.[42] Figure 5.15 shows training rates before eventual GED recipients earn their GED certificates. The GED opens doors to training, just as it opens doors to schooling. We do not have data on completion rates, but the greater participation in training of the GEDs does not appear to lead to enhanced life-cycle wage growth.

5.3.5 INDIRECT VERSUS DIRECT EFFECTS: THE RETURNS TO POSTSECONDARY EDUCATION

Some of the GED recipients who attend college benefit compared to other GED recipients. Figures 5.16–5.17 present estimates in a format similar to that used in Figures 5.6 and 5.7. They separate GED recipients who attend

42. Although Figure 5.14 shows training rates for eventual GED recipients, it does not distinguish between training received before or after GED certification.

Figure 5.15 Rates of Government-Sponsored Training, On-the-Job Training, and Vocational/Technical Training Before and After GED Receipt

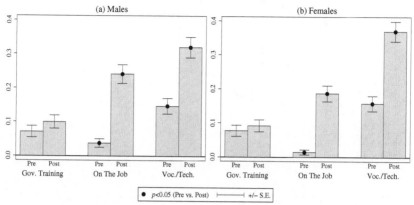

Source: National Longitudinal Survey of Youth, 1979, Nationally Representative Sample.
Notes: "Pre" and "Post" indicate periods before and after certification. The government training category includes skills training from a government-sponsored program such as CETA, Job Corps, or other programs targeted to young individuals who are not attending regular school. Company training is training received directly from one's employer. Vocational and technical training includes apprenticeship, barber/beauty, business college, correspondence, company training, flight school, nursing program, vocational or technical institute. The government training variable is only available between 1979 and 1987, so the estimates do not reflect averages through age 40. For more information, please see Table W5.3.9 of the Web Appendix.

college from those who never attend college.[43] The some-college category includes respondents who have attended any amount of college but do not necessarily receive a degree.

In general, female GED recipients who attend college perform better than other GED recipients, especially at older ages. Male GED recipients who attend some college do not perform much better than other GED recipients or dropouts. Although the point estimates of male post-GED benefits are generally positive, they are not statistically significantly different from those of GEDS who do not attain further education, or from dropouts. The higher

43. We estimate the benefits associated with various educational statuses relative to dropouts using the estimates from the following equation:
$Y_{it} = \alpha + \beta_1[(GED_{it}) \times (NOCOLL_{it})] + \beta_2[(GED_{it}) \times (SMCOLL_{it})] + \beta_3[(HSG_{it}) \times (NOCOLL_{it})] + \beta_4[(HSG_{it}) \times (SMCOLL_{it})] + \gamma X_{it} + \varepsilon_{it}$, where $NOCOLL_{it}$ and $SMCOLL_{it}$ indicate whether individual i has obtained no college or some college by time t. GED_{it} and HSG_{it} indicate whether a person is a GED recipient or high school graduate. X_{it} is a vector of background controls.

Figure 5.16 Background- and Ability-Adjusted Labor Market Differences, by Age and Postsecondary Education (Males)

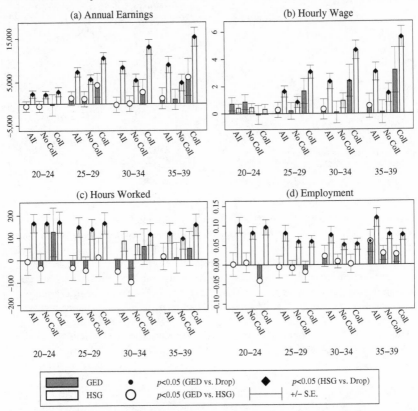

(a) Annual Earnings

(b) Hourly Wage

(c) Hours Worked

(d) Employment

▨ GED	• p<0.05 (GED vs. Drop)	◆ p<0.05 (HSG vs. Drop)
▢ HSG	○ p<0.05 (GED vs. HSG)	├──┤ +/– S.E.

Source: National Longitudinal Survey of Youth, 1979.

Controls: Age, region of residence, year, race, AFQT adjusted for schooling at time of test, broken home status at age 14, family income in 1979, mother's highest grade completed, urban residence at age 14, residence in the South at age 14, and factors based on adolescent risky behavior and criminal behavior. Regressions exclude those who report earning more than $300,000 (2005$), working more than 4,000 hours, or earning hourly wages less than $3 (2005$) or more than $200 (2005$).

Notes: "All" refers to the full sample. "No Coll" excludes people who ever attend a two- or four-year college. "Coll" includes only those who have attended a two- or four-year college. All regressions allow for heteroskedastic errors and, when appropriate, clustering at the individual level. For more information, please see Table W5.3.10 of the Web Appendix.

Figure 5.17 Background- and Ability-Adjusted Labor Market Differences, by Age and Postsecondary Education (Females)

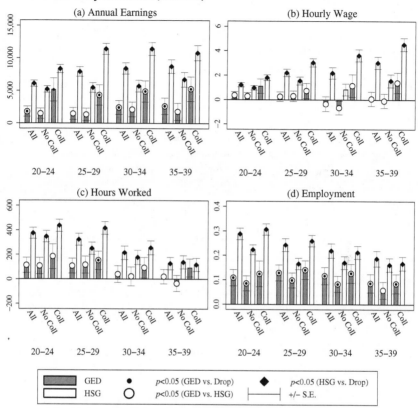

Source: National Longitudinal Survey of Youth, 1979.

Controls: Age, region of residence, year, race, AFQT adjusted for schooling at time of test, broken home status at age 14, family income in 1979, mother's highest grade completed, urban residence at age 14, residence in the South at age 14, and factors based on adolescent risky behavior and criminal behavior. Regressions exclude those who report earning more than $300,000 (2005$), working more than 4,000 hours, or earning hourly wages less than $3 (2005$) or more than $200 (2005$).

Notes: "All" refers to the full sample. "No Coll" excludes people who ever attend a two- or four-year college. "Coll" includes only those who have attended a two- or four-year college. All regressions allow for heteroskedastic errors and, when appropriate, clustering at the individual level. For more information, please see Table W5.3.11 of the Web Appendix.

returns to females who obtain post-GED education is consistent with the literature that finds that community college tends to provide higher returns to females, even when they do not earn degrees.[44]

Do the estimated GED effects arise because the GED has direct value in the labor market or because the GED opens the door to postsecondary education, which in turn improves labor market outcomes? To answer this question, we decompose the effect of GED certification into a "direct effect" (the effect of GED certification for people who have no postsecondary education) and an "indirect effect" (the benefits of GED certification on changing the probability of attending college multiplied by the gain from attending college).[45] As a benchmark we perform the same decomposition for high school graduates.

For GED recipients, the direct effect is the benefit of having a terminal GED with no postsecondary education. The indirect effect is the probability that a GED recipient attends college multiplied by the additional return to college beyond having a GED. The total effect is the sum of the indirect and direct effects.[46] The effects are defined analogously for high school graduates. We allow for the returns to postsecondary education to differ between GED recipients and high school graduates.

Figure 5.18 shows the estimates of the indirect and direct effects of GED certification and high school graduation on annual earnings. The first bar

44. See Belfield and Bailey (2011) for a review of the benefits of attending community college.

45. We present a brief formal description of this methodology in the Appendix to this chapter (Section 5.7). See the discussion surrounding equation (5.4).

46. For each age range, we estimate the benefit to various educational states relative to dropouts using the following equation: $Y_{it} = \alpha + \beta_1(GED_{it}) + \beta_2[(GED_{it}) \times (SMCOLL_{it})] + \beta_3(HSG_{it}) + \beta_4[(HSG_{it}) \times (SMCOLL_{it})] + \gamma X_{it} + \varepsilon_{it}$, where GED_{it} and HSG_{it} indicate whether individual i is a GED recipient or high school graduate at time t and $SMCOLL_{it}$ indicates whether individual i has obtained some college by time t. X_{it} is a vector of background controls. β_2 and β_4 are the additional returns to attending some college for GED recipients and high school graduates, respectively. At each age range, we also estimate the probability of having attended some college for GED recipients (p_{GED}) and high school graduates (p_{HSG}). The total effect of GED certification is decomposed as follows:

$$\text{Total effect} = \underbrace{\beta_1}_{\text{Direct effect}} + \underbrace{(p_{GED} \times \beta_2)}_{\text{Indirect effect}} ,$$

where p_{GED} is the probability of attending college for a GED. Methodological Appendix 5.7 discusses this decomposition in greater detail.

The standard errors are calculated using a bootstrap procedure that allows for arbitrary correlation of the error term within individuals over time but assumes that the error term is uncorrelated across individuals. We use 100 draws.

Figure 5.18 Background- and Ability-Adjusted Indirect and Direct Annual Earnings Effects, by Age, NLSY79

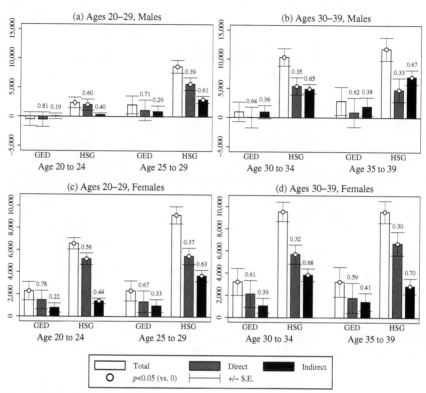

Source: National Longitudinal Survey of Youth, 1979.

Controls: Age, region of residence, year, race, AFQT adjusted for schooling at time of test, broken home status at age 14, family income in 1979, mother's highest grade completed, urban residence at age 14, residence in the South at age 14, and factors based on adolescent risky behavior and criminal behavior. *Notes:* Regressions exclude those who report earning more than $300,000 (2005$), working more than 4,000 hours, or earning hourly wages less than $3 (2005$) or more than $200 (2005$). The bars depict the total effect, the direct effect, and the indirect effect through some college. We estimate the returns to the educational states relative to dropouts using the following equation:
$Y_{it} = \alpha + \beta_1[(GED_{it}) \times (NOCOLL_{it})] + \beta_2[(GED_{it}) \times (SMCOLL_{it})] + \beta_3[(HSG_{it}) \times (NOCOLL_{it})] + \beta_4[(HSG_{it}) \times (SMCOLL_{it})] + \gamma X_{it} + \varepsilon_{it}$, where $NOCOLL_{it}$ and $SMCOLL_{it}$ indicate whether individual i has obtained no college or some college by time t. GED_{it} and HSG_{it} indicate whether a person is a GED recipient or high school graduate. X_{it} is a vector of background controls. The probabilities of being in educational states are estimated at the average value for the age range. The total effect is the sum of the estimated returns, weighted by the probabilities of each state. The direct effect is the estimated return to the no college state multiplied by the probability of attending no college. The indirect effect is the estimated return to the some college state multiplied by the probability of attending some college. The standard errors are calculated using a bootstrap procedure with 100 draws that allows for arbitrary correlation of the error term within individuals over time but assumes that the error term is uncorrelated across individuals. For more information, see Table W5.3.12 of the Web Appendix.

shows the total effect. The second and third bars show the relative contributions of no college and some college to the total effect. The numbers on top of the direct effect bars indicate the fraction of people who have not attended postsecondary education and the numbers on the indirect effect bars indicate the fraction who have attended postsecondary education. The decomposition for the other outcomes is presented in the Web Appendix.[47]

Both the direct and indirect effects of receiving a GED are small for male recipients at all ages. The total effect for male high school graduates increases over the life cycle, primarily due to growing returns by age for those who attend college. Between ages 20 and 24, most of the total GED effect for women comes from the direct effect. As women enroll in college at later ages, the indirect effect increases so that it is about half of the total effect by ages 35–39.

Tables 5.2 (men) and 5.3 (women) present the estimated benefits underlying Figure 5.18 and the analogous decomposition for hourly wage rates. They decompose the benefits of GED receipt and high school graduation into direct and indirect effects. They also show the probability of attending college and the benefit of attending college for GED recipients and high school graduates.

For males, there is little direct or indirect effect of GED certification on annual earnings or hourly wages. For female GED recipients, the effect of attending college on annual earnings is relatively high at young ages. The indirect effect is low because so few have attended college. As more female GED recipients attend college, the indirect effect of GED receipt on annual earnings increases so that by ages 35–39, the indirect effect accounts for nearly half of the estimated total effect of GED certification. For female GED recipients, the benefit of attending college comes through increased labor supply and not through increased hourly wages.

The indirect effect accounts for most of the effect of high school graduation on hourly wages. High school graduation opens the door to college and college leads to higher paying jobs. In contrast, the direct effect accounts for most of the effect of high school graduation on annual earnings. Why is the indirect effect more important for hourly wages than annual earnings? Much of the total effect of high school graduation on annual earnings comes through increased labor supply, rather than through higher hourly wages. In addition, attending college after graduating from

47. See Section W5.3.5.

Table 5.2 Direct and Indirect Effects and Their Components for Men

	Direct Effect	Effect of College	Probability of College	Indirect Effect	Total Effect
Annual Earnings					
GED (20–24)	−514	332	0.19	62	−453
	(1,254)	(2,634)	(0.03)	(503)	(1,187)
GED (25–29)	1,109	3,194	0.29	916	2,025
	(1,754)	(3,278)	(0.03)	(957)	(1,539)
GED (30–34)	14	2,646	0.36	953	968
	(1,790)	(3,138)	(0.04)	(1,140)	(1,681)
GED (35–39)	924	5,148	0.38	1,944	2,869
	(2,516)	(4,097)	(0.04)	(1,561)	(2,403)
HSG (20–24)	2,048	863	0.40	346	2,394
	(944)	(733)	(0.01)	(295)	(914)
HSG (25–29)	5,627	4,887	0.61	2,963	8,590
	(1,094)	(1,007)	(0.01)	(614)	(1,079)
HSG (30–34)	5,405	7,601	0.65	4,935	10,340
	(1,473)	(1,246)	(0.01)	(808)	(1,486)
HSG (35–39)	4,798	10,512	0.67	6,995	11,793
	(2,041)	(1,839)	(0.01)	(1,219)	(1,982)
Hourly Wages					
GED (20–24)	0.87	−0.94	0.18	−0.17	0.70
	(0.54)	(0.82)	(0.03)	(0.16)	(0.48)
GED (25–29)	0.19	1.47	0.29	0.42	0.62
	(0.60)	(1.07)	(0.04)	(0.32)	(0.54)
GED (30–34)	0.09	2.33	0.35	0.80	0.89
	(0.83)	(1.27)	(0.04)	(0.44)	(0.75)
GED (35–39)	0.10	3.08	0.37	1.12	1.23
	(0.83)	(1.82)	(0.04)	(0.70)	(0.89)
HSG (20–24)	0.42	−0.07	0.41	−0.03	0.39
	(0.31)	(0.31)	(0.01)	(0.13)	(0.32)
HSG (25–29)	0.84	2.23	0.60	1.35	2.19
	(0.42)	(0.41)	(0.01)	(0.25)	(0.39)
HSG (30–34)	0.94	3.72	0.64	2.40	3.34
	(0.57)	(0.51)	(0.01)	(0.33)	(0.60)
HSG (35–39)	1.50	4.11	0.67	2.72	4.22
	(0.68)	(0.71)	(0.01)	(0.47)	(0.62)

Source: National Longitudinal Survey of Youth, 1979. *Controls:* Age, region of residence, year, race, AFQT adjusted for schooling at time of test, broken home status at age 14, family income

(continued)

Table 5.2 (Continued)

in 1979, mother's highest grade completed, urban residence at age 14, residence in the South at age 14, and factors based on adolescent risky behavior and criminal behavior. *Notes:* Regressions exclude those who report earning more than $300,000 (2005$), working more than 4,000 hours, or earning hourly wages less than $3 (2005$) or more than $200 (2005$). We estimate the returns to educational states relative to dropouts using the following equation: $Y_{it} = \alpha + \beta_1(GED_{it}) + \beta_2[(GED_{it}) \times (SMCOLL_{it})] + \beta_3(HSG_{it}) + \beta_4[(HSG_{it}) \times (SMCOLL_{it})] + \gamma X_{it} + \varepsilon_{it}$, where GED_{it} and HSG_{it} indicate whether individual i is a GED recipient or high school graduate at time t and $SMCOLL_{it}$ indicates whether individual i has obtained some college by time t. X_{it} is a vector of background controls. At each age range, we also estimate the probability of having attended some college for GED recipients (p_{GED}) and high school graduates (p_{HSG}). β_1 and β_3 are the direct effects of GED receipt and high school graduation. β_2 and β_4 are the additional returns to attending some college for GED recipients and high school graduates. $p_{GED} \times \beta_2$ and $p_{HSG} \times \beta_4$ are the indirect effects of GED receipt and high school graduation. The standard errors are listed in parentheses and are calculated using a bootstrap procedure that allows for arbitrary correlation of the error term within individuals over time but assumes that the error term is uncorrelated across individuals. We use 100 draws.

Table 5.3 Direct and Indirect Effects and Their Components for Women

	Direct Effect	Effect of College	Probability of College	Indirect Effect	Total Effect
Annual Earnings					
GED (20–24)	1,490	3,652	0.22	790	2,280
	(836)	(1,861)	(0.03)	(412)	(825)
GED (25–29)	1,343	2,982	0.33	974	2,317
	(973)	(1,689)	(0.03)	(572)	(906)
GED (30–34)	2,127	2,762	0.39	1,071	3,199
	(1,206)	(1,698)	(0.03)	(668)	(1,214)
GED (35–39)	1,791	3,491	0.41	1,442	3,234
	(1,360)	(1,896)	(0.03)	(788)	(1,337)
HSG (20–24)	5,192	3,174	0.44	1,399	6,590
	(518)	(569)	(0.01)	(251)	(508)
HSG (25–29)	5,473	5,912	0.63	3,701	9,173
	(732)	(824)	(0.01)	(517)	(774)
HSG (30–34)	5,712	5,676	0.68	3,849	9,561
	(872)	(852)	(0.01)	(574)	(875)
HSG (35–39)	6,723	4,058	0.70	2,853	9,576
	(1,080)	(998)	(0.01)	(700)	(998)

Table 5.3 (Continued)

	Direct Effect	Effect of College	Probability of College	Indirect Effect	Total Effect
Hourly Wages					
GED (20–24)	0.29	0.82	0.23	0.19	0.48
	(0.32)	(0.64)	(0.03)	(0.16)	(0.30)
GED (25–29)	0.30	0.43	0.35	0.15	0.45
	(0.45)	(0.69)	(0.04)	(0.24)	(0.40)
GED (30–34)	−0.67	1.81	0.39	0.71	0.04
	(0.51)	(0.87)	(0.04)	(0.35)	(0.57)
GED (35–39)	−0.09	1.48	0.42	0.62	0.53
	(0.59)	(0.88)	(0.03)	(0.37)	(0.57)
HSG (20–24)	0.97	0.83	0.47	0.39	1.36
	(0.18)	(0.20)	(0.01)	(0.09)	(0.17)
HSG (25–29)	1.54	1.48	0.66	0.98	2.52
	(0.34)	(0.28)	(0.01)	(0.19)	(0.30)
HSG (30–34)	0.82	2.78	0.69	1.91	2.74
	(0.43)	(0.38)	(0.01)	(0.26)	(0.44)
HSG (35–39)	1.55	2.96	0.70	2.07	3.62
	(0.52)	(0.44)	(0.01)	(0.31)	(0.46)

Source: National Longitudinal Survey of Youth, 1979. *Controls:* Age, region of residence, year, race, AFQT adjusted for schooling at time of test, broken home status at age 14, family income in 1979, mother's highest grade completed, urban residence at age 14, residence in the South at age 14, and factors based on adolescent risky behavior and criminal behavior. *Notes:* Regressions exclude those who report earning more than $300,000 (2005$), working more than 4,000 hours, or earning hourly wages less than $3 (2005$) or more than $200 (2005$). We estimate the returns to educational states relative to dropouts using the following equation: $Y_{it} = \alpha + \beta_1(GED_{it}) + \beta_2[(GED_{it} \times (SMCOLL_{it})] + \beta_3(HSG_{it}) + \beta_4[(HSG_{it}) \times (SMCOLL_{it})] + \gamma X_{it} + \varepsilon_{it}$, where GED_{it} and HSG_{it} indicate whether individual i is a GED recipient or high school graduate at time t and $SMCOLL_{it}$ indicates whether individual i has obtained some college by time t. X_{it} is a vector of background controls. At each age range, we also estimate the probability of having attended some college for GED recipients (p_{GED}) and high school graduates (p_{HSG}). β_1 and β_3 are the direct effects of GED receipt and high school graduation. β_2 and β_4 are the additional returns to attending some college for GED recipients and high school graduates. $p_{GED} \times \beta_2$ and $p_{HSG} \times \beta_4$ are the indirect effects of GED receipt and high school graduation. The standard errors are listed in parentheses and are calculated using a bootstrap procedure that allows for arbitrary correlation of the error term within individuals over time but assumes that the error term is uncorrelated across individuals. We use 100 draws.

high school has little incremental effect on labor supply. These factors lead to a relatively small indirect effect on labor supply and therefore annual earnings.

5.3.6 PRESENT VALUES

Our cross-sectional analysis suggests that some groups of GED recipients benefit compared to other dropouts, especially those who complete some postsecondary education. But what is their lifetime benefit? Dropping out of high school delays final college attainment.

Figure 5.19 presents the difference in average annual earnings between high school graduates and GED recipients in the first five years after receiving an associate's degree or a bachelor's degree. The earnings of GED recipients constitute the baseline. For each type of degree, the first bar presents the unadjusted difference, and the second presents the difference after adjusting for ability and background. We only estimate the returns for the first five years because many GED recipients earn their degrees later in life and few of them have more than five years of experience with the degree in our sample. We cannot reject the hypothesis that GED recipients and high school graduates who obtain degrees have the same earnings. This finding differs from the results reported in Section 5.3.5 in which we combined all GED recipients who attended college, many of whom did not obtain degrees. However, many of the estimates used to generate Figure 5.19 are imprecisely determined because so few GED recipients receive degrees.

The few GED recipients who earn degrees obtain them later in life than high school graduates. As discussed in Chapter 4, there is considerable delay in the time between dropping out and obtaining GED certification. It averages five years for men and seven years for women. There is additional delay between GED certification and completion for those who obtain any degree. As shown in Figure 5.20, GED recipients tend to enroll in college much later than high school graduates. They also earn their degrees later. Male GED recipients tend to earn associate's degrees three years after high school graduates and bachelor's degrees seven to eight years after high school graduates. Female GED recipients earn associate's degrees and bachelor's degrees six to seven years after high school graduates.

The consequent delay in earnings produces a lower present value of earnings for GED recipients compared to high school graduates who obtain the same level of postsecondary education. Figure 5.21 shows estimates of

Figure 5.19 Annual Return to High School Graduate with Degree over GED Recipient with Degree

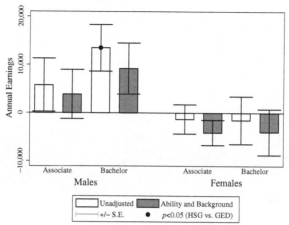

Source: National Longitudinal Survey of Youth, 1979, Cross-Sectional Sample.
Controls: Age, region of residence, year, race, AFQT adjusted for schooling at time of test, broken home status at age 14, family income in 1979, mother's highest grade completed, urban residence at age 14, residence in the South at age 14, and factors based on adolescent risky behavior and criminal behavior.
Notes: The figure presents the difference in annual earnings between high school graduates and GED recipients for the five-year period after the degree is earned. The sample excludes people once they have been to jail. The *p*-values test the null hypothesis of equality of average annual income of GED recipients who graduate with the comparable returns of high school graduates. For more information, please see Table W5.3.13 of the Web Appendix.

the present value of earnings of GED recipients and high school graduates relative to that of dropouts for different educational paths.

The present value of earnings is constructed by estimating the returns to various educational states and forming streams of the returns discounted to age 16. We analyze returns to educational experiences for different educational attainment levels: being a high school enrollee, being a high school dropout with no college, being a GED recipient with no college, being a high school graduate with no college, being a college enrollee (combining GED recipients and high school graduates), being a GED recipient with some college, being a high school graduate with some college, being a GED recipient with an associate's degree, being a high school graduate with an associate's degree, and being a bachelor's graduate (combining GED recipients and high school graduates). We allow the

Figure 5.20 Distribution of the Age of College Enrollment for GED Recipients and High School Graduates

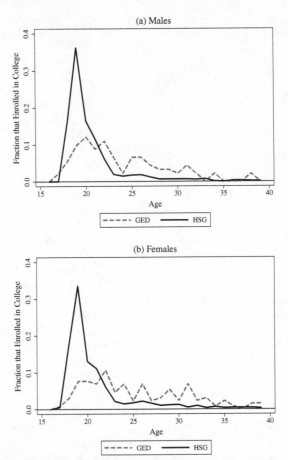

(a) Males

(b) Females

Source: National Longitudinal Survey of Youth, 1979, Nationally Representative Sample.
Note: The figure displays the distribution in the age for enrollment in college for GED recipients and high school graduates who ever enrolled in college by age 40.

returns within a state to depend on the experience in the state, and then we form sample averages.

We combine the estimates for different post-GED outcomes to estimate the present value of earnings. We assume that GED recipients drop out at age 16 and begin earning at the level of GED recipients at that time. Assuming a later age of dropping out or GED receipt would delay earnings further, decreasing the present value of earnings. Thus, our estimates are upper bounds on the benefits obtained from a GED. We assume that GED

Figure 5.21 Present Value of Annual Earnings for Different Educational Paths, Discounted to Age 16 (All Races, 10% Discount Rate)

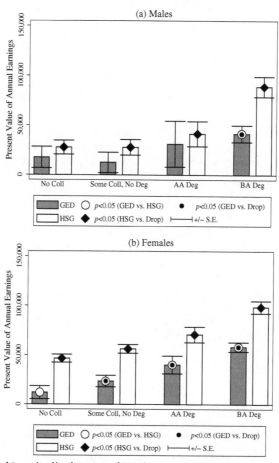

Source: National Longitudinal Survey of Youth, 1979.

Controls: Age, region of residence, year, race, AFQT adjusted for schooling at time of test, broken home status at age 14, family income in 1979, mother's highest grade completed, urban residence at age 14, residence in the South at age 14, and factors based on adolescent risky behavior and criminal behavior.

Notes: The sample excludes people once they have been to jail. All regressions allow for heteroskedastic errors and, when appropriate, clustering at the individual level. For more information about the methodology and estimates, please see Section W5.3.5 and Table W5.3.17 of the Web Appendix.

recipients earn their degrees after high school graduates and experience the average delay that GEDs who attain degrees experience.[48]

Figure 5.21 shows that the GED recipients who earn degrees have higher present discounted value of earnings compared to dropouts. The GED recipients, however, earn much less than high school graduates, in part because they earn their degrees so much later in life. This analysis shows that even the few GED recipients who obtain postsecondary degrees fare much worse than their high school graduate counterparts.

5.3.7 DIFFERENCES ACROSS RACES

With a few exceptions, the patterns of empirical results across races mirror those obtained from analyses of the combined sample. Figures 5.22–5.23 show labor market outcomes by race for GED recipients and high school graduates relative to high school dropouts.[49] For each age, the first pair of bars displays the estimate for whites, the second for blacks, and the third for Hispanics. The benefits of GED certification are estimated from regressions restricted to the indicated racial/ethnic group. Thus they are effects relative to the dropouts of that group.

After accounting for ability, white and Hispanic male GED recipients are nearly indistinguishable from other dropouts of the same ethnicity for all outcomes at all ages. Black male GED recipients have similar earnings, hourly wages, and hours worked conditional on employment as black male dropouts, but are slightly more likely to work than their dropout counterparts at older ages. Later in life, differences in employment lead to slightly higher earnings for black male GED recipients compared to their uncertified dropout counterparts.[50]

The regression coefficients plotted in Figure 5.22 do not show whether the probability of employment for black male GED recipients and high school graduates is increasing with age or whether the probability of employment for high school dropouts is decreasing. Figure 5.24 plots employment rates by age for dropouts, GED recipients, and high school graduates for different samples of black males who attain no postsecondary education. Panel (a) reveals that the increasing return to the GED with age to high school graduation and GED certification that is apparent in Figures

---

48. See Section W5.3.5 of the Web Appendix for a detailed description of the methodology and assumed educational paths underlying this calculation.

49. Unadjusted estimates and estimates separating by postsecondary education level are available in Section W5.3.6 in the Web Appendix.

50. See Web Appendix Section W5.3.6.

Figure 5.22 Background and Ability-Adjusted Labor Market Differences, by Age and Race, NLSY79 (Males, All Levels of Postsecondary Education)

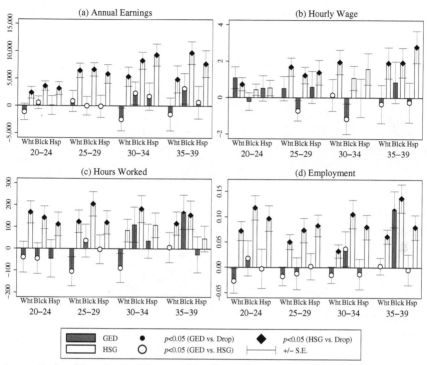

Source: National Longitudinal Survey of Youth, 1979.

Controls: Age, region of residence, year, race, AFQT adjusted for schooling at time of test, broken home status at age 14, family income in 1979, mother's highest grade completed, urban residence at age 14, residence in the South at age 14, and factors based on adolescent risky behavior and criminal behavior. Regressions exclude those reporting earning more than $300,000 or working more than 4,000 hours.

Notes: The figure reports background- and ability-adjusted estimates of the returns to the GED certificate and high school diploma by race. For each age, the first pair of bars is for whites, the second is for blacks, and the third is for Hispanics. The regressions are run separately for each race so that the baselines are estimates for that race. All regressions allow for heteroskedastic errors and, when appropriate, clustering at the individual level. For additional information, see Table W5.3.18 of the Web Appendix.

Figure 5.23 Background and Ability-Adjusted Labor Market Differences, by Age and Race, NLSY79 (Females, All Levels of Postsecondary Education)

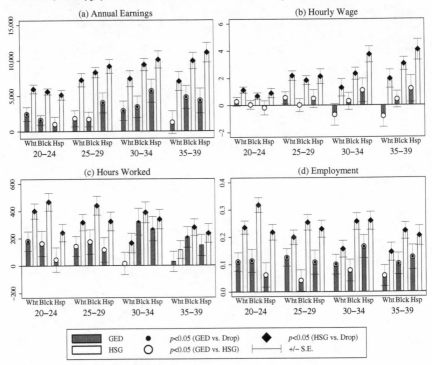

Source: National Longitudinal Survey of Youth, 1979.

Controls: Age, region of residence, year, race, AFQT adjusted for schooling at time of test, broken home status at age 14, family income in 1979, mother's highest grade completed, urban residence at age 14, residence in the South at age 14, and factors based on adolescent risky behavior and criminal behavior. Regressions exclude those reporting earning more than $300,000 or working more than 4,000 hours.

Notes: The figure reports background- and ability-adjusted estimates of the returns to the GED certificate and high school diploma by race. For each age, the first pair of bars is for whites, the second is for blacks, and the third is for Hispanics. The regressions are run separately for each race so that the baselines are estimates for that race. All regressions allow for heteroskedastic errors and, when appropriate, clustering at the individual level. For additional information, see Table W5.3.19 of the Web Appendix.

Figure 5.24 Black Male Employment and Supplemental Security Income
(No Postsecondary Education)

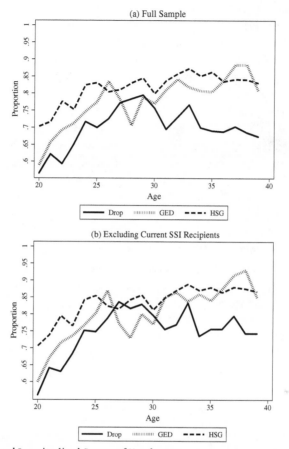

Source: National Longitudinal Survey of Youth, 1979.
Notes: Panel 5.24a includes the full sample of black males. Panel 5.24b excludes
people currently on supplemental social security income. The sample excludes people
once they have been to jail.

5.22–5.23 results from lower employment rates for high school dropouts
starting around age 30.

Why did many black male dropouts leave employment around age 30?
During the 1980s and 1990s, it became easier to qualify for social security.
In a sample that pools across age groups, Autor and Duggan (2003) show
how increases in unemployment coincided with changes in policies and the
greater uptake of Social Security Disability Income (SSDI). Panel (b) of Figure

5.24 shows the employment rates for black males excluding people who are currently on Supplemental Security Income (SSI). SSI recipients account for around half of the gap in employment rates between GED recipients and dropouts. This evidence is suggestive, but the sample sizes are relatively small. Other programs, such as SSDI, might account for more of the gap. Unfortunately, the NLSY79 does not have good measures of SSDI participation.

We supplement this analysis using the Current Population Survey (CPS) data that contains more information about disability. Figure 5.25 shows employment rates for black males including and excluding disabled populations. This data is for a cohort similar to that of the NLSY79 panel. The evidence is striking. In the full population, there is nearly a 30 percentage point gap between the employment rates of black male high school graduates and black male dropouts. Excluding the disabled, the gap is less than 5 percentage points. Unfortunately, the CPS does not distinguish between GED recipients and high school graduates, but our estimates in the NLSY79 suggest that GED recipients would follow trends similar to those for high school graduates. Why does welfare expansion not affect GED recipients and high school graduates as much as dropouts? SSDI eligibility depends on educational attainment. There are more restrictions for eligibility for people with high school equivalency degrees (including GED certificates) to obtain SSDI, because the Social Security Administration assumes that they are able to obtain jobs that would not be compromised by their disabilities.[51]

Male high school graduates of all races earn more, have higher hourly wages conditional on employment, work more hours conditional on employment, and are more likely to be employed than GEDs and dropouts. In general, white, black, and Hispanic female GED recipients have outcomes similar to those reported in the pooled group. GED recipients have higher earnings due to their greater labor supply but have the same wages.

5.3.8 DISTRIBUTIONS OF ESTIMATED EFFECTS
ACROSS SPECIFICATIONS

The cross-sectional estimates suggest that some groups might benefit from GED certification. As discussed in Section 5.2 and in greater detail in the Web Appendix,[52] different econometric specifications produce different

---

51. The Social Security Administration (2012) defines GED recipients as high school graduates for the purposes of determining SSDI eligibility. The Social Security Administration (2013) describes how high school education affects disability determination.

52. See Web Appendix Section W5.3.7 for discussion of robustness analyses.

Figure 5.25 Employment Rate of Black Males Born 1957–1964 (Age 20–40)

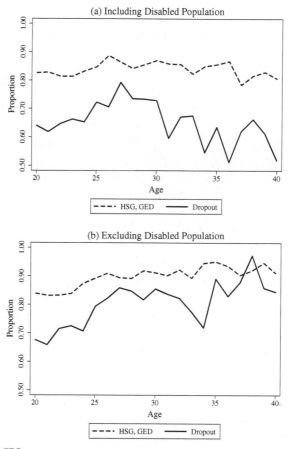

(a) Including Disabled Population

(b) Excluding Disabled Population

Source: March CPS, 1977–2005.

Notes: Employment rate is defined as the proportion of the population that has worked at least 80 hours in the previous year. A person is defined as disabled if his main reason for not working in the last year was "Disabled or Ill." Persons whose main reasons for not working in the last year were "Going to School" or "In the Armed Forces" are excluded from the analysis.

estimates of GED effects. The conventional practice of using econometric specification tests to pick a "correct" model is fraught with danger. The conventional practice is to "test down" to a model and to report p-values that ignore all of the testing that led to the final empirical model. This practice leads to badly biased inferences.

Estimates can appear to be statistically significant simply due to sampling variation. Approximately 5% of all estimates of the GED effect would appear to be "statistically significantly different from zero" at the 5% level, even if in actuality the GED had no effect. In an attempt to avoid this problem and summarize the cross-sectional results across a variety of plausible specifications, we estimate the distribution of estimated returns for over 100,000 different statistical models, using a variety of controls for different subpopulations. All models control for AFQT but use different combinations of other controls. We specify a set of other possible control variables that include mother's highest grade completed, urban residence at age 14, family income, residence in the South at age 14, smoked at 15, had sex by 15, committed a major crime, and ninth-grade GPA. We estimate the GED and high school graduate effects using each possible combination of these controls (without interaction terms). We run the regressions separately for separate subpopulations. All the subpopulations are partitions of race, postsecondary education, and age (measured in five-year categories) for males and females. The density of estimates for each subpopulation is weighted so that the figures report a nationally representative distribution.[53]

Figures 5.26–5.31 plot the estimates of returns across this large variety of specifications for annual earnings, hourly wages, employment, hours worked, and labor force participation. Figures 5.26, 5.27, and 5.28 present the distribution of the estimated effect for males of GED certification (dashed line) and high school graduation (solid line) for annual income, hourly wages, employment, hours worked, labor force participation, and the associated distributions of p-values.

Figure 5.26(a) shows that for male GEDs, the estimated coefficients capturing the effects of the GED on earnings compared with dropouts are centered at zero. Beneath this, Figure 5.26(c) plots the cumulative distribution of the p-values associated with tests of the null hypothesis of no GED effect for each model whose estimated effects are plotted in Figure 5.26(a). p-values are the probabilities that the estimated GED effects could arise from chance even if there is no effect of the GED on the indicated measure (earnings in Figure 5.26(a)). A well-known fact from statistics is that under the null hypothesis of no GED effect, the density of p-values is uniform—all p-values are equally likely to occur.

Figure 5.26(c) plots the cumulative distribution of the p-values. It is in the format of a Lorenz curve used to summarize departures of a variable from perfect equality. (The dotted line in the bottom panels of these figures is the line of perfect equality.) Under the null hypothesis of no GED

---

53. The exact procedure and a formal justification for this procedure are presented in Section W5.3.7 of the Web Appendix.

Figure 5.26 Distribution of the Estimated Effect of the GED Certificate and High School Graduation on Annual Earnings and Hourly Wage across Models for Males

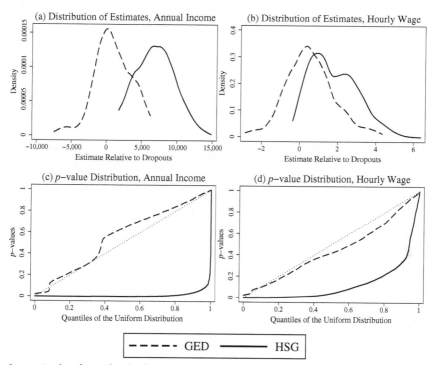

Source: National Longitudinal Survey of Youth, 1979.

Notes: The top panels plot the estimated coefficients from a series of linear regressions. The bottom panels plot the *p*-values from a series of estimates against quantiles of a uniform distribution with values between 0 and 1. For more information about the procedure, please see Section W5.3.7 of the Web Appendix. All models control for region, age, year, and AFQT score. The models differ in other controls and subpopulations of the data. The set of models includes all combinations of mother's highest grade completed, urban residence at age 14, family income, lives in the South at age 14, smoked at 15, has had sex by 15, has committed a major crime, and 9th grade GPA. The subpopulations are all partitions of race, postsecondary education (everyone, has some postsecondary education, no postsecondary education), and age (measured in five-year categories from 20 to 39) for males and females. The *p*-values are calculated allowing for heteroskedastic errors and, when appropriate, clustering at the individual level.

Figure 5.27 Distribution of the Estimated Effect of the GED Certificate and High School Graduation on Employment and Hours Worked across Models for Males

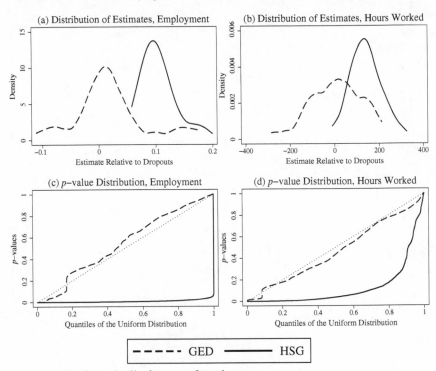

Source: National Longitudinal Survey of Youth, 1979.

Notes: The top panels plot the estimated coefficients from a series of linear regressions. The bottom panels plot the p-values from a series of estimates against quantiles of a uniform distribution with values between 0 and 1. For more information about the procedure, please see Section W5.3.7 of the Web Appendix. All models control for region, age, year, and AFQT score. The models differ in other controls and subpopulations of the data. The set of models includes all combinations of mother's highest grade completed, urban residence at age 14, family income, lives in the South at age 14, smoked at 15, has had sex by 15, has committed a major crime, and 9th grade GPA. The subpopulations are all partitions of race, postsecondary education (everyone, has some postsecondary education, no postsecondary education), and age (measured in five-year categories from 20 to 39) for males and females. The p-values are calculated allowing for heteroskedastic errors and, when appropriate, clustering at the individual level.

Figure 5.28 Distribution of the Effect of the GED Certificate and High School Graduation on Labor Force Participation across Models for Males

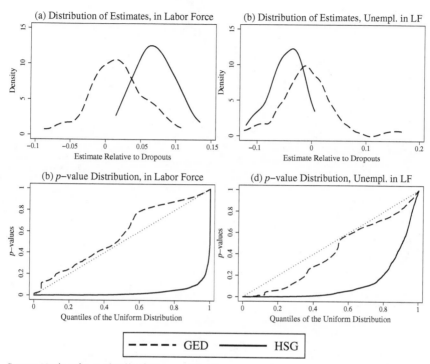

(a) Distribution of Estimates, in Labor Force

(b) Distribution of Estimates, Unempl. in LF

(b) p–value Distribution, in Labor Force

(d) p–value Distribution, Unempl. in LF

- - - - - GED ——— HSG

Source: National Longitudinal Survey of Youth, 1979.

Notes: The top panels plot the estimated coefficients from a series of linear regressions. The bottom panels plot the *p*-values from a series of estimates against quantiles of a uniform distribution with values between 0 and 1. For more information about the procedure, please see Section W5.3.7 of the Web Appendix. All models control for region, age, year, and AFQT score. The models differ in other controls and subpopulations of the data. The set of models includes all combinations of mother's highest grade completed, urban residence at age 14, family income, lives in the South at age 14, smoked at 15, has had sex by 15, has committed a major crime, and 9th grade GPA. The subpopulations are all partitions of race, postsecondary education (everyone, has some postsecondary education, no postsecondary education), and age (measured in five-year categories from 20 to 39) for males and females. The *p*-values are calculated allowing for heteroskedastic errors and, when appropriate, clustering at the individual level.

Figure 5.29 Distribution of the Effect of the GED Certificate and High School Graduation on Annual Earnings and Hourly Wage across Models for Females

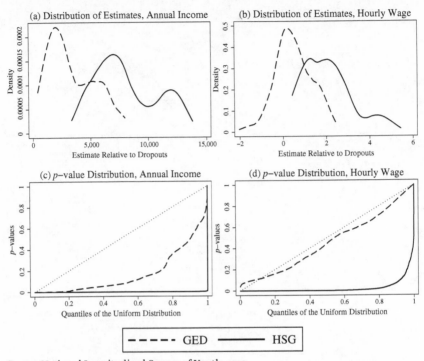

(a) Distribution of Estimates, Annual Income

(b) Distribution of Estimates, Hourly Wage

(c) p–value Distribution, Annual Income

(d) p–value Distribution, Hourly Wage

- - - - - GED　　———— HSG

Source: National Longitudinal Survey of Youth, 1979.

Notes: The top panels plot the estimated coefficients from a series of linear regressions. The bottom panels plot the p-values from a series of estimates against quantiles of a uniform distribution with values between 0 and 1. For more information about the procedure, please see Section W5.3.7 of the Web Appendix. All models control for region, age, year, and AFQT score. The models differ in other controls and subpopulations of the data. The set of models includes all combinations of mother's highest grade completed, urban residence at age 14, family income, lives in the South at age 14, smoked at 15, has had sex by 15, has committed a major crime, and 9th grade GPA. The subpopulations are all partitions of race, postsecondary education (everyone, has some postsecondary education, no postsecondary education), and age (measured in five-year categories from 20 to 39) for males and females. The p-values are calculated allowing for heteroskedastic errors and, when appropriate, clustering at the individual level.

Figure 5.30 Distribution of the Effect of the GED Certificate and High School Graduation on Employment and Hours Worked across Models for Females

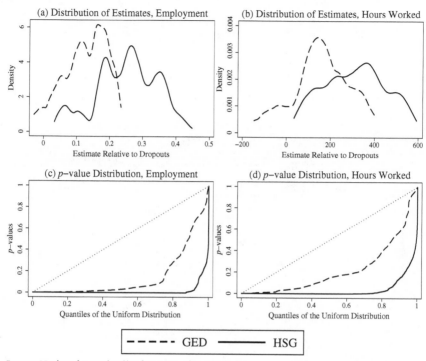

(a) Distribution of Estimates, Employment

(b) Distribution of Estimates, Hours Worked

(c) *p*–value Distribution, Employment

(d) *p*–value Distribution, Hours Worked

------ GED ———— HSG

Source: National Longitudinal Survey of Youth, 1979.
Notes: The top panels plot the estimated coefficients from a series of linear regressions. The bottom panels plot the *p*-values from a series of estimates against quantiles of a uniform distribution with values between 0 and 1. For more information about the procedure, please see Section W5.3.7 of the Web Appendix. All models control for region, age, year, and AFQT score. The models differ in other controls and subpopulations of the data. The set of models includes all combinations of mother's highest grade completed, urban residence at age 14, family income, lives in the South at age 14, smoked at 15, has had sex by 15, has committed a major crime, and 9th grade GPA. The subpopulations are all partitions of race, postsecondary education (everyone, has some postsecondary education, no postsecondary education), and age (measured in five-year categories from 20 to 39) for males and females. The *p*-values are calculated allowing for heteroskedastic errors and, when appropriate, clustering at the individual level.

Figure 5.31 Distribution of the Effect of the GED Certificate and High School Graduation on Labor Force Participation across Models for Females

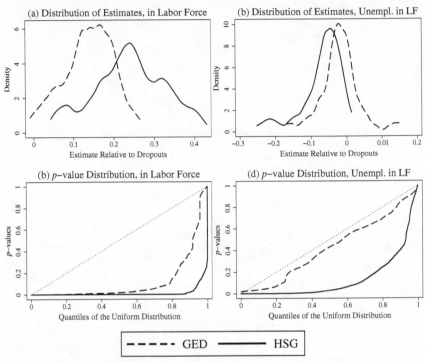

Source: National Longitudinal Survey of Youth, 1979.
Notes: The top panels plot the estimated coefficients from a series of linear regressions. The bottom panels plot the p-values from a series of estimates against quantiles of a uniform distribution with values between 0 and 1. For more information about the procedure, please see Section W5.3.7 of the Web Appendix. All models control for region, age, year, and AFQT score. The models differ in other controls and subpopulations of the data. The set of models includes all combinations of mother's highest grade completed, urban residence at age 14, family income, lives in the South at age 14, smoked at 15, has had sex by 15, has committed a major crime, and 9th grade GPA. The subpopulations are all partitions of race, postsecondary education (everyone, has some postsecondary education, no postsecondary education), and age (measured in five-year categories from 20 to 39) for males and females. The p-values are calculated allowing for heteroskedastic errors and, when appropriate, clustering at the individual level.

effect, the cumulative distribution of p-values should lie along a 45° line starting at the origin. The 45° degree line is the shape of the cumulative distribution of a uniform random variable. This would be the line of perfect equality for a Lorenz curve. Departure of a cumulative distribution from the 45° line indicates the strength of rejection of the null hypothesis. The evidence in Figure 5.26 across numerous models reveals that there is no GED effect.

In contrast, for high school graduation (compared to dropouts), the mean of the coefficients is shifted strongly upward and the cumulative distribution of the p-values departs strongly from the 45° line, suggesting large effects of high school graduation. The same pattern holds for estimated effects on hourly wages, hours worked, and employment.

For women, the pattern is different. (See Figures 5.29–5.31.) There is a strong estimated effect of GED certification and high school graduation on annual income (panels (a) and (c) of Figure 5.29), but not on hourly wages (see panels (b) and (d) of Figure 5.29). This effect arises through greater GED female labor supply (see Figures 5.30 and 5.31). This confirms the finding, previously demonstrated, that GED women work more and earn more but do not have higher hourly wages than other dropouts. High school graduates perform better on all dimensions.

This analysis bolsters the findings from the cross-sectional analyses previously reported. After controlling for their scores on an achievement test—the AFQT—the male GED recipients do not benefit compared to other dropouts on any labor market measure, whereas high school graduates benefit substantially. Female GED recipients have higher annual earnings but not higher hourly wages compared to other dropouts. They simply supply more labor than other dropouts.

5.3.9 THE PERSISTENCE OF BEHAVIOR

Life presents many opportunities to drop out. High school is one of the first; later opportunities arise in the military, employment, marriage, and college. Most GED recipients do not benefit from GED certification and remain lifelong dropouts. Character skills in adult life are relatively stable, although we show in Chapter 9 that they can be changed by intervention throughout childhood and adolescence. Section 5.3.5 demonstrated that few GED recipients who enroll in college make it past the first year. Few receive two- or four-year degrees. Chapter 6 shows that GED recipients are much more likely to drop out of the military compared to high school graduates.

In this section, we consider the persistence of GEDs and dropouts in a variety of life situations beyond high school. We first consider the survival

Figure 5.32 Survival Rates (Males, All Races, All Levels of Postsecondary Education)

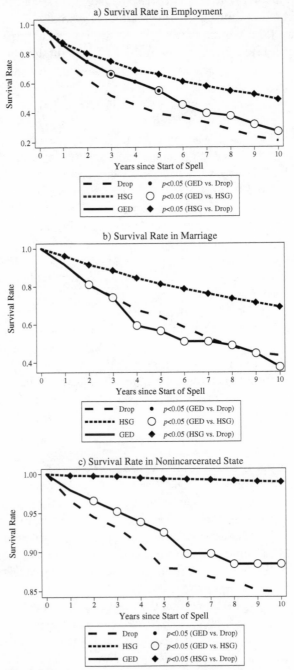

Source: National Longitudinal Survey of Youth, 1979 (NLSY79), Nationally Representative Cross-sectional Sample.

Note: For more information about the procedure, see Section W5.3.8 of the Web Appendix.

Figure 5.33 Survival Rates (Females, All Races, All Levels of Postsecondary Education)

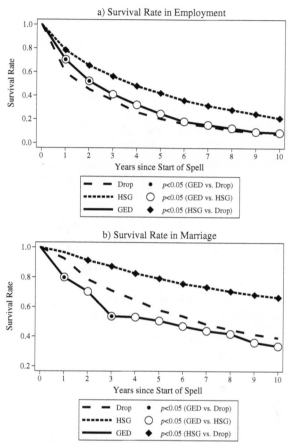

a) Survival Rate in Employment

b) Survival Rate in Marriage

Source: National Longitudinal Survey of Youth, 1979 (NLSY79), Nationally Representative Cross-sectional Sample.
Note: For more information about the procedure, see Section W5.3.8 of the Web Appendix.

rate of dropouts, GED recipients, and high school graduates in a variety of activities (the fraction of people who remain in a state as a function of time). Figures 5.32 and 5.33 present, for males and females respectively, survival rates in employment, marriage, and nonincarceration for dropouts, high school graduates, and GED recipients.[54] The black dots and diamonds on the

54. For more information on the calculation of survival rates, see Section W5.3.8 of the Web Appendix.

lines indicate whether the survivor functions are statistically significantly different from those of dropouts at the 5% level. The circles indicate whether or not GED survivor rates are statistically significantly different from those of high school graduates. GED recipients and dropouts leave jobs, marriage, and enter jail more frequently than high school graduates.[55] Male GED recipients are more likely to divorce than high school graduates. Although some GED recipients might change their ways, most continue throughout their lives dropping out of everything they start at much greater rates than high school graduates.[56]

Chapter 4 shows that during their adolescent years, children who eventually GED certify are as likely—or in some cases more likely—than other dropouts to engage in risky behaviors. Do GED recipients reform later in life? Figure 5.34 shows later-life rates of daily smoking, binge drinking, marijuana use, and self-reported depression for dropouts, GED recipients, and high school graduates. The measures of drug use are reported when respondents are between ages 29 and 37, and depression is reported when respondents are between ages 27 and 35. For all outcomes, GED recipients are similar to high school dropouts and much worse than high school graduates.

We supplement this analysis using the National Health Interview Survey (NHIS), a large, nationally representative data set that contains measures of risky behavior and health. Like some of the other data sources we use, the NHIS data only report the highest level of education attained, so we cannot identify whether college attendees are GED recipients or high school graduates. For this reason, we restrict our analysis to people who do not attend college. Additionally, the NHIS data do not include the time when the GED was received and the time when the outcome studied occurred. We analyze outcomes after age 35. By that age, most GED recipients have certified.

The top panels of Figure 5.35 show several outcomes from the NHIS data related to family structure and receipt of welfare. The top two figures plot rates of being single and living with children and divorce rates for all three groups. GED recipients are more likely than other dropouts or high school graduates to be in these categories. The evidence on divorce rates is consistent with the findings presented in Figures 5.32 and 5.33. The NHIS

---

55. When we eliminate black males from the sample, the survival rates in employment are the same for GEDs and dropouts.

56. Figure 5.33 settles an issue raised in Chapter 4. The higher employment rates of GED women compared to those of other dropouts reported there could have been due to the lower turnover rates or higher job-taking rates. Figure 5.33 shows that it is the latter reason.

Figure 5.34 Health and Personality Outcomes—NLSY79 (All Races, All Levels of Postsecondary Education)

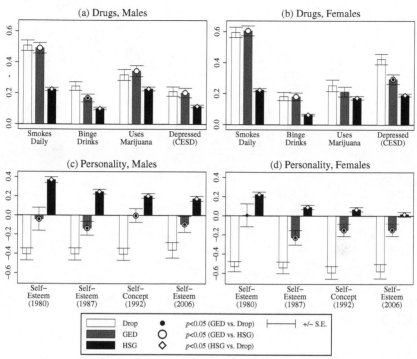

Source: National Longitudinal Survey of Youth, 1979 (NLSY79), Nationally Representative Cross-sectional Sample.

Notes: The estimates for daily smoking, binge drinking, and marijuana use are based on data from the 1992 and 1994 survey years when respondents are between 27 and 37. The estimate for depression are based on the 1992 survey when respondents are between 27 and 35. The sample excludes people who have been to jail. *Variable Definitions:* Smokes Daily—reports smoking daily. Binge Drinks—drinks and typically drinks 5 or more drinks per day when drinking for males or 4 or more drinks per day when drinking for females. Marijuana Last Year—has used marijuana in the past year. Depressed—greater than or equal to 16 on the 20-question version of the Center for Epidemiologic Studies Depression Scale (CES-D). Self-esteem is measured using the 10-item version of the Rosenberg Self-Esteem scale (Rosenberg, 1965). Self-concept is measured using the 7-item version of the Pearlin Mastery Scale (Pearlin et al., 1981). Higher scores represent higher levels of self-concept and self-esteem. The scores have been standardized over the whole population (combining males and females) for each year separately.

Figure 5.35 NHIS—Outcomes (All Races, Age 35–55)

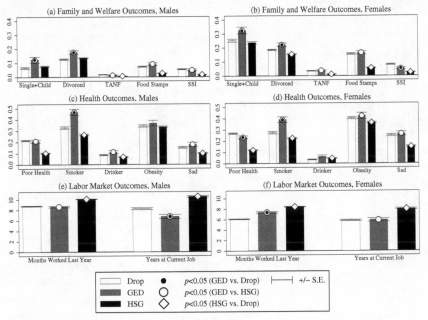

Source: National Health Interview Survey (NHIS), 2004–2007.
Notes: The data collected in the NHIS are obtained through a complex sample design involving stratification, clustering, and multistage sampling. For this reason weights were used in our analysis for means calculation. In addition, STRATUM and PSU were used to estimate variance correctly. For more information about the method, see NHIS user guide. Divorced and Separated were considered as the same category. Single + Child—Proportion of single families with children under age 18 out of all the families with children. TANF and Food Stamps—Proportion of individuals who received any income last year from these welfare programs. SSI—Proportion of individuals who receive Supplemental Security Income. Poor Health—Proportion of people with "Poor" and "Fair" self-reported health. Smoker—Percent of people who are current everyday smokers. Drinker—Proportion of heavy drinkers: for males >14 drinks per week in past year and females >7 drinks per week in past year. Obesity—Proportion of people with BMI≥ 30. Sad—Percent of people who "felt so sad that nothing cheers them up" all/most/some of the time during the past 30 days.

data, however, do not allow us to distinguish whether divorce precedes or follows GED certification, so its interpretation is less clear. GED recipients are as likely to receive welfare as other dropouts.

The middle two panels of Figure 5.35 show that the pattern of differences in adolescent behavior among high school dropouts, GED recipients, and high school graduates persist into adulthood. Compared to high school graduates, GED recipients are more likely to report having poor or fair health (as opposed to good, very good, or excellent health), smoking daily, drinking heavily, being obese, or being depressed. Most of these differences are statistically significant. For most outcomes, GED recipients are similar to other dropouts, but GED recipients are about 10% more likely to smoke daily than other dropouts.

The NHIS data has some information on labor market outcomes. The bottom two panels of Figure 5.35 show the number of months worked in the past year and the number of years worked at the current job for dropouts, GED recipients, and high school graduates who attend college. Male GED recipients work similar hours as high school dropouts. They also spend fewer years at their current job, suggesting that they have higher turnover rates.[57] This is consistent with the data from the NLSY79 displayed in Figure 5.32. In contrast, female GED recipients work more months than high school dropouts, but spend a similar number of years at their current job as other dropouts.

5.4 Panel Data Estimates of Life-Cycle Dynamics

Up to this point we have analyzed outcomes by educational attainment using cross sections of people at different ages. Connecting estimates across ages produces "synthetic" life-cycle profiles that are averages over many different life-cycle trajectories. Profiles constructed in this fashion may not represent the actual life-cycle profiles of any person.[58]

This concern is especially relevant for the study of the impact of GED certification. There are many routes to GED certification, and recipients certify at very different ages (see Figure 4.11). The work experience gained in the years after attaining the GED may have a higher payoff than work experience gained prior to certification. The primary benefit of GED certification may be that it opens doors to career advancement and enhances life-cycle wage growth.

Instead of averaging across different life-cycle trajectories, it would be better to estimate the effect of GED certification longitudinally. The trajectories before and after certification could in principle be compared to those for persons who never certify, who certify later, or both.[59] Many interesting counterfactual comparisons might be made. One could in principle compare persons with different ages of certification and different levels of

57. For their sample of young males, Cameron and Heckman (1993) report similar estimates.

58. See Web Appendix Section W5.4 for a more formal description of the analysis presented in this section.

59. The same people appear at different ages in our cross sections, but we do not observe full life cycles for anyone.

pre- and post-GED work experience. Such a comparison could reveal how the age at which people attain the GED affects their payoff stream. Those receiving GEDs at younger ages might experience more rapid career advancement and hence more rapid wage growth than those receiving GEDs at older ages who have diminished post-GED working lives.

Making such comparisons presents two major problems. The first is that they place great demands on the data. Many possible profiles are associated with different ages of GED certification and levels of pre-GED and post-GED work experience. Even with the large samples at our disposal, we need to simplify the set of possible trajectories to obtain estimates with any precision. The second problem is that the timing of the receipt of a GED and the levels of work experience pre- and postcertification are choice variables. The variables at our disposal may not be sufficient to control for all of the attributes that shape these choices. This creates the potential for serious endogeneity problems.

This section uses the panel data at our disposal to analyze the life-cycle dynamics associated with GED certification. We find that cross-sectional analyses give a fairly reliable guide to the life cycle of men. They are much less accurate for women, who have more complex and diverse patterns of life-cycle dynamics.

We present two distinct analyses based on different measures of work experience. For each analysis, we distinguish the performance of different types of female GED recipients. Our analyses are motivated by the research of Jacob Mincer (1974), who made a fundamental contribution to understanding life-cycle wage dynamics by demonstrating how wages and earnings increase with work experience. He interpreted the growth in wages as arising from on-the-job investments. Another possible interpretation of the same phenomenon is that people are learning by doing.[60]

We follow Mincer and analyze the effect of work experience on labor market outcomes. Our two measures of work experience are (a) cumulative hours of actual work experience and (b) potential experience (age at survey minus the age at which the person left school). The latter measure is widely used in applied work and has the advantage that it only depends on one choice—the age at which a person leaves school. Cumulative "actual experience" is vulnerable to multiple sources of endogeneity. However, "potential experience" is vulnerable to mismeasurement of experience.

---

60. See Heckman, Lochner, and Cossa (2003) for an analysis distinguishing the sources of life cycle wage growth.

The major findings from our analyses are as follows. (1) For both men and women there is no evidence that GED certification boosts the rate of earnings growth with experience regardless of the measure of work experience analyzed. (2) Using potential work experience, we find estimates that are consistent with cross-sectional results established in previous sections of this chapter. (3) Using actual work experience, our panel estimates are consistent with the cross-sectional results for men, but not for women. With the exception of women at the lowest levels of actual experience, female GED recipients do not have higher earnings at each level of experience.

For each measure of experience, we conduct two analyses. The first builds on the work of Mincer and assumes that the rate of growth of earnings with work experience is the same for persons at all educational levels. The second estimates separate effects for pre-GED and post-GED work experience to determine whether certification boosts wage and earnings growth. We find no evidence of such a boost.

5.4.1 ANALYSIS BY ACTUAL WORK EXPERIENCE

We first analyze labor market outcomes by educational attainment at different levels of *actual* work experience. Initially, we do not distinguish between pre- and post-GED work experience. Actual work experience is defined as cumulative hours worked since age 18 divided by 2,000, making the units one full year of work experience.[61]

Figures 5.36 and 5.37 (for males and females, respectively) display labor market outcomes by educational attainment at different levels of actual work experience.[62,63] We use the NLSY79 histories up to age 40 to measure educational attainment and work histories. There are only four bins in each figure. The first bin is for persons with 0–4 years of work experience, pre- or post-GED. The icons denoting outcomes are shifted slightly at different levels of experience in the graph to improve the visual display. The lines connecting the bins are drawn to enhance the reader's perception of the graphs. We do not plot outcomes for each year of experience.[64]

Outcomes are reported for all people with the indicated levels of education and work experience. The same person may show up in multiple bins. Thus a person with 4–8 years of actual experience would show up in at least

---

61. We assume that work experience below 18 has negligible effects on wages.
62. Due to the sparsity of the data, we create bins of experience.
63. See Web Appendix Section W5.4 for a more complete discussion of this analysis.
64. For each bin, the average years of actual work experience generally differs by educational status. It also varies across bins.

Figure 5.36 Ability- and Background-Adjusted Labor Market Outcomes by Actual Experience (OLS)—(Males, All Levels of Postsecondary Education)

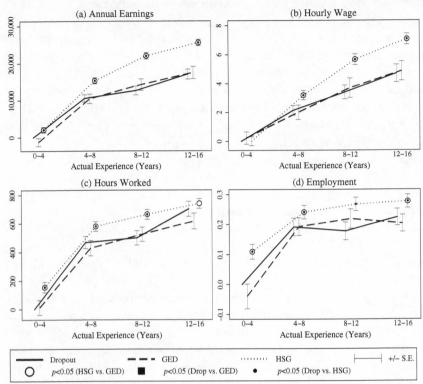

Sources: National Longitudinal Survey of Youth, 1979, Nationally Representative Sample.
Controls: Region of residence, race, AFQT adjusted for schooling at time of test, broken home status at age 14, family income in 1979, mother's highest grade completed, urban residence at age 14, residence in the South at age 14, and factors based on adolescent risky behavior and criminal behavior.
Notes: Respondents are classified as GED recipients if they earn a GED before the age of 40. The sample excludes people once they have been to jail. Actual experience is the cumulative hours worked divided by 2,000. All regressions allow for heteroskedastic errors and, when appropriate, clustering at the individual level. For more information about the methodology, please see Web Appendix Section W5.4.

Figure 5.37 Ability- and Background-Adjusted Labor Market Outcomes by Actual Experience (OLS)—(Females, All Levels of Postsecondary Education)

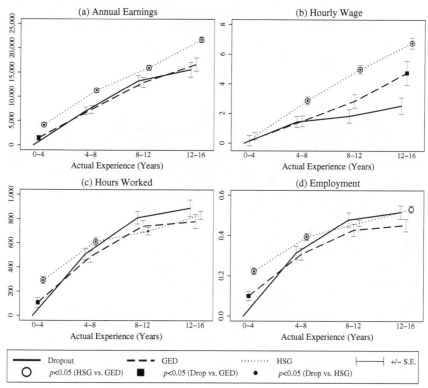

Source: National Longitudinal Survey of Youth, 1979, Nationally Representative Sample.
Controls: Region of residence, race, AFQT adjusted for schooling at time of test, broken home status at age 14, family income in 1979, mother's highest grade completed, urban residence at age 14, residence in the South at age 14, and factors based on adolescent risky behavior and criminal behavior.
Notes: Respondents are classified as GED recipients if they earn a GED before the age of 40. The sample excludes people once they have been to jail. Actual experience is the cumulative hours worked divided by 2,000. All regressions allow for heteroskedastic errors and, when appropriate, clustering at the individual level. For more information about the methodology, please see Web Appendix Section W5.4.

two bins and possibly more if followed further over the life cycle. The level of education reported in each bin is the highest level attained by the person, although the work experience is aggregated across all educational attainment levels (at the time the experience was achieved) for each person. Everyone appears at least once in the category 0–4 years of actual experience.[65]

These graphs are to be compared with their age counterparts in Figures 5.6 and 5.7. In Figures 5.6 and 5.7, persons age 20–24 can have very different years of actual work experience. For males, the estimates based on actual work experience show a very similar pattern to what is obtained from the cross-sectional analyses. Male GED recipients and high school dropouts have nearly identical outcome measures, whereas high school graduates outperform both.

For females, the two analyses tell different stories. In the cross-sectional analyses, female GED recipients have higher annual earnings than other dropouts at each age because they are more likely to be in the labor force and be employed (see Figure 5.7). In contrast, in the panel estimates based on actual experience, only at 0–4 years of actual experience do female GED recipients have higher annual earnings than other dropouts. At 12–16 years of actual experience, female GED recipients earn somewhat higher hourly wages than other dropouts, but the estimated effect of the GED on earnings is not statistically significant.[66]

For women, the difference between an analysis based on actual work experience and a cross-sectional analysis is due to a group of dropouts who are rarely employed. Figure 5.38 shows the fraction of women who never accrue more than four years (8,000 hours) of actual work experience between ages 18 and 40.[67] Permanent dropouts who do not GED certify are about 15 percentage points more likely to be in this category than GED recipients. These persistent nonworkers show up at every age in Figure 5.7 but appear only in the first experience category of Figure 5.37. Most of the women not working at ages 20–24 are not working at ages 35–39, producing a roughly constant estimated GED effect on labor supply in cross-sectional estimates. If persons with low lifetime hours supplied to the market do not GED certify (and few do), the presence of a group that does not acquire work experience makes the benefits of GED certification on labor supply and earnings

65. Persons with no work experience are dropped. Very few observations are dropped for this reason. For women it is less than 1%; for men it is even smaller.

66. This is a very small and select group of women.

67. The analogous figure for males is in Section W5.4 of the Web Appendix. For males, there are no statistically significant differences between GED recipients and permanent dropouts.

Figure 5.38 Fraction of Females with Less Than 4 Years (8,000 Hours) of Actual Experience by Educational Status

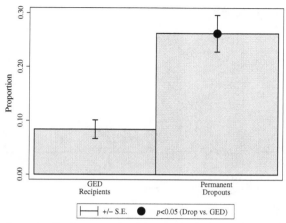

Source: National Longitudinal Survey of Youth, 1979, Nationally Representative Sample.
Notes: Respondents are classified as GED recipients if they earn a GED before the age of 40. The sample excludes people once they have been to jail.

appear to be larger in the cross section at each age. This finding explains why the employment rates and annual earnings of female GED recipients are only high in the interval 0–4 years of actual experience. This interval includes some women who will have many more years of work experience as well as those who will not. For women who work more than four years, there is no estimated effect of the GED on labor supply.

5.4.2 ANALYSES BASED ON POTENTIAL EXPERIENCE

Actual experience is endogenous. Our conditioning variables may not be sufficient to control for it. A commonly used alternative measure of work experience that circumvents the endogeneity problem is to use "potential experience"—the number of years since leaving school.[68] Figures 5.39 and 5.40 present estimates based on potential work experience analogous to those of Figures 5.36 and 5.37.[69] The estimates based on potential experience are very similar to the estimates obtained from cross sections. Age is a good approximation to potential experience. In this case, they are similar because GED recipients and dropouts leave school at roughly the same age (slightly less than a year apart on average) and most males work at each age.

68. See Mincer (1974) where this measure is used.
69. See Web Appendix Section W5.4 for a further description of the analysis.

Figure 5.39 Ability- and Background-Adjusted Labor Market Outcomes by Potential Experience (OLS)—(Males, All Levels of Postsecondary Education)

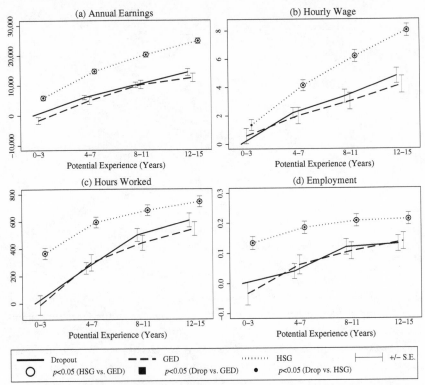

Source: National Longitudinal Survey of Youth, 1979, Nationally Representative Sample.
Controls: Region of residence, race, AFQT adjusted for schooling at time of test, broken home status at age 14, family income in 1979, mother's highest grade completed, urban residence at age 14, residence in the South at age 14, and factors based on adolescent risky behavior and criminal behavior.
Notes: Respondents are classified as GED recipients if they earn a GED before the age of 40. The sample excludes people once they have been to jail. Potential experience is the number of years since exiting high school. All regressions allow for heteroskedastic errors and, when appropriate, clustering at the individual level. For more information about the methodology, please see Web Appendix Section W5.4.

Figure 5.40 Ability- and Background-Adjusted Labor Market Outcomes by Potential Experience (OLS)—(Females, All Levels of Postsecondary Education)

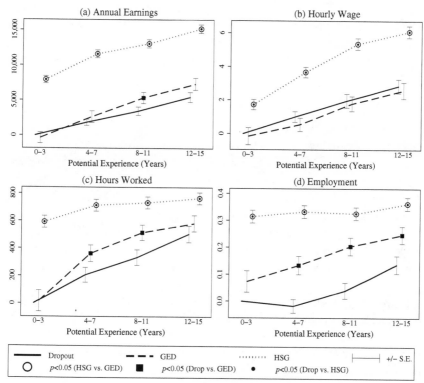

Source: National Longitudinal Survey of Youth, 1979, Nationally Representative Sample.
Controls: Region of residence, race, AFQT adjusted for schooling at time of test, broken home status at age 14, family income in 1979, mother's highest grade completed, urban residence at age 14, residence in the South at age 14, and factors based on adolescent risky behavior and criminal behavior.

Notes: Respondents are classified as GED recipients if they earn a GED before the age of 40. The sample excludes people once they have been to jail. Potential experience is the number of years since exiting high school. All regressions allow for heteroskedastic errors and, when appropriate, clustering at the individual level. For more information about the methodology, please see Web Appendix Section W5.4.

Male high school graduates have higher levels of earnings, hours worked, and wages compared to those of GED recipients or dropouts. Adjusting for their greater ability, male GED recipients and other dropouts have virtually identical outcomes at each level of potential experience. As is found in the cross section, female GED recipients appear to have higher earnings at each age because they are more likely to work than other dropouts.[70]

5.4.3 DOES PRE-GED EXPERIENCE HAVE THE SAME EFFECT AS POST-GED EXPERIENCE?

The analyses reported in the previous two subsections do not distinguish between the effect of work experience pre-GED and the effect of post-GED work experience. It may be that the GED confers benefits to wage and earnings growth that accrue only gradually. The analysis in this section makes this distinction. We find no difference in levels or rates of growth of wages and earnings pre- and post-GED certification except for one group of women, but even for this group the effect comes through their labor supply. This section also provides an implicit test of the validity of our set of control variables.

Although the NLSY79 contains many measures of background and ability, it might not include all relevant background characteristics that affect the decision to take the GED, to work, or the other outcomes studied. There might be unobserved differences among dropouts, GED recipients, and high school graduates that affect their labor market outcomes and their certification and labor supply choices for which we do not properly control. Differences could also arise if people change their behavior after the age at which our measures of their background and abilities are recorded. This change in behavior could be associated with receiving a GED or other life events.

To investigate these possibilities and to examine whether receipt of a GED boosts wage growth, we compare the labor market outcomes of eventual GED recipients before and after they receive their GED. We estimate a statistical model in which we allow persons who will eventually earn a GED but are currently dropouts to have different rates of growth of earnings (and other outcomes) with experience before and after they GED certify.[71] If we have properly controlled for unobservables, we should find no evidence of differences or differential growth rates.

---

70. As previously discussed, this effect arises from the core group of persistent dropouts in the category 0–4 years of actual work experience.

Figures 5.41–5.42 present labor market outcomes by actual experience for dropouts who never earn a GED, dropouts who will eventually earn a GED but have not yet earned one, GED recipients, and high school gradu-ates.[72] In these figures, persons can be in only one category, unlike the categories used to create Figures 5.36–5.37 and 5.39–5.40. In constructing these figures, we use histories up to age 40. The post-GED estimate in the interval 8–12 is for someone who has been in the labor market for a total of 8–12 years and has also had a GED for 8–12 years. The pre-GED estimate in this interval is for a person with 8–12 years of work experience who does not have a GED but will eventually obtain one.

At each experience level, we test the difference between the pre- and post-GED experience profiles. A "*" indicates that the difference between the pre-GED and post-GED estimate is statistically significant. We stop the analysis at 12 years of actual experience. Few GED recipients work for more than 12 years before earning a GED.

Using actual work experience, on average, GED recipients do not per-form better than pre-GED recipients. There is no evidence that the GED produces greater wage growth with work experience. At 0–4 years of actual experience, male pre-GED recipients have higher annual earnings than post-GED recipients.[73]

For women, the only statistically significant differences between the out-comes of pre- and post-GED recipients arise from persons with 0–4 years of la-bor market experience. Post-GED females are more likely to be employed than pre-GED females. This estimated effect is closely related to the pattern previ-ously discussed in our analysis of Figure 5.37. For women, receipt of the GED is associated with entry into the labor market. Figure 5.37 suggests that the GED may produce moderate boosts in hourly wages for females with high levels of actual experience. However, Figure 5.42 shows that in fact, female GED recipients do not perform any better than dropouts who later earn a GED.

Figures 5.43 and 5.44 show results parallel to the ones just discussed for estimates based on potential experience. For men at the same level of

71. We estimate a standard model of outcomes partitioned by mutually exclu-sive education and experience categories. We normalize the estimates against the category of permanent (through age 40) dropouts with 0–4 years of actual work experience.

72. "Never" means through age 40. See Web Appendix Section W5.4 for a further description of the analysis.

73. This is consistent with the phenomenon of Ashenfelter's dip associated with men's receipt of the GED noted in Chapter 4. Many men earn their GED when they are unemployed, and hence their pre-GED earnings are depressed.

Figure 5.41 Ability- and Background-Adjusted Labor Market Outcomes by Actual Experience (OLS)—(Males, All Levels of Postsecondary Education)

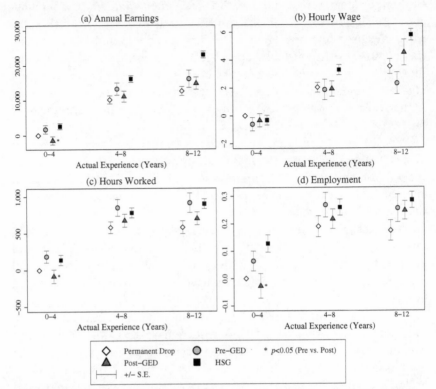

Source: National Longitudinal Survey of Youth, 1979, Nationally Representative Sample.
Controls: Region of residence, race, AFQT adjusted for schooling at time of test, broken home status at age 14, family income in 1979, mother's highest grade completed, urban residence at age 14, residence in the South at age 14, and factors based on adolescent risky behavior and criminal behavior.
Notes: Respondents are classified as GED recipients if they earn a GED before the age of 40. The sample excludes people once they have been to jail. Actual experience is the cumulative hours worked divided by 2,000. All regressions allow for heteroskedastic errors and, when appropriate, clustering at the individual level. For more information about the methodology, please see Web Appendix Section W5.4.

experience, there are no differences in labor market outcomes between pre- and post-GED recipients. In contrast, women at the same level of experience who have a GED supply more labor than women who will eventually earn one.

This finding is consistent with our previous discussion of the employment patterns surrounding receipt of a GED for women. Many women earn

Figure 5.42 Ability- and Background-Adjusted Labor Market Outcomes by Actual Experience (OLS)—(Females, All Levels of Postsecondary Education)

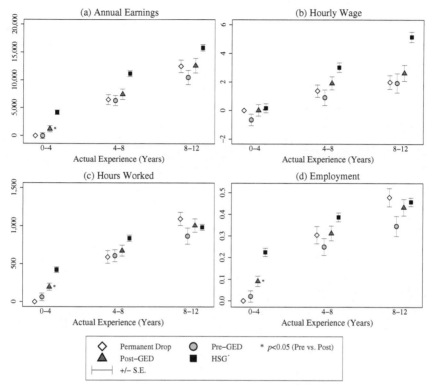

Source: National Longitudinal Survey of Youth, 1979, Nationally Representative Sample.
Controls: Region of residence, race, AFQT adjusted for schooling at time of test, broken home status at age 14, family income in 1979, mother's highest grade completed, urban residence at age 14, residence in the South at age 14, and factors based on adolescent risky behavior and criminal behavior.
Notes: Respondents are classified as GED recipients if they earn a GED before the age of 40. The sample excludes people once they have been to jail. Actual experience is the cumulative hours worked divided by 2,000. All regressions allow for heteroskedastic errors and, when appropriate, clustering at the individual level. For more information about the methodology, please see Web Appendix Section W5.4.

a GED as they are entering the labor market. There are no hourly wage benefits of certification for any groups. These analyses suggest little effect of the GED, except possibly on female labor supply. Even for labor supply, the estimates might not reflect a causal effect of the GED. The data are consistent with the interpretation that the women who chose to take the GED are also the ones who want to work more in the future. The estimated

Figure 5.43 Ability- and Background-Adjusted Labor Market Outcomes by Potential Experience (OLS)—(Males, All Levels of Postsecondary Education)

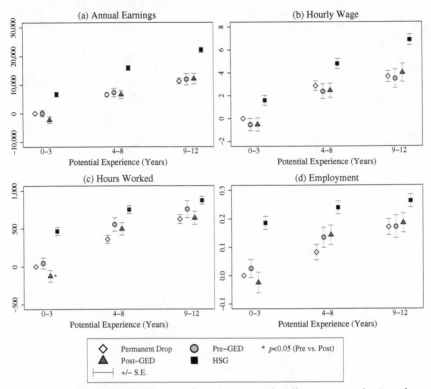

Source: National Longitudinal Survey of Youth, 1979, Nationally Representative Sample.
Controls: region of residence, race, AFQT adjusted for schooling at time of test, broken home status at age 14, family income in 1979, mother's highest grade completed, urban residence at age 14, residence in the South at age 14, and factors based on adolescent risky behavior and criminal behavior.
Notes: Respondents are classified as GED recipients if they earn a GED before the age of 40. The sample excludes people once they have been to jail. Potential experience is the number of years since exiting high school. All regressions allow for heteroskedastic errors and, when appropriate, clustering at the individual level. For more information, please see Web Appendix Section W5.4.

Figure 5.44 Ability- and Background-Adjusted Labor Market Outcomes by Potential Experience (OLS)—(Females, All Levels of Postsecondary Education)

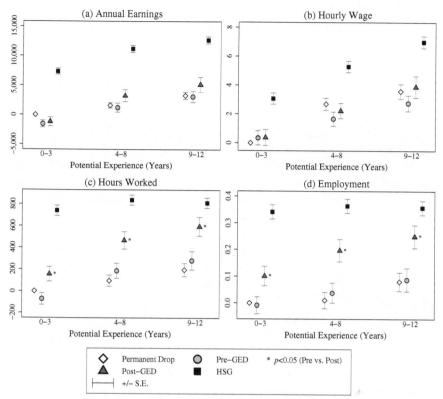

Source: National Longitudinal Survey of Youth, 1979, Nationally Representative Sample.
Controls: Region of residence, race, AFQT adjusted for schooling at time of test, broken home status at age 14, family income in 1979, mother's highest grade completed, urban residence at age 14, residence in the South at age 14, and factors based on adolescent risky behavior and criminal behavior.
Notes: Respondents are classified as GED recipients if they earn a GED before the age of 40. The sample excludes people once they have been to jail. Potential experience is the number of years since exiting high school. All regressions allow for heteroskedastic errors and, when appropriate, clustering at the individual level. For more information, please see Web Appendix Section W5.4.

GED effect might be a selection effect, where certification is a marker for tastes for work.[74,75]

5.4.4 DISTINGUISHING AMONG DIFFERENT FEMALE GED RECIPIENTS

Female GED recipients differ among themselves in their life experiences. Approximately 40% of female GED recipients drop out of high school to have a child. As shown in Chapter 4, these women have traits different from those of other GED recipients. On average they have the same AFQT scores, but they are less likely to commit crimes, smoke, or drink. They also complete more grades in school before they drop out.

Figure 5.45 shows annual earnings for four different types of female GED recipients compared to permanent (through age 40) dropouts: (1) GED recipients who are pregnant before dropping out and attend any postsecondary education, any time before age 40, (2) GED recipients who are pregnant before dropping out and do not attend postsecondary education before age 40, (3) GED recipients who are not pregnant before dropping out and attend college at some time before age 40, and (4) all other female GED recipients. The percentage of GED recipients in each group is displayed in the legend.

This graph shows that female GED recipients who eventually attend college and females who drop out of high school due to pregnancy benefit from GED certification. The remaining category of female GED recipients do about as well as other dropouts who do not certify.[76] The evidence for women who drop out due to pregnancy is consistent with two possible, and not mutually exclusive, explanations. First, as shown in Chapter 4, these women have higher levels of character skills compared to other female GEDs who drop out for other reasons. When we adjust for our measures of these skills, we do not eliminate the benefits received by pregnant dropouts. Second, these women might change their preferences or motivations due to

74. This selection effect could arise whether or not there is a causal effect of the GED. Selection could arise because some women anticipate a real benefit from certification or because the same tastes for future work drive the certification decision and the decision to work in the future.

75. In all of these analyses, we compare people at fixed ages or levels of actual experience. A more complete analysis would condition simultaneously on both dimensions. Unfortunately, the small sizes of the samples at our disposal limit our capacity to do so.

76. "College" is defined as ever attending any level of college, including vocational training programs—measured through age 40.

Figure 5.45 Annual Earnings by Type of Female GED Recipient (All Races, Background- and Ability-Adjusted)

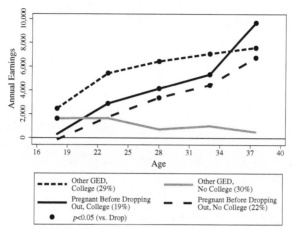

Source: National Longitudinal Survey of Youth, 1979, Nationally Representative Sample.
Controls: Age, region of residence, year, race, AFQT adjusted for schooling at time of test, broken home status at age 14, family income in 1979, mother's highest grade completed, urban residence at age 14, residence in the South at age 14, and factors based on adolescent risky behavior and criminal behavior.
Notes: Respondents are classified as GED recipients if they earn a GED before the age of 40. The sample excludes people once they have been to jail. Regressions exclude those who report earning more than $300,000 (2005$). All regressions allow for heteroskedastic errors and, when appropriate, clustering at the individual level.

the birth of their children.[77] Unfortunately, we do not have measures of their character skills over the life cycle, so we cannot identify whether they have experienced a change in their cognitive or character skills.[78]

5.4.5 IS THERE A CAUSAL EFFECT OF THE GED FOR WOMEN?

We find no evidence of a causal effect of the GED for men. The evidence from our cross-sectional analysis suggests that the GED might have a causal effect for women that arises from their greater labor force participation and employment. The evidence from our panel analysis substantially qualifies our cross-sectional analysis for women. Any estimated

77. Preferences and expectations may change. Constraints surely change when they have a child.

78. A third explanation is that the women are subject to financial constraints because they need to support their children, and this induces changes in their behavior. We cannot distinguish between changes in constraints and changes in preferences or skills.

female GED labor supply effects arise from a group of female dropouts who rarely work.

We cannot rule out the possibility that GED certification induces greater labor supply for women. A natural question is, why is there no effect for men? An alternative explanation of our evidence that we find more plausible is that women who have greater preferences for work, however arrived at, are more likely to GED certify as a way to facilitate employment and gain the educational credentials that improve employability.[79] GED certification signals their greater taste for work. The evidence in Chapter 4 shows that women who drop out of high school due to pregnancy are more likely to attain GEDs after their youngest children can safely be placed in child care. Many go on to attend some form of postsecondary education. These more motivated female GEDs obtain their credentials earlier in life and work more than permanent dropouts or most other GEDs who eventually attain their certificates. Many have better character skills before they drop out of school. Our evidence of an estimated GED effect may be a consequence of the inadequacy of our measures of skills leading to selection bias or because of a change in skills that occurs after our measures are taken. In our view, the weight of the evidence favors a selection story.

5.5 The Female Advantage

A consistent finding of the analyses in this book is that female GED recipients generally have better social skills (relative to uncertified dropouts) than male GED recipients. This pattern shows up more generally in the sorting of males and females into occupations classified by their average skills (see Figures 5.46 and 5.47). O*NET[80] provides data on the average level of cognitive, character, and physical skills in the occupations selected by persons of different educational attainment and gender. Using the ACS data (which only reports final educational attainment and hence cannot distinguish between college graduates who earned a GED certificate from those who earned a high school degree), we plot the O*NET occupational scores of men and women classified by education. Observe that female

---

79. Our study suggests that women who pass the GED are more motivated. Their decision to take the GED might also reflect motivation to enter the workforce. Jepsen, Mueser, and Troske (2011), using a sample of women who attempt the GED, find that those who pass and those who fail earn the same. They include nonworkers, so their analysis captures employment effects. Controlling for motivation in this fashion, they find no GED effect.

80. More information on O*NET is available at http://www.doleta.gov/reports /DESA_skill.cfm.

Figure 5.46 Average Occupational Factor Scores by Final Education—Males

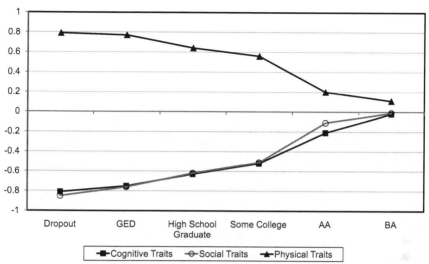

Source: The American Community Survey, 2009, and O*NET. (More information on O*NET is available at http://www.doleta.gov/reports/DESA_skill.cfm.)
Notes: All educational categories are final education at time of interview. Each factor is based on the following O*NET occupational importance scores: Cognitive—active learning, analytical thinking, complex problem solving, critical thinking, deductive reasoning, inductive reasoning, interpretation of meaning, math reasoning, mathematics, processing information, reading comprehension, creative thinking, updating knowledge, and visualization. Social—communicate to outside organizations, concern for others, customer or personal service, establish relationships, leadership, oral expression, persuasion, social perceptiveness, speaking, writing, written expression, active listening, and cooperation. Physical Traits—arm and hand steadiness, control and precision, coordination, depth perception, explosive strength, finger dexterity, gross body coordination, gross body equilibrium, manual dexterity, multi-limb coordination, reaction time, spatial orientation, stamina, static strength, stress tolerance, trunk strength, and wrist and finger speed.

GED scores on social traits are much higher than male GED scores—a pattern that holds true for other education levels as well.

Not surprisingly, more educated people sort into jobs requiring less physical strength and more cognitive and personality skills. For males, the occupations selected by GED recipients (as measured by average traits of workers in the occupation) are barely different from those selected by dropouts. For females, there is a much sharper difference, especially in personality (social skills) sorting. Females generally sort into more non-cognitively demanding occupations than do their male counterparts.

Figure 5.47 Average Occupational Factor Scores by Final Education—Females

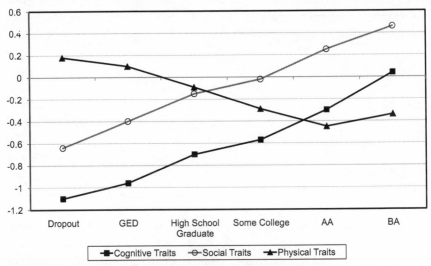

Source: The American Community Survey, 2009, and O*NET. (More information on O*NET is available at http://www.doleta.gov/reports/DESA_skill.cfm.)
Notes: All educational categories are final education at time of interview. Each factor is based on the following O*NET occupational importance scores: Cognitive—active learning, analytical thinking, complex problem solving, critical thinking, deductive reasoning, inductive reasoning, interpretation of meaning, math reasoning, mathematics, processing information, reading comprehension, creative thinking, updating knowledge, and visualization. Social—communicate to outside organizations, concern for others, customer or personal service, establish relationships, leadership, oral expression, persuasion, social perceptiveness, speaking, writing, written expression, active listening, and cooperation. Physical Traits—arm and hand steadiness, control and precision, coordination, depth perception, explosive strength, finger dexterity, gross body coordination, gross body equilibrium, manual dexterity, multi-limb coordination, reaction time, spatial orientation, stamina, static strength, stress tolerance, trunk strength, and wrist and finger speed.

5.6 Summary and Conclusions

This chapter summarizes and extends the previous literature on the effects of GED certification. It estimates the social and economic benefits of GED certification for numerous adult outcomes using a variety of major data sets. Consistent with the previous literature, we find that GED certification is a poor substitute for high school graduation. After accounting for differences in their preexisting ability, GED recipients are virtually identical to other dropouts on almost all of the outcomes we study.

After controlling for their higher cognitive ability, male GED recipients are nearly indistinguishable from other male dropouts with regard to labor market outcomes, including annual earnings, hourly wages, employment, and hours worked. Female GED recipients have higher annual earnings than other dropouts because they are more likely to be employed, not because they earn higher hourly wages. Our analysis shows that female GED recipients are more likely to participate in the labor force compared to other dropouts, but are not more likely to be employed if they do participate in the labor force. This finding is consistent with the interpretation that women who do not plan to work in the future have no incentive to earn a GED. Estimated effects of certification on annual earnings are primarily for women who attend college or are pregnant before dropping out. Many in this group have high levels of measured cognitive and character skills prior to dropping out of school. Even for these groups, any differences between GEDs and dropouts are largely confined to their effects on labor supply and so the interpretation of the estimated female effect is ambiguous. It may be due to a selection effect, or it may reflect a causal effect of certification. We feel that the weight of the evidence supports the interpretation of the estimated GED effect as arising primarily from a selection effect.

Many GED recipients attend a two- or four- year college, but only around 4% complete a bachelor's degree. GED recipients who obtain bachelor's degrees have annual earnings similar to those of high school graduates with bachelor's degrees, but the GED recipients earn their degrees later, which reduces the present value of their earnings by over 30%.

We find little evidence that the economic benefits to GED certification increase with work experience. GED recipients and dropouts have very similar life cycle hourly wage profiles. The GED certificate does not send a positive signal in the labor market. With the exception of labor supply for women, GED recipients perform the same in the labor market before and after they obtain a GED. For women, obtaining a GED appears to coincide with their decision to enter the labor force.

GED recipients are very similar to other high school dropouts on a variety of nonlabor market outcomes, including divorce, incarceration, health, welfare receipt, and measures of later life personality. Although some GED recipients might change their skills and motivations as part of the process of obtaining a GED, for most the deficits in skills that led GED recipients to drop out of high school appear to persist over their life cycles. These conclusions survive across many different model specifications and demographic groups.

5.7 Methodological Appendix

In making valid inferences about the effect of the GED on outcomes, it is important to control for differences in characteristics between GED recipients and other dropouts that exist prior to the certification decision.[81] Failure to do so could produce substantially biased estimates of the effect of GED certification. It would be ideal in studying the average benefits of GED certification to be able to randomly assign dropouts to GED status and compare their outcomes to those of dropouts randomly denied the opportunity to take the exam. Random assignment would, on average, equalize preexisting differences between treatments and controls.[82] Since we do not have access to experimental data on GED certification, we are forced to use nonexperimental or "quasi-experimental" methods that adjust for preexisting differences.

Quasi-experimental methods operate in the following fashion. Denote Y as an outcome studied. For specificity, let it be earnings. Let D denote receipt ($D=1$) or nonreceipt ($D=0$) of a GED. A standard econometric model writes

$$Y = \alpha_0 + \alpha_1 D + U, \qquad (5.1)$$

where U represents unobserved (or uncontrolled) factors that help to determine Y and that might in part also determine D. "α_1" is the causal effect of the GED. A least-squares regression of Y on D estimates the mean difference between GED recipients and dropouts ($E(Y|D=1) - E(Y|D=0)$), which is not necessarily the same as the causal effect of D on Y holding U fixed (α_1). The problem is that the least-squares effect of D on Y includes α_1 and any effect of U on Y that is mediated through D.[83]

A standard procedure for constructing causal estimates is to control for the biasing effect of U on D using a variety of plausible, exogenous determinants of Y and D, which we denote by X. For example, a standard procedure is to estimate a model where $U = \alpha_2 X + V$ and V is assumed to be uncorrelated with D and X. Substituting this expression for U, we can write the model of Equation (5.1) as

$$Y = \alpha_0 + \alpha_1 D + \alpha_2 X + V. \qquad (5.2)$$

81. See Heckman, LaLonde, and Smith (1999) for one survey of the methodologies used in this chapter.

82. Random assignment, however, can only answer a limited set of policy-relevant questions. See, for example, Heckman (1992), Heckman and Smith (1998), Heckman, LaLonde, and Smith (1999), and Heckman and Vytlacil (2007).

83. See, for example, Haavelmo (1943).

Under the stated conditions, controlling for X allows analysts to identify the *ceteris paribus* causal effect of D on Y.[84] Another procedure that is available if the analyst has access to panel data is to compute the difference in earnings before and after persons obtain the GED. This approach eliminates components of U that are present before and after certification is obtained, thereby eliminating this source of bias.

5.7.1 ROBUST EVIDENCE

One problem with conventional analyses is that analysts may not agree on which variables to include in X. Such choices can critically affect the estimates of α_1. There is no purely statistical criterion for selecting X, although some pretend otherwise.[85] We use economic theory and previous research in empirical economics to guide the selection of X, but it is an inherently controversial exercise.

Equation (5.2) is a version of what economists call an hedonic model. It relates the outcome measure Y to market determinants of productivity, which in this instance are D and X. If Y is income, one can interpret α_1 and α_2 as prices—rewards per unit attributes of D and X respectively.

A large and well-established literature shows the benefits for earnings of human capital investments such as schooling and post-school training (see, e.g., Mincer, 1974; Rubinstein and Weiss, 2006). There is ample evidence that measures of both cognitive and noncognitive ability affect earnings (see, e.g., Almlund et al., 2011; Borghans et al., 2008; Heckman and Kautz, 2012).

In order to minimize any controversy surrounding the adjustments employed in the analysis of this chapter, we use a variety of samples and standard measures of productivity and motivation to adjust for preexisting differences among persons that should not be attributed to the GED. We also use a variety of econometric methods to adjust for differences among the different educational groups in their backgrounds. We avoid relying on any particular methodology or data set to shape our conclusions. We place our estimates in the context of the received literature.[86,87]

---

84. The method of matching is a nonparametric version of this procedure. See Heckman (2008b).

85. Using all of the available X can produce substantial bias. See Heckman and Navarro (2004).

86. This methodology is used in all careful empirical research in economics. Nobel Laureates Simon Kuznets and his student, Robert Fogel, both preached and practiced this approach. See Fogel (1987).

87. An additional problem that plagues any study of wages and hours worked is that analysts can only measure wages for working persons. See Heckman (2001).

5.7.2 AVOIDING PRETESTING BIAS

In the text and in the Web Appendix, we summarize literally thousands of estimates of GED effects using multiple data sets with a variety of specifications. In reporting statistically significant "effects" from any particular empirical specification, one must address the problem that arises from "fishing" the data, that is, searching among alternative models (with different X and different functional forms) to find a set of "statistically significant" outcomes. This is a standard practice in social science that is used in many of the studies reviewed in the Web Appendix.[88]

Even though many models are fit, the standard errors and significance levels of coefficients typically reported ignore the messy process that leads to their selection. Few studies conduct extensive sensitivity studies that examine how variations in sets of adjustment variables and specifications affect the reported outcomes and whether reported estimates hold up in other data sets. Choosing one model from a candidate set of models and ignoring the consequences of the search process that leads to the final choice of a model spuriously distorts true p-values and produces biased estimates (see Bancroft, 1944; Judge and Bock, 1978).

In truth, a lot of fishing goes on in most studies in empirical social science. Reported p-values are substantially downward biased. No simple procedure is available for addressing this problem since most analysts do not tabulate all of the preliminary models that are estimated prior to reporting a final specification. The standard errors and p-values assume that the reported model is the first and only empirical model that is estimated.

Prisoners do not report wages, nor do persons who choose not to work. The measured wages of workers may or may not overstate the potential wages of all persons of a given educational category. This gives rise to *selection bias*, a pervasive problem in the analysis of social science data. Those who work are likely to be those who have good wage offers from the market. Selection can also work the other way. For example, evidence presented in Heckman (1980), and, recently reconfirmed in Mulligan and Rubinstein (2008), shows that for educated women, it is more likely that high-wage women stay at home to raise their kids. Such selection reduces the level of the measured wages of female workers. But how this effect operates in distorting comparisons of the wages of GED recipients and dropouts is far from obvious, since there is selective nonparticipation in both educational categories. Low-wage men are more likely to be incarcerated, for example. Such selection inflates the measured wages of all men compared to what would be observed if it were possible to obtain market wages for the incarcerated, but how it affects the difference in measured wages between GED recipients and dropouts is far from obvious. Such selection problems also plague experiments. We use a variety of methods to correct for this fundamental problem in an effort to produce a robust analysis.

88. See Web Appendix Section W5.2.

We address this problem by estimating a large collection of possible models reporting the distributions of a variety of fitted models.

5.7.3 DIRECT AND INDIRECT EFFECTS

We estimate both direct and indirect effects of GED certification. The direct effect is the effect on an outcome of attaining a GED and stopping there. The indirect effect is the effect that arises from the options created by GED certification. It arises from two components that are multiplied to produce the indirect effect: (a) the effect of GED certification on attaining any subsequent education and (b) the effect of that education on the outcome studied above and beyond the direct effect. In principle we could compute indirect effects for a variety of post-GED educational decisions. Practical considerations force us to lump all post-GED educational decisions into one category.

More precisely,

Let $D_1 = 1$ if a person gets a GED,
$= 0$ otherwise.
Let $D_2 = 1$ if a person who gets a GED goes on to a higher level of schooling,
$= 0$ otherwise.

Let p_{GED} be the probability of getting some education beyond the GED. Keeping the other covariates implicit, write

$$Y = \beta_0 + \beta_1 D_1 + \beta_2 D_1 D_2 + V.$$

β_1 is the direct effect of the GED. It is what agents would receive if they stopped their education at the GED. β_2 is the effect of attaining further education on earnings above and beyond the direct effect. Assuming that V is uncorrelated with D_1 and $D_1 D_2$, and $E(V) = 0$,

$$E(Y|D_1 = 1) = \beta_0 + \beta_1 + \beta_2 E(D_2|D_1 = 1)$$
$$= \beta_1 + (p_{GED} \times \beta_2),$$
$$E(Y|D_1 = 0) = \beta_0.$$

The total effect of the GED $E(Y|D_1 = 1) = E(Y|D_1 = 0) = \beta_1 + (p_{GED} \times \beta_2)$ is broken down to the direct effect β_1 and the value of further education multiplied by the probability of attaining further levels of education $(p_{GED} \times \beta_2)$.

$$\text{Total effect} = \underbrace{\beta_1}_{\text{direct effect}} + \underbrace{(p_{GED} \times \beta_2)}_{\text{indirect effect}}.$$

Indirect effects are a substantial component of any estimated GED effect.

BIBLIOGRAPHY

Almlund, Mathilde, Duckworth, Angela, Heckman, James J., and Kautz, Tim. 2011. "Personality Psychology and Economics." In *Handbook of the Economics of Education*, edited by E. A. Hanushek, S. Machin, and L. Wößmann, vol. 4, 1–181. Amsterdam: Elsevier.

Autor, David H., and Duggan, Mark G. 2003. "The Rise in the Disability Rolls and the Decline in Unemployment." *Quarterly Journal of Economics* 118(1):157–206.

Bancroft, T. A. 1944. "On Biases in Estimation Due to the Use of Preliminary Tests of Significance." *The Annals of Mathematical Statistics* 15(2):190–204.

Becker, Gary Stanley. 1964. *Human Capital: A Theoretical and Empirical Analysis, With Special Reference to Education.* New York: National Bureau of Economic Research.

Belfield, Clive R., and Bailey, Thomas. 2011. "The Benefits of Attending Community College: A Review of the Evidence." *Community College Review* 39(1):46–68.

Boesel, David, Alsalam, Nabeel, and Smith, Thomas M. 1998. *Educational and Labor Market Performance of GED Recipients.* Washington, DC: U.S. Department of Education, Office of Educational Research and Improvement, National Library of Education.

Borghans, Lex, Duckworth, Angela L., Heckman, James J., and ter Weel, Bas. 2008. "The Economics and Psychology of Personality Traits." *Journal of Human Resources* 43(4):972–1059.

Boudett, Katheryn Parker, Murnane, Richard J., and Willett, John B. 2000. " "Second-Chance" Strategies for Women Who Drop Out of School." *Monthly Labor Review* 123(12):19–32.

Cameron, Stephen, and Heckman, James J. 1994. "Determinants of Young Males' Schooling and Training Choices." In *Training and the Private Sector: International Comparisons*, edited by Lisa M. Lynch, chap. 7, 201–232. Chicago: University of Chicago Press.

Cameron, Stephen V. 1996. "Three Essays on the Economics of Education." Ph.D. thesis, University of Chicago.

Cameron, Stephen V., and Heckman, James J. 1993. "The Nonequivalence of High School Equivalents." *Journal of Labor Economics* 11(1, Part 1):1–47.

Cameron, Stephen V., and Heckman, James J. 2001. "The Dynamics of Educational Attainment for Black, Hispanic, and White Males." *Journal of Political Economy* 109(3):455–499.

Cao, Jian, Stromsdorfer, Ernst W., and Weeks, Gregory. 1996. "The Human Capital Effect of General Education Development Certificates on Low Income Women." *Journal of Human Resources* 31(1):206–228.

Carroll, Joseph M. 1990. "The Copernican Plan: Restructuring the American High School." *Phi Delta Kappan* 71(5):358–365.

Clark, Melissa A., and Jaeger, David A. 2006. "Natives, the Foreign-Born, and High School Equivalents: New Evidence on the Returns to the GED." *Journal of Population Economics* 19(4):769–793.

Fogel, Robert. 1987. "Some Notes on the Scientific Methods of Simon Kuznets." Working Paper 2461, NBER.

Haavelmo, Trygve. 1943. "The Statistical Implications of a System of Simultaneous Equations." *Econometrica* 11(1):1–12.

Heckman, James J. 1980. "Sample Selection Bias as a Specification Error with an Application to the Estimation of Labor Supply Functions." In *Female Labor Supply: Theory and Estimation*, edited by James P. Smith and John F. Cogan, 206–248. Princeton, NJ: Princeton University Press.

Heckman, James J. 1987. "Selection Bias and Self-Selection." In *The New Palgrave: A Dictionary of Economics*, edited by John Eatwell, Murray Milgate, and Peter Newman, 287–297. London: Palgrave Macmillan Press.

Heckman, James J. 1992. "Randomization and Social Policy Evaluation." In *Evaluating Welfare and Training Programs*, edited by C. Manski and I. Garfinkel, 201–230. Cambridge, MA: Harvard University Press.

Heckman, James J. 2001. "Micro Data, Heterogeneity, and the Evaluation of Public Policy: Nobel Lecture." *Journal of Political Economy* 109(4):673–748.

Heckman, James J. 2008a. "Econometric Causality." *International Statistical Review* 76(1):1–27.

Heckman, James J. 2008b. "The Principles Underlying Evaluation Estimators with an Application to Matching." *Annales d'Economie et de Statistiques* 91–92:9–73.

Heckman, James J. 2010. "Building Bridges Between Structural and Program Evaluation Approaches to Evaluating Policy." *Journal of Economic Literature* 48(2):356–398.

Heckman, James J., Humphries, John Eric, and Mader, Nicholas. 2011. "The GED." In *Handbook of the Economics of Education*, edited by Eric A. Hanushek, Stephen Machin, and Ludger Wößmann, vol. 3, chap. 9, 423–484. Amsterdam: North Holland, Elsevier.

Heckman, James J., Humphries, John Eric, Urzúa, Sergio, and Veramendi, Gregory. 2011. "The Effects of Educational Choices on Labor Market, Health, and Social Outcomes." Unpublished manuscript, University of Chicago, Department of Economics.

Heckman, James J., and Kautz, Tim. 2012. "Hard Evidence on Soft Skills." *Labour Economics* 19(4):451–464, Adam Smith Lecture.

Heckman, James J., and LaFontaine, Paul A. 2006. "Bias Corrected Estimates of GED Returns." *Journal of Labor Economics* 24(3):661–700.

Heckman, James J., LaLonde, Robert J., and Smith, Jeffrey A. 1999. "The Economics and Econometrics of Active Labor Market Programs." In *Handbook of Labor Economics*, edited by Orley Ashenfelter and David Card, vol. 3A, chap. 31, 1865–2097. New York: North-Holland.

Heckman, James J., Lochner, Lance J., and Cossa, Ricardo. 2003. "Learning-by-Doing versus On-the-Job Training: Using Variation Induced by the EITC to Distinguish between Models of Skill Formation." In *Designing Social Inclusion: Tools to Raise Low-End Pay and Employment in Private Enterprise*, edited by Edmund S. Phelps, 74–130. Cambridge, England: Cambridge University Press.

Heckman, James J., and Navarro, Salvador. 2004. "Using Matching, Instrumental Variables, and Control Functions to Estimate Economic Choice Models." *Review of Economics and Statistics* 86(1):30–57.

Heckman, James J., and Rubinstein, Yona. 2001. "The Importance of Noncognitive Skills: Lessons from the GED Testing Program." *American Economic Review* 91(2):145–149.

Heckman, James J., and Smith, Jeffrey A. 1998. "The Sensitivity of Nonexperimental Evaluation Estimators: A Simulation Study." Unpublished working paper, University of Chicago, Department of Economics.

Heckman, James J., and Vytlacil, Edward J. 2007. "Econometric Evaluation of Social Programs, Part II: Using the Marginal Treatment Effect to Organize Alternative Economic Estimators to Evaluate Social Programs and to Forecast Their Effects in New Environments." In *Handbook of Econometrics*, edited by J. Heckman and E. Leamer, vol. 6B, chap. 71, 4875–5143. Amsterdam: Elsevier.

Jepsen, Christopher, Mueser, Peter, and Troske, Kenneth. 2011. "Labor Market Returns to the GED Using Regression Discontinuity Analysis." Working Paper 1014, Department of Economics, University of Missouri.

Judge, George G., and Bock, M. E. 1978. *The Statistical Implications of Pre-test and Stein-Rule Estimators in Econometrics*, vol. 25. Amsterdam: North-Holland.

Killingsworth, Mark R. 1983. *Labor Supply.* Cambridge, England: Cambridge University Press.

Means, B., and Laurence, Janice H. 1984. "Characteristics and Performance of Recruits Enlisted with General Educational Development (GED) Credentials." Tech. Rep. FRPRD-84-6, Human Resources Research Organization, Alexandria, VA.

Mincer, Jacob. 1962. "On-the-job Training: Costs, Returns, and Some Implications." *Journal of Political Economy* 70(5, Part 2: Investment in Human Beings):50–79.

Mincer, Jacob. 1974. *Schooling, Experience and Earnings.* New York: Columbia University Press for National Bureau of Economic Research.

Mulligan, Casey B., and Rubinstein, Yona. 2008. "Selection, Investment, and Women's Relative Wages over Time." *Quarterly Journal of Economics* 123(3):1061–1110.

Murnane, Richard J., Willett, John B., and Boudett, Kathryn Parker. 1995. "Do High School Dropouts Benefit from Obtaining a GED?" *Educational Evaluation and Policy Analysis* 17(2):133–147.

Murnane, Richard J., Willett, John B., and Boudett, Kathryn Parker. 1997. "Does a GED Lead to More Training, Post-secondary Education, and Military Service for School Dropouts?" *Industrial and Labor Relations Review* 51(1):100–116.

Murnane, Richard J., Willett, John B., and Boudett, Kathryn Parker. 1999. "Do Male Dropouts Benefit from Obtaining a GED, Postsecondary Education, and Training?" *Evaluation Review* 23(5):475–502.

Murnane, Richard J., Willett, John B., and Tyler, John H. 2000. "Who Benefits from Obtaining a GED? Evidence from High School and Beyond." *Review of Economics and Statistics* 82(1):23–37.

Pearl, Judea. 2000. *Causality.* Cambridge, England: Cambridge University Press.

Pearlin, Leonard I., Menaghan, Elizabeth G., Lieberman, Morton A., and Mullan, Joseph T. 1981. "The Stress Process." *Journal of Health and Social Behavior* 22(4):337–356.

Rosenberg, Morris. 1965. *Society and the Adolescent Self-Image.* Princeton, NJ: Princeton University Press.

Rubinstein, Yona, and Weiss, Yoram. 2006. "Post Schooling Wage Growth: Investment, Search and Learning." In *Handbook of the Economics of Education*, edited by Eric Hanushek and Finis Welch, *Handbooks in Economics*, vol. 1, chap. 1, 1–67. Amsterdam: North-Holland.

Smith, James P., and Cogan, John F. 1980. *Female Labor Supply: Theory and Estimation.* Princeton, NJ: Princeton University Press.

Social Security Administration. 2012. "DI 25001.001 Medical-Vocational Quick Reference Guide," last accessed February 4, 2013 from https://secure.ssa.gov /poms.nsf/lnx/0425001001.

Social Security Administration. 2013. "Evaluation Considering Age, Education, and Work Experience." In *Social Security Handbook*, § 609. Washington, DC: Social Security Administration.

Spence, A. Michael. 1974. *Market Signalling: The Informational Structure of Job Markets and Related Phenomena.* Cambridge, MA: Harvard University Press.

Taubman, Paul. 1977. *Kinometrics: Determinants of Socioeconomic Success Within and Between Families.* New York: North-Holland.

Theil, H., and Boot, J. C. G. 1962. "The Final Form of Econometric Equation Systems." *Revue de l'Institut International de Statistique/Review of the International Statistical Institute* 30(2):136–152.

Tyler, John H., and Kling, Jeffrey R. 2006. "Prison-Based Education and Re-Entry into the Mainstream Labor Market." NBER Working Paper 12114.

Tyler, John H., Murnane, Richard J., and Willett, John B. 2000. "Estimating the Labor Market Signaling Value of the GED." *Quarterly Journal of Economics* 115(2):431–468.

Tyler, John H., Murnane, Richard J., and Willett, John B. 2003. "Who Benefits from a GED? Evidence for Females from High School and Beyond." *Economics of Education Review* 22(3):237–247.

Zgoba, K., Haugebrook, S., and Jenkins, K. 2008. "The Influence of GED Obtainment on Inmate Release Outcome." *Criminal Justice and Behavior: An International Journal* 35(3):375–387.

Zhang, Jizhi, Guison-Dowdy, Anne, Patterson, Margaret Becker, and Song, Wei. 2011. "Crossing the Bridge: GED Credentials and Postsecondary Educational Outcomes." Year two report, GED Testing Services.

6

THE MILITARY PERFORMANCE OF GED HOLDERS

JANICE H. LAURENCE

6.1 The Issue

With high school dropout rates at almost 25% nationally (Heckman and LaFontaine, 2010), prevention programs are hard at work promoting graduation. After all, high school graduation is associated with higher earnings and better quality of life. This chapter provides yet another reason for earning a traditional high school diploma: without one, it's hard to enlist in the military.

The military's credential consciousness stems from the results of decades of performance studies showing that high school diploma holders adjust to the rigors of service life better than nongraduates and alternative credential holders (Laurence, 1993). Enlistees who have not completed high school at the time of enlistment experience more disciplinary, administrative, and retraining actions (Brady et al., 1991; Department of Defense, 1974). Perhaps the most important indicator of adjustment is first-term attrition—failure to complete a contracted term of enlistment. Nongraduates and alternative credential holders are about twice as likely as high school diploma graduates to leave service prematurely. Such findings are consistent with patterns outside the military where high school diploma graduates are more successful on the job and in their personal lives (see Chapter 5, this volume).

6.2 The Attrition Problem in Perspective

Each year, approximately 200,000 new recruits enlist in the active duty military. Each and every entering soldier, sailor, marine, and airman agrees to serve on active duty for a specified number of years (typically, from three to six years). Failure to fulfill this obligation is a serious problem for the military services, given the high cost of training and other investments (e.g., recruiting and salary costs, veterans benefits expenditures, payment of unemployment compensation). Furthermore, there are nonmonetary costs such as force instability, lowered morale, and reduced readiness.

On average, around one-third of accessions (as entering recruits are called) leave service prematurely, and a disproportionate share of attrition occurs early on—during training (General Accounting Office, 1997).

First-term attrition occurs for a variety of reasons, most of which (about 75%) is categorized as failure to meet minimum behavior or performance criteria (Laurence, Naughton, and Harris, 1996; Laurence, Ramsberger, and Arabian, 1996). This category includes a host of reasons for separation, including character or behavior disorder, motivational problems, ineptitude, alcoholism, use of drugs, discreditable incidents, misconduct, unsuitability, pattern of disciplinary infractions, and fraudulent entry. Half of the remaining instances of attrition appear to be medically related, and the rest are for dependency, hardship, or other reasons. Such designators may seem innocuous; however, in some cases, behavioral delinquency may be the real reason for separation. Among the most prevalent causes noted on personnel records are problems in the areas of work/duty, training, minor offenses, and mental health (Klein, Hawes-Dawson, and Martin, 1991). There is considerable flexibility as to exactly what constitutes grounds for discharge, how a discharge is coded, and the ease with which a discharge is given (Foch and King, 1977; General Accounting Office, 1980, 1997). In contrast to "stinginess" in granting early separations under the draft, since 1973, under the All Volunteer Force, a person who seeks to sever the enlistment contract can do so by displaying a pattern of disciplinary infractions tantamount to openly requesting a discharge.

6.3 Managing Attrition

A primary means of managing first-term attrition of enlisted personnel is by the selection of applicants who possess a traditional high school diploma or similar credential. Informed by research results, in the 1960s, the Services began emphasizing the enlistment of high school graduates and required nongraduates to meet higher aptitude and moral character standards to be considered for enlistment. Initially, no distinction was made between traditional and alternative secondary school diploma graduates. For example, persons with credentials based on General Educational Development (GED) high school equivalency testing were treated the same as high school diploma graduates. However, subsequent research revealed that the rate of attrition among GED recipients was more consistent with that of nongraduates than traditional graduates. Thus, in the mid-1970s, the Services no longer considered GED holders as high school graduates for enlistment purposes (Eitelberg, Laurence, and Waters, 1984). Instead, a third credential category was established, with GEDs sandwiched between traditional graduates and nongraduates.

Ultimately, this scheme faltered as the number and types of secondary schools proliferated throughout the 1970s and 1980s. In response to the

plethora of credentials, the Department of Defense (DoD) sponsored research to examine the attrition behavior among individuals holding various
alternate credentials in addition to the GED, such as adult diploma holders,
the home schooled, and those with other equivalency certificates (Laurence,
1983, 1987). After collecting and analyzing data from a 1983 sample of almost
75,000 service applicants and recruits, DoD and the Services unified and
modified the categorization scheme for education credentials in 1988.

A new and improved three-tier system was adopted, with credentials
placed within tiers according to average attrition rates (Laurence, 1993).
That is, traditional high school diploma graduates and college attendees
(regardless of traditional high school completion) received Tier 1 or preferred enlistment status. Alternative credential holders and those without
any credential were relegated to Tiers 2 and 3, respectively, and enlisted
sparingly. The categorization of credentials, with an enlistment advantage
for those in Tier 1, was, to say the least, contentious. Despite the empirical
basis of the taxonomy, issuers of credentials relegated to a lower tier were
piqued over what they viewed as a snub of their educational programs
(see Laurence, 1993). Although attrition data from the 1983 education credential tier sample suggested a Tier 2 placement for adult education diploma holders, lobbyists for such educational programs were relentless
and ultimately successful in having Congress intervene and obtain Tier 1
placement at least until operational data suggested otherwise. Since the
adoption of the tier system in 1988, DoD has accumulated data and peri-
odically examines the attrition rates of the various credential holders so as
to report on the value of its credential tier categories.

Cutting to the chase, Table 6.1 shows 36-month attrition for fiscal year
(FY) 1988 through 2005 accessions by education credential for each Service
and for all Services combined. Of particular note is Tier 2, which comprises
predominantly high school equivalency credential holders (Laurence, Ramsberger, and Arabian, 1996). The official DoD definitions of this credential
code and the less common codes within Tier 2 follow (see: http://www.mep
com.army.mil/docs/680-3A-E_Instructions_May_11.doc).

Test-Based High School Equivalency: A diploma or certificate of general educational development (GED) or other test-based high credential. A state or
locally issued secondary school diploma obtained solely on the basis of
testing and not graded day coursework.

National Guard Youth ChalleNGe Program: An individual who completed a
22-week National Guard Youth ChalleNGe Program (NGYCP) and passed

the General Educational Development (GED). Must be identified separately from other GED holders for tracking purposes.

Occupational Program: An individual who completed at least 11 years of graded day high school and received a certificate of completion of a six-month non-correspondence vocational-technical program.

High School Certificate of Attendance/Completion: An attendance-based high school diploma or certificate or credential based on an Individualized Education Program (IEP) that involves community experiences, employment, training, daily living skill and post-school transition skills that differ from the traditional high school graduation requirements.

Home School Diploma: A home school diploma from the parent, guardian, or home school association, with certification and transcripts issued in compliance with applicable state laws. The curriculum must involve parental instruction and supervision and closely pattern the normal credit hours per subject used in the traditional high school. At a minimum the last academic year (nine months) must be completed in a home school environment.

Other Nontraditional High School Credential: A secondary school credential issued for completing a public alternative school/program that differs in course content and curriculum from the traditional high school diploma program. Public schools/programs that are accelerated and issue a diploma based on a combination of testing, independent study, adult basic education (ABE), and/or competencies are classified as Tier 2, regardless of whether the credential was issued by a secondary or postsecondary institution. Applicants from private (nonpublic) alternative programs who meet this criteria will also be able to enlist under this category. However, their credential will require a formal individual tier evaluation prior to enlistment.

Practically all persons (88%) within the test-based high school equivalency credential code are GED recipients (see Means and Laurence, 1984). Across Services, the 36-month attrition rates for GED holders is 45%, compared to 28% for traditional diploma graduates.[1] Furthermore, attrition

---

1. Given the large number of cases that are in fact population counts for the years reported, confidence intervals and statistical significance are not reported. Confidence intervals are provided for an earlier version of these data (based on 24-month attrition for 1988–1993 accessions) in Laurence, Ramsberger, and Arabian (1996).

Table 6.1 36-Month Attrition for FY 1988–2005 NPS Accessions by Education Credential and Service

Tier/Education Credential[a]	Army		Navy	
	N	% Attrition	N	% Attrition
Tier 1				
High school Graduate	1,146,429	31	884,028	29
College				
One semester	35,711	42	21,788	43
2 years or more	62,829	22	21,131	21
Adult Education	17,094	43	24,196	43
Failed Exit Exam	601	32	346	20
Tier 2				
H.S. Equivalency	118,341	45	36,030	48
ChalleNGe GED	3,454	44	1,498	53
Occupational Program Certification[b]	4,144	44	257	32
Certification of Attendance or Completion	217	38	1,811	47
Correspondence School Diploma	194	40	313	40
Home School Diploma	2,669	41	2,282	48
Other Nontraditional H.S. Credential	174	26	195	31
Tier 3				
Less Than H.S. Diploma	9,629	52	25,458	50
Total	**1,409,636**	**32**	**1,030,722**	**30**

Source: Defense Manpower Data Center.
[a]Credentials do not sum to total because retired, missing, and inapplicable codes were included only in the Total row.
[b]The Army uses this code for Job Corps program graduates.
[c]Cell size 20 or fewer, attrition rate not calculated.

for GEDs tends to be stable and higher than the levels for most other Tier 2 credentials and is very similar to the rate found for nongraduates in Tier 3 (50%). Attrition is even high for those who earned their GED through the National Guard ChalleNGe program, which included a 5½-month residential phase and a weekly meeting with a mentor over a 14-week period. The levels of attrition vary by Service and are influenced by job character-

Marine Corps		Air Force		Total DoD	
N	% Attrition	N	% Attrition	N	% Attrition
564,835	26	592,126	24	3,187,418	28
7,758	39	6,652	20	71,909	40
5,933	21	16,079	16	105,972	21
8,423	36	588	36	50,301	42
164	25	241	17	1,352	28
12,455	45	4,253	33	171,079	45
1,096	35	100	52	6,148	45
80	44	293	34	4,774	43
6,086	40	274	19	8,388	41
359	40	29	14	895	39
1,182	31	857	27	6,990	40
109	33	c	c	487	29
1,784	45	551	34	37,422	50
611,985	**27**	**623,580**	**24**	**3,675,923**	**29**

istics, other environmental and organizational factors (e.g., duty location, leadership style), separation policies, and recruit characteristics, in addition to education (e.g., level of aptitude, gender, marital status). Regardless of the fact that the Air Force has relatively low attrition rates, the patterns by tier are the same. Tier 2 and "misplaced" Tier 1 credential holders leave or are discharged to a greater degree than high school graduates. In fact, high school equivalency recruits in the Air Force are more likely to "attrit" than diploma graduates in any of the other Services.

6.4 The Reliability of Education Credential Attrition Differences

The tabulated attrition findings are neither new nor spurious. The relationship between high school graduation status and attrition rate is consistent. For example, the 36-month attrition rates for nongraduates, GEDs, and diploma holders who enlisted in FY 1979 were 43%, 45%, and 24%, respectively. The corresponding rates for those enlisted in FY 1983 were 52%, 45%, and 23% (Laurence, 1987). The absolute level of attrition has remained fairly constant, as has the magnitude of differences between credential groups. These findings are not only reliable across cohort, but behavioral and demographic factors do not explain these attrition differences (Laurence, 1997).

Although modest correlations can be found between attrition and level of aptitude, preservice employment, and preservice arrest record, such characteristics do not account for the differences in attrition among education credential holders. In fact, to be considered for enlistment, GEDs are required to meet higher minimum aptitude requirements relative to diploma graduates.[2] Thus, it is particularly notable that GED holders with relatively high aptitude levels are more likely to "quit" the military than lower aptitude high school graduates. Table 6.2 shows 36-month attrition by tier within aptitude category. These categories represent score ranges (I = highest; IV = lowest)[3] on the Armed Forces Qualification Test (AFQT)— the math and verbal test composite of the Armed Services Vocational Aptitude Battery (ASVAB), the military's enlistment screening instrument. Monotonic relationships can be seen across AFQT categories and credential tiers (AFQT Category I and Tier 1 recruits have lower attrition). However, by far the stronger relationship is between credential and attrition. In fact, as has been shown in the past, Tier 1 accessions in the lowest aptitude category (Category IV) had *lower* attrition rates than Category I accessions in either Tiers 2 or 3.

Attrition patterns by credential also hold regardless of gender, race, age, geographic region, and socioeconomic status. And although attrition

---

2. Waivers of moral character standards (e.g., traffic offenses, misdemeanors, and the like) also are less likely to be granted for Tier 2 and 3 recruits.

3. There are actually five main categories with percentile score ranges, as follows: I = 93–99; II = 65–92; IIIA = 50–64; IIIB = 31–49; IV = 10–30; V = 1–9. Category V applicants are ineligible, by law, for enlistment. The ability distribution is based on a nationally representative sample of youth ages 18–24.

Table 6.2 36-Month Attrition for FY 1988–1993 Nonprior Service Accessions by Education Credential Tier and AFQT Category (N in parenthesis)

Tier Credential	AFQT Category					
	I	II	IIIA	IIIB	IV	Total[a]
Tier 1	21.4	25.7	30.0	32.4	34.3	28.8
	(58,652)	(481,559)	(350,702)	(370,335)	(40,187)	(1,309,518)
Diploma graduate	21.5	25.5	29.5	32.0	33.8	28.5
	(51,106)	(453,237)	(335,599)	(354,111)	(38,709)	(1,240,394)
Tier 2	40.9	45.6	49.9	47.4		47.7
	(842)	(16,652)	(21,958)	(4,287)	[b]	(44,095)
GED	43.1	46.9	50.4	49.5		48.7
	(722)	(14,880)	(20,053)	(2,787)	[b]	(38,778)
Tier 3	43.4	49.4	54.8	56.1		52.6
	(327)	(8,060)	(11,204)	(1,750)	[b]	(21,459)
All	21.7	26.7	31.8	32.7	34.4	29.8
	(60,062)	(508,964)	(385,548)	(378,684)	(41,045)	(1,382,807)

Source: Defense Manpower Data Center.
[a]Totals contain obsolete codes, whereas AFQT category entries do not; thus rows may not sum to totals.
[b]Cell entries are not shown because of unreliability, given that fewer than 50 people were enlisted with these characteristics over the course of the six years depicted.

varies by job, the patterns remain steadfast within occupational categories (Laurence, 1987). For example, the four most populous occupational areas are: (1) infantry, guncrews, and seamanship; (2) electrical or mechanical equipment repair; (3) service and supply; and (4) functional support and administration. The percentages of FY 1982/1983 male enlistees who remained in service three years later are shown in Table 6.3.

6.5 GED Attrition: Why High?

Time and again, even after controlling for potential confounds, military members who did not hold a traditional high school diploma at the time of enlistment have been shown to be greater attrition risks. Despite the robustness of this finding, the question remains: Why do nongraduates and GEDs, in particular, have greater difficulty adjusting to the military, and why are they more likely to leave prematurely? There are no firm answers, but a trail of evidence is available.

One axiom in the behavioral sciences is that past behavior is the best predictor of future behavior. For whatever reasons, whether due to poor grades,

Table 6.3 Percent of FY 1982 and 1983 Male Nonprior Service Accessions Who Completed at Least Three Years of Service by Credential Category for Selected Occupation Groups

Occupation Group	High School Graduates		GEDs		Nongraduates	
	1982	1983	1982	1983	1982	1983
Infantry	80	79	57	64	53	54
Equipment Repair	88	87	71	73	65	65
Service/Supply	83	79	64	63	53	55
Administration	88	85	68	69	63	63

Source: Laurence (1987).
Note: Credential category designators are those in effect prior to the establishment of the 1988 tier system.

other academic deficiencies, disciplinary trouble, lack of motivation, or the like, GED holders quit high school. They "failed" within the structured classroom environment with its rules, regulations, and requirements. Military training also begins in a structured, classroom setting. Following about six weeks of basic training or "boot" camp, the majority of new soldiers, sailors, marines, and airmen go on to receive technical training for a few months or over a year depending on the assigned occupational specialty. Indeed, regular attendance, books, lectures, notes, homework, classroom participation, and tests are part of the enlistment package.

Given the typical training experiences upon entry and because attrition is higher for GED recipients even after controlling for level of aptitude, noncognitive factors can be assumed to account for most of the diploma's predictiveness. That is, the personal and social skills, experiences, and attributes that enable students to complete high school also enable them to complete their first terms. A high school diploma signifies attributes such as maturity, perseverance, and tolerance for rules and regulations, which are important for success in the military (Laurence, 1984). To graduate, students must learn to cooperate with their instructors and to get along with their peers. A high school diploma not only represents a certain level of academic success, but more importantly, a degree of discipline (Cheatham, 1978). Data from the 1983 Educational and Biographical Information Survey (EBIS) support these notions. Tables 6.4 and 6.5 provide the summary statistics and structure coefficients from an "exploratory" dis-

Table 6.4 Summary Statistics for Discriminant Analysis of Education Credential Groups

Summary Statistic	Function 1	Function 2	
Group Centroids			Percent Correct Classification
High School Diploma (n = 18,994)	0.26184	−0.00349	84.6
GED/Alternate Credential (n = 1749)	−1.46269	0.22002	37.9
No Credential (n = 1326)	−1.82144	−0.24023	48.0
			Overall = 78.7
Eigenvalue	0.42796	0.00732	
Relative Percentage	98.32	1.68	
Canonical Correlation	0.55	0.09	
Wilks' Lambda	0.695	0.993	
df	114	56	

criminant analysis[4] of a subsample of military recruits who took the EBIS. Linear composites (functions) of the EBIS variables were used to predict credential categories.

The first function or factor accounts for practically all of the variance among groups (98.32%) and differentiates high school diploma graduates from the other credential groups. On the basis of the resulting functions, around 85% of high school graduates were correctly classified as such. GED holders and nongraduates were less likely to be classified correctly because of the confusion between these two "nondiploma groups." The second function (for the little that it is worth as a group discriminator) attempts

4. Discriminant analysis can be described as a "turned around" Multiple Analysis of Variance (MANOVA) (see Tabachnick and Fidell, 2001). A set of 66 out of 121 EBIS variables was used for this stepwise, Rao discriminant analysis. This set was derived from previous research that examined items in relation to attrition. It was neither expanded nor winnowed down or otherwise refined for the present analysis, which was not published previously. The data set was not available for reanalysis at the time this chapter was prepared.

Table 6.5 Pooled Within-Group Structure Coefficients Showing Correlation between EBIS Variables and Discriminant Functions

Variable*	Function 1	Function 2
Never thought of quitting school	.76651	−.22517
Quit—work full time	.50765	.05571
Quit—not graduating on time	.45507	.00867
Quit—bored	.41212	−.13436
Quit—other reasons	.40513	−.17743
Days absent last year h.s.	.35999	.06042
Age first ran away	.30882	.12235
Ever in trouble in school—skipping	.29745	.07285
Grades in English	.29584	.17802
Quit—getting bad grades	.28772	.14403
Quit—family needed money	.28158	.10404
Quit—didn't get along with teachers	.25885	.15199
Ever in trouble in school—missing class	.23398	.17114
Ever expelled from school	.23214	.13878
Never in trouble in school	.22757	.14843
Ever in trouble in school—smoking	.21826	.11959
Courses taken most—gen., acad., voc., other	.21516	−.18707
Grades in science	.19268	.17675
Left job—went back to school	.17481	−.10877
Age first dated	.16984	.14979
Age first got drunk	.16841	.15549
Age first used marijuana	.16694	.02107
Age first smoked cigarettes	.15560	.02013
Ever in trouble in school—fighting	.14571	.11786
Grades in vocational subject	.14033	−.08372
Longest time in part-time job	.13347	−.0161
Grades in math	.12446	.02395
Where lived most between ages 8 and 17	.12365	−.04542
Ever arrested—unauthorized vehicle use	.12241	.03016
Ever in trouble in school—talking back	.11548	.03078
Ever arrested—disorderly conduct	.11132	.01795
Times ever used marijuana	.10954	−.03169
Times used other narcotics	.10274	.02543
Times used downers	.10220	.06298
Grade 1–6 suspensions	.09914	.09241
High school participation—athletic teams	.09884	−.07132
Times used other drugs	.09444	−.01030
Ever arrested—assault/battery	.09410	−.01121
Ever arrested—drunken driving	.09026	−.08430

Table 6.5 (Continued)

Variable*	Function 1	Function 2
Left job—bad working conditions	.06602	−.04605
Left job—joined military	.06069	.05793
Age first held paying job	.05138	.01263
Ever arrested/convicted of felony	.03505	−.01342
Left job—didn't get along with supervisor	.01953	−.00452
Grade 9–12 suspensions	.26660	.36740
Left job—pay not good	.03239	−.27499
Quit—expelled or suspended	.22021	.26786
Physical fights—how often last 3 years	.21384	.25659
Grade 7–8 suspensions	.20820	.25505
Ever in trouble in school—other	.06756	.24241
Left job—laid off	.02684	−.22803
Left job—fired	.03940	−.21171
Left job—found better job	−.01829	−.16458
Ever in trouble in school—bad language	.11710	.15422
Ever arrested—theft	.13006	−.14598
Mother's discipline (lenient–strict)	.07459	−.13448
Times used cocaine	.07514	.12859
Ever convicted of misdemeanor	.08764	−.12490
Family income level—ages 14–17	.05489	−.11983
Ever in trouble in school—disorderly	.07943	.10863
Times used uppers	.09572	.10542
Left job—other reasons	.04286	.10045
Ever arrested—drug-related offense	.08658	.09048
Father's discipline (lenient–strict)	.08535	−.08571
Left job—moved	.03784	−.05243
Left job—no chance to get ahead	.01998	−.02015

*Response alternatives were keyed relative to completion of term of service (i.e., the inverse of attrition). That is, the item score is the percent of "completers" who selected each option. Thus, variables such as "Quit—work full time" are not counterintuitive but reflect the fact that diploma graduates were more likely to choose the more heavily weighted option "no." For details on item coding see Steinhaus (1988).

to distinguish between GEDs and those with no credential. The structure coefficients (Table 6.5) indicate the strength of the relationship between the EBIS variables and functions and can be used to describe or name the function (Klecka, 1980). In conjunction with the group centroids (Table 6.4) these coefficients show ways in which the credential groups differ. When interpreting the discrimination between credential groups, it is important to keep in mind that institutional and self-selection likely affected these results. Renegade recruits, especially from the nonpreferred tiers, are not likely to have made it into the sample.

All in all, GED holders and nongraduates were more likely to have thought about quitting high school for a variety of reasons, were in more trouble in school (including expulsion), got poorer grades, were more likely to engage in deviant (and some delinquent) behavior and at an earlier age, and were less likely to hold on to a part-time job. They quit school (and jobs) and disobeyed the rules to a greater extent than diploma graduates. The second function is not terribly elucidating, but suggests that relative to *nongraduates*, GEDs were less likely to be suspended or disrespectful in school but were more likely to have left a job for varying reasons. These patterns are consistent with the literature on the characteristics of dropouts (Smith, 1996), including evidence that conduct disorders and substance abuse are more prevalent among those who do not complete high school (Kessler et al., 1995). The civilian literature shows similar findings regarding attrition of GED holders and the noncognitive factors that underlie their poorer job performance (see Chapter 5 and Heckman and Rubinstein, 2001).

These findings are supported by subsequent data on a 1990 sample of Army recruits who were administered a survey upon reception into service (see Sipes et al., 2000). Tables 6.6 and 6.7 present the results of a

Table 6.6 Summary Statistics for Discriminant Analysis of Education Credential Groups (Army Recruit Survey)

Summary Statistic	Function 1	
Group Centroids		Percent Correct Classification
High School Diploma (n = 21,375)	−0.195	95.1
GED/Alternate Credential & No Credential (2,822 & 17; n = 2,839)	1.970	49.3
		Overall = 90.9
Eigenvalue	0.385	
Canonical Correlation	0.53	
Wilks' Lambda	0.722	
df	38	

Table 6.7 Pooled Within-Group Structure Coefficients Showing Correlation between Army Recruit Survey and Discriminant Function

Variable	Function 1
Never thought about quitting HS	−.799
Thought about quitting: Work full time	.504
Thought about quitting: Other reasons	.503
Thought about quitting: Wasn't going to graduate on time	.459
Thought about quitting: Bored, not learning anything	.393
Thought about quitting: Family need	.293
How often smoke before DEP	.278
Thought about quitting: Didn't get along with authorities	.266
Number of types of trouble in school	.261
Thought about quitting: Expelled or suspended	.261
Thought about quitting: Getting bad grades	.261
Were you ever expelled	.237
Thought about quitting: Got married or became a parent	.233
Thought about quitting: Didn't get along with students	.222
Left job—moved	.219
Average grades in high school	−.207
Left job—laid off	.186
Were you ever suspended	.172
Left job—found better job	.170
Left job—no chance to get ahead	.169
Left job—pay was not good	.151
White/Nonwhite	.146
Years active duty service expected	.142
Participation in high school activities	−.141
Join the Army: Patriotism	.127
Left job—fired	.102
Thought about quitting: Rules were too strict	.096
Left job to go back to school	−.088
Participated in athletic teams	−.088
Average fitness level before Army	−.086
How often drink alcohol before DEP	.084
Left job—bad working conditions	.081
Left job for other reasons	.068
Haven't had job outside the home	−.066
Would leave: Injuries during training	−.065
Left job—conflict with supervisor	.058

(continued)

Table 6.7 (Continued)

Variable	Function 1
Would leave: Better job outside the Army	−.056
Would leave: Problems adjusting to Army life	−.054
Confident—adapt to Army life	.053
Join the Army: Bad environment	.053
Left job—arrested	.048
Would leave: Homesickness	−.045
Would leave: Lack of motivation, boredom	−.041
Would leave: Racial discrimination	−.039
Would leave: Illness/medical condition	−.036
Unsure about Army career: Changes in the Army mission	−.032
Would leave: Not getting desired military job	−.030
Would leave: Sexual harassment	−.030
Don't have any uncertainty about Army career	.030
Would leave: Sexual or gender discrimination	−.029
Join the Army: Adventure	−.028
Would leave: Poor academic performance	.025
Join the Army: Family/friends influence	.025
Join the Army: Values	.024
Would leave: Disciplinary problems	.023
Confident—earn promotions in Army	.023
Join Army: Benefits	.022
Level of strain, conflict, or stress (low to high)	.022
AFQT category	.017
Unsure about Army career: Sexual or racial discrimination	.015
Would leave: Pregnancy	.015
Would leave: One or more serious offenses	−.014
Left job to join the military	−.012
Unsure of chances for promotion	.011
Would leave: Problems with supervisors	−.010
Unsure about Army career: Unclear career goals	−.008
Confident—success in basic training	.008
Join the Army: Economic factors	.008
Would leave: Not getting along with others	.006
Expected of you in the Army?	.004
Confident—meet physical req.	.004
Unsure about Army career: Changes in Army job opportunities	−.002
Would leave: Fail physical requirements	.001

Notes: Pooled within-group correlations between discriminating variables and standardized canonical discriminant functions. Variables ordered by absolute size of correlation within function.

discriminant analysis performed to differentiate between regular gradu-ates and others. (Note that because there were so few nongraduates—17—this group was combined with the GED group.)

In contrast to traditional diploma graduates, GED recipients considered quitting school for a multitude of reasons, were more likely to have been expelled or suspended from school, quit their jobs, and were less likely to participate in school activities. Again, the caveat regarding the "selected" nature of this sample applies. Greater differentiation between groups might well be realized within a more representative sample of education credential groups.

Regardless of the controversy over the cognitive or academic equiva-lency of a regular secondary school diploma and passing the GED tests, the military experience suggests that the two are not equal in other, non-academic ways. Although it might be argued that it is unfair to judge the "staying power" of GED holders by their adaptation to the hardships, structure, and discipline of the active duty military, similar dropout pat-terns are evident in the Selected Reserve (Buddin and Kirby, 1997) and in other nonmilitary settings. By definition, this group has quit high school. In addition, they have been found to be more likely to drop out of technical school and college (both two- and four-year institutions) and are more likely to quit a job than high school completers (Boesel, Alsalam, and Smith, 1998; Cameron and Heckman, 1993; and Chapter 5, this volume). Indeed, there is ample evidence that a diploma by any other name is not as sweet.

6.6 Controlling Attrition: Efficiency, Effectiveness, and Equity
The military does not eschew GED holders on the basis of cognitive achievement or abilities. Rather, the military limits their enlistment based on their poor persistence and incompatibility with military order and dis-cipline. Although attitude rather than aptitude is the key to lasting in the military, the military considers level of aptitude more strongly for GED candidates. All applicants must take the ASVAB; however, there are higher composite score minimums for applicants in Tiers 2 and 3. Although aptitude does not eliminate the attrition problem, it promotes better training and job performance. GEDs may be more likely to leave service early, but while in uniform, their relatively high aptitude levels make them more trainable, assignable, and proficient on the job.

Although selection policies permit GEDs and nongraduates to enlist if they make the grade, relatively few have gained access to the military's rank and file. With few exceptions, since the mid-1980s, over 90% of new recruits have been traditional diploma holders. Among FY 2009 incoming recruits, almost 93% were traditional diploma graduates, around 7% were in Tier 2, and less than 1% were in Tier 3 (Department of Defense, 2009).[5]

When recruiting becomes more difficult for the military, restrictions on the enlistment of GED holders tends to be eased a bit, though not eliminated. In FY 1999—a tough recruiting year—for example, approximately 91% of accessions were in Tier 1, almost 8% were in Tier 2, and just over 1% were in Tier 3 (Department of Defense, Various). The Army initiated the trial GED-Plus Program through which up to 4,000 otherwise highly qualified nongraduates are sponsored for GED testing prior to enlisting.[6] This test segued into the GED ChalleNGe program piloted in 1993 and permanently established in 1998.[7] Such GED programs are by no means an indication that GED holders will find easy access to the military perpetually. When goals can be met by recruiting those in Tier 1, even this modest interest in GEDs likely will wane.

The GED Testing Service, which manages the GED program, has not been silent with regard to the *persona non grata* treatment and high hurdles to enlistment faced by GED holders. Among their arguments in opposition to the limitations are that most GEDs are successful in the military and that numerically (in contrast to proportionately) more attrition cases are from Tier 1. Further, they have protested that GED credential holders have been unfairly denigrated and that other alternative credentials unjustifiably have made it to Tier 1 status. They have lobbied Congress to push DoD toward other means of attrition screening in lieu of using broad education categories (Laurence, 1993).

Such arguments are not without merit, but from DoD's institutional (rather than individual) perspective, using three education categories is an efficient and effective way to reduce attrition. Any denigration of the credential on the military's part is unintentional. Unfortunately, it is rather difficult for those who are not ensconced in the technical aspects of attrition prediction and control to separate a credential's academic achievement signal from its comportment value. The Services have clarified their

5. These statistics are reported by the Defense Manpower Data Center. Other official statistics submitted to DoD by the Services after "cleaning" may not match these figures exactly.

6. Among the additional screens were aptitude level, moral character, participation in scouting, Junior ROTC, and score on the Assessment of Individual Motivation (AIM). In addition to 4,000 active duty accessions, the program was also available to 2,000 reservists.

7. See Chapter 9 in this volume for a more thorough discussion of the ChalleNGe program.

policies to the public and the recruiting community as part of their efforts to avoid misstatements regarding, and indelicate treatment of, alternate credential holders.

Of course, most attrition is experienced by the most populous group—the traditional high school graduates. However, this fact does not invalidate the predictive power of credential groups and does not detract from the cost savings (to the tune of tens of thousands of dollars per person)[8] of limiting the enlistment of persons in Tiers 2 and 3. Aside from an attrition "floor" effect introduced by consistently high percentages of high school diploma graduates, steady attrition rates may be influenced by continuing cases of credential confusion,[9] political intervention regarding credential placement within tiers, apparent declines in physical and moral character fitness of the recruitment pool, and the increasing enlistment of women, who experience higher attrition rates than men. These and other factors mitigate the positive effects of diploma status. Another potential reason why attrition has not declined appreciably with high proportions of diploma graduates is that the Services have come to "count on" a certain level of attrition and recruit accordingly. Thus, to some extent, the worst third of an entering cohort gets cut even if today's worst third is better than yesterday's worst third (Laurence, Naughton, and Harris, 1996; Laurence, Ramsberger, and Arabian, 1996).

DoD and the Services have researched other selection measures, most notably, biographical and temperament inventories (see Trent and Laurence, 1993). Regardless of the *apparent* power of biodata, technical, practical, and political concerns precluded its operational adoption. Among the nullifying issues is concern about the realistic potential for recruiter coaching and applicant faking of a self-report biodata inventory. In the early 1990s, the Navy tested a Compensatory Screening Model (CSM) and included factual background information rather than a self-administered, self-report biographical inventory. The Army turned to a temperament measure as part of its GED-Plus test program. Enlistment candidates sponsored for GED testing were evaluated with regard to their scores on the Assessment of Individual Motivation (AIM), among other factors. Such screening did not replace

8. Using 1987 dollars, the estimated cost was $18,400 for each person who left service prematurely (see Laurence, 1987).

9. In addition to occasional but systematic credential coding errors, there are reported instances of intentional efforts to make alternative credentials indistinguishable from a traditional high school diploma. For example, some states issue a state high school diploma on the basis of GED results.

reliance on education credential but was used to expand the recruiting market by identifying the "least risky" from among the set of risky candidates (Young, Heggestad, and Nason, 1999). Regardless of the verifiability of the attrition screens, operational tests have yielded little success. Biodata and CSM-type instruments have limited viability and utility.

Using biodata or a temperament measure for Tier 1 would reduce attrition, but it might very well jeopardize the supply of new recruits. Injecting verifiable characteristics that are found to be more highly related to attrition (e.g., gender, race/ethnicity) is contraindicated from an equity perspective. Education credential screening, on the other hand, has been evaluated as valid and equitable for these and other population subgroups (Laurence, 1987). It should also be noted that, although the Services restrict the enlistment of alternative credential holders, they continue to enlist such individuals in representative proportions. Liberally estimated, GEDs comprise roughly 5.2% of the 18- to 24-year-old population as of 1994.[10] Recall that among FY 2009 accessions, 7% were categorized within Tier 2.

6.7 Conclusions and Prescriptions

Whereas it is important to consider whether the military should focus on recruiting Tier 1 applicants, this chapter has a more basic message. According to evidence from the nation's largest employer—the military—the GED program does not adequately prepare its "graduates" for work, particularly the noncognitive or nonacademic demands of the job. Despite the fact that GED recipients are screened more thoroughly (and thus may be atypical of GEDs overall), they are more likely to create discipline problems and as a result are twice as likely as traditional diploma holders to be dismissed from or quit the military.

The GED purportedly documents whether or not a dropout possesses academic knowledge equivalent to the level acquired by an average high school graduate. Being prepared for a military career, or more generally the world of work, involves much more than minimum preparation for a day's worth of testing. Proof of persistence, teamwork, adaptability, work ethic, and the like are needed as well. Training and instruction toward these ends would be fitting goals of the GED program in addition to marketing a test.

10. This estimate was derived by applying the age distribution of GED test takers to data on the number of GEDs issued annually from 1989 through 1994, as contained in *Digest of Education Statistics 1996*, U.S. National Center for Education Statistics, U.S. Department of Education, Office of Educational Research and Improvement, NCES 96-133, Table 100 (National Center for Education Statistics, Various).

In response to the relegation of the GED to Tier 2 status, the Testing Service has been quick to remind DoD of the military origins of the program. What they fail to realize or at least mention is that the GED tests were used to certify military members for college *after* they successfully completed their time in service. Employers are looking not only for basic skills but for prosocial skills, attitudes, and behaviors as well (Nelson, 1997). Likewise, the military provides occupational training in exchange for maintaining personal discipline and commitment—for at least a few years. Failure to fully equip those looking for a second chance is not good from both individual and organizational perspectives.

BIBLIOGRAPHY

Boesel, David, Alsalam, Nabeel, and Smith, Thomas M. (1998). *Educational and Labor Market Performance of GED Recipients.* (Washington, DC: U.S. Department of Education, Office of Educational Research and Improvement, National Library of Education).

Brady, E. J., Busciglio, H. H., White, L. A., and Young, M. C. (1991). "The Relationship of Education Credentials to Enlisted Job Performance." (Unpublished manuscript. Presented at the Military Testing Association).

Buddin, Richard J., and Kirby, Sheila Nataraj. (1997). *GED Accessions in the Selected Reserve: How Long Do They Serve?* (Santa Monica, CA: RAND).

Cameron, Stephen V., and Heckman, James J. (1993). "The Nonequivalence of High School Equivalents." *Journal of Labor Economics* 11(1, Part 1): 1–47.

Cheatham, C. W. (1978). *The High School Graduate: An Indicator of a Quality Marine?* (Fort Levenworth, KS: U.S. Army Command and General Staff College).

Department of Defense. (1974). *Defense Manpower Quality Requirements.* (Washington, DC: Office of the Assistant Secretary of Defense) (Manpower, Reserve Affairs, and Logistics).

Department of Defense. (Various). *Population Representation in the Military Services.* (Washington, DC: Office of the Assistant Secretary of Defense).

Eitelberg, M. J., Laurence, Janice H., and Waters, B. K. (1984). *Screening for Service: Aptitude and Education Criteria for Military Entry.* (Washington, DC: Office of the Assistant Secretary of Defense) (Manpower, Installations, and Logistics).

Foch, C., and King, N. (1977). "Gatekeepers: First Term Enlisted Attrition Policies and Practices." in *First Term Enlisted Attrition.* H. W. Sinaiko, ed. 1. (Arlington, VA: Office of Naval Research).

General Accounting Office. (1980). *Attrition in the Military: An Issue Needing Management Attention.* (Washington, DC: U.S. Government Printing Office).

General Accounting Office. (1997). *Military Attrition: DOD Could Save Millions by Better Screening Enlisted Personnel.* (Washington, DC: U.S. Government Printing Office).

Heckman, James J., and LaFontaine, Paul A. (2010). "The American High School Graduation Rate: Trends and Levels." *Review of Economics and Statistics* 92(2): 244–262.

Heckman, James J., and Rubinstein, Yona. (2001). "The Importance of Noncognitive Skills: Lessons from the GED Testing Program." *American Economic Review* 91(2): 145–149.

Kessler, Ronald, Foster, Cindy, Saunders, William, and Stang, Paul. (1995). "Social Consequences of Psychiatric Disorders, I: Educational Attainment." *American Journal of Psychiatry* 152(7): 1026–1032.

Klecka, William R. (1980). *Discriminant Analysis.* (Beverly Hills, CA: Sage Publications).

Klein, Stephen P., Hawes-Dawson, Jennifer, and Martin, Thomas. (1991). *Why Recruits Separate Early.* (Santa Monica, CA: RAND).

Laurence, Janice H. (1983). *Secondary Education Credentials: A Military Enlistment Policy Dilemma.* (Alexandria, VA: Human Resources Research Organization, FR-PRD-83-22).

Laurence, Janice H. (1984). "Education Standards for Military Enlistment and the Search for Successful Recruits." (Alexandria, VA: Human Resources Research Organization, FR-PRD-84-4).

Laurence, Janice H. (1987). "Military Enlistment Policy and Education Credentials: Evaluation and Improvement." (Alexandria, VA: Human Resources Research Organization, FR-PRD-87-33).

Laurence, Janice H. (1993). "Education Standards and Military Selection: From the Beginning." in *Adaptability Screening for the Armed Forces.* T. Trent and J. H. Laurence, eds. (Washington, DC: Office of Assistant Secretary of Defense) (Force Management and Personnel).

Laurence, Janice H. (1997). *Education Credential Tier Evaluation.* (Alexandria, VA: Human Resources Research Organization).

Laurence, Janice H., Naughton, Jennifer, and Harris, Dickie A. (1996). *Attrition Revisited: Identifying the Problem and Its Solutions.* (Alexandria, VA: U.S. Army Research Institute for the Behavioral and Social Sciences).

Laurence, Janice H., Ramsberger, P. F., and Arabian, J. M. (1996). "Education Credential Tier Evaluation." (Alexandria, VA: Human Resources Research Organization, FR-EADD-96-19).

Means, B., and Laurence, Janice H. (1984). "Characteristics and Performance of Recruits Enlisted with General Educational Development (GED) Credentials." (Alexandria, VA: Human Resources Research Organization, FR-PRD-84-6).

National Center for Education Statistics. *Digest of Education Statistics.* (Washington, DC: National Center for Education Statistics).

Nelson, B. (1997). "Should Social Skills Be in the Vocational Curriculum? Evidence from the Automotive Career Field." in *Transitions in Work and Learning: Implications for Assessment, Papers and Proceedings.* A. M. Lesgold, M. J. Feuer, and A. M. Black, eds. (Washington, DC: National Academy Press).

Sipes, D. E., Strickland, W. J., Laurence, Janice H., DiFazio, A. S., and Wetzel, E. S. (2000). "Training Base Attrition: Analysis and Findings." (Alexandria, VA: Human Resources Research Organization, FR-00-38).

Smith, T. M. (1996). *Origins of the Social Value of the GED: Economic and Sociological Perspectives on Individual Support and State Sanction of the General Educational Development Test.* (Washington, DC: National Center for Education Statistics).

Steinhaus, S. D. (1988). "Predicting Military Attrition from Educational and Biographical Information." (Alexandria, VA: Human Resources Research Organization, FR-PRD-88-06).

Tabachnick, Barbara G., and Fidell, Linda S. (2001). "Using Multivariate Statistics. Boston: Allyn and Bacon.

Trent, Thomas, and Laurence, Janice H. (1993). *Adaptability Screening for the Armed Forces.* (Washington, DC: Office of Assistant Secretary of Defense) (Force Management and Personnel).

Young, M. C., Heggestad, E., and Nason, E. (1999). "A.I.M. Pre-Implementation Research and Implementation Plans." (Presented to: Working Group 4: Screening, Selection, Attrition, and Retention of the Military Operations Research Society Mini-Symposium).

IV

THE GED CREATES PROBLEMS

7

THE GED TESTING PROGRAM INDUCES
STUDENTS TO DROP OUT

JAMES J. HECKMAN, JOHN ERIC HUMPHRIES, PAUL A. LAFONTAINE,
AND PEDRO L. RODRÍGUEZ

7.1 Introduction

This chapter studies how changes in the availability and difficulty of the
General Education Development (GED) test affect high school dropout rates.
GED certification allows dropouts to earn state-issued GED credentials.[1]

As noted in Chapter 1, GED credentials account for approximately 12%
of high school credentials issued in the United States in 2008. Test takers
are required to pass a five-part, 7.5-hour test to earn a state-issued GED
credential. Obtaining a GED certificate is easier for most students than
graduating in the traditional fashion. The option may be especially attractive for cognitively able students who lack credits or face other challenges.
As noted in Chapter 1, the median study time of GED test takers who study
is 32 hours.[2] Chapter 5 documents the small average labor market returns
to GED certification.[3]

Few papers have considered whether the availability of the GED option
induces students to drop out rather than graduate. Chaplin (1999) and
Lillard (2001) estimate the effect of the availability of the GED on high
school continuation and dropout rates by exploiting cross-state variation in GED testing policies over time. Controlling for state-, year-, and
age-fixed effects, both studies find that state GED policies are statistically
significant predictors of high school dropout rates. In particular, policies

---

1. This chapter is based on Heckman et al. (2012).

2. See Zhang, Han, and Patterson (2009). We do not know the amount of time spent
studying by those who do not pass the exam. Data from 1989 (Boesel, Alsalam, and
Smith, 1998) shows that 56% of people reported studying 40 hours or less and 24%
reported studying over 100 hours. Classroom attendance for a typical school year
is over 1,000 hours per year, and most GEDs are a year or more below twelfth grade
when they drop out of school.

3. See Chapter 5 for a review of the literature.

that provide exemptions to age restrictions for GED testing or lower passing standards promote dropping out of high school. Furthermore, states with lower requirements for the GED have higher GED test-taking rates.

The identification strategy employed in previous studies could be compromised if cross-state variation in GED-testing requirements is not exogenous. If states change GED requirements in response to trends in state-level dropout rates, estimates of the GED effect will be biased. States might respond to increased dropout rates by lowering GED requirements. Estimates that do not account for this response would tend to overstate the effect of lower passing standards.

This chapter presents three studies of the incentive effects of the GED program. The first study uses an identification strategy based on a nationally mandated change in GED passing standards imposed in 1997 by the GED Testing Service. All states were required to comply with new score requirements. This national mandate forced some states to raise passing standards, while other states were unaffected. This strategy addresses the endogeneity problem because the timing and magnitude of the one-time change in requirements is exogenous to any state-specific trends or policy changes.

Students react strongly to the change in the difficulty of the GED test. Difference-in-difference estimates show that a 6 percentage point decrease in the probability of passing the GED causes a statistically significant 1.3 percentage point decline in the overall dropout rate. The policy has its greatest effect on older students who are less restricted in their educational decisions. In states that were required to change their policies, the graduation rate increased by 3 percentage points more than in states that did not change their policies. GED policy changes have larger effects on minorities because at any grade they tend to be older and hence less subject to minimum school-leaving age requirements. They are also more likely to be behind majority students in meeting graduation requirements.

In a second study, we examine the effect of introducing GED Option programs in Oregon. First introduced in 2001, these programs offer GED preparation and certification in high schools. They target students who are perceived to be at risk of dropping out of high school and guide them into GED certification. These programs reduce high school graduation rates. Using panel data, we show that graduation rates declined by 4% in districts which implemented programs in regular high schools.

In a third study, we examine the impact of introducing the GED in California. In 1974, California became the last state to extend GED certification to civilians.[4] Prior to adopting the GED program, California had higher graduation rates than other states in the United States. After adopting the GED program, California's graduation rates quickly fell to levels similar to those in other states. Difference-in-difference estimates suggest that adoption of the GED led to a 3 percentage point decline in high school graduation rates.

Our findings are consistent with previous studies showing that the GED induces youth to drop out of school. We expand on previous studies by showing that minorities and males are more strongly affected by GED policy changes. We provide the first empirical estimate of the effect of introducing the GED program on high school graduation rates.

This chapter and the next show that students respond to the incentives created by schools and the options to drop out of school. When high-stakes testing in public schools becomes more stringent, more students drop out, and many take the GED.[5] When the GED is introduced or made easier, more students take it and drop out of schools, incurring the wage penalties discussed in Chapter 5.

This chapter proceeds in the following way. Section 7.2 presents a background discussion of the relationship between GED policies and dropout rates. Section 7.3 analyzes the impact of the 1997 GED policy change on the dropout rate. Section 7.4 estimates the effect on the dropout rate of introducing the GED as an option for at-risk high school students in Oregon. Section 7.5 estimates the effect of introducing the GED program for civilians on California dropout rates. Section 7.6 concludes with a discussion of our main findings and their implications for policy.

7.2 Evidence on the Effects of GED Policies and Incentives

As discussed in Chapter 2, the GED Testing Service (GEDTS) promotes its credential as being equivalent to a traditional high school diploma. A recent NCES study shows that many students view taking the GED credential as an attractive alternative to graduating from high school. It found that over 40% of dropouts stated they did not complete high school because they "thought it would be easier to get a GED." This was the second most cited reason behind "missed too many school days" (43.5%). It also placed far above the reasons that are commonly believed to be the primary ones

---

4. Prior to 1974, the GED program in California was restricted to veterans and military personnel.

5. See Warren, Jenkins, and Kulick (2006) and Chapter 8 of the present volume.

Table 7.1 Percentage of Spring 2002 HS Sophomores Who Had Not Completed a HS Degree by Spring 2004, by Reason for Leaving School

Reason for Leaving School (Not Mutually Exclusive)	Percent
Missed too many school days	43.5
Thought it would be easier to get GED	40.5
Getting poor grades/failing school	38.0
Did not like school	36.6
Could not keep up with schoolwork	32.1
Became pregnant[a]	27.8
Got a job	27.8
Thought could not complete course requirements	25.6
Could not get along with teachers	25.0
Could not work at same time	21.7
Had to support family	20.0
Did not feel belonged there	19.9
Could not get along with other students	18.7
Was suspended from school	16.9
Had to care for a member of family	15.5
Became father/mother of a baby	14.4
Had changed schools and did not like new one	11.2
Thought would fail competency test	10.5
Did not feel safe	10.0
Was expelled from school	9.9
Got married/planned to get married	6.8

Source: Reproduced from U.S. Department of Education, National Center for Education Statistics, Education Longitudinal Study of 2002 (ELS:2002/04), "First Follow-up, Student Survey, 2004," previously unpublished tabulation (January 2006).
[a]Percentage of female respondents only. The reason could only be selected by female respondents.

for dropping out of school, notably pregnancy (27.8%), work (27.8%), and marriage (6.8%).[6] See Table 7.1.

There is a close relationship between trends in GED test taking and the national dropout rate. Figure 7.1 plots two versions of the dropout rate by both including and excluding GED recipients as graduates. It also plots the percentage of GED test takers ages 19 or under in each year. Increases in the fraction of high school dropouts are associated with increasing GED test taking among secondary school–age youth. The two time series move together in response to national GED policy changes. When GED

6. Answers are not mutually exclusive and therefore percentages do not sum to 100.

Figure 7.1 U.S. High School Dropout Rate Including and Excluding GED Recipients, 1968–2005

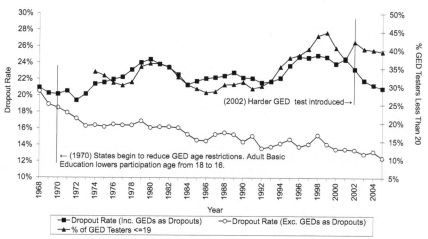

Notes: The dropout rate is calculated as the fraction of public and private school 8th graders who do not obtain a regular high school diploma. Public school enrollment and public and private high school diploma counts come from the NCES Digest of Education Statistics (various years). Annual private school enrollment is estimated from CPS October data. The NCES dropout rate is one minus the status completion rate. The status completion rate is computed from CPS October data as the percentage of 18- through 24-year-olds who are not enrolled in high school and who have any type of high school credential. High school credential includes a high school diploma or equivalent credential such as a GED.

age requirements are lowered, more youth take the GED and more students drop out. When standards are increased, the opposite occurs.

If GED recipients are counted as high school graduates, the dropout rate has steadily declined since 1970. If they are counted as dropouts, the high school dropout rate increased until the early twenty-first century. In the first few years of the graph, the two dropout measures are nearly equal. They begin to diverge sharply after 1970, coinciding with the rapid expansion of the GED testing program shown in Figure 1.1 of Chapter 1.

Expansion of the GED testing program is associated with a number of important policy changes that made the GED more accessible to school-age youth. As noted in Chapter 2, during the early 1970s, states began to eliminate age restrictions on GED testing in an attempt to make GED credentials more accessible to young dropouts. Previously, most states required that individuals be at least 20 years old in order to take the GED. Additionally, in 1970 Adult Education (AE) programs began targeting younger populations

Figure 7.2 Average Age of GED Test Takers from the GED Testing Service, 1960–2006

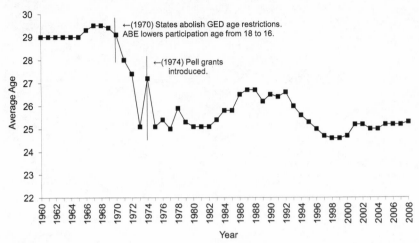

Source: American Council on Education, General Educational Development Testing Service Statistical Reports.

by lowering the minimum age requirement for participation from 18 to 16. In the same year, Adult Secondary Education (ASE) programs were introduced, targeting those lacking secondary education. These programs produced many GED credentials. AE programs issued 20% of GED credentials in 1972 and 40% by 1980.[7]

Following these changes, both the dropout rate and the percentage of young GED test takers began to rise. Figure 7.2 shows that the average age of GED test takers dropped precipitously in the early 1970s, declining from 29 in 1970 to 25 in 1973.[8] The average age has remained low since then, except for a sharp increase in 1974 that coincides with the introduction of Pell Grants financing higher education, which initially required at least a GED to qualify.[9]

7. See Chapter 3 and Heckman, Humphries, and Mader (2011).

8. Heckman and LaFontaine (2010) show that the baby boom and the subsequent baby bust accounts for only a small portion of the variation in the average age of GED test takers.

9. The Federal Pell Grant Program provides need-based grants to low-income undergraduate and certain postbaccalaureate students to promote access to post-secondary education (U.S. Department of Education Website, http://www.ed.gov/programs/fpg/index.html). The sharp rise in the average age in 1974 was possibly due to a pent-up demand for college among older dropouts.

7.3 The Effect of the 1997 GED Policy Change

The survey and time-series evidence suggests that incentives to take the GED test are related to youth dropout behavior. Are the observed relationships causal? In the first of the three studies reported in this chapter, we address this question by exploiting exogenous variation in the difficulty of passing the GED arising from a nationally mandated toughening of GED passing score requirements in 1997. Prior to 1997, states fell into one of three groups: (1) 19 states with a requirement of a minimum score of 40 on each subtest and a mean score of 45 across all subtests; (2) 26 states with a 35 minimum and 45 mean requirement; and (3) a group of 5 states where GED candidates had to achieve a 40 minimum on each test *or* a mean score of 45 across all tests.

Starting in 1997, all states had to meet the new standard of a minimum score of 40 on each test and a mean score of 45. This standard forced the second group of states to raise their minimum score requirement on each test from 35 to 40 and the third group of states to require a minimum of 40 *and* a mean of 45. The first group of states that already met the new standards did not change their requirements. Figure 7.3 shows the geographic distribution of the states by category.

According to a norming study conducted by the American Council on Education, only 67% of graduating high school seniors are able to meet a minimum score requirement of 40 and a mean score requirement of 45. A minimum of 35 and a mean of 45 was obtained by 69%, and 73% scored at the 40 or mean of 45 threshold (Table 7.2). Thus, the change in difficulty of passing the GED was far greater in the third group relative to the other two. Observed changes in pass rates in the three types of states before and after 1997 reflect this difference (see the far right-hand column of Table 7.2).

The third group of five states serves as our "treatment" group. The states that did not change their standards serve as the "control" group.[10] We compare GED testing and dropout rates in treatment and control states in 1994–1996 to the same rates measured in 1998–2000. We exclude 1997 from our empirical analysis because the change in GED requirements occurred in the middle of the school year. The reform could have caused some students to drop out and take the GED early in the year and others to stay in school after the requirements were changed later in the same year.

10. In Web Appendix Section W7.4, we use as our control group the states that were required to minimally raise the difficulty of obtaining a GED to test the exogeneity assumption. The results from this analysis are consistent with the results reported in the text. This Web Appendix mentioned in this note and subsequent notes is found at http://jenni.uchicago.edu/Studies_of_GED.

Figure 7.3 States That Were Required to Raise GED Passing Standards in 1997

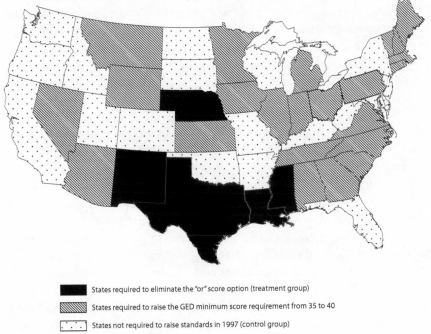

■ States required to eliminate the "or" score option (treatment group)

▨ States required to raise the GED minimum score requirement from 35 to 40

⬚ States not required to raise standards in 1997 (control group)

Source: GED Testing Service: 2001 GED Statistical Report.

Table 7.2 Percentage of High School Seniors Meeting Various GED Score Requirements and the Actual Change in Pass Rates Pre– and Post–1997

GED Score Standard	Number of States Prior to 1997 Change	% of HS Seniors Meeting Requirements[a]	Actual Change in Pass Rate[b]
Minimum 40 or Mean 45	5	73%	–7.43%
Minimum 35 and Mean 45	26	69%	–1.68%
Minimum 40 and Mean 45	19	67%	–1.26%

Source: The percentage of high school seniors in the GED norming study meeting the given score requirement is from the 1987 GED statistical report. The actual change in pass rates are from authors' calculation based on various GED statistical reports.

[a]GED norming studies are based on the performance of a representative sample of high school seniors. Depending on their performance, GED scores are normalized to obtain a normal distribution of mean 50 and standard deviation 10.

[b]In states that went from indicated requirement pre–1997 to Minimum 40 and Mean 45 post–1997.

We compute three measures of annual dropout rates using the Common Core of Data (CCD) and a methodology similar to that developed by Kominski (1990).[11] The measures are: (1) the *overall* dropout rate, defined as the percentage of students enrolled in the tenth, eleventh, and twelfth grades in year t who are not enrolled and have not graduated in year $t + 1$; (2) the *lower level* dropout rate, defined as the percentage of students enrolled in tenth and eleventh grades in year t who are not enrolled in year $t + 1$; and (3) the *upper level* dropout rate, given by the percentage of students enrolled in twelfth grade in year t who did not graduate in year $t + 1$.[12] These rates are yearly exit rates from school and therefore differ in levels from more commonly reported cohort dropout rates (see, e.g., Heckman and LaFontaine, 2010). All dropout rate calculations are weighted by the fraction of the U.S. 15- to 17-year-old population that resides in each state for our sample period. Figure 7.4 plots these rates of GED test taking and dropout by year in treatment and control states during our sample period.[13]

We define dropout rates this way for the following reasons. First, we need to compute yearly exit rates from schooling to capture the timing of the school-leaving decision before and after the GED policy change. Second, we seek to examine whether there are differential effects by grade and age.[14] If students drop out to take the GED, we would expect to find larger effects for students enrolled in upper-grade levels since they are older and, as a group, less restricted by compulsory schooling laws and state-level GED testing age requirements. Third, these measures are less sensitive to migration than cohort rates at the state level because they are defined over shorter intervals. Cohort dropout and graduation rates are generally calculated using up to five-year lags of enrollment and diploma counts (e.g., diplomas issued in the spring of year t over fall eighth-grade enrollment in

11. The Common Core of Data (CCD) are collected from state departments of education and contain the number of students enrolled in each grade level in a given year in each state, as well as the number of high school diplomas issued in that year. See Web Appendix Section W7.1 for details. From these annual counts, approximate annual exit rates from each grade can be computed. See Web Appendix Section W7.2 for more details on the construction of these measures.

12. The labels "overall," "lower," and "upper" are our own and are not based on any official definitions. All formulas used to compute each of the dropout rate measures are included in Section W7.2 of the Web Appendix.

13. The plots by race are available in the Web Appendix, Section W7.2. Data on GED testing by age is from the 1994–2000 GED Statistical reports (see GED Testing Service, 1959–2008). Population totals by age are obtained from the Census Bureau.

14. The age of students is not available in CCD data, so we use the grade level as a proxy measure.

Figure 7.4 GED Testing and Dropout Rates by Year, Treatment versus Control States

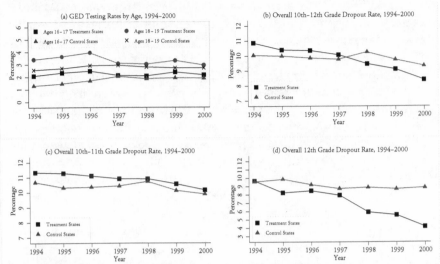

Notes: GED testing rates are calculated from yearly GED Statistical Reports as the percentage of the state population in the given age range who take the GED in that year. Dropout rates are calculated from the Common Core of Data (CCD) as the exit rate for those in the indicated grades in the given year. See Sections W7.2 and W7.3 of the Web Appendix for further details. States required to raise GED pass requirements (treatment states) are: LA, MS, NE, NM, TX. States that did not change pass requirements (control states) are: AR, CA, CO, DE, DC, FL, ID, KY, MD, MO, NJ, NY, ND, OK, OR, SD, UT, WA, WV, WI. NJ is excluded in all dropout calculations due to data errors.

year $t-5$). Our exit rates are lagged one year and therefore are less sensitive to migration.[15] Finally, we exclude ninth graders because high rates of retention at that grade make it difficult to calculate yearly exit rates between ninth and tenth grade. Most ninth graders are younger than 16, so they are not eligible to take the GED in any state.

Conley and Taber (2005) show that standard asymptotic results do not apply to many difference-in-difference studies due to the small number of observed policy changes. They develop a permutation test methodology

15. A 1997 immigration reform bill generally made it more difficult to migrate and reside in the United States. To test the sensitivity of our Hispanic estimates to this reform, we compare Hispanic dropout rates in high-immigration control states to the large estimates we find in treatment states. We find no significant declines in dropout rates in these control states, suggesting that bias due to migration is minimal. See Web Appendix Table W7.52 for this analysis.

that consistently estimates the asymptotic distribution of the treatment effect under the null hypothesis of no treatment effect. Since our sample is limited to only five states that were required to change GED testing policies, we follow their methodology when computing our test statistics. We also report robust standard errors clustered at the state level for purposes of comparison.

Figure 7.5 presents the average GED test-taking rate by age pre- and post-1997. The unadjusted mean difference-in-difference estimates and standard errors are also reported for each age group at the top of the figure. For the control group, average GED testing rates remained essentially flat over the two periods for all age groups. In contrast, treatment group states exhibit a sharp decline in GED testing after 1997, especially for the older cohorts (ages 18–19) that face fewer restrictions in both leaving school and taking

Figure 7.5 Average Pre– and Post–1997 GED Test-Taking Rate by Age Group

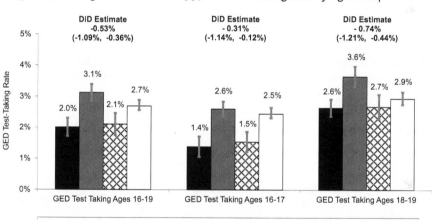

Source: GED Testing Service Annual Reports: "Who Took the GED?" (1994–2000).
Note: GED test-taking rates are defined as the ratio between total number of test takers of a given age and total population of that age. The plot above shows the average GED test-taking rate for the period pre–1997 (i.e., 1994–1996) and post–1997 (i.e., 1998–2000). For more information, see Section W7.2 and Tables W7.2 and W7.7 in the Web Appendix. All estimates are weighted by the 15- to 17-year-old population by state. Conley-Taber-adjusted confidence intervals in parentheses, while standard error bars show robust standard errors clustered at the state level. The treatment group consists of states that were required to eliminate the and/or score option. These include LA, MS, NE, NM, TX. The control group consists of states that already had high enough standards by 1997. These include: AR, CA, CO, DE, DC, FL, ID, KY, MD, MO, NJ, NY, ND, OK, OR, SD, UT, WA, WV, WI. The state of NJ is dropped in order for test-taking rates to be consistent with dropout rate regressions.

the GED test. These estimates suggest that the policy change led to a 0.74 percentage point reduction in GED test taking ($p < 0.05$). This is a 20% decline relative to the average GED test-taking rate in treatment states prior to the change. Also, before raising passing requirements, treatment group states had much higher GED testing rates than did states in the control group. This difference in GED testing levels is nearly eliminated once the treatment states increased their standards.

The overall dropout rates pre- and post-1997 across all races in both control and treatment states are presented in Figure 7.6. Unadjusted difference-in-difference estimates and standard errors are reported at the top of each set of figures. In the treated states, the overall dropout rate declines sharply across all race groups. The largest declines occur for blacks and Hispanics.[16]

In contrast, younger students did not drop out at higher rates, likely because they did not meet the minimum age requirements for the GED.[17] For younger students, dropout rates decline in both treatment and control states for whites, blacks, and Hispanics, but none of the difference-in-difference estimates are statistically significantly different from zero.

The estimated effect of the GED testing reform on school dropout rates is much larger for older students (see Figure 7.7). The estimated change in the twelfth-grade dropout rate across all race groups combined is 3.1 points and is statistically significant at the 5% level. Again, we observe larger effects among minority students. Whereas the twelfth-grade dropout for whites decreases by 1.4 points, black and Hispanic dropout rates decline by 4.4 and 7 points more in treatment states, respectively. Declines in the twelfth-grade dropout rate account for nearly all of the decline in the overall dropout rate in states that increased GED standards. Chapter 8 reports a similar pattern of greater sensitivity of minority students' GED certification to changes in the stringency of high school exit exams. Minority students are more likely to be on the margin for dropping out of school entirely as they are typically behind their group in grade attainment (see Cameron and Heckman, 2001).

Students enrolled in lower grade levels in treatment states effectively provide a second control group in our analysis. Most of the students in this group are not affected by changes in GED requirements because they

16. The estimates by race are not directly comparable with the "all races" category since estimates by race include fewer states as a result of missing enrollment data by race. All estimates by race are restricted to the same subsample of states.

17. See Figure W7.1 in the Web Appendix.

Figure 7.6 Average Pre– and Post–1997 10th–12th Grade Dropout Rate for Treatment and Control Group

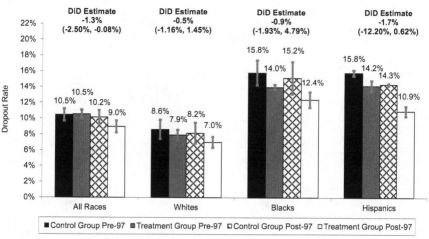

Source: Common Core of Data (CCD).

Notes: The dropout rate is defined as the ratio of students enrolled in a given grade(s) in year t and the number of students enrolled in the previous grade(s) in year $t-1$, where $t = 1994$–2000. All estimates are weighted by the 15- to 17-year-old population in the given state. The plot above shows the average dropout rate for the period pre–1997 (i.e., 1994–1996) and post–1997 (i.e., 1998–2000). For more information, see Section W7.2 and Tables W7.1 and W7.7 in the Web Appendix. Conley-Taber-adjusted confidence intervals are in parentheses, while standard error bars show robust standard errors clustered at the state level. Treatment states are those states that were required to eliminate the and/or score option. These include: LA, MS, NE, NM, TX. Control states are those that already had high enough standards by 1997. These include: AR, CA, CO, DE, DC, FL, ID, KY, MD, MO, NJ, NY, ND, OK, OR, SD, UT, WA, WV, WI. States with fewer than two observations per period are dropped for "all races" category. States with fewer than two observations per period for any of the dropout rate measures by race are dropped for by race categories. Control states dropped from "all races" regressions due to missing and negative dropout rates include: NJ. Control states dropped from regression by race due to missing and negative dropout rates include: AR, ID, KY, MO, ND, NJ, NY, SD, UT, WA, WV. No treatment states are dropped from any regressions. Since there are more missing in the dropout rates by race, the "all races" category is not directly comparable to the categories by race.

Figure 7.7 Average Pre– and Post–1997 12th Grade Dropout Rate for Treatment and Control Group

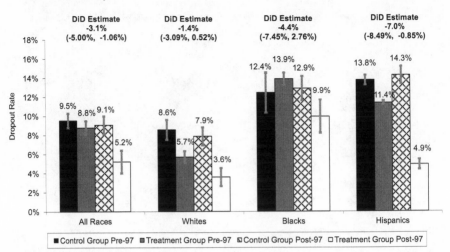

Source: Common Core of Data (CCD).

Notes: The dropout rate is defined as the ratio of students enrolled in a given grade(s) in year *t* and the number of students enrolled in the previous grade(s) in year *t* – 1, where *t* = 1994–2000. All estimates are weighted by the 15- to 17-year-old population in the given state. The plot above shows the average dropout rate for the period pre–1997 (i.e., 1994–1996) and post–1997 (i.e., 1998–2000). For more information, see Section W7.2 and Tables W7.1 and W7.7 in the Web Appendix. Conley-Taber-adjusted confidence intervals in parentheses, while standard error bars show robust standard errors clustered at the state level. Treatment states are those states that were required to eliminate the and/or score option. These include: LA, MS, NE, NM, TX. Control states are those that already had high enough standards by 1997. These include: AR, CA, CO, DE, DC, FL, ID, KY, MD, MO, NJ, NY, ND, OK, OR, SD, UT, WA, WV, WI. States with fewer than two observations per period are dropped for "all races" category. States with fewer than two observations per period for any of the dropout rate measures by race are dropped for by race categories. Control states dropped from "all races" regressions due to missing and negative dropout rates include: NJ. Control states dropped from regression by race due to missing and negative dropout rates include: AR, ID, KY, MO, ND, NJ, NY, SD, UT, WA, WV. No treatment states are dropped from any regressions. Since there are more missings in the dropout rates by race, the "all races" category is not directly comparable to the categories by race.

Figure 7.8 Percentage of HS Students 18 or Older by Grade and Race, CPS, October 1994–2000

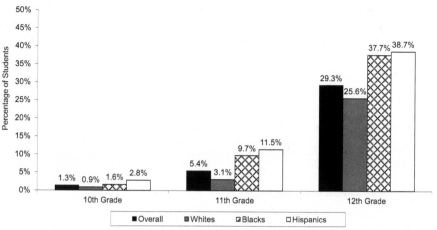

Notes: Authors' calculations from CPS, October 1994–2000 data. The sample is restricted to those who report being enrolled in high school between the ages of 12 and 20.

are too young to take the GED test without obtaining a special exemption.[18] The greater decline in dropout rates for older students suggests that the relationship between students' behavior and the reform does not stem from a confounding factor that would affect all students (e.g., increased spending per pupil or number of teachers per pupil).

If high school students respond to changes in GED score requirements, GED testing rates would likely increase immediately before increases in the standards and decline immediately afterward, artificially increasing our estimate of the dropout effect. In order to check that our estimates are not produced from a surge in test taking in 1996 and a subsequent decline induced by the shift to higher standards in 1997, we delete the 1996 observations. This barely affects our estimates.[19]

Figure 7.8 shows that differences in age between whites and minority students might explain why the reform had greater impact on minority

18. Special exemptions to age requirements vary by state and include such conditions as teenage pregnancy, residence in a juvenile detention facility, and enrollment in Job Corps programs. The 2006 GED Statistical Report contains additional information on this topic (see GED Testing Service, 1959–2008).

19. See Web Appendix W7.4.4 for this and other sensitivity analyses. In Section W7.4.5 of the Web Appendix we show that the trends prior to 1994 and post–2000 are in line with the trends displayed in Figure 7.4. The trends in the time period studies are not anomalous.

students. For whites, 25.6% of the students are 18 and above in the fall of twelfth grade. The corresponding figures for blacks and Hispanics are 37.7% and 38.7%, respectively. Far more minority students are in the age group that is not restricted by mandatory school-leaving age requirements or GED minimum age requirements. Thus, minority students are at higher risk of being induced to drop out of school by the GED at all grade levels. In addition, minority students have fewer credits than white students at each grade level, making the GED a more attractive option for them (see Agodini and Dynarski, 1998). Availability of the GED will induce more students to drop out as more students delay entry into school or are held back in school.[20] Restricting the minimum age of GED test taking is one way to prevent early exit from secondary education.[21]

7.4 GED Option Programs

Our second strategy evaluates the effect of introducing school-sanctioned GED preparation programs into high schools. As previously noted, a large and growing number of people earn GEDs before age 20 and before their high school class graduates. This is a shift away from the "traditional" concept of the GED as a second chance for older dropouts.

As shown in Chapter 3, 16-to-19-year-olds are the largest and fastest growing age group of GED test takers. Furthermore, the bulk of the growth in the 16-to-19-year-old age category comes from 16-to-17-year-olds, which grew from 10% of all GED test takers in 1980 to 15% in 2008. The GED certificate may be inducing students to leave high school.

7.4.1 THE EFFECT OF GED OPTION PROGRAMS

The American Council on Education (ACE), the organization that promotes and administers the GED test, allows some states to offer GED Option programs. These programs offer GED preparation and certification in high schools. They aim to target students who are at a high risk of dropping out and to guide them into GED certification as an alternative. The definition of high risk varies by state, but typically it means that the student is at risk of not graduating with his class or is a year behind in credits.

Introduced in 1989, the details of the Option programs vary greatly by state. Virginia requires 15 hours of academic preparation per week and

---

20. Heckman and LaFontaine (2010).

21. Section W7.5 of the Web Appendix presents a fixed-effect analysis of the introduction of higher passing standards on dropout rates, which corroborate the analysis of Section 7.3.

work- or career-based training for 10 hours a week, for a median of 12 weeks. Virginia also requires scores of 450 on each subsection of the official practice test. This is higher than the passing standard. In contrast, Oregon reports a median of 20 study hours and median enrollment of 75 days.[22,23] The majority of Option program participants graduate before their high school class. For them, the Option program may provide an expedited route out of high school.[24]

The GED Option programs offer a mixed bag. The programs may teach valuable skills to students who would otherwise drop out. However, introducing the GED directly into the high school may induce some students to earn GEDs rather than graduate. It may do this in several ways. Its presence in regular high schools lowers the information costs of learning about, preparing for, and taking the GED. Integrating it into the school system also gives the GED credential credibility. Teachers and counselors may encourage at-risk students to pursue the GED, not knowing the evidence of its minimal beneficial impact. School districts can count GED Option participants for funding purposes and remove them from the classroom. Administrators may encourage disruptive students to take the GED Option. The GED Option program may have peer effects, as many preparing for the GED are still attending their local high school. The credibility of the GED Option is further bolstered because in many states the GED credential is semantically indistinguishable from a high school diploma.[25]

7.4.2 OREGON'S GED OPTION PROGRAMS

Using administrative records, we evaluate the effect of Oregon's GED Option programs on high school graduation rates. Oregon implemented GED Option programs in 2001. The requirements of Oregon's programs are lower than those of many other states.

Oregon allows school districts to petition the state for permission to implement GED Option programs. School districts typically implement the program in one of the following ways: (1) district-wide; (2) in specific high schools in the district; or (3) only in nontraditional high schools or community colleges in the district. By 2005, 54% of districts had some form

---

22. GED Testing Service (2009).

23. Figures W7.6 and W7.7 in the Web Appendix show that the state Option programs vary greatly in terms of average days enrolled and average preparation.

24. See Figure W7.8 in the Web Appendix.

25. See Table W7.8 in the Web Appendix. However, No Child Left Behind legislation prohibits states from issuing actual diplomas based on GED certification.

of an Option program. Of the districts with programs, 49% have Option programs in some schools and 28% have district-wide Option programs.

7.4.3 THE EFFECT OF THE GED OPTION PROGRAM ON COHORT COMPLETION RATES

Using the Common Core of Data, we construct eighth-grade, ninth-grade, and tenth-grade cohort completion rates, where the eighth-grade cohort completion rate is the number of diplomas issued in a year divided by the number of eighth graders enrolled four years earlier. Ninth- and tenth-grade cohort completion rates are constructed in the same manner, but using ninth-grade enrollment lagged three years or tenth-grade enrollment lagged two years. We use all three cohort completion rates to check the robustness of our estimates. Using Oregon Department of Education ad-ministrative data, we construct three variables to capture the presence of a GED Option program: (1) a dummy for district-wide implementation, (2) a dummy variable indicating if the district has any regular high schools offering GED Option programs, and (3) a dummy for implementation of a GED Option program, but not in regular high schools. Districts with GED Option programs outside of regular high schools typically have GED Option programs in local community colleges or second-chance schools for expelled students. School districts with Option programs in regular schools typically have a large number of schools offering the program and resemble district-wide programs. We present evidence on the exogeneity of the presence of these programs in districts in Section 7.4.4.

We regress each of our three cohort completion rates on each of the three measures of the GED Option program, a set of district controls, and district and year fixed effects:

$$Y_{i,t} = \alpha GED_{i,t} + \beta_1 X_{i,t} + \beta_2 Year_t + \beta_3 District_i + \varepsilon_{i,t}, \quad i = 1, \ldots, I; \quad t = 1, \ldots, T,$$

where $Y_{i,t}$ is either eighth-, ninth-, or tenth-grade cohort completion rates; $GED_{i,t}$ is a binary variable indicating the presence or absence of a GED Option program; $X_{i,t}$ is a vector of time-variant district characteristics; $Year_t$ is a year fixed effect; and $District_i$ is a district fixed effect. The $X_{i,t}$ include percent black enrollment, percent Hispanic enrollment, percent free lunch eligible, percent free or reduced lunch eligible, the pupil–teacher ratio, total expenditure per pupil, and total revenue per pupil. State and federally operated districts, charter districts, vocational or special needs districts, and nonoperating districts are excluded from our analysis. We include data from 2000 through 2008 in our analysis, with 2002 being the first year programs were offered.

The presence of district-wide GED Option programs in schools decreases cohort completion rates. Eighth-, ninth-, and tenth-grade cohort completion rates decrease by 4.2%, 3.0%, and 4.2% after districts implement a district-wide program (Figure 7.9a). These estimates are all statistically significant.[26] We find similar results ranging from 3% to 4% for districts that have any Option program in a regular high school.[27] Cohort completion rates are not affected in districts with Option programs implemented outside of regular high schools (see Figure 7.9b). This evidence supports the notion that information and availability play key roles in the decision to earn a GED.

Not all students induced to drop out of high school by the Option program GED certify. We find an increase in GED certification rates[28] across cohorts in districts that adopt some version of a GED Option program. The presence of a district-wide Option program is associated with a 1.7% increase in the cohort GED certification rate for the eighth-, ninth-, and tenth-grade cohorts.[29] This increase is only half of the estimated decrease in cohort diploma rates.[30]

7.4.4 WHICH DISTRICTS ADOPT OPTION PROGRAMS?
Districts select into Option programs. Such selection may bias our results. Using NCES Common Core of Data and district-level 2000 Census data, we compare districts prior to the 2001 introduction of the GED Option. We find only small differences between districts that adopt GED Option programs and those that do not, suggesting that selection does not play a role.[31]

7.5 Eliminating the GED Option in California
The third study we conduct examines the effect of introducing the GED for civilians on dropout rates in California. In 1974, California became the

---

26. Estimates are statistically significant at the 0.05 level for eighth- and tenth-grade cohort completion rates and the 0.1 level for ninth-grade rates.

27. See Figure W7.9 in the Web Appendix.

28. GED certification rates are measured by the number of "other completers" reported by a district, which includes individuals who GED certify through school or state preparation programs.

29. These estimates are each statistically significant at the 0.10 level.

30. We find no statistically significant effect of the Option program on dropout rates when it is placed in alternative schools. This provides evidence that its presence in ordinary high school advertises its availability and possibly fosters iatrogenic peer effects.

31. See Figure W7.10 and Figure W7.11 in the Web Appendix.

Figure 7.9 The Effect of the GED Option Program on High School Cohort Completion Rates

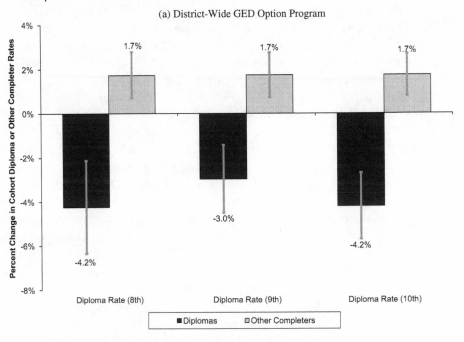

(a) District-Wide GED Option Program

last state to offer a state-recognized credential for GEDs.[32] The California legislature amended the state education code to include provisions for the issuance of the California High School Equivalency Certificate to be given on the basis of GED test scores.[33] According to the new law, this certificate would be "deemed to be a high school diploma for the purpose of meeting the requirements of employment by all state and local public agencies."

In 1974, the GED testing program was neither as large as it is today nor as popular among school-age youth. However, even then it accounted for nearly 9% of all high school credentials issued and 34% of the GED test takers were ages 16 to 19.[34]

To assess the impact of introducing the GED program, we compare the high school graduation rate in California with that of all other states in the three years before and after 1974. Since enrollment counts by grade are not available on a state-by-state basis in this period, we use an esti-

32. See Allen and Jones (1992).
33. California Legislature (1973).
34. See Figures 1.1 and 7.1.

Figure 7.9 (Continued)

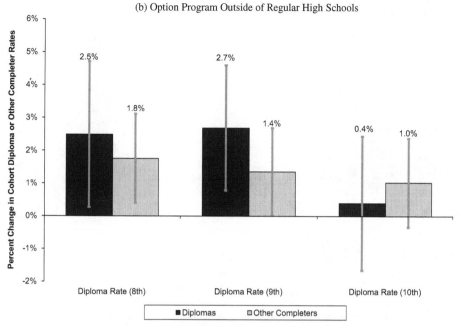

(b) Option Program Outside of Regular High Schools

Source: National Center for Education Statistics, Common Core Data and Oregon School Districts Administrative Data.

Notes: Cohort completion rates are defined as the number of diplomas issued divided by 8th, 9th, or 10th grade enrollment lagged the appropriate number of years. The definition of other completers includes students who GED certify through a district- or state-sanctioned certification program, and thus should capture students who GED certify through the GED Option program. Regressions include controls for percent black enrollment, percent Hispanic enrollment, percent free lunch eligible, percent free or reduced lunch eligible, pupil–teacher ratio, expenditures per pupil, revenue per pupil, and district- and year-fixed effects. Regressions include 2001–2002 school year through 2007–2008 school year. The bars show standard errors. For more information, see Tables W7.9–W7.12 in the Web Appendix.

mate of the 14-year-old population as a proxy for the entering ninth-grade enrollment.[35]

Figure 7.10 displays the overall, male, and female mean high school graduation rates pre- and post-1974 in both California and the rest of the

35. Population estimates for California were obtained from the California Demographic Research Unit. They provide estimates of the state population by age for the resident population on July 1 of each year. We use the July 1 15-year-old population in the next year to proxy for the previous year's fall 14-year-old population. U.S. population estimates by age are from the Census Bureau and are also estimates of the resident population on July 1.

Figure 7.10 Graduation Rate Before and After Implementing the GED Program, California versus All Other States

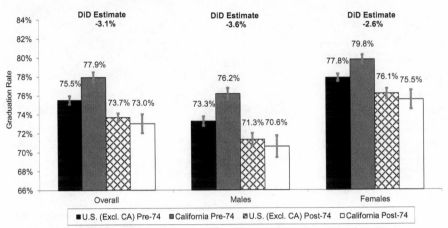

Notes: Authors' calculations based on NCES data. The graduation rate is the number of regular public and private high school diplomas issued over the 14-year-old population four years previously. Population totals for the United States were obtained from the U.S. Census Bureau. California population estimates were obtained from the California Demographic Research Unit. Huber-White robust standard errors in parentheses. State 15-year-old population are used as weights. Pre-period is defined as 1971–1973 and post-period as 1975–1977.

country.[36] Difference-in-difference estimates are also reported. Prior to the introduction of the GED program, California had a high school graduation rate that was higher than that in the rest of the United States. Once the GED was introduced, California graduation rates immediately fell to the levels of other states. While graduation rates fell both in California and the rest of the United States during this time, difference-in-difference estimates show that introducing the GED program resulted in a 3 percentage point greater drop in California relative to other states in the period from 1975 to 1977.

The adverse effect of introducing the GED program on graduation rates was larger for males than for females.[37] Male graduation rates fell by 3.6 percentage points, while the graduation rate for females declined by 2.6 points. One possible reason for this differential is that males might have

36. Figure W7.12 in the Web Appendix for this chapter displays completion rates by year for California and the rest of the country for the years 1971–1977.

37. Data for this period are not available by race.

better immediate employment opportunities and would, therefore, find an early exit from high school through GED certification a more attractive option. Additionally, males tend to be further behind in school than females at any given age. This finding is also consistent with the evidence reported in Heckman and LaFontaine (2010), who show that male graduation rates have declined more than female rates since the early 1970s.

Evidence from the late introduction of the GED program in California further suggests that the GED induces youth to drop out of school. Eliminating the GED option would increase high school graduation rates. Arguably, estimates based on 1974 data understate the effect we would observe today if the GED were not available to students. Since 1974, the GED program has expanded and become more popular with adolescents and young adults. In addition, high school standards, as measured by mandatory courses and high-stakes testing requirements, have increased substantially since the mid-1980s (see Lillard and DeCicca, 2001). These changes increase the cost of graduating from high school and the attractiveness of the GED. For these reasons, it is plausible that our estimates based on California in the mid-1970s understate the potential impact of enacting this reform under current conditions.

7.6 Conclusion

This chapter presents three studies of the effect of the GED program on the high school graduation rate. In the first study, we find that increasing the passing requirements of the GED test reduces dropout rates. A nationally mandated increase in GED passing standards in 1997 resulted in a 1.3 percentage point drop in the overall dropout rate in states that were required to change their standards relative to those that were not required to do so. The reduction in dropout rates was stronger for students enrolled in upper grade levels since these individuals are less restricted in both school leaving and GED testing. The twelfth-grade high school dropout rate fell by 3 percentage points following the 1997 reform.

Minorities are more sensitive to the availability of GED credentials than are whites. Minority students tend to be further behind than majority students. This factor makes obtaining a GED credential more attractive for minorities than high school graduation. Minority dropout rates exhibit the sharpest declines following the increase in GED passing standards. Black twelfth-grade dropout rates declined by 4.8 percentage points, those for Hispanics by 6.2 points, and those for whites by 1.3 percentage points. There are smaller changes in dropout behavior for younger students not eligible to drop out.

In a second study, we examine the effect of introducing the GED into high schools. GED Option programs integrate GED test preparation and certification for struggling students into the high school curriculum. The introduction of GED Option programs in Oregon led to a 4% decrease in graduation rates in districts that introduced programs in regular high schools.

In a third study, we show that introducing the GED reduces overall graduation rates. Prior to the introduction of the GED program in 1974, California had higher graduation rates than most other states in the country. When the California legislature established credentials for civilian dropouts passing the GED test, graduation rates fell by 3 points in California relative to the rest of the United States, and graduation levels dropped to those of the other states. Eliminating the GED option today would likely have much larger effects given the wider acceptance of the program.

Taken together, these studies suggest that the GED program induces students to drop out of school. The program has expanded from its original intention of providing a second chance to adults to providing high school–age students an alternative to a traditional high school degree.

BIBLIOGRAPHY

Agodini, R., and M. Dynarski (1998, June). Understanding the trend toward alternative certification for high school graduates. Document PR98-39, 37, Mathematica Policy Research, Inc., Princeton, NJ.

Allen, C. A., and E. V. Jones (1992). *GED Testing Program: The First Fifty Years.* Washington, D.C.: American Council on Education.

Boesel, D., N. Alsalam, and T. M. Smith (1998). *Educational and Labor Market Performance of GED Recipients.* Washington, DC: U.S. Department of Education, Office of Educational Research and Improvement, National Library of Education.

California Legislature (1973). Chapter 6 of division 6 of the education code, article 9. In *West's Education Code, Chapter 872*, pp. 1594. Sacramento: State of California.

Cameron, S. V., and J. J. Heckman (2001, June). The dynamics of educational attainment for black, Hispanic, and white males. *Journal of Political Economy 109*(3), 455–499.

Chaplin, D. (1999, November). GEDs for teenagers: Are there unintended consequences? Presented at the 1999 annual meeting of the Association for Public Policy Analysis and Management, Washington, DC.

Conley, T., and C. Taber (2005, June). Inference with "difference in differences" with a small number of policy changes. Technical Working Paper 312, NBER.

GED Testing Service (1959–2008). *Who Took the GED?: GED Statistical Report.* Washington, DC: American Council on Higher Education.

GED Testing Service (2009, December). *2008–2009 GED Option Statistical Report.* Washington, DC: American Council on Education.

Heckman, J. J., J. E. Humphries, P. A. LaFontaine, and P. L. Rodríguez (2012). Taking the easy way out: How the GED testing program induces students to drop out. *Journal of Labor Economics, 30*(3), 495–520.

Heckman, J. J., J. E. Humphries, and N. Mader (2011). The GED. In E. A. Hanushek, S. Machin, and L. Wößmann (Eds.), *Handbook of the Economics of Education*, Volume 3, Chapter 9, pp. 423–484. Amsterdam: North Holland, Elsevier.

Heckman, J. J., and P. A. LaFontaine (2010, May). The American high school graduation rate: Trends and levels. *Review of Economics and Statistics 92*(2), 244–262.

Kominski, R. (1990, May). Estimating the national high school dropout rate. *Demography 27*(2), 303–311.

Lane Community College (2008). Online GED preparation, GED 2002 changes. https://teach.lanecc.edu/ged/ged2002.htm (accessed May 9, 2008).

Lillard, D. R. (2001). Do general educational development certificate policies induce youth out of high school? Unpublished manuscript, Cornell University.

Lillard, D. R., and P. DeCicca (2001). Higher standards, more dropouts? Evidence within and across time. *Economics of Education Review 20*(5), 459–473.

National Center for Education Statistics (Various). *Digest of Education Statistics.* Washington, DC: National Center for Education Statistics.

Van Slyke, C. (2005). *GED 2005–2006 (Kaplan).* New York: Simon and Schuster.

Warren, J. R., K. N. Jenkins, and R. B. Kulick (2006, Summer). High school exit examinations and state-level completion and GED rates: 1975 through 2002. *Educational Evaluation and Policy Analysis 28*(2), 131–152.

Zhang, J., M. Y. Han, and M. B. Patterson (2009). Young GED examinees and their performance on the GED tests. GED Testing Service Research Studies 2009-1, GED Testing Service, Center for Adult Learning and Educational Credentials, American Council on Education, Washington, DC.

8

HIGH-STAKES TESTING AND THE RISE OF THE GED

ANDREW HALPERN-MANNERS, JOHN ROBERT WARREN,
AND ERIC GRODSKY

Between 1980 and 2009 the General Educational Development (GED) Testing Service issued nearly 25 million GEDs, representing approximately one-sixth of all high school-leaving credentials awarded during that time period (GED Testing Service, 2010). Although a GED certificate may benefit some portions of the population, most economists and social scientists agree that the credential is not a profitable alternative to standard high school diplomas for the majority of youth and young adults (Cameron and Heckman, 1993; Heckman, Humphries, and Mader, 2011; Heckman and LaFontaine, 2006). Given the comparatively modest return to the GED, it is natural to wonder *why* the test has become such a popular route to high school completion.

In this chapter, we consider whether the growing prominence of state-mandated high school exit examinations (HSEEs) has contributed to the rise in GED testing over the past several decades. Many states have adopted HSEEs in recent years, and existing HSEEs have become increasingly challenging (Center on Education Policy, 2012). Sound empirical evidence shows that exit exams reduce high school graduation rates (see, e.g., Holme et al., 2010), but few studies explore their consequences for rates of GED testing. To remedy this situation, we use state-level data from the GED Testing Service, the American Community Survey (ACS), and various other sources to estimate the effects that state HSEE policies have had on rates of GED testing since the early 1980s.

8.1 Background
Many states use high-stakes achievement tests to hold students, schools, and school districts accountable for meeting state-mandated academic standards. Exit exams are one type of high-stakes test. In states with HSEE policies, students must pass an exam or a series of exams before they can receive their regular high school diploma. The exams are usually administered during the tenth or eleventh grade, depending on the state, and range in difficulty from "basic skills" tests to more challenging tests aligned to

high school-based standards. Most include multiple-choice assessments of students' reading and math skills, although some also contain writing and/or other components. If students are unable to score above the passing threshold on their first attempt, they are typically allowed to retake the exam (or the portion of the exam that they failed) in subsequent years.[1]

Increasingly, states are using HSEEs as a way to verify that students have acquired certain skill sets before they finish high school. As indicated by the dashed line in Figure 8.1, the number of states requiring students to pass HSEEs before graduating rose sharply over the past three decades, to the point that nearly three out of every four public high school students are now subject to a binding HSEE policy (see, e.g., Center on Education Policy, 2012; Dee and Jacob, 2007; Holme et al., 2010; Warren and Kulick, 2007). Barring unexpected changes, this figure should continue to grow for the foreseeable future (or at least hold steady), as states that are currently in the process of phasing-in HSEEs begin to withhold diplomas on the basis of students' exam results (for up-to-date implementation timetables, see Center on Education Policy, 2012).

As we show in Figure 8.1, this shift toward heightened accountability has been accompanied by a fairly pronounced increase in rates of GED testing—*especially among high school–aged individuals* (see, e.g., Humphries's discussion in Chapter 3 of the GED testing program, its origins, and its expansion since the mid- to late 1970s). Within the 28-year period from 1974 and 2002, the number of test takers between the ages of 16 and 19 more than doubled, rising from a low of 180,000 examinees per year to a high of just over 400,000 (Heckman, Humphries, and Mader, 2011). Because of this increase, teenagers now make up nearly 40% of all test takers nationwide, putting them well ahead of 20- to 24-year-olds as the most frequently tested age group (according to the GED Testing Service, 20- to 24-year olds represent approximately 25% of the total test-taking population).

Theoretically, it makes sense to think that these two time trends are related. By design, HSEEs serve as a barrier to high school completion. Students must demonstrate mastery of various skills in order to satisfy state-mandated standards. The failure to do so can produce feelings of

1. The number of retake opportunities that students are allowed varies considerably from state to state. Some states, like Alabama, give students four chances to meet the required score before completing the twelfth grade. Other states, like Mississippi, give students five chances *per year*. Neither of these numbers are hard caps, however, as students are generally given an unlimited number of retests once they have completed all of their other graduation requirements (Center on Education Policy, 2009).

Figure 8.1 GED Test Takers and the Proliferation of State-Mandated High School Exit Exams (HSEEs), 1974–2009

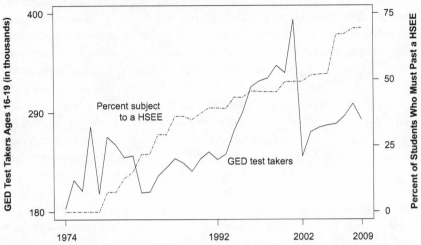

Notes: Data on GEDs were obtained from the American Council on Education's Annual Statistical Reports (various years). Data on state HSEEs were obtained from public records, legal archival resources, and personal communications with officials in state education agencies and legislative archives. Note that a new, more challenging edition of the GED test was introduced in 2002, leading to a sharp decline in examinees of all ages. See text for further details.

anxiety and discouragement (Cornell, Krosnick, and Chang, 2006; Holme et al., 2010), particularly among at-risk students from socially or economically disadvantaged backgrounds (Reardon et al., 2010).[2] As students run out of retest opportunities, they must confront the possibility that a conventional diploma is unobtainable (Dee and Jacob, 2007; Ou, 2010; Papay, Murnane, and Willett, 2010). In these situations, nontraditional pathways to high school completion may become increasingly appealing (Heilig and Darling-Hammond, 2008; Hughes and Bailey, 2001).

Nontraditional pathways may also hold some appeal from the school's perspective. Teachers and school administrators typically face strong ex-

2. Pass rates vary substantially from state to state and subject to subject. In 2011, for example, the pass rate on Florida's Comprehensive Assessment Test among first-time test takers was 58% in math and 50% in reading. The percentages in Arizona for these same subjects were 60% and 80%, respectively (Center on Education Policy, 2012).

ternal pressure to raise pass rates on HSEEs (and other state-mandated tests). In the era of No Child Left Behind, salaries, job security, and even local control of schools are often tied to specific performance targets. The nature of this incentive structure may prompt some schools to "push out" low-achieving students whose scores are unlikely to exceed the required passing threshold (Heilig and Darling-Hammond, 2008).[3] Recent qualitative evidence suggests that these difficult-to-educate students are sometimes channeled toward alternative testing programs like the GED (Sipple, Killeen, and Monk, 2004).[4]

How large of an effect these "push factors" have on rates of GED testing is not entirely clear. Although research shows that HSEEs increase dropout rates by approximately 1–2% (Holme et al., 2010), data limitations have made it difficult to quantify potential GED effects (see, e.g., Bishop and Mane, 2001; Dee and Jacob, 2007; Marchant and Paulson, 2005; Ou, 2010; Papay, Murnane, and Willett, 2010; Reardon et al., 2010). In his study of exit exams and high school persistence, for example, Jacob (2001) defined a dropout as any student who left school and did not reenroll prior to their senior year, and a non-dropout as any student who remained in school after their junior year. No exceptions were made for "dropouts" who went on to obtain a GED, or for "nondropouts" whose eventual high school-leaving credential was something other than a traditional diploma.

Unfortunately, the few studies that have distinguished GEDs from other outcomes have tended to use information particular to specific states (Jacob, 2001), time periods (Bishop and Mane, 2001; Bishop et al., 2001; Warren and Edwards, 2005), or both (Martorell, 2004), often leading to inconsistent and contradictory results. One recent exception is a study

3. This practice contributed to the so-called Texas miracle in Houston, which recorded a dropout rate of 1.5% in the 2000–2001 school year. An audit of administrative records in Houston later showed that the district had substantially understated the actual dropout rate by removing low-performing students from their calculations (Schemo, 2003).

4. In October 2008, U.S. Secretary of Education Margaret Spellings announced new requirements regarding states' measures of high school completion rates as a part of the No Child Left Behind regulations. Under the new rules, states are required to calculate and report four-year graduation rates that (1) only count regular high school diploma recipients in the numerator of the graduation rate; and (2) include students who leave high school to pursue a GED in the denominator. These new requirements are designed to minimize the sorts of "gaming" practices that were described above.

by Warren, Jenkins, and Kulick (2006), who used state-level data to model the relationship between HSEEs, high school completion statistics, and GED test-taking rates among high school–aged youth. Their results suggest that exit exam policies are associated with lower graduation rates—particularly in states with harder tests, larger minority populations, and more poverty—and higher rates of GED test taking.

In the present study, we update and extend Warren, Jensen, and Kulick's (2006) research in a variety of ways. In addition to expanding our time series to include data on more recent graduating classes, we also use a conceptually improved measure of GED test taking that allows us to better differentiate between students in adjacent cohorts who (may or may not have) faced different HSEE testing requirements. With this measure, and with the database of states' HSEE policies that we introduce in the next section, we are able to (1) estimate the impact of exit exams on rates of GED testing among high school–aged individuals; and (2) consider the degree to which such effects depend on the difficulty of HSEEs and/or the sociodemographic characteristics of the students who must pass them.

8.2 Data and Measures

In this section, we describe our measure of states' HSEE policies, our indicator of GED test taking, and various other covariates that we include in our models. We then outline our basic research design. Throughout, our unit of analysis is state-years, which we constructed by cross-classifying 50 states and the District of Columbia by the 28 years from 1981 to 2008. Note that our use of the term *years* refers only to graduating classes, not calendar years. Thus, when we say that Minnesota had an HSEE in 2002, we mean that the graduating class of 2002 was subject to that policy in that state.

8.2.1 STATE HIGH SCHOOL EXIT EXAMS

To estimate the effect of state HSEE policies on rates of GED test taking, we began by compiling a record of which states made passage of an exit exam a prerequisite for graduation and in which years. We obtained this information from a combination of sources, including public records, legal archival resources, and personal communications with officials in state education agencies (see Warren and Kulick, 2007, for more details). With this data, we were able to determine whether an HSEE policy was in effect for a given class, and whether the HSEE was a "minimum competency" test or a "more difficult" examination. If any component of the HSEE assessed

Figure 8.2 Timeline of State High School Exit Examination Policies, 1980–2009

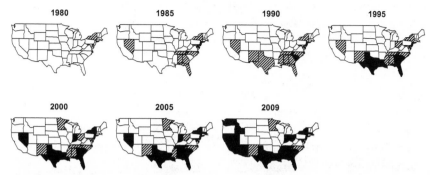

Notes: White indicates states without an exam, cross-hatching indicates states with a "minimum competency exam," and black indicates states with a "more difficult" exam aligned to high school-based standards. See text for further details.

materials typically introduced during or following the ninth grade, we categorized the exam into the latter category. All other state HSEEs were classified as minimum competency.[5]

Figure 8.2 provides a graphical representation of our HSEE data. For the graduating class of 1980, only one state (New York) required its students to pass an exit exam (the Regents Competency Test). By 2000, this figure had grown to 18, and by 2009 there were 24 states with active HSEE policies and at least five more with policies scheduled to soon take effect (Center on Education Policy, 2009, 2012). Until the late 1980s, these exams mostly assessed minimum competencies in the basic skills of reading, writing, and arithmetic. However, beginning in the early 1990s—and particularly after a prominent 1991 Department of Labor report (Secretary's Commission on Achieving Necessary Skills, 1992)—many states shifted to more challenging tests aligned to higher curriculum standards; these states are shown in black.[6]

8.2.2 GED TESTING

To create our measure of GED test taking, we collected annual state-level data on (1) the number of GED tests taken by 17- to 19-year-olds and (2) the

5. Though rudimentary, this two-tiered approach has proved useful in prior research. Warren, Jenkins, and Kulick (2006) and Dee and Jacob (2007), for example, showed that the negative association between more difficult HSEEs and the completion of high school is stronger than the association between the same outcome and minimum-competency exams.

6. Members of Tennessee's graduating class of 2008, for instance, had to pass exams in English, algebra, geometry, biology, chemistry, and U.S. history.

number of high school–aged youth by single year of age.[7] We then used this data to construct a yearly, graduating class-specific indicator of GED test-taking rates for each state-year:

$$\frac{TT(\text{age }17)_{s,t-1} + TT(\text{age }18)_{s,t} + TT(\text{age }19)_{s,t+1}}{POP(\text{age }18)_{s,t}}, \tag{8.1}$$

where s indexes states; t indexes years; TT denotes counts of test takers of different ages; and POP represents an estimate of how many students were eligible to graduate in each class.[8] Conceptually, this measure represents the percentage of students in each graduating class who took the GED test during or immediately following their high school years.[9]

The benefit of this approach is that it allows us to calculate test-taking rates across individuals who were all subject to the same HSEE policy (because they were all members of the same graduating class).[10] This is an improvement over previous state-level analyses (Warren, Jenkins, and Kulick, 2006), which group individuals from different cohorts into a single test-taking category under the assumption that they all faced identical graduation requirements. The downside is that state-level data on test takers by single year of age are not available prior to 1990; for these years, the GED Testing Service combined information on 16- and 17-year-old test takers into one category and 18- and 19-year-olds into another. To circumvent this problem, we calculated the average ratio of 16- to 17-year-old test takers and 18- to 19-year-old test takers for each state during the *post*–1990 period. Using these ratios, we then allocated the aggregated *pre*-1990 counts provided by the GED Testing Service into a single year of age categories.[11]

7. We exclude individuals ages 16 and under from our analysis because, in some states, they are not eligible to take the GED test.

8. For the years between 1980 and 1999, we obtained annual state-level population estimates by single year of age from the U.S. Census Bureau's Population Estimates Program. For the years between 2000 and 2009, these data come from the decennial census and the ACS.

9. Because a small fraction of examinees take the GED test more than once before turning 20, the cohort-based estimates produced by equation (8.1) may be slightly inflated.

10. We make no adjustments for grade retention or red-shirting. These issues are not likely to affect our estimates in a meaningful way, but they do introduce a slight amount of imprecision.

11. This technique requires us to assume that the ratio of 16- to 17-year-old test takers and 18- to 19-year-old test takers remained relatively stable over time within states. As a rough check of this assumption, we examined within-state changes in each of the respective ratios between 1990 and 2009. In both cases, the mean differ-

Although our main interest is the relationship between HSEE policies and rates of GED testing, we also include an extensive set of time-varying covariates in our analysis to reduce the possibility that the observed associations are spurious. As we describe below, we employ state and year fixed-effects models that account for (1) variables that remain constant over time but vary across states, and (2) variables that are constant across states but vary over time. This means that the only factors that could induce spuriousness are those that vary both across states and over time. Table 8.1 presents a list of measures that fit this description, provides the source of information for each, and gives descriptive statistics for all of the variables in our analysis.

Our first set of time-varying covariates includes a series of state education policy variables (other than state HSEE policies). Based on evidence that course graduation requirements affect dropout rates (Lillard and DeCicca, 2001), we include a measure of the number of Carnegie units that states require students to complete in order to graduate. Because some states have only recently adopted mandatory course requirements, we also include a dummy variable that indicates whether state-years have a minimum course policy in place; when they do not, the value of the Carnegie unit variable is set to 0. In addition, we include a measure of states' maximum compulsory age of school attendance and an indicator reflecting the difficulty of states' GED passing standards.[12] These latter two variables allow us to control for some of the structural factors that young people must consider when evaluating the feasibility of different high school-leaving options.

The second set of covariates allows us to adjust for state-level characteristics that are known to influence the likelihood of HSEE adoption *and* high school completion (Warren and Kulick, 2007). Using data from the U.S. Census Bureau, we include annual state poverty rates, which are highest in states with "more difficult" HSEEs and lowest in states with no HSEEs. Using data from the U.S. Bureau of Labor Statistics, we include measures of per capita income (expressed in thousands of constant 2008 dollars), state unemployment rates, and the percentage of jobs in each state that are manufacturing. Finally, using data from the March CPS and

---

ence between the two years (0.22 for 18- to 19-year-olds and 0.11 for 16- to 17-year-olds) was centered near zero with a relatively tight distribution.

12. Our measure of GED difficulty was derived from *GED Examiner's Manuals* (various years), which include information on each state's requirements for GED receipt. For more details, see the description included in Chapter 3.

Table 8.1 Source and Description of Dependent and Independent Variables

Variable	Source	Min	Max	No High School Exit Exam (N = 998) Mean	(SD)	Minimum Competency Exam (N = 243) Mean	(SD)	More Difficult Exam (N = 171) Mean	(SD)
Dependent Variable									
Percent of Cohort Taking the GED	American Council on Education; U.S. Census Bureau	1.23	17.12	6.95	(2.51)	7.89	(2.93)	7.58	(2.52)
Time-varying Covariates									
Poverty Rate	March Current Population Surveys	2.87	27.75	13.32	(4.10)	13.05	(4.04)	14.19	(4.41)
Unemployment Rate	U.S. Bureau of Labor Statistics	2.30	17.40	5.88	(2.21)	5.63	(1.50)	5.21	(1.11)
Percent Manufacturing	March Current Population Survey	1.60	33.76	15.51	(6.53)	14.74	(7.33)	13.02	(5.29)
Percent Non-Hispanic Black	March Current Population Survey American Community Survey	0.00	87.70	9.76	(13.98)	20.53	(12.25)	22.63	(11.73)
Percent Hispanic	March Current Population Survey American Community Survey	0.00	51.89	6.00	(8.15)	8.16	(12.57)	13.67	(12.55)
Per Capita Income (in 1000s of 2008 dollars)	U.S. Bureau of Economic Analysis	18.28	68.12	31.85	(6.73)	32.40	(5.79)	36.35	(6.36)
Compulsory Age of School Attendance	National Center for Education Statistics	14.00	18.00	16.55	(0.86)	16.62	(0.87)	16.67	(0.78)
Carnegie Units Required for Graduation	National Center for Education Statistics	12.00	24.00	18.54	(2.66)	20.31	(1.93)	22.18	(1.27)
GED Difficulty (estimated pass rate among seniors)	GED Examiner's Manual	51.00	81.00	66.88	(4.51)	67.03	(4.16)	62.68	(4.81)

Notes: The data set used to generate these estimates was created by cross-classifying 50 states and the District of Columbia by 28 years. Due to missing data on GED test taking, we were forced to drop 16 of these state-years from our analysis, resulting in a final sample size of 1,412. For the years between 1980 and 1999, our measures of percent non-Hispanic black and percent Hispanic represent four-year moving averages generated using data from the CPS; in all subsequent years we created these variables using annual data from the ACS. See text for further details.

the ACS, we construct state-year specific measures of the percentage of 14- to 21-year-olds who are non-Hispanic black and of the percentage of 14- to 21-year-olds who are Hispanic. As noted above, prior work has shown that these two indicators moderate the association between HSEE testing policies and states' high school completion rates. Whether the same is true for rates of GED testing is a question that we shall return to later.

8.2.4 RESEARCH DESIGN

To identify the "GED effect" attributable to HSEE testing policies, we examine changes in such policies within states over time. The basic estimating equation that we use is:

$$Y_{s,t} = \alpha + \mathbf{H}_{s,t}\beta + \mathbf{X}_{s,t}\lambda + \gamma_s + v_t + \varepsilon_{s,t}, \tag{8.2}$$

where $Y_{s,t}$ represents GED test-taking rates in state s and year t; $\mathbf{H}$ is a matrix of variables describing states' HSEE policies in a given year; $\mathbf{X}$ is a matrix containing the time-varying covariates described above; γ_s and v_t are state and year fixed effects, respectively; α, β, and λ are parameters to be estimated; and ε_{st} is a random error term that is assumed to be correlated within states.

The state fixed effects specified in equation (8.2) account for unmeasured, time-constant differences that exist between states; the year fixed effects account for changes in GED test-taking rates that are common across states within years (including those that resulted from the introduction of a new testing policy in 2002). In supplementary analyses, we estimate variants of this model where the sample is restricted to different time periods and different subsets of the population. These additional analyses, which we describe in detail below, help to establish the robustness of our findings and the validity of our identification strategy. In all analyses, observations are weighted by population size, where population size is set equal to the size of the graduating cohort in that state-year.

8.3 Results

Our first set of results is presented in Table 8.2, which shows point estimates and standard errors from a series of models predicting GED test-taking rates. The models vary in terms of how HSEEs are operationalized and whether year, state, or year and state fixed effects are included.[13] The findings

13. For the sake of space, we do not present estimates for the time-varying covariates listed in Table 8.1. Results for these variables and for models with no fixed effects are available in the online appendix to this volume.

Table 8.2 Estimated Effects of State HSEE Policies on Rates of GED Test Taking, 1981–2008

	Percent of Graduating Cohort Who Took the GED Test							
	(1)	(2)	(3)	(4)	(5)	(6)	(7)	(8)
Exit Exam of Any Difficulty	**0.979**	**1.103**	**0.675**	**0.659**	—	—	—	—
	(0.146)	(0.135)	(0.136)	(0.114)				
Minimum Competency Exam	—	—	—	—	**0.926**	**1.062**	**0.463**	**0.393**
					(0.158)	(0.146)	(0.149)	(0.125)
More Difficult Exam	—	—	—	—	**1.090**	**1.187**	**0.952**	**1.007**
					(0.192)	(0.178)	(0.158)	(0.133)
Constant	**15.176**	**21.527**	3.398	**13.505**	**15.222**	**21.543**	3.509	**13.274**
	(2.079)	(2.026)	(2.176)	(1.985)	(2.080)	(2.027)	(2.165)	(1.967)
State Fixed Effects?	No	No	Yes	Yes	No	No	Yes	Yes
Year Fixed Effects?	No	Yes	No	Yes	No	Yes	No	Yes
R-squared	0.399	0.512	0.759	0.839	0.399	0.512	0.761	0.842

Notes: Our analysis file was created by cross-classifying 50 states and the District of Columbia by 28 years (corresponding to the graduating classes of 1981–2008). Standard errors are shown in parentheses below each point estimate; bolded coefficients are at least twice their standard error. Although not shown, all models include time-varying covariates indicating state unemployment rate, state poverty rate, percent of jobs that are manufacturing, percent non-Hispanic black, percent Hispanic, the state's compulsory age of school attendance, the number of Carnegie units required for graduation, and the difficulty of the state's GED passing requirements. See text for further details.

are consistent across specifications. In Models 1–4, the estimates indicate that the presence of an HSEE policy significantly increased rates of GED test taking among graduating cohorts (coefficients that are at least twice their standard error are shown in bold), with effect sizes ranging from 0.66 to 1.10 percentage points depending on model specification. Given that the mean test-taking rate among cohorts was approximately 7.2% during the time period we examined, these estimates imply relative increases in test-taking rates of between 9.2% and 15.3%.

Do the effects associated with state HSEEs vary depending on their difficulty? To answer this question, we replaced the generic HSEE measure that we used in Models 1–4 with indicators of whether the exit exam was designed to assess minimum competency skills or more difficult curricular material. Here, the results are more variable across specifications. In Model 5, which does not include controls for unobserved state- or year-specific factors, there appears to be little difference between the two types of exam: both show significant and positive effects of roughly equivalent magnitude. Once we enter the state and year fixed effects, however, the story changes. In our fully specified model (Model 8), the point estimate associated with "more difficult" exams is twice as large as the estimate for "minimum competency" HSEEs, suggesting that harder tests lead relatively more students to seek alternative credentials like the GED.

How big are these effects? Using the measure described in equation (8.2), we calculate that for the graduating classes of 1981 through 2008, there was a cumulative total of 6,995,521 GED examinees between the ages of 17 and 19. Assuming everything else remained unchanged, what do our estimates imply would have happened had no states implemented HSEEs? Using the coefficients obtained from Model 8 and annual state-level data on the number of GED test takers, we computed the expected number of examinees under the counterfactual situation in which no states implemented HSEE requirements. Using this procedure, we estimate that approximately 350,000 fewer young people in the graduating classes of 1981 through 2008 would have taken GED tests had there been no state HSEEs. This is a reduction of about 5.0% in the total number of GED test takers.

8.3.1 SUPPLEMENTARY MODELS

To evaluate the robustness of the findings reported in Table 8.2, we conducted two sets of supplementary analyses. In the first analysis, we broke our time series into two evenly sized intervals: one corresponding to the graduating classes of 1981 to 1994 and the other corresponding to the graduating classes of 1995 to 2008. We then re-ran our fully specified model

(Model 4) using each subseries. This estimation strategy allows us to adjust for state-level factors that remain constant over a somewhat shorter period of time (e.g., 14 graduating classes instead of 28), while retaining the same collection of time-varying covariates and year fixed effects. If the results are consistent across the subseries, it would further strengthen the inferences we drew in the previous section.

We display the results in Figure 8.3. The y-axis gives the estimated HSEE effect on rates of GED test taking; the filled circles give point estimates for different cohorts; and the attached line segments give the 95% confidence intervals associated with those estimates. What should immediately jump out is the high degree of consistency across time periods in the HSEE-GED relationship. Having an HSEE increases the rate of GED test taking, with slightly smaller effects in the earlier period (when most HSEEs were minimum competency) and slightly larger effects in more recent years (when a greater share of HSEEs assessed higher-order skills). That these effects are both positive and significant suggests that time-invariant confounds pose only a minimal concern.

In the second set of supplementary models, we repeated our analysis using a somewhat different population of GED test takers: adults between

Figure 8.3 Estimated HSEE Effect by Graduating Class

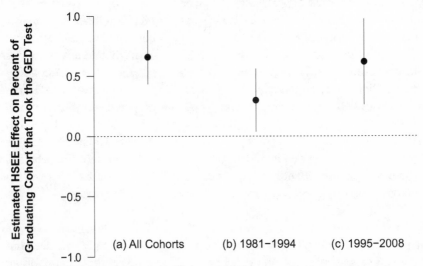

Notes: The filled circles give point estimates for different graduating cohorts, and the attached line segments give the 95% confidence intervals associated with those estimates. All models include state and year fixed effects, as well as the full set of time-varying covariates shown in Table 8.1. See text for more details.

the ages of 25 and 29. Because these individuals may or may not have been subject to the same exit exam policy (either because the policy was not in effect when they were in high school or because they were living in a different state at the time), and because there is little reason to anticipate lagged effects, we would expect to observe a substantially weaker relationship between high school exit exams and rates of GED test taking for this age group. Evidence to the contrary (e.g., nonzero effects) would suggest that factors other than state HSEEs are at least partially responsible for the HSEE effects that we described earlier.

The results are reported in Table 8.3, with coefficient estimates again arranged into eight columns according to model specification. As expected, the association between state-mandated HSEEs and rates of GED test taking is severely attenuated in each of the models. Adults between the ages of 25 and 29 are, statistically speaking, no more or less likely to take the GED test if they reside in a state that requires its *high school students* to pass an exit exam prior to graduation, regardless of the test's level of difficulty. As we mentioned earlier, this is a reassuring finding for our purposes: it lessens the possibility that our inferences about high school–aged individuals are being driven by a spurious association between state-mandated HSEEs and unmeasured (time-varying) GED testing policies and/or more general test-taking trends.

8.3.2 HETEROGENEITY IN HSEE EFFECTS ACROSS STATES

The results that we have presented to this point provide information about the average effect of enacting an HSEE policy during the years following implementation. To augment these findings, we fit a series of interactive models to evaluate the degree to which these effects vary across states with different sociodemographic profiles. The key interactions are between (1) states' HSEE policies and poverty rates, and (2) states' HSEE policies and their racial/ethnic composition. For these analyses, we have mean centered our measures of exit exams, poverty rates, and percentage minority. To ease interpretation, we only consider whether the passage of a HSEE was required for students to obtain a high school diploma; no distinctions are made concerning the exam's difficulty.

We summarize the results in Table 8.4. Consistent with prior research on high school dropouts, the effect of HSEEs on rates of GED test taking appears to be larger in states with more poverty and greater shares of racial/ethnic minorities, as indicated by the positive and significant interactions in columns 2 and 3. A 4 percentage point increase in the state poverty rate (roughly one standard deviation), for example, leads to a quarter of a

Table 8-3 Estimated Effects of State HSEE Policies on GED Test Taking among 25- to 29-year-olds

	(1)	(2)	(3)	(4)	(5)	(6)	(7)	(8)
				Percent of 25- to 29-year-olds Who Took the GED Test				
Exit Exam of Any Difficulty	0.012	0.007	0.035	0.020	—	—	—	—
	0.011	0.010	0.019	0.011	—	—	—	—
Minimum Competency Exam	—	—	—	—	0.023	0.022	0.032	0.019
					0.012	0.011	0.018	0.013
More Difficult Exam	—	—	—	—	−0.008	−0.023	0.041	0.021
					0.015	0.014	0.025	0.014
Constant	**0.709**	**1.134**	**−0.436**	**0.478**	**0.739**	**1.169**	**−0.442**	**0.476**
	(0.147)	(0.157)	(0.189)	(0.181)	(0.148)	(0.157)	(0.189)	(0.181)
State Fixed Effects?	No	No	Yes	Yes	No	No	Yes	Yes
Year Fixed Effects?	No	Yes	No	Yes	No	Yes	No	Yes
R-squared	0.176	0.341	0.587	0.697	0.178	0.346	0.587	0.697

Notes: Our analysis file was created by cross-classifying 50 states and the District of Columbia by 28 years (corresponding to the graduating classes of 1981–2008). Standard errors are shown in parentheses below each point estimate; bolded coefficients are at least twice their standard error. Although not shown, all models include time-varying covariates indicating state unemployment rate, state poverty rate, percent of jobs that are manufacturing, percent non-Hispanic black, percent Hispanic, the state's compulsory age of school attendance, the number of Carnegie units required for graduation, and the difficulty of the state's GED passing requirements. See text for further details.

Table 8.4 Alternative Model Specifications

	Model		
	(1)	(2)	(3)
Exit Exam of Any Difficulty	**0.635**	**0.564**	**0.468**
	(0.150)	(0.153)	(0.160)
Exit Exam by Poverty Rate Interaction	–	**0.058**	–
	–	(0.023)	–
Exit Exam by % Non-Hispanic Black Interaction	–	–	0.012
	–	–	(0.011)
Exit Exam by % Hispanic Interaction	–	–	**0.033**
	–	–	(0.010)
Constant	**6.262**	**6.633**	**5.961**
	(2.333)	(2.333)	(2.347)

Notes: Our analysis file was created by cross-classifying 50 states and the District of Columbia by 28 years (corresponding to the graduating classes of 1981–2008). Standard errors are shown in parentheses below each point estimate; bolded coefficients are at least twice their standard error. All models include state and year fixed effects, as well as time-varying covariates indicating state unemployment rate, state poverty rate, percent of jobs that are manufacturing, percent non-Hispanic black, percent Hispanic, the state's compulsory age of school attendance, the number of Carnegie units required for graduation, and the difficulty of the state's GED passing requirement. See text for further details.

percentage point increase in the expected effects of implementing a state HSEE on the GED test-taking rate. Likewise, a 10 percentage point increase in the share of state residents who are Hispanic (roughly a standard deviation) leads to about a third of a percentage point increase in the expected effects of implementing a state HSEE on the GED test-taking rate. Although we can only speculate, we suspect that these findings reflect the state-specific proportions of students who are both "at risk" of being prevented from obtaining a diploma and also sufficiently motivated to pursue GED credentials. State HSEEs may matter more for GED test-taking rates in state-years with more disadvantaged and (nonblack) minority students because a greater fraction of students in those state-years are "on the bubble," achieving at a low enough level to experience HSEEs as a real obstacle but sufficiently talented to view the GED as a viable alternative.

8.4 Discussion

We began this chapter by asking whether increases in GED test taking over the past three decades can be explained, in part, by the proliferation of state-mandated high school exit exams. Based on the evidence that we just presented, the answer appears to be a decided "yes." All else equal, high school–aged individuals who live in states with binding HSEE requirements have a higher likelihood of seeking out an alternative high school-leaving credential like the GED. Our results indicate that this effect is felt most strongly in high-poverty states with more demanding tests and larger racial/ethnic populations. As shown in the previous section, these inferences are robust to a variety of model specifications and are supported by supplementary analyses.

To what underlying mechanisms should we attribute these findings? As we described earlier, it seems likely that students' decisions to pursue a GED are governed by a combination of individual- and school-level factors. In some cases, the requirements imposed by HSEEs may cause marginal students to reevaluate their chances of obtaining a regular high school diploma. Already facing other barriers to high school completion, these individuals may come to view the GED as a less taxing, more realistic way to obtain a high school credential. In other cases, a desire to manipulate their state's accountability system may drive educators to remove low-scoring students from their school's high-stakes testing pool. As work by Sipple et al. (2004) and others demonstrates, one increasingly easy way to do this is to encourage them to enroll in a GED program.

Regardless of which of these explanations carries the most weight, exit exams almost certainly divert at least some students' educational pathways, rerouting them away from conventional classroom settings and toward alternative testing programs such as the GED. The costs associated with this shift should not be borne lightly. By now, it is well established that the GED has low economic returns and little influence on most recipients' postsecondary educational attainment (Cameron and Heckman, 1993; Heckman, Humphries, and Mader, 2011; Heckman and LaFontaine, 2006), especially when compared to a conventional high school degree. If it is true that high-stakes testing policies increase the attractiveness of the GED vis-à-vis more traditional routes to high school completion, as our results suggest, then these policies may actually be doing harm to a large number of students.

Whether or not this harm is justified is beyond the scope of our analysis, but we believe there is good reason to be skeptical. Prior work, including our own, has consistently shown that HSEEs have no effect on students' academic achievement, college preparedness, college completion, or workforce productivity (Bishop and Mane, 2001; Dee and Jacob, 2007; Holme et al., 2010; Reardon et al., 2010; Warren and Edwards, 2005; Warren and Grodsky, 2009; Warren, Grodsky, and Lee, 2008). At the same time, the direct costs to taxpayers of developing, implementing, scoring, and sustaining HSEEs, as well as the indirect costs of denying conventional high school diplomas to thousands of otherwise eligible students, are potentially quite large (Bhanpuri and Sexton, 2006). The fact that a subset of these students later goes on to take the GED test does little to balance out the equation.

To further investigate the questions that we raised in this chapter, future work should proceed in at least two directions. First, it would be instructive to model HSEE effects on rates of GED *certification*, not GED *testing*. Such analyses would allow researchers to provide a fuller accounting of the effect HSEE policies have on students' educational attainments. Are young people who leave the school system due to high-stakes tests successful in their attempts to obtain an equivalency degree? Or do they fare as poorly on the GED as they did on their exit exam? Unfortunately, we were unable to answer these questions in the present study because the GED Testing Service did not report state-by-age counts of GED recipients for many of the state-years under consideration. These tabulations may be available, however, through GED administrators in individual states.

Second, it would be useful to know whether the consequences of HSEEs depend on how they are administered. Within the past few years, comprehensive exit exams have begun to give way to end-of-course tests designed to gauge student learning at the completion of specific classes. Flexible scoring systems, remediation programs, and alternative forms of assessment have also become increasingly common (Center on Education Policy, 2012). With access to more recent data, researchers will be able to determine whether these policy modifications help to mitigate any of the negative consequences that we observed in our analysis. In our view, this is an important next step in clarifying the relationship between states' high-stakes testing policies, schools' responses to those policies, and students' eventual educational outcomes.

BIBLIOGRAPHY

Bhanpuri, Hoor, and Sexton, Susan K. (2006). "A Look at the Hidden Costs of High School Exit Exams." Center on Education Policy, CEP Policy Brief.

Bishop, John H., and Mane, Ferran. (2001). "The Impacts of Minimum Competency Exam Graduation Requirements on High School Graduation, College Attendance and Early Labor Market Success." *Labour Economics* 8(2): 203–222.

Bishop, John H., Mane, Ferran, Bishop, Michael, and Moriarty, Joan. (2001). "The Role of End-of-Course Exams and Minimum Competency Exams in Standards-Based Reforms." In *Brookings Papers on Education Policy*. D. Ravitch, ed. (Washington, DC: Brookings Institution), 267–345.

Cameron, Stephen V., and Heckman, James J. (1993). "The Nonequivalence of High School Equivalents." *Journal of Labor Economics* 11(1, Part 1): 1–47.

Center on Education Policy. (2009). *State High School Exit Exams: Trends in Test Programs, Alternate Pathways, and Pass Rates*. (Washington, DC: Center on Education Policy).

Center on Education Policy. (2012). *State High School Exit Exams: A Policy in Transition*. (Washington, DC: Center on Education Policy).

Cornell, Dewey G., Krosnick, Jon A., and Chang, LinChiat. (2006). "Student Reactions to Being Wrongly Informed of Failing a High-Stakes Test: The Case of the Minnesota Basic Standards Test." *Educational Policy* 20(5): 718–751.

Dee, Thomas S., and Jacob, Brian A. (2007). "Do High School Exit Exams Influence Educational Attainment or Labor Market Performance?" in *Standards-Based Reform and the Poverty Gap: Lessons for No Child Left Behind*. A. Gamoran, ed. (Washington, DC: Brookings Institution Press), 154–197.

GED Testing Service. (2010). *2009 GED Testing Program Statistical Report*. (Washington, DC: American Council on Education).

GED Testing Service. (Various). *GED Examiner's Manual: For the Tests of General Educational Development*. (Washington, DC: American Council on Education).

Heckman, James J., Humphries, John Eric, and Mader, Nicholas S. (2011). "The GED." in *Handbook of the Economics of Education*. E. A. Hanushek, S. Machin, and L. Woessmann, eds. 3. (Amsterdam: Elsevier), 423–483.

Heckman, James J., and LaFontaine, Paul A. (2006). "Bias Corrected Estimates of GED Returns." *Journal of Labor Economics* 24(3): 661–700.

Heilig, Julian Vasquez, and Darling-Hammond, Linda. (2008). "Accountability Texas-Style: The Progress and Learning of Urban Minority Students in a High-Stakes Context." *Educational Evaluation and Policy Analysis* 30(2): 75–110.

Holme, Jennifer Jellison, Richards, Meredith P., Jimerson, Jo Beth, and Cohen, Rebecca W. (2010). "Assessing the Effects of High School Exit Examinations." *Review of Educational Research* 80(4): 476–526.

Hughes, Shannon, and Bailey, Jason. (2001). "What Students Think about High-Stakes Testing." *Educational Leadership* 59(4): 74–76.

Jacob, Brian A. (2001). "Getting Tough? The Impact of High School Graduation Exams." *Educational Evaluation and Policy Analysis* 23: 99–121.

Lillard, Dean R., and DeCicca, Philip. (2001). "Higher Standards, More Dropouts? Evidence within and across Time." *Economics of Education Review* 20(5): 459–473.

Marchant, Gregory J., and Paulson, Sharon E. (2005). "The Relationship of High School Graduation Exams to Graduation Rates and Sat Scores." *Education Policy Analysis Archives* 13(6): 1–17.

Martorell, Francisco. (2004). "Do High School Graduation Exams Matter? A Regression Discontinuity Approach." (Accessed from http://www.utdallas.edu /research/tsp-erc/pdf/wp_martorell_2004_high_school_graduation_exams.pdf. Unpublished manuscript, University of California, Berkeley).

Ou, Dongshu. (2010). "To Leave or Not to Leave? A Regression Discontinuity Analysis of the Impact of Failing the High School Exit Exam." *Economics of Education Review* 29(2): 171–186.

Papay, John P., Murnane, Richard J., and Willett, John B. (2010). "The Consequences of High School Exit Examinations for Low-Performing Urban Students:

Evidence from Massachusetts." *Educational Evaluation and Policy Analysis* 32(1): 5–23.

Reardon, Sean F., Arshan, Nicole, Atteberry, Allison, and Kurlaender, Michal. (2010). "Effects of Failing a High School Exit Exam on Course Taking, Achievement, Persistence, and Graduation." *Educational Evaluation and Policy Analysis* 32(4): 498–520.

Schemo, Diana J. (2003). "Questions on Data Cloud Luster of Houston Schools." *New York Times*, July 11, 2003: A1.

Secretary's Commission on Achieving Necessary Skills, U.S. Department of Labor. (1992). *Learning a Living: A Blueprint for High Performance: A SCANS Report for America 2000.* (Washington, DC: U.S. Government Printing Office).

Sipple, John W., Killeen, Kieran, and Monk, David H. (2004). "Adoption and Adaptation: School District Responses to State Imposed Learning and Graduation Requirements." *Educational Evaluation and Policy Analysis* 26(2): 143–168.

Warren, John Robert, and Edwards, Melanie R. (2005). "High School Exit Examinations and High School Completion: Evidence from the Early 1990s." *Educational Evaluation and Policy Analysis* 27: 53–74.

Warren, John Robert, and Grodsky, Eric. (2009). "Exit Exams Harm Students Who Fail Them—and Don't Benefit Students Who Pass Them." *Phi Delta Kappan* 90(9): 645–649.

Warren, John Robert, Grodsky, Eric, and Lee, Jennifer C. (2008). "State High School Exit Examinations and Postsecondary Labor Market Outcomes." *Sociology of Education* 81(1): 77–107.

Warren, John Robert, Jenkins, Krista N., and Kulick, Rachael B. (2006). "High School Exit Examinations and State-Level Completion and GED Rates: 1975 through 2002." *Educational Evaluation and Policy Analysis* 28(2): 131–152.

Warren, John Robert, and Kulick, Rachael B. (2007). "Modeling States' Enactment of High School Exit Examination Policies." *Social Forces* 86(1): 215–229.

V

WHAT CAN BE DONE TO PROMOTE CHARACTER?

9

FOSTERING AND MEASURING SKILLS

INTERVENTIONS THAT IMPROVE CHARACTER

AND COGNITION

JAMES J. HECKMAN AND TIM KAUTZ

9.1 Introduction

The GED program does not solve the high school dropout problem. While GED certification appears to offer benefits for some groups, it does not confer the same benefits as a high school degree. Worse, the GED program conceals and fuels the dropout problem. The failure of the GED program is a symptom of a deeper problem in American society: its failure to produce essential life skills. As a group, GED recipients lack the character skills required for success in the classroom and in life. Skills, not certificates, matter.

Character skills are universally valued across all cultures and societies. Recognition of the importance of skills other than raw intelligence is deeply embedded in folk wisdom. Children everywhere are taught character-building stories like *The Tortoise and the Hare* and *The Little Engine That Could.* Even the enthusiastic creators of the early IQ tests, such as Alfred Binet, Charles Spearman, and Edward Webb, recognized the importance of character skills beyond cognition in predicting academic success.[1]

This chapter reviews the recent evidence from economics and personality psychology on the predictive power of cognition and character and the best available evidence on how to create them. A growing body of empirical research shows that character skills rival IQ in predicting educational attainment, labor market success, health, and criminality.[2]

Skills are not set in stone at birth. They can be improved. Cognitive and character skills change with age and with instruction. Interventions to improve skills are effective to different degrees for different skills at different ages.

Skills enable people. They are capacities to function. Greater levels of skill foster social inclusion and promote economic and social mobility. They

---

1. Binet and Simon (1916); Webb (1915).
2. See Almund et al. (2011), Borghans et al. (2008a), Heckman and Kautz (2012), and Roberts et al. (2007) for reviews.

generate economic productivity and create social well-being. Skills give agency to people to shape their lives in the present and to create future skills.

An effective strategy for promoting human development should be based on three factually based insights:

1. The powerful role of families in shaping skills;
2. The multiplicity of skills required for successful functioning in society. A core set of skills promotes success in many aspects of life. Different tasks require different skills in different levels and proportions. People tend to pursue the tasks where their skills give them comparative advantage;
3. The technology of skill formation: skills together with investment beget further skills.

Effective policies to promote skills straddle the missions of cabinet agencies and draw on the wisdom of many academic disciplines. They require broad thinking. Both cognition and character are important ingredients of successful lives. They are malleable to different degrees at different stages of the life cycle. They cross-fertilize each other. Focusing on one dimension of human skills to the exclusion of other dimensions misses fundamental aspects of human performance and development. Narrowly focused policies fail to capture synergisms in the expression and development of skills.

Many policymakers share a common desire to develop human potential. However, current policy discussions focus on promoting skills by improving schools. In this very narrow view, the success of schools is measured by scores on achievement tests as exemplified by the GED exam or the exams used to monitor performance under No Child Left Behind. This focus is a consequence of a very limited conceptualization of human capabilities that assumes that achievement tests capture the important life skills.

This emphasis misses important dimensions of human flourishing. It does not recognize that skills are multiple in nature. Nor does it recognize the importance of families and communities in creating skills. While schools are important, they are not the sole producers of the skills that matter.

Both cognitive and character skills are crucial to success in economic and social life. Character skills include perseverance ("grit"), self-control, trust, attentiveness, self-esteem and self-efficacy, resilience to adversity, openness to experience, empathy, humility, tolerance of diverse opinions, and the ability to engage productively in society.

Our emphasis on character skills does not arise from any agenda to impose Western middle-class values on society. A strong base of cognitive and character skills is universally valued across different cultures, religions, and societies. There are reliable ways to measure them, and there are proven ways to enhance them and to evaluate efforts to foster them.

Recent research establishes the existence of critical and sensitive periods in the formation of skills over the life cycle. Sensitive periods are those when investment is especially productive; critical periods are those when investment is essential. Critical and sensitive periods differ across skills. Investments should target those periods.

In designing effective human development strategies, it is essential to discard obsolete views about the origin and malleability of "traits." What used to be regarded as traits fixed at conception are now understood to be skills that can be augmented through guidance and instruction. Raw intelligence is not fixed solely by parental genes, although heritability plays an important role. It is boosted by quality parenting and by caring environments. It becomes solidified around the time of puberty. Character skills can also be shaped. Compared to raw intelligence, they are more malleable until later ages. Neuroscience shows that this malleability is associated with the slow development of the prefrontal cortex.[3] When attempted, adolescent remediation should focus on boosting character skills.

Skill development is a dynamic process. For example, boosting character skills early in life increases the benefits of education later in life: More persistent students learn more. The levels of cognitive and character skills at any age depend on levels of those skills at younger ages and earlier investments.[4]

Inequality among families in parenting and lack of support given to children in schools are major contributors to inequality in skills. In light of this evidence, it is of great concern that so many American children are being born into disadvantage as measured by the quality of parenting and that the trend appears to be accelerating.[5] The traditional family with its secure environment for rearing children is under challenge. A major casualty of this trend is the quality of parenting available to disadvantaged children. It is unreasonable to expect schools to take on the huge burden of supplementing compromised family environments in addition to their traditional job of educating children.

3. Walsh (2005).
4. Cunha and Heckman (2007, 2008); Cunha, Heckman, and Schennach (2010).
5. See Heckman (2008) and McLanahan (2004).

Evidence from the social and biological sciences establishes the importance of the early years in fostering the skills that promote human flourishing. Families do much more than pass on their genes or put food on the table. Human development is a dynamic process of nature/nurture interactions that starts in the womb. Environments and skills interact to foster the development of later life skills and create who we are and what we become.

The foundations for adult success are laid down early in life. Many children raised in disadvantaged environments start behind and stay behind. Poverty has lasting effects on brain development, health, cognition, and character. Gaps in skills emerge early, before formal schooling begins. Waiting until kindergarten to address these gaps is too late. It creates achievement gaps for disadvantaged children that are costly to close.

Family disadvantage is poorly assessed by conventional measures of poverty that focus on family income flows and parental education. The absence of parental guidance, nourishment, and encouragement is the most damaging condition for child development. Absence of quality parenting—stimulation, attachment, encouragement, and support—is the true measure of child poverty.

Consistent with a large literature that emphasizes the importance of the early years, Chapter 4 establishes that differences in cognitive and character skills among dropouts, GED recipients, and high school graduates emerge as early as age 6. Children from disadvantaged homes are much more likely to drop out of high school. Compared to high school graduates, dropouts and GED recipients are more likely to come from single-parent families. Single-parent families, compared to two-parent families, give less cognitive and emotional stimulation to their children (Moon, 2012), and as a consequence their children have diminished cognitive and character skills.[6] The evidence summarized in this chapter suggests that skill deficits can be prevented by improving the early lives of disadvantaged children.

Yet, while important and often neglected in American public policy, the early years do not fully determine adult success. Children are resilient and quality parenting throughout childhood fosters the development and expression of skills. Schooling shapes both cognitive and character skills. Certain adolescent remediation programs appear to be effective.

---

6. See, for example, Carneiro and Heckman (2003), Cunha et al. (2006), and Cunha and Heckman (2009).

A variety of adolescent interventions attempt to remediate early-life skill deficits. Alternatives to the traditional high school curriculum provide potential dropouts with training suitable to their interests and skills. Such programs can mold character, even if it is not their primary goal. Other interventions attempt to directly remediate character deficits after students drop out of school.

We aim to provide a sober account of what is known. We compare different skill enhancement strategies and consider the features that make some programs more successful than others. Unfortunately, the field of human development is marred by overzealous advocates who claim miracle fixes from their favored programs. They focus on one slice of the life cycle to the exclusion of others.

Slogans often replace hard evidence. Most evaluations of interventions have only short-term follow-ups. Many differ in their measures of outcomes and skills and target different demographic groups, so it is difficult to compare alternative programs. Despite these limitations, several studies suggest that interventions during the preschool years or in kindergarten improve character in a lasting way, some with annual rates of return (per annum yields) that are comparable to those from investment in the stock market in normal times.[7] Several adolescent interventions are promising, particularly those that combine education with work-related experience.[8]

This chapter is organized as follows. Section 9.2 defines cognitive and character skills and discusses how they are measured. Section 9.3 summarizes the evidence on the predictive power of character skills. Section 9.4 presents an analysis of the skills needed in the workforce, as garnered from surveys of employers. Section 9.5 presents a framework for analyzing investment in skills over the life cycle. Sections 9.6–9.12 review evidence about the efficacy of education, parental investment, and interventions in improving character skills from preschool, elementary school, and adolescence. Section 9.13 summarizes the chapter.

9.2 Measures of Cognitive and Character Skills
9.2.1 COGNITIVE SKILLS
Measures of cognition have been developed and refined over the past century. Cognitive ability has multiple facets.[9] Psychologists distinguish between fluid intelligence (the rate at which people learn) and crystallized

---

7. See Heckman et al. (2010a).
8. See, for example, Kemple and Willner (2008) and Roder and Elliot (2011).
9. See Ackerman and Heggestad (1997) and Carroll (1993) for discussions.

intelligence (acquired knowledge).[10] Achievement tests are designed to capture crystallized intelligence,[11] whereas IQ tests like Raven's progressive matrices (1962) are designed to capture fluid intelligence.[12,13]

This new understanding of cognition is not widely appreciated. Many use IQ tests, standardized achievement tests, and even grades as interchangeable measures of "cognitive ability" or intelligence.[14] As shown in Chapter 1, scores on IQ tests and standardized achievement tests are strongly correlated with each other and with grades. However, these general indicators of "cognition" measure different skills and capture different facets of cognitive ability.[15,16] In the following section we show that scores on these tests are also influenced by effort and character skills.

9.2.2 MEASURING CHARACTER

Throughout this book we use the term *character skills* to describe the personal attributes not thought to be measured by IQ tests or achievement tests. These attributes go by many names in the literature, including soft skills, personality traits, non-cognitive skills, non-cognitive abilities, character, and socio-emotional skills. These different names connote different properties.[17] "Traits" suggests a sense of permanence and possibly also of heritability. "Skills" suggests that these attributes can be learned. In reality, the extent to which these personal attributes can change lies on a spectrum. Both cognitive and character skills can change and be changed over

10. See, for example, Nisbett et al. (2012).

11. Roberts et al. (2000).

12. Raven, Raven, and Court (1988). The high correlation between scores on intelligence tests and scores on achievement tests is in part due to the fact that both require intelligence and knowledge. Fluid intelligence promotes the acquisition of crystallized intelligence. Common developmental factors affect the formation of both skills.

13. Ackerman and Heggestad (1997) and Carroll (1993) discuss more disaggregated facets of cognitive ability.

14. This practice is true even among leading professional psychologists. For example, all of these measures are used as measures of intelligence in Flynn (2007), Nisbett (2009), and Nisbett et al. (2012).

15. See Borghans et al. (2011a).

16. It is an irony of the testing literature that high school grades are more predictive of first-year college performance than SAT scores (Bowen, Chingos, and McPherson, 2009). The SAT and related tests were once thought to be a more objective measure of student quality than high school grades (Lemann, 1999).

17. See Almlund et al. (2011) and Borghans et al. (2008) for comparisons of some of these different taxonomies.

the life cycle, but through different mechanisms and with different ease at different ages. We generally use the term *skill* throughout this chapter because all attributes can be shaped.

Although character skills are overlooked in most contemporary policy discussions and in economic models of choice behavior, personality psychologists have studied these skills for the past century. Psychologists primarily measure character skills by using self-reported surveys or observer reports. They have arrived at a relatively well-accepted taxonomy of character skills called the Big Five, with the acronym OCEAN, which stands for: Openness to Experience, Conscientiousness, Extraversion, Agreeableness, and Neuroticism. Table 9.1 defines these skills and their multiple facets.[18] Some argue that the Big Five are the longitude and latitude of character skills, by which all more narrowly defined skills may be categorized.[19]

While the Big Five measures are now widely used in psychology, there are several other taxonomies, including the Big Three, the MPQ, and the Big Nine. They are conceptually and empirically related to the Big Five.[20] Other taxonomies, including psychopathology as measured by the DSM-IV and measures of temperament, have also been related to the Big Five.[21] Almlund et al. (2011) and Becker et al. (2012) summarize evidence showing that economic preference parameters are not closely related to the Big Five measures and apparently represent different skills that, along with the skills measured by psychologists, govern behavior.[22]

9.2.3 A TASK-BASED FRAMEWORK FOR IDENTIFYING AND MEASURING SKILLS

One leading personality psychologist defines personality (character) traits (skills) as follows:

18. See for example, Borghans et al. (2008).

19. Costa and McCrae (1992a).

20. See Borghans et al. (2008a) and Almlund et al. (2011) for comparisons of these taxonomies.

21. See, for example, Cloninger et al. (1999).

22. A deeper issue, as yet not systematically investigated in the literature in economics or psychology, is whether the "traits" captured by the alternative measurement systems are the expression of a deeper set of preferences or goals. McAdams (2006) adds goals to the list of possible traits. Almlund et al. (2011) and Heckman and Kautz (2012) develop a model in which preferences and endowments of skills determine the effort applied to tasks. As shown in the next section, performance on tasks is the source of any measurement of a trait. Hence, in their framework, measures of traits are determined, in part, by preferences.

Table 9.1 The Big Five Domains and Their Facets

Big Five Personality Factor	American Psychology Association Dictionary Description	Facets (and correlated skill adjective)	Related Skills	Analogous Childhood Temperament Skills
Conscientiousness	"The tendency to be organized, responsible, and hardworking"	Competence (efficient), Order (organized), Dutifulness (not careless), Achievement striving (ambitious), Self-discipline (not lazy), and Deliberation (not impulsive)	Grit, Perseverance, Delay of gratification, Impulse control, Achievement striving, Ambition, and Work ethic	Attention/(lack of) distractibility, Effortful control, Impulse control/ delay of gratification, Persistence, Activity*
Openness to Experience	"The tendency to be open to new aesthetic, cultural, or intellectual experiences"	Fantasy (imaginative), Aesthetic (artistic), Feelings (excitable), Actions (wide interests), Ideas (curious), and Values (unconventional)		Sensory sensitivity, Pleasure in low-intensity activities, Curiosity
Extraversion	"An orientation of one's interests and energies toward the outer world of people and things rather than the inner world of subjective experience; characterized by positive affect and sociability"	Warmth (friendly), Gregariousness (sociable), Assertiveness (self-confident), Activity (energetic), Excitement seeking (adventurous), and Positive emotions (enthusiastic)		Surgency, Social dominance, Social vitality, Sensation seeking, Shyness*, Activity*, Positive emotionality, and Sociability/affiliation

Agreeableness	"The tendency to act in a cooperative, unselfish manner"	Trust (forgiving), Straight-forwardness (not demanding), Altruism (warm), Compliance (not stubborn), Modesty (not show-off), and Tender-mindedness (sympathetic)	Empathy, Perspective taking, Cooperation, and Competitiveness	Irritability*, Aggressiveness, and Willfulness
Neuroticism/ Emotional Stability	Emotional stability is "Predictability and consistency in emotional reactions, with absence of rapid mood changes." Neuroticism is "a chronic level of emotional instability and proneness to psychological distress"	Anxiety (worrying), Hostility (irritable), Depression (not contented), Self-consciousness (shy), Impulsiveness (moody), Vulnerability to stress (not self-confident)	Internal versus External, Locus of control, Core self-evaluation, Self-esteem, Self-efficacy, Optimism, and Axis I psychopathologies (mental disorders) including depression and anxiety disorders	Fearfulness/ behavioral inhibition, Shyness*, Irritability*, Frustration, (Lack of) soothability, Sadness

Source: Table adapted from John and Srivastava (1999).
Notes: *These temperament attributes may be related to two Big Five factors. Facets specified by the NEO-PI-R personality inventory (Costa and McCrae, 1992b). Adjectives in parentheses from the Adjective Check List (Gough and Heilbrun, 1983).

Personality traits are the relatively enduring patterns of thoughts, feelings, and behaviors that reflect the tendency to respond in certain ways under certain circumstances. (Roberts, 2009, 140)

Roberts's definition of personality ("character") suggests that all psychological measurements are calibrated on measured behavior or "tasks" broadly defined. A task could be an IQ test, a personality questionnaire, job performance, school attendance, completion of high school, participation in crime, or performance in an experiment. Figure 9.1 depicts how performance on a task can depend on incentives, effort, and cognitive and character skills. Performance on different tasks depends on these components to different degrees. People can compensate for their shortfalls in one dimension by having strengths in other dimensions.

Many believe that personality skills can only be assessed by self-reported questionnaires that elicit skills like the Big Five. However, performance on any task or any observed behavior can be used to measure skills.[23] This book uses that approach. When comparing GED recipients and high school graduates, we control for their cognitive ability as measured by achievement tests (performance on one task) and consider how completing high school (performance on another task) predicts life outcomes. Performance on the task of completing high school reveals valuable character skills and is highly predictive of later-life outcomes. Completing high school requires many other skills besides those measured by achievement tests, including showing up in school, paying attention, and behaving in class.[24]

Figure 9.1 suggests that inferring skills from performance on tasks requires standardization for all of the other contributing factors that produce the observed behaviors. The inability to parse and localize behaviors that depend on a single skill or ability gives rise to a fundamental problem of assessing the contribution of any skill to successful performance on a task. This problem is commonly ignored in empirical research that studies how psychological skills affect outcomes.[25]

---

23. See Almlund et al. (2011).

24. The idea of using behaviors to measure character is old. Ralph Tyler suggested using measures of behavior to capture character skills in his first proposal for the National Assessment of Educational Progress tests. See Rothstein et al. (2008); Tyler (1973). This idea is being pursued in the recent literature (Heckman et al., 2011; Jackson, 2013).

25. See Almlund et al. (2011), Borghans et al. (2011a), and Heckman and Kautz (2012) for discussions of this problem.

Figure 9.1 Determinants of Task Performance

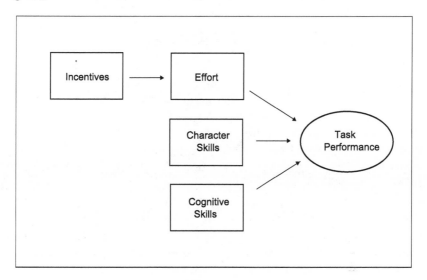

There are two issues here. First, behavior depends on incentives created by situations. Different incentives elicit different amounts of effort on the tasks used to measure skills. Accurately measuring character skills requires standardizing for the effort applied in any task. Second, performance on most tasks depends on many skills. Not standardizing for incentives and other relevant skills can produce misleading estimates of any particular skill.

These problems are empirically important. For example, incentives partly determine scores on IQ tests. A series of studies conducted over the past 40 years show that incentives, like money or candy, can increase IQ scores, particularly among low-IQ individuals. The black–white gap in IQ can be completely eliminated by giving M&M candies for correct answers.[26] However, there is no evidence that this performance persists. It has not been shown that creating incentives for performance on one test improves performance on subsequent tests, and there is some evidence that it, in fact, may worsen subsequent performance (Deci and Ryan, 1985; Ryan and Deci, 2000). Duckworth et al. (2011) have supplemented these studies by showing that observer-rated motivation predicts IQ scores.

26. See Ayllon and Kelly (1972); Borghans, Meijers, and ter Weel (2008); Breuning and Zella (1978); Clingman and Fowler (1976); Edlund (1972); Holt and Hobbs (1979); Larson, Saccuzzo, and Brown (1994); Segal (2008). This evidence is summarized in Almlund et al. (2011) and Borghans et al. (2008).

Not all persons respond to incentives with equal strength. Research by Borghans, Meijers, and ter Weel (2008) and Segal (2008) shows that the responsiveness of persons to incentives on IQ and achievement tests depends on their character skills.

The recent literature shows that character skills predict standardized achievement test scores, which many analysts assume are good measures of intelligence.[27] Figures 9.2 and 9.3 show how the variance in the scores on two achievement tests, the Armed Forces Qualification Test (AFQT) and the closely related Differential Aptitude Tests (DAT),[28] can be decomposed into IQ and character measures. Character skills explain a substantial portion of the variability in both AFQT scores and DAT scores.[29] Character skills explain the variance in achievement scores above and beyond the variance that IQ explains when both character and IQ are included in a regression. These findings caution the interpretation that standardized achievement tests only measure cognitive ability. They also capture character skills.[30] Ironically, *The Bell Curve* by Herrnstein and Murray, which uses achievement tests as a measure of intelligence, implicitly shows the power of both character and cognition in shaping life outcomes.

9.2.4 REFERENCE BIAS

Answers from self-reports can be misleading when comparing levels of personality skills across different groups of people. Most personality assessments do not anchor their measurements in any objective outcome.[31] For example, the German Socio-Economic Panel (GSOEP) survey asks respondents to rate themselves on the following statement: *"I see myself as someone who tends to be lazy"* (Lang et al., 2011). The scale ranges from 1 = "strongly disagree" to 7 = "strongly agree." In answering this question, people must interpret the definition of *"lazy,"* which likely involves comparing themselves to other people. If different groups have differ-

27. See, for example, Nisbett (2009).

28. The correlation between DAT and AFQT scores in the National Longitudinal Study of Youth 1979 (NLSY79) is 0.75 (Borghans et al., 2011b). Friedman and Streicher (1985) estimate correlations between 0.65 and 0.82 in a sample of high school sophomores and juniors. Kettner (1976) estimates correlations between DAT and the AFQT subtests of 0.76 to 0.89 in a sample of juniors and seniors.

29. The lower explained variance in the sample with DAT is likely a consequence of restriction on range. The DAT data come from a single school, whereas the AFQT data come from a national sample.

30. In the Stella Maris data, Openness to Experience is strongly correlated with IQ. See Borghans et al. (2011b).

31. These are called Likert scales (Likert, 1932).

Figure 9.2 Decomposing Variance Explained for Achievement Tests and Grades into IQ and Character [NLSY79]

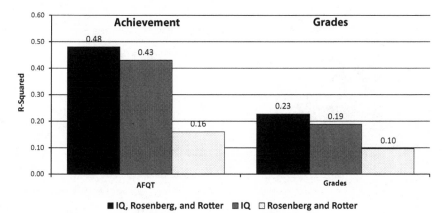

Source: Borghans et al. (2011a).

Notes: Personality is measured by the Rotter and Rosenberg personality inventories. These are only a subset of the personality inventories described in Table 9.1. Locus of Control is based on the four-item abbreviated version of the Rotter Internal-External Locus of Control Scale. This scale is designed to measure the extent to which individuals believe that they have control over their lives through self-motivation or self-determination (internal control) as opposed to the extent to which individuals believe that the environment controls their lives (external control). The self-esteem scale is based on the 10-item Rosenberg Self-Esteem Scale. This scale describes a degree of approval or disapproval toward oneself. Rotter was administered in 1979. The ASVAB and Rosenberg were administered in 1980. AFQT is constructed from the Arithmetic Reasoning, Word Knowledge, Mathematical Knowledge, and Paragraph Comprehension ASVAB subtests. IQ and GPA are from high school transcript data. AFQT, Rosenberg, and Rotter have been adjusted for schooling at the time of the test conditional on final schooling, as laid out in Hansen, Heckman, and Mullen (2004). IQ is pooled across several IQ tests using IQ percentiles. GPA is the individual's core subject GPA from 9th grade. Sample excludes the military oversample. R-squared is a measure of the proportion of variance in the outcome explained by the designated variable.

ent standards or reference points, comparing traits across groups can be highly misleading. Laziness may mean different things to different groups of people.

This measurement problem—sometimes called reference bias—is empirically relevant.[32] Schmitt et al. (2007) administer a Big Five personality questionnaire to groups of people in a variety of different countries. Using

32. Reference bias is also problematic in health surveys that use self-reported, subjective health assessments. See Groot (2000).

Figure 9.3 Decomposing Variance Explained for Achievement Tests and Grades into IQ and Character: Stella Maris Secondary School, Maastricht, Holland

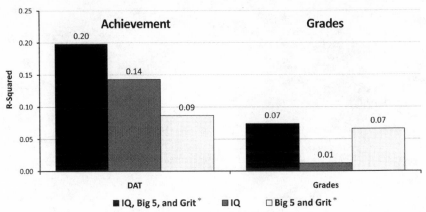

Source: Borghans et al. (2011a).
Note: Grit is a measure of persistence on tasks (Duckworth et al., 2007).

their estimates, Figure 9.4 shows how Organization of Economic Cooperation and Development (OECD) countries rank in Conscientiousness (from high to low). The bars display the average number of hours that people work in the country. The results are surprising. South Korea ranks second to last in terms of Conscientiousness but also ranks first in the number of hours worked. South Korea is not an anomaly. Country-level reports of Big Five Conscientiousness are unrelated to the number of hours worked. The rank correlation between hours worked and Conscientiousness across countries is negative, though statistically insignificant.[33]

These findings are relevant for constructing measurements of character skills. This book shows that achievement tests miss important skills, suggesting that students, teachers, and schools should not be evaluated solely by achievement tests. Would the self-reported Big Five be a useful supplement to school evaluations? The possibility of reference bias suggests that it might not. Self-reports of Conscientiousness might measure different things for different schools.

Psychologists have attempted to address the problem of reference bias.[34] Some surveys include vignette-based questions that attempt

33. $r = -0.07$ ($p = 0.73$).

34. For further discussion of reference bias, see Duckworth (2012) and her references: Goldammer (2010); Heine, Buchtel, and Norenzayan (2008); Heine et al.

Figure 9.4 National Rank in Big Five Conscientiousness and Average Annual Hours Worked

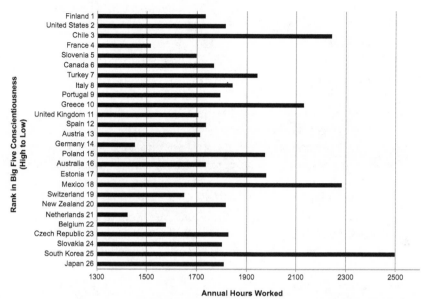

Source: The Conscientiousness ranks come from Schmitt et al. (2007). These measures were taken in 2001 (Schmitt, 2002). The hours worked estimates come from Organization of Economic Cooperation and Development (2001).
Note: Several countries are omitted due to lack of data.

to standardize for aspects of the culture or situation. They attempt to frame questions so that the people in the survey answer within a common situation. However, this approach might not work well for evaluating schools, especially if teachers have incentives to coach children on taking these tests so that they score better and give answers perceived to be positive. Direct use of standard psychological measures can be problematic.[35]

(2001, 2002); Naumann and John (2011); Peng, Nisbett, and Wong (1997); and Schmitt et al. (2007).

35. In an attempt to address reference bias, some psychologists measure skills using behaviors. Heine, Buchtel, and Norenzayan (2008) examine cross-country differences in Conscientiousness using objective measures, including walking speed, postal workers' speed, and the accuracy of clocks in public banks. To measure walking speed, researchers timed how long it took for a random sample of people to walk 60 feet in public areas. Postal workers' speed was assessed by measuring how long it took for postal workers to sell stamps.

Ralph Tyler, a pioneer of achievement testing, recognized its limitations. He suggested using measures of behavior such as performance, participation in student activities, and other observations by teachers and school administrators to complement achievement tests when evaluating students and schools. Several recent papers show that this is a promising approach. Heckman, Pinto, and Savelyev (2013) show that teacher ratings of elementary schoolchildren's behaviors are strong predictors of adult outcomes and that early childhood interventions promote the character skills measured by these ratings. Heckman et al. (2011) estimate the causal effect of cognitive and socio-emotional (character) skills on a variety of outcomes. They measure socio-emotional (character) skills using risky and reckless behaviors measured in the adolescent years.[36] Motivated by findings such as those reported in Figure 9.2 and Figure 9.3, they develop and apply methods to use high school grades to measure both cognition and character. They show that character skills promote educational attainment, beneficial labor market outcomes, and health.

Jackson (2013) studies the effect of teachers on student cognition and character. In a fashion similar to Heckman et al. (2011), Jackson measures cognitive skills using achievement test scores, while measuring noncognitive (character) skills using absences, suspensions, grades, and grade progression. These measures of character predict adult outcomes with a strength similar to measures of cognitive ability. His measures of character are commonly available from the administrative records of schools.

Similar to Ralph Tyler's suggestion to use participation in extracurricular activities, Lleras (2008) measures noncognitive (character) skills in part by using tenth-grade participation in sports, academic clubs, and fine arts activities. Participation in these activities predicts educational attainment 10 years later, even after controlling for cognitive ability as measured by achievement tests.

Criminologists have also debated about whether it is better to measure self-control with self-reported psychological scales or with objective behaviors. The publication of Gottfredson and Hirschi's *A General Theory of Crime* (1990) launched a series of studies on the link between self-control

---

36. The measure of risky and reckless behavior is based on whether adolescents engaged in any of the following behaviors: stealing from a store, purposefully damaging property, taking something worth less than $50, or conning someone.

and crime. In that study, they posit that a single factor, self-control, predicts much of the variance in criminal outcomes.

There is a divide in this literature. Subsequent studies have measured self-control using psychological scales, while others have used behavioral measures. A meta-analysis by Pratt and Cullen (2000) finds that behavioral measures are at least as good at predicting crime as are measures based on self-reported taxonomies. In a similar vein, Benda (2005) uses both types of measures in the same study and finds that behavioral measures predict crime better than psychological scales.

Hirschi and Gottfredson (1993) suggest that objective behavioral measures might be preferred to self-reports, partly because the act of filling out a survey requires some level of self-control. Answering survey questions is another task that relies on skills beyond the ones targeted by the survey.

Some criticize this approach and argue that it is tautological to use measures of behavior to predict other behavior, even though the measures are taken early in life to predict later life behaviors.[37] As suggested by Figure 9.1, all tasks or behaviors can be used to infer a skill as long as the measurement accounts for other skills and aspects of the situation. Self-reported scales should not be assumed to be more reliable. The question is which measurements are most predictive and can be implemented in practice. The literature suggests that there are objective measurements of character that are not plagued by reference bias.

9.2.6 ARE CHARACTER SKILLS STABLE?

Many have questioned whether there are stable character skills. The publication of Walter Mischel's 1968 book, *Personality and Assessment*, gave rise to a heated "personality–situation" debate within psychology, which pitted social psychologists who favored situational factors as primary determinants of behavior against personality psychologists who considered stable personality (character) traits (skills) as more consequential. Mischel argued that aspects of situations overshadow any effect of personality (character) traits (skills) on behavior.[38] Ironically, Mischel himself later demonstrated the stability of character skills over the life cycle in his celebrated "marshmallow experiment."[39]

---

37. See the discussion in Benda (2005) and Pratt and Cullen (2000).

38. This point is echoed in behavioral economics. See Thaler (2008).

39. A participant (usually a child) was given a marshmallow. The experimenter left the room and told the participant that he or she would receive a second

A large body of evidence reviewed in Almlund et al. (2011) shows that stable character skills exist and are predictive of many behaviors.[40] An early paper by Epstein (1979) presents compelling evidence that, averaging over tasks and situations, people act in a predictable fashion with a high level of reliability of average behavior ("measured character") across situations.[41] The analysis of Chapter 5 shows that most GED recipients also exhibit stable patterns of behavior: they do not persist in a variety of later life tasks.

In addition, measures of character skills tend to be about 30%–60% heritable, suggesting that something tied to the person, rather than the situation, influences behavior (Bouchard and Loehlin, 2001).[42] Evidence from neuroscience suggests that expression of different skills is linked to different regions of the brain (see Canli, 2006; and DeYoung et al., 2010).

9.3 Predictive Power of Character

A substantial body of evidence shows that character skills predict a wide range of life outcomes, including educational achievement, labor market outcomes, health, and criminality. For many outcomes, the predictive power of character skills rivals that of measures of cognitive ability. Of the Big Five, Conscientiousness—the tendency to be organized, responsible, and hardworking—is the most widely predictive across a variety of outcomes.[43]

Given that school requires hard work and perseverance, it is not surprising that Conscientiousness is associated with educational attainment. Figure 9.5 shows standardized coefficients from a regression of the Big Five on educational attainment from the German Socio-Economic Panel (GSOEP). The darker lines show effects without adjusting for measures of

---

marshmallow if he or she resisted consuming the marshmallow until the experimenter returns. The length of time that the participant waits is a measure of short-term discounting. The children who could wait had much better lifetime outcomes. (For a recent discussion of this study, see Mischel et al., 2011.)

40. See the special issue of *Journal of Research in Personality* (43) entitled "*Personality and Assessment at Age 40*" for a recent discussion.

41. R^2 of 0.6–0.8, where R^2 is a measure of variance explained.

42. Devlin, Daniels, and Roeder (1997) suggest that traditional estimates of the heritability of IQ may be inflated because they fail to take into account the effect of the environment on conditions in the maternal womb. See also Rutter (2006) and an emerging literature on epigenetics (Jablonka and Raz, 2009).

43. See Almlund et al. (2011); Borghans et al. (2008); Heckman and Kautz (2012); Roberts et al. (2007).

Figure 9.5 Association of the Big Five and Intelligence with Years of Schooling in GSOEP

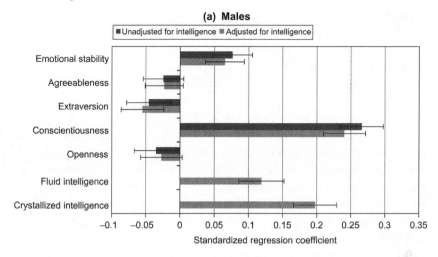

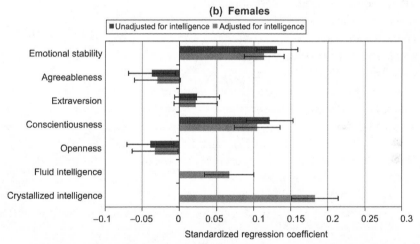

Source: German Socio-Economic Panel (GSOEP), wages 2004–2008, Almlund et al. (2011). *Notes:* The figure displays standardized regression coefficients from a multivariate regression of years of school attended on the Big Five and intelligence, controlling for age and age squared. The bars represent standard errors. The Big Five coefficients are corrected for attenuation bias. The Big Five were measured in 2005. Years of schooling were measured in 2008. Intelligence was measured in 2006. The measures of intelligence were based on components of the Wechsler Adult Intelligence Scale (WAIS). The data is a representative sample of German adults between the ages of 21 and 94.

intelligence, and the lighter lines show effects after additionally adjusting for measures of fluid and crystallized intelligence. Conscientiousness predicts years of schooling with the same strength as the measures of intelligence.

Aspects of job performance are also related to academic performance. Both require completing work on a schedule and involve intelligence to varying degrees. As with academic performance, numerous studies and meta-analyses have found that Conscientiousness is associated with job performance and wages (Barrick and Mount, 1991; Hogan and Holland, 2003; Nyhus and Pons, 2005; Salgado, 1997). Figure 9.6 presents correlations of the Big Five and IQ with job performance. Of the Big Five factors, Conscientiousness is the most strongly associated with job performance but is about half as predictive as IQ. Conscientiousness, however, may play a more ubiquitous role than IQ. The importance of IQ increases with job complexity (the information processing requirements of the job). Cognitive skills are more important for professors, scientists, and senior managers than for semiskilled or unskilled laborers (Schmidt and Hunter, 2004). The importance of Conscientiousness does not vary much with job complexity (Barrick and Mount, 1991); this suggests that it applies to a wider spectrum of jobs.

Measures of character skills rival IQ and measures of socioeconomic status in predicting longevity.[44] Roberts et al. (2007) review evidence from 34 different studies on the predictive validity of the Big Five personality measures, relative to that of cognitive ability and socioeconomic status. Most studies in their meta-analysis control for relevant background factors, including gender and severity of disease. Roberts and colleagues convert the results of each study into correlation coefficients that can be compared across studies. Figure 9.7 presents results from their analyses. Conscientiousness is a stronger predictor of longevity than any other Big Five trait and a stronger predictor than either IQ or socioeconomic status.[45] In general, skills related to Conscientiousness, Openness to Experience, and Agreeableness are associated with longer lives, whereas those related to Neuroticism are associated with shorter lives.[46] The magnitudes of the relationships vary across studies.

44. For a recent study, see Friedman and Martin (2011).
45. The timing of the measurements of character relative to the outcomes varies by study.
46. See Boyle et al. (2005); Friedman and Martin (2011); Kern and Friedman (2008); Kubzansky et al. (2001); Martin, Friedman, and Schwartz (2007); Mroczek and Spiro (2007); Schulz et al. (1996).

Figure 9.6 Associations with Job Performance

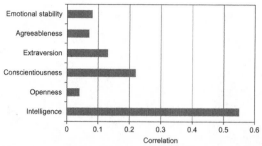

Sources: The correlations reported for personality traits come from a meta-analysis conducted by Barrick and Mount (1991). The correlation reported for intelligence comes from Schmidt and Hunter (2004).

Notes: The values for personality are correlations that were corrected for sampling error, censoring, and measurement error. Job performance was based on performance ratings, productivity data, and training proficiency. The authors do report the timing of the measurements of personality relative to job performance. Of the Big Five, the coefficient on Conscientiousness is the only one statistically significant, with a lower bound on the 90% credibility value of 0.10. The value for intelligence is a raw correlation.

Figure 9.7 Correlations of Mortality with Character, IQ, and Socioeconomic Status (SES)

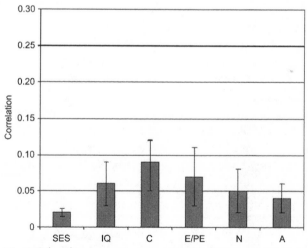

Source: Roberts et al. (2007).

Notes: The figure represents results from a meta-analysis of 34 studies. Average effects (in the correlation metric) of low socioeconomic status (SES), low IQ, low Conscientiousness (C), low Extraversion/Positive Emotion (E/PE), Neuroticism (N), and low Agreeableness (A) on mortality. Error bars represent standard errors. The lengths of the studies represented vary from 1 year to 71 years.

Figure 9.8 Juvenile Delinquency and the Big Five

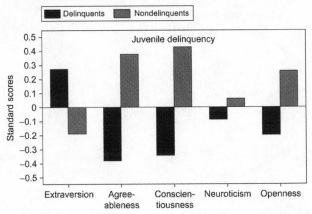

Source: John et al. (1994).

Notes: Delinquents are those who have committed at least one of the following: breaking and entering, strong-arming, or selling drugs. Nondelinquents have committed no more than the following crimes: stealing at home, vandalism at home, or theft of something less than $5. The y-axis reports mean differences in standardized scores of the Big Five measures based on mothers' reports. The measures were taken at ages 12–13 and reflect cumulative delinquent behavior.

Of the Big Five, Conscientiousness and Agreeableness are most predictive of criminality. Figure 9.8 illustrates that in a sample of at-risk youth, boys who committed severe delinquent behaviors were more than three quarters of a standard deviation lower in Agreeableness and Conscientiousness, as measured by mothers' reports at age 12 or 13, than boys who had minor or no delinquent behaviors up to that age (John et al., 1994).

As with most studies in personality psychology, the evidence presented in Figures 9.5–9.8 does not address the question of causality; that is, do measured skills *cause* (rather than just predict) outcomes? Empirical associations are not a reliable basis for policy analysis. As previously noted and summarized in Figure 9.1, multiple skills, effort, and acquired skills generate performance in a given task. Many studies in personality psychology do not control for all of the factors that produce performance on measured tasks. They equate measures of outcomes with the skill being measured.[47]

47. Selecting measures and verifying them is part of the mysterious and inherently subjective process of "construct validity" in psychology. For a discussion, see Borghans et al. (2008).

This practice can lead to a substantial bias in inference about the importance of any particular skill. Our survey of the intervention literature in the next sections presents evidence on the causal relationship between skills and outcomes.

9.4 The Skills Needed for Success in the Labor Market[48]

Another perspective on the importance of character skills comes from surveys of employers and workers. In 1991, the Secretary's Commission on Achieving Necessary Skills (SCANS) conducted an extensive analysis of which skills workers needed in the American workforce.[49] The Commission researched the literature, consulted with experts, and conducted detailed interviews with workers and/or supervisors in 50 occupations. The interviews rated the importance of various skills in the context of illustrative tasks and tools on the job. Using these sources, the Commission categorized necessary skills into basic skills, thinking skills, personal qualities, and a set of workplace competencies. In addition to reading, writing, and math skills, basic skills include listening and speaking. The thinking skills cover creative thinking, decision making, problem solving, reasoning, and the ability to learn. SCANS specifies that personal qualities include responsibility, self-esteem, sociability, self-management, integrity, and honesty. SCANS identifies five groups of workplace competencies: the ability to allocate resources (time, money, facilities), interpersonal skills (such as teamwork, teaching others, leadership), the ability to acquire and to use information, the ability to understand systems, and the ability to work well with technology.

Employer surveys reinforce the importance of skills that go well beyond academic skills. In a survey of 3,200 employers in four large metropolitan areas conducted in the 1990s, employers reported that such personal qualities as responsibility, integrity, and self-management are as important as or more important than basic skills (Holzer, 1997). In another employer survey undertaken in the mid-1990s of 3,300 businesses (the National Employer Survey), employers ranked attitude, communication skills, previous work experience, employer recommendations, and industry-based credentials above years of schooling, grades, and test scores as part of the skills needed for success in the workplace (Zemsky, 1997).

---

48. We have benefited from the commentary of Robert Lerman in preparing this section. See Lerman (2013).

49. Secretary's Commission on Achieving Necessary Skills (1992).

Nonacademic skills are especially critical for entry level and hourly workers. Of employers drawn from a national sample in the United States in 1996, 69% reported rejecting hourly applicants because they lacked basic employability skills, such as showing up every day, coming to work on time, and having a strong work ethic. This percentage is more than double the percentage of rejecting applicants due to inadequate reading and writing skills. Rejections for not passing a drug test were almost as common as rejections for lack of literacy skills.[50] In a 2007 survey of employers in Washington State, about 60% reported difficulty in hiring. They experienced less difficulty finding workers with adequate reading, writing, and math skills than with appropriate occupational, problem solving, teamwork, communication, and adaptability skills as well as positive work habits and a willingness to accept supervision.[51]

Evidence from the United Kingdom supports these findings. A 1998 survey of 4,000 employers found that the four skills found most lacking in 16- to 24-year-olds were technical and practical skills, general communication skills, customer handling skills, and teamwork skills.[52] At the bottom of the list were numeracy and literacy skills. In a 2002 survey of 4,000 employers in the UK, 23% of employers reported a significant number of their staff were less than fully proficient at their jobs. Skill shortfalls were most common in communication, teamwork, other technical and practical skills, customer handling, and problem solving and least common in numeracy and literacy.[53]

Consistent with these findings, the Confederation of British Industry defines employability as (1) values and attitudes compatible with the work, including a desire to learn, to apply that learning, to improve, and to take advantage of change; (2) basic skills (literacy and numeracy); (3) key skills (communication, application of numbers, information technology, improving one's own learning and performance, working with others, problem solving) sufficient for the needs of the work; (4) other generic skills such as modern language and customer service skills; and (5) job-specific skills and the ability to manage one's own career.

An ethnographic approach provides some revealing examples of how skills are used in context and how nonacademic skills are often de-

50. Barton (2006).
51. Washington Workforce Training Board (2008).
52. Westwood (2004).
53. Hillage et al. (2002).

veloped and used as part of a community of practice.[54] In addition to formal knowledge, Nelsen (1997) points out that workplaces require not only formal knowledge, facts, principles, theories, and math and writing skills, but also informal knowledge embodied in heuristics, work styles, and contextualized understanding of tools and techniques. In her revealing case study of auto repair workers, Nelsen argues that social skills of new workers are very important for learning the informal knowledge of experienced workers, as captured in stories, advice, and guided practice.

9.5 A Framework for Understanding Interventions

A variety of strategies have been advocated for promoting character and cognitive skills. Different advocates press their favorite strategies. Policymakers have limited resources, so it is important to identify which programs are most effective. The rate of return—the per-period yield of an investment—provides a convenient and interpretable summary of the efficacy of competing programs. An alternative to funding an early education program might be to invest the resources in the stock market and to use the resources plus the accrued interest to fund a program for adolescents.

In this section, we present a conceptual scheme for understanding the dynamics of skill development.[55] Figure 9.9 illustrates the basic idea. In this framework, cognitive and character skills are produced by investments at different stages of the life cycle. Skills at birth depend on prenatal investments and inherited traits. Skill formation at later ages depends on the stock of skills acquired earlier as well as prior investments. For example, a child who has a better attention span more easily acquires more cognitive skills from classroom instruction. This concept is called *self-productivity* and is summarized by the motto "skills beget skills."

Investments (parenting, environment, and schools) also affect skills. The efficacy of investment is moderated by the stock of skills at any age. The benefits of an investment depend on the current level of skills—a phenomenon that economists call *static complementarity*. More motivated children learn more. In addition, investment today increases the stock of future skills, which in turn increases the return to future investments.

---

54. Stasz (2001).

55. These ideas are formalized in Cunha and Heckman (2007, 2008); Cunha, Heckman, and Schennach (2010).

Figure 9.9 Framework for Understanding Skill Development

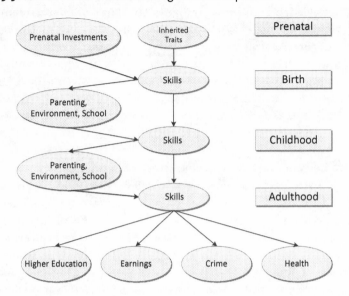

Economists call this phenomenon *dynamic complementarity.* This channel increases the returns to early investments because it makes future investments more productive. For this reason, Cunha, Heckman, and Schennach (2010) show that it is economically efficient to invest in the most disadvantaged young children because it raises their payoffs from future investments.

This framework recognizes that different skills might be relatively easy to shape at different stages of the life cycle. *Sensitive periods* for a given skill are periods when investments are relatively more productive. *Critical periods* for a particular skill are periods when investment during any other period is not productive.

Figure 9.9 illustrates why understanding the effects attributable to specific interventions is such a challenging task. Most of the empirical studies that we review only investigate the interventions received in a slice of the life cycle. They do not connect the links or correct for the effects of later investment in producing the outcomes attributed to early investments.

9.6 Summary of Empirical Evidence on the Efficacy of Interventions

This section summarizes the empirical evidence from a variety of interventions ranging from targeting prenatal infants to targeting young adults. In the subsequent sections, we discuss some of these programs in greater detail. In these discussions, we focus on programs that have been well studied, have long-term follow-ups, have been widely adopted, or offer unique insights. Descriptions and discussions of other programs can be found in the Web Appendix.[56]

For three reasons, evaluating and comparing the evidence from intervention programs is challenging. First, many interventions are only evaluated with short-term follow-ups, which could lead to upward-biased estimates of returns if the benefits eventually dissipate or to downward-biased estimates of the returns if the effects of the programs appear later in life. Second, not all studies measure the same outcomes. Ideally, all studies would report outcomes in terms of the rate of return of the program. Reported outcomes often differ across studies. Many studies only consider the effect of an intervention on a few outcomes. Without knowing the range of outcomes affected, it is difficult to calculate a rate of return. Third, many programs target specific demographic groups. Applying the findings from one group to another might be problematic if groups differentially benefit from programs. The evidence presented in this book suggests substantial heterogeneity in program effects across groups.

Table 9.2 summarizes the effects of each intervention discussed in this section. The table displays information about the nature of the intervention, the quality of the evaluation, the effects on later life outcomes, and estimates of the rate of return and cost-benefit ratio when available. The squares in the "Components" columns indicate the extent to which the program and the evaluation of it have the features defined in the table. The dots in the "Effects on Outcomes" columns indicate the extent to which the program influenced skills and outcomes. (The notes at the bottom of the table define the symbols and abbreviations used.)

Three striking patterns emerge about the nature of the programs and the quality of the available evaluations of them. First, as a group, early childhood and elementary school programs have longer follow-ups. All of the early childhood or elementary school programs in Table 9.2 have evaluations that follow participants for at least 10 years and many follow them more than 20 years, whereas only two evaluations of adolescent programs follow participants at least 10 years (the longest is 12).

Second, early childhood programs tend to measure cognitive and character skills in addition to a variety of later-life outcomes, whereas many

---

56. See http://jenni.uchicago.edu/Studies_of_GED/chapter_09_appendix.pdf.

Table 9.2 Summary of Effects for Main Interventions

Program	Age	Duration	Target	Selection	Follow-Up	Sample	Home	Health	Parental
			Participant/Evaluation Characteristics					*Components*	
Early									
NFP	<0	2Y	SES	Prgrm	19Y	640	☒	☒	☒
ABC	0	5Y	SES	Refer	30Y	90	☐	☒	☒
IHDP	0	3Y	Health	Prgrm	18Y	640	☒	☐	☒
FDRP	0	5Y	SES	Prgrm	15Y	110	☒	☒	☒
PCDC	1	2Y	SES	Prgrm	15Y	170	☒	☐	☒
JSS	1–2	2Y	Health	Prgrm	22Y	160	☒	☒	☒
Perry	3	2Y	SES, IQ	Prgrm	37Y	120	☒	☐	☒
Head Start	3	2Y	SES	Prnt	23Y	4,170	☒	☒	☒
CPC	3–4	2Y	SES	Prnt	25Y	1,290	☐	☒	☒
TEEP	3,5	2Y	SES	Prgrm	22Y	260	☒	☒	☒
STAR	5–6	4Y	SES	Prgrm	22Y	11,000	☐	☐	☐
Elementary									
LA's Best	5–6	6Y	SES	Schl	12Y	19,320	☐	☒	☒
CSP	5–13	5Y	Behav	Refer	35Y	510	☒	☒	☒
SSDP	6–7	6Y	Crime	Prgrm	21Y	610	☐	☒	☒
Adolescence									
BBBS	10–16	1Y	SES	Self	1Y	960	☐	☐	☐
IHAD	11–12	7Y	SES	Prgrm	8Y	180	☐	☒	☒
EPIS	13–15	3Y	Schl	Schl	2Y	45,070	☐	☐	☐
xl club	14	2Y	Schl	Schl	2Y	261,420	☐	☐	☐
SAS	14–15	5Y	Schl, SES	Schl	6Y	430	☐	☐	☐
STEP	14–15	2Y	Schl, SES	Self	4Y	4,800	☐	☒	☐
QOP	14–15	5Y	Schl	Prgrm	10Y	1,070	☐	☒	☐
Academies	13–16	4Y	Schl, SES	Self	12Y	1,460	☐	☐	☐
ChalleNGe	16–18	1Y	Dropout	Self	3Y	1,200	☐	☒	☐
Job Corps	16–24	1Y	SES	Self	9Y	15,300	☐	☒	☐
Year-Up	18–24	1Y	SES	Self	2Y	200	☐	☐	☐

| | | Effects on Outcomes | | | | | | | Return/Benefits | |
On Site	Group	IQ	School	Character	Education	Health	Crime	Earnings	Return	Benefit/Cost
☐	☐	●	◑	●	○	◍	◑	·		2.9
☒	☒	●	●	◑	◑	◍	◑	◑		3.8
☒	☒	◑	◑	◑	○	○	○	·		
☒	☒	○	◑	◍	·	◍	●	·		
☒	☒	◍	◍	●	·	·	·	·		
☐	☐	●	●	●	◍	●	·	●		
☒	☒	◍	●	●	◑	○	●	◑	7–10	7.1–12.2
☒	☒	◍	◍	○	●	●	◑	●		
☒	☒	·	●	●	●	●	●	●	18	10.8
☒	☐	◍	●	●	●	·	·	·		
☒	☒	·	◍	●	●	·	·	●	6.2	
☒	☒	·	◍	·	●	·	○	·		0.9
☒	☒	·	·	○	·	⊗	○	·		
☒	☒	·	●	●	●	●	◍	○		3.1
☐	☐	·	◑	○	·	◑	○	·		1.0
☒	☒	·	·	·	●	·	·	·		
☒	☒	·	●	·	·	·	·	·		0.9–3.0
☒	☒	·	○	·	·	·	·	·		
☐	☐	·	◍	○	●	·	·	·		
☒	☒	·	○	·	○	·	·	○		
☒	☒	·	○	·	◍	○	⊗	○		0.42
☒	☒	·	◍	○	○	○	●	◑		
☒	☒	·	·	◍	●	◑	◍	●	6.4	2.66
☒	☒	·	·	·	○	◍	◍	◍		0.22
☒	☒	·	·	·	·	·	·	●		

(continued)

Table 9.2 (Continued)

Notes: □ – Does not include intervention component. ⊠ – Includes intervention component. ○ – No effects. ● – Positive effects. ◍ – Weakly positive effects. ◑ – Mixed effects (either different studies find different results or only particular sub-populations benefited). ⊗ – Negative effects. "•" – Not measured. "Age" – The age at which participants entered the program. For programs that targeted grades, rather than ages, it was assumed that children entered kindergarten at ages 5–6 and the age range advanced one year for each subsequent grade. "Duration" – Length of the treatment. In cases where the treatment length varied for participants, the longest duration was presented. "Target" – Population that was targeted by the program. SES – socioeconomic status or disadvantage. Behav – Behavior. Schl – School Performance. Crime – local crime rates. IQ – low IQ. "Selection" – The party that acted first in joining the sample. Prgrm – Evaluation program contacted participants. Refer – Other party referred participants to program. Prnt – Parent applied to program. Self – Participant applied to program. Schl – School selected participants. "Follow-Up" – duration of longest follow-up evaluation in years. "Sample" – Largest sample size from the studies examined (rounded to nearest 10). "Home" – Included home visits. "Health" – Included a nutritional component. "Parental" – Involved parents. "On Site" – Took place at an on site location. "Group" – Whether the intervention combined participants in groups. "IQ" – IQ score. "School" – school performance. "Character" – measured character skills. "Education" – educational attainment. "Health" – health (including drug use). "Crime" – crime. "Earnings" – earnings or related outcomes. "Return" – Annual rate of return. "Benefit/Cost" – Estimated benefits divided by costs.

Sources: **NFP** – Eckenrode et al. (2010); Kitzman et al. (2010); Olds (2006); Olds et al. (2004a, 2004b, 2007, 2010). **ABC** – Breitmayer and Ramey (1986); Heckman et al. (2012); Temple and Reynolds (2007). **IHDP** – McCormick et al. (2006). **FDRP** – Lally, Mangione, and Honig (1987). **PCDC** – Besharov et al. (2011); Bridgeman, Blumenthal, and Andres (1981); Johnson and Walker (1991). **JSS** – Gertler et al. (2013); Grantham-McGregor et al. (1991); Walker et al. (2005); Walker et al. (2007). **Perry** – Heckman et al. (2010a, 2010b, 2012). **Head Start** – Carneiro and Ginja (2012); Currie and Thomas (1995); Deming (2009); Garces et al. (2002); Ludwig and Miller (2007); Westat (2010). **CPC** – Niles, Reynolds, and Nagasawa (2006); Reynolds (1994); Reynolds and Temple (1998); Reynolds et al. (2002, 2011a, 2011b). **TEEP** – Kagitcibasi, Sunar, and Bekman (2001); Kagitcibasi et al. (2009). **STAR** – Chetty et al. (2011); Krueger (2003). **LA's BEST** – Goldschmidt and Huang (2007); Huang et al. (2000, 2005). **CSP** – McCord (1978). **SSDP** – Hawkins et al. (1999, 2005, 2008). **BBBS** – Tierney et al. (1995). **IHAD** – Kahne and Bailey (1999). **EPIS** – Martins (2010). **XL Club** – Holmlund and Silva (2009). **SAS** – Johnson (1999). **STEP** – Walker and Vilella-Velez (1992). **QOP** – Rodríguez-Planas (2010, 2012). **Academies** – Kemple and Snipes (2000); Kemple and Willner (2008). **ChalleNGe** – Bloom et al. (2009); Millenky et al. (2010, 2011). **Job Corps** – Schochet et al. (2001, 2008). **Year Up** – Roder and Elliot (2011).

of the adolescent evaluations focus solely on labor market outcomes. Because of these features of data availability, we can better understand the sources of the effects on adult outcomes of early childhood programs by considering how these interventions produce skills. Due to the absence of measures of skills for many adolescent interventions, understanding these programs requires examining the curricula of the programs themselves, for example, whether the program seeks to foster cognitive or character skills.

Third, selection into programs differs by the age of intervention. In most early childhood evaluations, the programs first contact parents to participate and then parents opt into the program. In contrast, in most adolescent evaluations, participants themselves chose to enter the program.

Table 9.2 also suggests certain features of effective programs. Only very early interventions (before age 3) improve IQ in a lasting way, consistent with the evidence that early childhood is a critical period for cognitive development (see Knudsen et al., 2006). The most successful interventions target preschoolers and primary school children. They improve later-life outcomes by developing character skills.

Programs that target adolescents have not been established to be as effective as programs that target earlier ages, in part because there have been fewer long-term evaluations of them. Several of the successful adolescent mentoring or residential programs improve labor market and social outcomes, but have relatively short follow-ups. The two programs with the longest follow-ups improve outcomes in the short run, but the benefits fade after a few years. These programs alter participants' environments and incentives during the intervention, which could influence their behavior in the short term without having a lasting effect.

The most promising adolescent programs integrate aspects of work into traditional education. Such programs break down the rigid separation between school and work that characterizes the American high school.

High schools create an adolescent society with values distinct from those of the larger society and removed from the workplace.[57] Even in affluent communities, the adolescent society has an anti-academic, anti-achievement bias. It was not until 1940 that more than half of each birth cohort graduated from high school.[58] In earlier times, adolescents took apprenticeships and jobs where they were supervised and mentored by adults. Mentoring involved teaching valuable character skills—showing up for work, cooperating with others, and persevering on tasks. These skills could be fostered in high schools, but with the relaxation of discipline in the schools, it is more difficult to do so.[59]

57. See Coleman (1961).
58. See Goldin and Katz (2008).
59. See Arum (2005).

The apparent success of apprenticeship programs might arise in part from their cultivation of character skills. The attachment of a supervisor to an apprentice helps create character in a version of the attachment bond between parent and child.[60]

9.7 Early-Life Interventions That Begin before Formal Schooling

This section discusses the most influential interventions listed in Table 9.2 that start before children enroll in kindergarten. We divide the early interventions into two categories: (1) infant programs and model preschools that target infants by directly providing cognitive and socio-emotional stimulation to children, by instructing young mothers or by providing center-based care to a specific population and (2) large-scale programs that have been implemented in schools and are relatively less expensive than center-based care. Many early interventions have successfully boosted cognitive skills, character skills, or both.

Given that there are more differences among evaluations than there are evaluations, it is difficult to understand exactly *why* some programs are more successful than others. Nevertheless, certain patterns emerge. Only programs that start before the age of 3 have had lasting impacts on IQ. Some of the most successful programs have had no long-term impact on IQ but have improved later-life outcomes by improving character skills. Evidence from these programs indicates that one viable alternative to the GED program is to prevent the emergence of character deficits before students enter kindergarten. As a general rule, large-scale programs have been less successful than smaller-scale programs, but the large-scale programs differ from small-scale programs in important ways.

9.7.1 INFANT PROGRAMS AND MODEL PRESCHOOLS

9.7.1.1 *Nurse-Family Partnership*

Evidence from the Nurse-Family Partnership (NFP) program shows how improving prenatal conditions and early parenting can improve child skills and outcomes. NFP aims at first-time, low-income, unmarried, and/or adolescent mothers without previous births. In the program, nurses visit young mothers from the first or second trimester of the mother's pregnancy until the second birthday of her first child. The program encourages mothers to reduce smoking, teaches mothers how to care for their children, and helps mothers to pursue education and find jobs. It was introduced, as a pilot, at Elmira,

---

60. See Bowlby (1951); Sroufe (1997); Sroufe et al. (2005).

New York. Later, the program was introduced at Memphis, Tennessee, and Denver, Colorado.[61] At Elmira and Memphis, mothers receive around 30 to 35 visits of around 75–90 minutes each. By 2006, it operated in 26 states and served more than 20,000 families each year. It is evaluated by the method of randomized assignment (Howard and Brooks-Gunn, 2009; Olds, 2006).

NFP reduces risky behaviors of mothers and their children (see Table 9.3). Children exhibit persistently higher IQ scores through age 6 (Olds et al., 2004).[62] At age 12, the children in the treatment group have lower rates of substance abuse and exhibit lower levels of internalizing behavior (e.g., anxiety, depression, and withdrawal).[63] When the children are 12, mothers are much less dependent on welfare.[64] By age 19, children are less likely to engage in crime.[65,66] Importantly, the program improves measures of criminal activity, even though there are only weak effects on achievement test scores or grades in the long run. This suggests that the program works by improving character skills.

9.7.1.2 Jamaican Study

Many childhood programs have been introduced in less developed countries. The Jamaican Supplementation Study was one of the few with a long-term follow-up.[67] This randomized program consisted of a two-year nutritional and stimulation program for stunted children (low height for age), aged 9–24 months at the start of the program. Participants either received

---

61. Our discussion will focus on the effects of the program up to age 12 for the Memphis sample and the effects at age 19 for the Elmira sample.

62. Measured by the mental processing domain of the Kaufman Assessment Battery for Children (KABC).

63. Kitzman et al. (2010). The measure of internalizing behavior is based on self-reports from the Achenbach Child Behavior Checklist (Achenbach and Rescorla, 2001). See Almlund et al. (2011) for a discussion of the relationship between internalizing behavior and the Big Five.

64. Olds et al. (2010).

65. Eckenrode et al. (2010).

66. Illustrated by the strong discrepancy in Table 9.3 between estimates for "Ever Arrested" versus "Arrested in Last Year."

67. Most programs lack long-term follow-ups (even beyond age 10), or any follow-up at all, and few employ methods of random assignment. Short-term effects are generally positive; intervention leads to better cognitive skills and, in most cases, lower grade retention in the early years of primary school. For an overview, see Engle et al. (2007, 2011); Grantham-McGregor et al. (1991, 2007); Jolly (2007); Lake (2011); Myers (1992); Walker et al. (2005, 2007, 2011a, 2011b); and Young (1996).

Table 9.3 Summary of Treatment Effects of the Nurse–Family Partnership

Outcome	Treatment	Control	Treatment Effect
Age 6[1]			
Vocabulary Skills(ES)			0.17**
Internalizing Disorders(%)	12.6	14.7	−2.1
Externalizing Disorders(%)	17.4	20.2	−2.8
Age 9[2]			
GPA(ES)			0.09
Antisocial Behavior(%)			−0.03
Grade Retention(%)	16.0	12.4	3.6
Age 12[3]			
GPA			0.08
Achievement Tests[a]			1.09
Grade Retention(%)	24.9	20.8	4.1
Internalizing Disorders(%)[b]	22.1	30.9	−8.8**
Externalizing Disorders(%)[c]	19.7	17.8	1.9
Used Substance Last 30 Days(%)	1.7	5.1	−3.4**
Ever Arrested(%)	3.1	3.1	0.0
Welfare Benefits Mother[d]	8772	9797	−1025**
Age 19[4]			
Ever Arrested(%)	21.3	37.4	−16.1**
Arrested in Last Year(%)	8.2	5.5	2.7
Illicit Drug Use(%)	48.7	51.9	−3.2
Has HS Diploma(%)	70.6	74.5	−3.9
Economically Productive(%)[e]	71.4	68.3	3.1

Sources: (1) The estimates at Age 6 come from Olds et al. (2004). (2) The estimates at Age 9 come from Olds et al. (2007). (3) The estimates at Age 12 come from Kitzman et al. (2010) and Olds et al. (2010). (4) The estimates at Age 19 come from Eckenrode et al. (2010).
Notes: The estimates are coefficients from regressions that control for sample member characteristics. % refers to treatment effects in terms of changes in prevalence in outcome variable in percentage points. ES indicates Effect Size, reporting the treatment effect in standard deviations of the outcome variable. The Age 6–12 estimates come from the Memphis site. The Age 19 estimates come from the Elmira site. (a) Is based on group reading and math achievement test scores and is in percentile units. (b) Uses student self-reports on domains such as anxiety, depression, somatization, and withdrawal to assess if students pass a clinical threshold, based on the Achenbach Child Behavior Checklist (Achenbach and Rescorla, 2001). (c) Uses student, teacher, and parent reports on domains such as conduct problems, aggression, and total problems to assess if students pass a clinical threshold, based on the Achenbach Child Behavior Checklist. (d) Measures the average yearly receipt of welfare during the child's first 12 years of life, in US$. (e) Measures if someone is involved in education, a job, the military, or job training. **Attains 5% significance level.

supplementation (milk formula), stimulation (encouraged mother to play with kids in an effective manner), or both (Grantham-McGregor et al., 1991).

In general, the stimulation intervention outperformed the supplementation intervention (see Table 9.4). Both interventions improved early cognitive development in the short-term, but only the stimulation intervention improved cognitive and character skills in the long run (Gertler et al., 2013; Grantham-McGregor et al., 1991). As with the NFP program, the stimulation

Table 9.4 Summary of Treatment Effects from the Jamaican Study

Outcome	Supplementation	Stimulation
Age 2[1]		
Mental Development(ES)[a]	0.76***	0.91***
Age 17–18[2]		
Full Scale IQ(ES)	−0.03	0.58**
Performance IQ(ES)	0.04	0.51*
Verbal IQ(ES)	−0.05	0.50**
Reading Score(ES)[b]	−0.05	0.66***
Internalizing Behavior(ES)		0.39**
Externalizing Behavior(ES)		0.22
Age 20–22[3]		
Years of Education		0.66
Currently in Education(ES)		0.14*
Log Earnings of Last Job		0.33**
Employment(%)		8.0

Sources: (1) The estimates at Age 2 come from Grantham-McGregor et al. (1991). (2) The estimates at Age 17–18 come from Gertler et al. (2013) and Walker et al. (2005). (3) The estimates at Age 20–22 come from Gertler et al. (2013).

Notes: The estimates are coefficients from regressions that control for sample member characteristics. Grantham-McGregor et al. (1991) and Walker et al. (2005) test and do not reject the hypothesis that "stimulation only" and "supplementation only" treatment effects add to produce the "both" treatment effect. We report the effects of separate treatment streams: "stimulation only" and "supplementation only." Gertler et al. (2013) do not use the supplementation group at all and pool the stimulation and "both" groups into a single treatment group. % refers to treatment effects in terms of changes in prevalence in outcome variable in percentage points. ES indicates Effect Size, reporting the treatment effect in standard deviations of the outcome variable. (a) Assessed with Griffiths Mental Development Scales (Griffiths, 1954). The values have been divided by the standard deviation of the control group. (b) The reading score is based on the sentence completion portion of the Group reading test 2, revised. The effect is divided by the standard deviation of the control group.

*10% significance; **5% significance; ***1% significance.

program improved internalizing behavior (Walker et al., 2005). The stimulation intervention improved educational attainment and earnings.[68] The effects on migration and earnings at age 22 are substantial (Gertler et al., 2013).

9.7.1.3 Perry Preschool Program

As discussed in Chapter 1, evaluations of the Perry Preschool program provide some of the most compelling evidence that character skills can be boosted in ways that produce adult success. The Perry Preschool program enriched the lives of 3- and 4-year-old low-income black children with initial IQs below 85 at age 3.[69] They attended 2.5 hours of center-based preschool five days a week for two years. In addition, home visits promoted parent–child relationships. The program ended after two years of enrollment, and both treatment and control groups entered the same school.

Participants were taught social skills in a daily "plan-do-review" sequence in which children first planned a task, executed it, and then reviewed it with teachers and fellow students. They learned to work with others when problems arose.[70] The program was evaluated by the method of random assignment.

The program did not improve IQ scores in a lasting way. Figure 9.10 shows that, by age 10, treatment and control groups had the same average IQ scores. Many critics of early childhood programs seize on this finding and related evidence to dismiss the value of early intervention studies.

Nevertheless, the program improved outcomes for both boys and girls, resulting in a statistically significant rate of return of around 7%–10% per annum for both boys and girls (see Heckman et al., 2010b). These returns are in the range of the post–World War II, pre–2008 meltdown stock market returns to equity in the U.S. labor market, estimated to be 6.9% per annum.[71]

Heckman, Pinto, and Savelyev (2013) show that the Perry treatment effects arise primarily from lasting changes in character skills, not from

---

68. The supplementation program might have been ineffective in the long run because the supplement was relatively weak, contained few micronutrients, and had no fortified formula. Some of the interventions referred to in Myers (1992) and Young (1996) also reported stronger effects of stimulation over supplementation.

69. We draw on the analysis of Heckman et al. (2010a, 2010b, 2012).

70. Sylva (1997) describes the Perry program as a program that fosters character skills. It has features in common with the Tools of the Mind intervention discussed below. See Bodrova and Leong (2007) for the Tools of the Mind curriculum. See Heckman, Pinto, and Savelyev (2013) for a discussion of the Perry curriculum and the Tools of the Mind curriculum.

71. See DeLong and Magin (2009).

Figure 9.10 Perry Preschool Program: IQ, by Age and Treatment Group

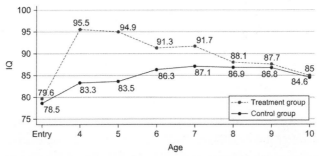

Source: Cunha et al. (2006) and Heckman and Masterov (2007), based on data provided by the High Scope Foundation.

Notes: IQ measured on the Stanford-Binet Intelligence Scale (Terman and Merrill, 1960). The test was administered at program entry and at each of the ages indicated.

changes in IQ. Figure 9.11 shows histograms of measures of character skills for the treatment and control groups. The treatment groups of both genders improved their teacher-reported externalizing behavior, a skill related to Agreeableness and Conscientiousness. For girls, the program also improved Openness to Experience (proxied by academic motivation). Figure 9.11 also shows that the program improved scores on the California Achievement Test (CAT), even though it did not have a lasting effect on IQ. This evidence is consistent with the evidence summarized in Figures 9.2 and 9.3 showing that achievement test scores depend strongly on character skills (see Borghans et al., 2008a, 2009). Achievement tests measure general knowledge. The acquisition of general knowledge (crystallized intelligence) depends on persistence, curiosity, and focus.

9.7.1.4 Abecedarian Program

The Abecedarian (ABC) program was another program aimed at disadvantaged black children. It started earlier, lasted much longer, and was much more intensive than the Perry program, combining a preschool intervention that started when children were as young as 6 weeks old with school-age treatment through grade three.[72] The preschool component was full-day child care 5 days per week, 50 weeks a year. The curriculum focused

---

72. It is easy to exaggerate the difference in intensity between the Perry program and the ABC program. While ABC starts earlier, and spends more time each day with the child, the amount of time per day spent on essentially the same type of learning activities is very similar at ages 3 and 4. See Griffin et al. (2013).

Figure 9.11 Histograms of Indices of Noncognitive Skills and CAT Scores

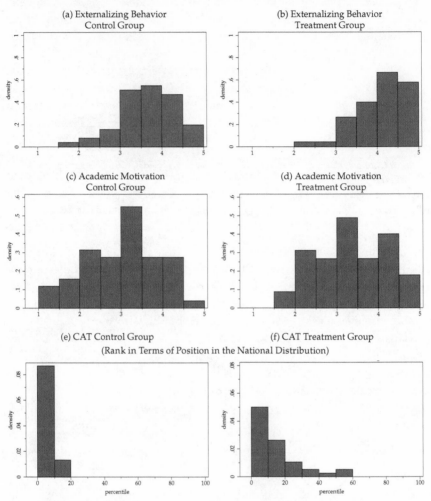

Source: Heckman et al. (2013).

Notes: Indices for Externalizing Behavior and Academic Motivation are based on items of the Pupil Behavior Inventory (PBI), teacher ratings of student behavior. The units are expressed in terms of standard deviations. The scale on "Externalizing Behavior" is normalized so that a higher score corresponds to better behavior. The PBI includes whether the student disrupts classroom. "CAT" is the California Achievement Test score expressed in percentiles of the general population distribution of the scores. The one-sided *p*-values for difference in means are 0.001, 0.043, and 0.000 for Externalizing Behavior, Academic Motivation, and CAT scores, respectively. Histograms are based on the pooled sample of males and females.

on a series of "educational games" that emphasized language, emotional development, and the development of cognitive skills. It also had a medical and nutritional component.[73] For grades one through three, the curriculum was tailored to the individual strengths of the students. During this phase, teachers and parents interacted on a bi-weekly basis.

In contrast to Perry, ABC led to lasting improvements in IQ.[74] For girls, the program improved IQ through age 21 (see Figure 9.12). The effect for boys was positive but was less precisely estimated. Girls and boys also scored better on achievement tests. ABC likely improved IQ because it started at an earlier age than Perry. Very early childhood appears to be a critical period for shaping IQ.

As with Perry, the benefits of the ABC program differ across genders. For girls, the program improved educational attainment, reduced participation in criminal activity, decreased substance abuse, and improved internalizing and externalizing behavior. Like the Perry program, ABC improved employment and health for males and produced substantial improvements in character skills.[75] Campbell et al. (2012) report substantial beneficial effects of the program on adult health for both genders.

9.7.2 LARGE-SCALE INFANT AND YOUNG CHILD PROGRAMS
9.7.2.1 Head Start
The Head Start program receives considerable attention both in the evaluation literature and in public discussion. Head Start children are eligible for enrollment from ages 3 to 5, although they generally enter at age 4 and receive one year of treatment. In addition to a center-based (preschool) intervention, Head Start includes medical services and parental assistance (Ludwig and Miller, 2007). Its implementation differs greatly across sites, making it difficult to evaluate its overall effectiveness (Deming, 2009). Parental participation was not mandatory, and there is some evidence that many do not participate.[76]

There have been no long-term evaluations of Head Start based on randomized assignment. Instead, most evaluations of Head Start compare siblings with different enrollment statuses[77] or use regression discontinuity designs.[78] Empirical evidence on Head Start is mixed. Many studies

73. See Campbell et al. (2001, 2002).
74. We report on the treatment effects of the preschool component from Heckman, Moon, and Pinto (2012).
75. See Campbell et al. (2013).
76. Schumacher (2003).
77. For example, Deming (2009); Garces, Thomas, and Currie (2002).
78. For example, Carneiro and Ginja (2011); Ludwig and Miller (2007).

Figure 9.12 Cognitive Tests by Gender and Daycare Treatment Status

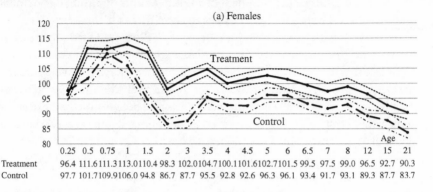

(a) Females

	0.25	0.5	0.75	1	1.5	2	3	3.5	4	4.5	5	6	6.5	7	8	12	15	21
Treatment	96.4	111.6	111.3	113.0	110.4	98.3	102.0	104.7	100.1	101.6	102.7	101.5	99.5	97.5	99.0	96.5	92.7	90.3
Control	97.7	101.7	109.9	106.0	94.8	86.7	87.7	95.5	92.8	92.6	96.3	96.1	93.4	91.7	93.1	89.3	87.7	83.7

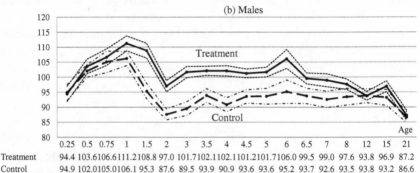

(b) Males

	0.25	0.5	0.75	1	1.5	2	3	3.5	4	4.5	5	6	6.5	7	8	12	15	21
Treatment	94.4	103.6	106.6	111.2	108.8	97.0	101.7	102.1	102.1	101.2	101.7	106.0	99.5	99.0	97.6	93.8	96.9	87.2
Control	94.9	102.0	105.0	106.1	95.3	87.6	89.5	93.9	90.9	93.6	93.6	95.2	93.7	92.6	93.5	93.8	93.2	86.6

Source: Heckman et al. (2012).

Notes: All the cognitive tests have been standardized to population mean of 100 and standard deviation of 15. The measures used in this figure are Bayley Mental Development Index at age 0.25, 0.5, 0.75, 1, and 1.5; Stanford Binet Intelligence Scale at age 2, 3, 4, 5, and 6; McCarthy Index at age 3.5, 4.5, and 7; WPPSI IQ Score at age 5; WISC-R Intelligence Scale at age 6.5, 8, 12, and 15; WAIS-R Adult Intelligence Scale at age 21.

find that Head Start improves IQ scores and achievement test scores, but that the improvements fade by age 10 (Deming, 2009; Ludwig and Miller, 2007). For some subgroups, there is evidence of persistent gains in test scores and reductions in retention rates.[79] Garces, Thomas, and Currie

79. Deming (2009) reports persistent gains for males and those with higher ability mothers as measured by summary test score that includes the Peabody Picture Vocabulary Test (PPVT), Peabody Individual Achievement Math (PIATMT), and Reading Recognition (PIATRR). Retention rates were lower for boys, blacks, and students with low maternal AFQT.

(2002) find that Head Start improves outcomes for educational attainment for whites and reduces criminality for blacks, whereas Deming (2009) finds that Head Start improves educational attainment for blacks.

A short-term experimental study by Westat (2010) based on randomized assignment offers a more pessimistic view. The study finds that most positive impacts on achievement tests[80] and socio-emotional development[81] fade by first grade. This evaluation likely underestimates the true program effects. Many members of the control group joined the program at sites other than where they initially applied or were enrolled in other childhood programs that were more intensive than Head Start.

9.7.2.2 Chicago CPC

The Chicago Child–Parent Center (CPC) is an apparently successful large-scale preschool program. It is directed toward disadvantaged, predominantly black, inner-city children in Chicago. The program provides a half- or full-day preschool program for 3- and 4-year-olds. The program was designed to develop basic reading, writing, and math skills. In contrast to other large-scale programs, parents are required to visit the centers and receive advice on good parenting behavior (Reynolds, 2000).

CPC has not been evaluated by the random assignment method. All evaluations are based on samples of children attending CPC kindergarten matched to "comparable" children attending non-CPC kindergarten. Based on these methods, the program appears to improve education and reduce criminal behavior (see Table 9.5). Although it is difficult to tell what causes the improvement in adult outcomes, some evidence suggests that boosts in character play a role. At age 13, the participants have higher levels of social and emotional competence. The program also improves achievement test scores (Iowa Tests of Basic Skills),[82] but improvements in character can lead to improvements in achievement tests without affecting IQ, as was the case with the Perry program.

---

80. Including the Peabody Picture Vocabulary Test and several batteries of the Woodcock-Johnson III test.

81. Including parent- and teacher-reported measures of aggression, hyperactivity, withdrawn behavior, and total problem behavior. They use several test batteries, including the Achenbach Classroom Behavior Checklist (CBCL; Achenbach and Rescorla, 2001) and the Adjustment Scales for Preschool Intervention (ASPI; Lutz, Fantuzzo, and McDermott, 2000).

82. Hieronymus, Lindquist, and Hoover (1980).

Table 9.5 Summary of Treatment Effects from the Chicago Child–Parent Center

Outcome	Treatment	Control	Treatment Effect
Age 13[1]			
Reading Achievement(ES)			0.36***
Math Achievement(ES)			0.32***
Social and Emotional Competence(ES)			0.19*
Problem Behavior(ES)			−0.17
Grade Retention(ES)			−0.3***
Age 18–20[2]			
Has HS Diploma(%)	49.7	38.5	11.2***
Number of Arrests	0.45	0.78	−0.33**
Number of Violent Arrests	0.22	0.35	−0.13**
Age 22–26[3]			
Has HS Diploma(%)	79.7	72.9	6.8***
Number of Adult Felony Arrests	0.32	0.44	−0.12**
Substance Abuse(%)	14.3	18.8	−4.5**
Full-time Employment (%)	36.8	33.5	3.3
Age 28[4]			
On Time HS graduation(%)	44.3	36.6	7.7**
Any Adult Arrest(%)	47.9	54.3	−6.4**
Substance Abuse(%)	13.7	18.9	−5.2**
Annual Income($)	11,582	10,796	786**

Notes: The estimates are coefficients from regressions that control for sample member characteristics. Estimates apply to the pre-school part of CPC, excluding extended treatment. ES indicates Effect Size, reporting the treatment effect in standard deviations of the outcome variable.
* 10% significance; ** 5% significance; *** 1% significance.
Sources: (1) The estimates at Age 13 come from Niles et al. (2006) and Reynolds (1995). (2) The estimates at Age 18–20 come from Reynolds et al. (2001). (3) The estimates at Age 22–26 come from Reynolds et al. (2011). (4) The estimates at Age 28 come from Reynolds et al. (2011).

CPC might have been more successful than other similar programs, like Head Start, because it encouraged parental involvement. Parents are induced to visit the centers, and the staff teaches them various forms of stimulative play that they can do at home and assists parents interested in pursuing further education and seeking jobs (Reynolds, 2000).

9.8 Education and Interventions in Kindergarten and Elementary School

As noted in the first chapter of this book, 150 years ago, moral education, rooted in Protestant Christianity, was taught in American public schools. For reasons given in Chapter 1, moral and character education disappeared from the curriculum of public schools. However, moral education is featured in Catholic education. Some private schools teach a secular version of moral education. For example, the Knowledge Is Power Program (KIPP) Charter Schools enforce strict codes of discipline and give character training to their participants (The KIPP Foundation, 2011). In contemporary society, discussions of moral and character education provoke controversy even among its advocates. Scholars disagree about the origins of character and morality and how they can best be fostered.[83]

In this section of the chapter we survey the evidence on secular versions of moral and character education. This does not reflect any antireligious bias on our part. Instead, it reflects the absence of convincing evaluations of the effectiveness of character education/moral development programs in religious schools.

9.8.1 TARGETED CHARACTER INTERVENTIONS

Few well-evaluated interventions have targeted children in elementary school. Durlak et al. (2011) present a meta-analysis of 213 school-based social and emotional learning programs. While their study suggests that these programs have been successful, many of the evaluations they review suffer from substantial methodological problems. For example, only 15% of the studies have follow-ups that last beyond 6 months. For the studies with longer follow-up, the mean impact is positive and statistically significant. However, these follow-ups are still short compared to those for

---

83. The conceptualizations of morality and character differ in the literature. Character is usually viewed as a skill acquired through habituation and practice. In its perfected state it becomes a gut reaction. Morality is viewed as a consequence of conscious choices. Many dismiss discussions of morality and character out of hand because of their religious connotations or because they suggest a prudish vision of society that does not tolerate cultural pluralism. Lapsley and Yeager (2012) survey the controversies in the field, the curricula available, and evidence on their effectiveness.

the Perry Preschool program and ABC.[84] Although these programs appear promising, evidence on their long-run effectiveness is lacking.

9.8.1.1 The Seattle Social Development Project (SSDP)

Of all of the programs reported by Durlak et al. (2011), the Seattle Social Development Project (SSDP) has been evaluated the most thoroughly. The program targeted public elementary schools in high-crime areas of Seattle. The full program lasted from first grade through sixth grade.

The program emphasized attachment between children and their parents and teachers. Throughout elementary school, the participants' teachers received five days of training per year that included proactive classroom management, interactive teaching, and cooperative learning. The first-grade teachers received additional lessons based on the Cognitive Problem-Solving curriculum, which teaches children to resolve conflicts with peers (Shure and Spivack, 1988). In first and second grade, parents were offered a seven-session course on behavioral management training.[85] In second and third grade, parents were offered a four-session course to support their children's academic achievement.[86] Finally, in fifth and sixth grade, parents were offered a five-session course designed to reduce drug use.[87] Parents of 43% of the children participated in parenting classes.[88]

The program improved a variety of long-run outcomes. Table 9.6 shows that SSDP improved grades and behavior during adolescence. At age 21, participants were 10 percentage points more likely to have graduated from high school (or have earned an equivalency degree). By age 24, this effect faded, but this likely occurred because members of the control group earn GED certificates.[89] By ages 24 and 27, the participants were 12 percentage points more likely to earn an associate's degree. The treatment group had higher earnings at ages 24 and 27, although treatment

---

84. The largest federal study to date on character education programs failed to find evidence for improvements in behavior or academic performance (see Social and Character Development Research Consortium, 2010).

85. The course followed the "Catch 'Em Being Good" curriculum (Hawkins, Von Cleve, and Catalano, 1991).

86. The course consisted of four sessions that followed the "How to Help Your Child Succeed in School" curriculum (Abbott et al., 1998).

87. The course followed the "Preparing for the Drug (Free) Years" curriculum (Haggerty et al., 1999).

88. Hawkins et al. (1999).

89. Few people earn a traditional high school degree between age 21 and 24.

Table 9.6 Summary of Treatment Effects from the Seattle Social Development Project

Outcome	Age 18[h]	Age 21[i]	Age 24[j]	Age 27[j]
			Age	
GPA	0.24*			
CAT(ES)[a]	0.05			
Grade Repetition(%)	−8.7**			
Dropout(%)	−7.3			
School Misbehavior[b]	−1.41**			
Violent Crime(%)	−11.4**			
Ever Arrested(%)	−6.0			
Arrested past year(%)		−2.0	1.0	1.0
Smoking(%)	−0.7			
Pregnancy(%)	−9.3*		−9.0	−8.0
Anxiety(%)[c]		−2.0		
Depression(%)[c]		−8.0*		
High School Graduate/GED(%)		10.0***	6.0	6.0
More than 2 Years of College(%)		8.0***		
Self-efficacy[d]		0.17***	0.13*	−0.01
Associate's Degree(%)			12.0*	12.0*
Bachelor's Degree(%)			7.0	6.0
Substance Abuse Index[e]			3.0	−3.0
Mental Health Disorder Index[f]			−9.0*	−11.0**
Income(in thousands)[g]			3.51	3.12

Notes: The estimates are coefficients from regressions that control for sample member characteristics. % refers to treatment effects in terms of changes in prevalence in outcome variable in percentage points. ES indicates Effect Size, reporting the treatment effect in standard deviations of the outcome variable. (a) CAT stands for California Achievement Test score and combines reading, language, and mathematics subtests. It has been standardized based on the sample of ninth-grade Seattle students. (b) Measures frequency of occurrence of skipping, cheating, and being sent from class. (c) Anxiety, social phobia, and depression were measured using the *DSM-IV* (American Psychiatric Association, 1994). The mental health disorder index groups this for anxiety, social phobia, posttraumatic stress disorders, and major depressive episodes. (d) Measured as mean score on six items concerning perceived future opportunities, on a scale of 1–4. (e) The Substance Abuse Index measures dependence on substances (tobacco, alcohol, and illicit drugs) using *DSM-IV* criteria. (f) The Mental Health Disorder Index summarizes problems of anxiety, social phobia, posttraumatic stress and depression, using *DSM-IV* criteria. (g) Refers to income from all sources, before taxes. Includes zero-earners; income is top-coded at $200,000. (h) Hawkins et al. (1999). (i) Hawkins et al. (2005). (j) Hawkins et al. (2008).
* 10% significance; ** 5% significance; *** 1% significance.

effects on income are not precisely determined. The program improved self-efficacy at age 21 and 24 but did not have a statistically significant effect on achievement test scores. The program improved mental health in the long run. Like many other programs, if one judged it solely on the basis of achievement tests, SSDP would be unsuccessful. Considering meaningful life outcomes and character outcomes presents a far more positive picture.

9.8.1.2 Cambridge-Somerville Program

The Cambridge-Somerville Program is an example of a primary school program that harmed participants. This five-year intervention targeted 5- to 13-year-old boys with behavioral problems. The program was evaluated by the method of random assignment. The treatment differed among participants but included medical assistance, tutoring, access to summer camps, and meetings with parents (McCord and McCord, 1959). A 30-year follow-up showed that participants exhibited worse drinking habits, more serious mental diseases, more heart problems, higher blood pressure, (modestly) higher crime rates, and died younger (McCord, 1978). Despite the negative effects, participants reported that they thought the program helped them. McCord (1978) speculates that the program failed because it did not create a sense of autonomy among participants. It gave intensive assistance to participants. When the assistance was removed, they fell back into unfavorable behaviors. These were aggravated by feelings of rejection and resentment for lack of support.

9.8.1.3 Project STAR

Project STAR provides evidence that higher quality kindergarten classes improve later-life outcomes by improving character. From kindergarten through third grade, children and teachers were randomly assigned to classrooms of differing class sizes. In an analysis that builds on the work of Heckman et al. (2013), Chetty et al. (2011) examine the Project STAR program and find that students placed in higher quality kindergarten classes tended to have higher test scores at the end of kindergarten. They measure quality by peer average performance on the Stanford Achievement Test. The effect on test scores faded over time. By eighth grade, students in better kindergarten classes performed no differently on tests.

As with the Perry program, benefits emerge later in life. Children placed in better kindergarten classrooms had significantly higher earnings in early adulthood. Furthermore, kindergarten classroom quality also predicts better fourth- and eighth-grade behavior as measured by teacher-assessed effort, initiative, interest in the class, and disruptive behavior. In turn, measured behavior predicts earnings in adulthood, suggesting that improvement in character skills is the main channel through which better kindergarten classrooms improve earnings. Several studies suggest that smaller class sizes per se do not improve long-run outcomes.[90]

The analyses of the Perry Preschool program and Project STAR highlight the importance of long-term follow-ups and measuring outcomes that depend on character skills. If these studies had only measured short-run improvements in cognitive ability, the programs would appear to have had little effect.[91]

9.9 Education and Interventions Targeted toward Adolescents and Young Adults

Compared to early-childhood programs, the evidence on adolescent programs is less abundant. There are, however, some well-documented and promising interventions. We divide adolescent programs into four main categories: (1) mentoring programs for at-risk students; (2) residential-based education programs for high school dropouts; (3) in-school, professional training; and (4) incentives for student performance. Several mentorship programs and residential-based programs appear promising but have relatively short follow-ups. Somewhat similar programs with long follow-ups have had no long-term effects. These programs appear to achieve their short-term effects by closely monitoring participants and removing them from their usual environments.[92] Programs that combine work and education are more promising and have been shown to have lasting effects. A few programs that combine long-term mentoring with financial support to attend college have improved educational attainment but do not measure other outcomes.

Few programs that target adolescents have long-term follow-ups. As Table 9.2 shows, only two evaluations of adolescent programs have follow-ups of at least 10 years, compared to 14 early-childhood and elementary

90. Chetty et al. (2011); Hanushek (2003).
91. However, the estimates reported in Chetty et al. (2011) appear to be implausibly large for the effect of one teacher in one class on the lifetime earnings of students.
92. These are called "incapacitation" effects in criminology.

school evaluations. Most adolescent intervention programs tend to measure fewer outcomes and focus mainly on schooling and employment.

Our framework on the life-cycle development of skills provides an interpretation of the relative failure of adolescent programs. Early childhood is a sensitive period for the development of both cognitive and character skills—prevention is more effective than remediation. Early investments are productive because early skills promote the development of later skills and, through dynamic complementarity, make later investments more productive. The finding that short-term benefits fade away quickly in most adolescent interventions might indicate the importance of incentives and situations in affecting behavior. As previously noted, several adolescent programs temporarily supervise and control the environments of adolescents, thereby changing their incentives which beneficially, but temporarily, affects their behavior.

9.9.1 ADOLESCENT MENTORSHIP PROGRAMS

9.9.1.1 *Quantum Opportunity Program*

The Quantum Opportunity Program (QOP) is one of the few adolescent mentorship programs with a long-term follow-up. Rodríguez-Planas (2012) estimates the effect of the QOP on labor market outcomes, educational attainment, and risky behaviors. The program was an intensive after-school program that provided mentoring, educational services, and financial incentives during the four years of high school (plus one additional year in case students fell behind). The program targeted low-performing high school students. QOP was evaluated by the method of random assignment.

QOP was not successful in improving risky behaviors, and, if anything, caused harm for males. Table 9.7 summarizes the effects of the program. Ten years after the start of the program, males in the treatment group were *more* likely to have been recently arrested. Males were more likely to have completed two years of college or training, but the increased educational attainment did not translate into higher earnings in the follow-up period. Female participants had better educational outcomes during the first follow-up near the end of the program, but the control group caught up by the end of the three-year follow-up.

Because the program had many components, it is difficult to pinpoint why the program failed. Rodríguez-Planas (2010) suggests four reasons. First, increasing awareness about the consequences of risky behavior could have caused teens to become fatalistic; for example, some might feel that drug addiction was inevitable. Second, the mentors might have served as

Table 9.7 Summary of Treatment Effects from the Quantum Opportunity Program

Outcome since Assignment	Males			Females		
	5Y	7Y	10Y	5Y	7Y	10Y
Education and Employment						
High School Diploma (%)	3.5	3.2	2.9	7.4*	3.7	0.7
Obtained GED(%)	−2.2	1.2	1.7	1.2	0.7	−0.7
Math Test Score (percentile)[a]	0.7	—	—	0.2	—	—
Reading Test Score (percentile)[a]	0.7	—	—	0.2	—	—
Ever in College	—	7.3	7.4	—	5.1	2.0
Completed 2 Years of College or Training	—	—	7.7*	—	—	6.2
Earned BA	—	—	0.3	—	—	2.4
Has a Job	—	−6.5	−2.9	—	0.2	5.5
Hourly Wage[b]	—	−1.2*	−1.3	—	0.8	0.2
Annual Earnings[b]	—	—	230	—	—	1,397
Risky Behaviors and Welfare						
Binge Drinking in Past 30 Days	5.0	−10.1**	−2.4	−0.9	−0.5	3.5
Used Illegal Drugs in Past 30 Day	5.9	−6.3	−2.2	6.7	−2.0	1.9
Arrested or Charged[c]	−8.3**	1.8	7.8**	2.7	−2.2	0.2
Receiving Welfare	—	5.8*	4.5	—	−1.0	1.5

Source: Rodríguez-Planas (2012).
Notes: The estimates show the difference in means between the treatment and control groups, regardless of whether they participated in QOP. Weights were used to account for nonresponse and survey design. The years at in the columns indicate time since the start of the program. (a) The tests were developed from National Education Longitudinal Study (NELS) tests and scored by the Educational Testing Service (ETS). (b) Nonworkers were assigned values of "0." (c) For the 5-year follow-up, the value indicates percentages of ever being arrested or charged. For the 7-year follow-up, the value indicates percentages over the past 3 months. For the 10-year follow-up, the value indicates percentages over the past 2 years.
*10% significance; **5% significance; ***1% significance.

advocates when students were in trouble at school or with the law, lowering the cost of engaging in problem behaviors. Third, students might have used their stipends to purchase drugs or alcohol. Fourth, the program organized group activities among the participants, which could have induced negative peer-effects.

9.9.1.2 Big Brothers Big Sisters

The Big Brothers Big Sisters (BBBS) mentoring program effectively improves educational outcomes (Tierney, Baldwin-Grossman, and Resch, 1995). The program is aimed at children (ages 10–16) living in unstable

Table 9.8 Summary of Treatment Effects from Big Brother Big Sister Program 18 Months after Assignment

	Treatment Effects	
Outcome	Males	Females
Start Drug Use (Odds Ratio)	0.58**	0.77
Start Alcohol Use (Odds Ratio)	0.83	0.68
Number of Times Hit Someone	−0.67	−1.17*
Number of Times Stole Something	−0.07	−0.02
Number of Times Damaged Property	−0.04	−0.03
Perceived Ability to Complete Schoolwork	0.39	1.25***
Grade Point Average	0.03	0.17**
Number of Times Skipped Class	−0.18	−1.07***
Number of Times Lied to Parent	−0.83	−2.24
Global Self-Worth[a]	0.24	0.37
Social Acceptance[a]	0.54	0.09
Self-Confidence[b]	0.01	0.46

Source: Tierney et al. (1995).
Notes: The estimates come from models that control for baseline characteristics. The effects for "Start Drug Use" and "Start Alcohol Use" were estimated using a logit model. All other effects were estimated using ordinary least squares. (a) From "Self-Perception Profile for Children" (Harter, 1985). (b) From "Self-Image Questionnaire for Young Adolescents" (Petersen et al., 1984).
*10% significance; **5% significance; ***1% significance.

family environments, which generally are single-parent households. Volunteer mentors have regular and lengthy meetings with the enrollees for an average treatment length of one year. Mentors have flexibility in their guidance, but the program emphasizes five primary goals: developing a successful relationship; providing social, cultural, and recreational enrichment; improving peer relationships; improving self-concept; and improving motivation.

Tierney et al. (1995) evaluate the program by comparing treated children to a control group that was put on a waiting list for the program. As Table 9.8 shows, BBBS has positive impacts on academic outcomes but only for girls. The effects on direct measures of character skills related to Big Five Neuroticism (Self-Worth, Social Acceptance, and Self-Confidence) are positive but not statistically significant. The treatment group children are less likely to hit other children or lie to their parents. The follow-up lasted only 18 months after random assignment. Given the results from QOP, this follow-up is too short to determine whether the effects are persistent. However, BBBS differed in important ways from QOP. BBBS features one-on-one mentorship, which allows mentees and mentors to form stronger attachments and might help avoid the negative peer effects of grouping at-risk youth together.

9.9.1.3 EPIS Program

Martins (2010) analyzes data from EPIS, a program developed to improve student achievement of 13- to 15-year-olds in Portugal. Unlike many other interventions, EPIS emphasizes character skills, aiming to increase motivation, self-esteem, and study skills. The program consists of one-on-one meetings with a trained staff member or meetings in small groups. The intervention is tailored to each participant's individual skill deficit. EPIS decreases grade retention by 10 percentage points, in a cost-effective way. Unfortunately, other outcomes are not reported.

9.9.2 RESIDENTIAL-BASED PROGRAMS

9.9.2.1 Job Corps

The Job Corps is the largest residential training program in the United States for at-risk youth. Youth spend one year in training and remedial education, and receive counseling and training in social skills. About 90% of participants live at a residential facility throughout the program (Schochet, Burghardt, and Glazerman, 2001). Early evaluations found that the program improved many outcomes, including wages, welfare dependence, college attendance, health, and crime.[93] However, more recent evaluations report that gains in earnings fade away rather quickly and that the reduced crime effects came primarily during the program and only for the residential participants (Schochet, Burghardt, and Glazerman, 2001; Schochet, Burghardt, and McConnell, 2008). Figure 9.13 shows that net earnings effects are basically zero.[94]

This program provides useful insights into the ineffectiveness of the GED program. The Job Corps promoted GED certification. Early, optimistic evaluations of the program (Schochet, Burghardt, and Glazerman, 2001) treated GED recipients as equivalent to high school graduates and projected substantial earnings gains. Later evaluations based on realized earnings showed the ineffectiveness of the Job Corps and implicitly the GED.

The program's emphasis on job search might explain the temporary increase in earnings after participants leave it. Job Corps centers use placement outcomes in their evaluation of vocational instructors and other

---

93. See, for example, Mallar et al. (1982).

94. For males ages 20–24 there appear to be modest Job Corps effects. However, these findings do not survive adjustments for multiple hypothesis testing (Schochet, Burghardt, and McConnell, 2008).

Figure 9.13 The Treatment Effect of Job Corps on Annual Earnings

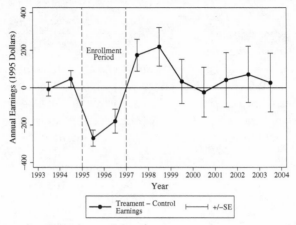

Source: Estimates from Schochet et al. (2008).
Notes: The values in the graph are the difference between the annual earnings in
the treatment group and the control group. The dashed interval indicates the
period when most participants were enrolled in the program. The earnings data come
from the social security earnings SER records. Earnings include zero earnings for
nonworkers.

staff. Staff from Job Corps centers often remain in contact with former participants to assist in subsequent job searches.

9.9.2.2 *National Guard ChalleNGe*

The National Guard Youth ChalleNGe program is a 17-month intervention
for youth who have dropped out of high school. Although the program
does not require that participants enroll in the military, it stresses aspects of military discipline. Like the Job Corps, most training occurs in a
residential facility removed from the usual environments of participants.
The program features a two-week residential orientation and assessment
period, a 20-week residential program often conducted at a military base,
and a one-year, nonresidential mentoring program. There have been three
major evaluations of the program: one occurring nine months after random assignment, another 21 months after random assignment, and a third
evaluation three years after random assignment (Bloom, Gardenhire-
Crooks, and Mandsager, 2009; Millenky, Bloom, and Dillon, 2010; Millenky
et al., 2011).

Table 9.9 shows the estimated treatment effects of the program. Nine
months after the program, participants are more likely to have a GED or

Table 9.9 Summary of Treatment Effects from the National Guard ChalleNGe Program

Outcome	Time since Assignment		
	9 Months[1]	21 Months[2]	3 Years[3]
Has HS Diploma(%)	12.0***	5.7**	3.7
Has GED(%)	23.4***	26.5***	22.4***
Earned Any College Credit	—	15.1***	16.1***
Currently Working(%)	9.1***	4.9*	7.1**
Earnings (Annual)[a]	—	2,028***	2,226***
Working or in Training(%)	–1.9	5.7**	4.6
Arrested(%) [b]	–5.8**	0.9	–0.8
Convicted(%)[b]	–4.4**	–4.2**	2.8
High Self-Efficacy	4.0**	—	—
Low Self-Efficacy	–9.6***	—	—
Serious Psychological Distress[c]	—	0.3	–1.1
Always Uses Birth Control	—	0.3	–8.0**
Overweight	4.2	1.0	6.1**
Obese	–4.3**	–1.5	–0.7

Sources: (1) The estimates after 9 months come from Bloom et al. (2009). (2) The estimates after 21 months come from Millenky et al. (2010). (3) The estimates after 3 years come from Millenky et al. (2011).

Notes: The estimates are coefficients from regressions that control for sample member characteristics. The headers in the columns indicate the duration since random assignment. (a) For the 21-month survey, annual earnings are approximated by multiplying the estimates for weekly earnings by 52. Nonworkers are included as "0's." (b) For the 9-month survey, the value is for differences since random assignment. For the 21-month and 3-year follow-ups the value indicates differences for the past 12 months. (c) The psychological distress score is based on the K6 scale, which ranges from 0 to 24. Serious psychological distress is a score of 13 points or more.
*10% significance; **5% significance; ***1% significance.

high school diploma and be employed. They are less likely to have been arrested or convicted. Three years after the intervention, the effects for criminal behavior and high school graduation decline and become statistically insignificant. The initial reduction in crime likely occurs because participants are housed in a residential program (an incapacitation effect). However, the employment and earnings effects persist. Given the similarities between the Job Corps and the ChalleNGe program, the three-year follow-up might not be long enough to determine whether the labor market effects are truly persistent.

In-depth interviews of the participants shed light on why some of the effects of the program might fade. Most participants were glad that they had entered the program, but explained that friends made it difficult to maintain the discipline that they had learned once they returned to their original environments (Millenky, Bloom, and Dillon, 2011). The authors suggest that it might be important to maintain stronger attachment with participants after they leave the residential facility. The high rate of GED certification for treatment group members is a bad omen for any hope of finding a long-run benefit from the program.

9.9.3 WORKPLACE-BASED ADOLESCENT INTERVENTION PROGRAMS

Workplace-based internships and apprenticeships can boost skills.[95] A hundred and fifty years ago, apprenticeships and workplace-based education were standard for most adolescents. Apprenticeships offer in-depth, work-based learning combined with related academic course work. Few rigorous studies have examined how entering and completing apprenticeships in the United States affects the educational attainment, job skills, nonacademic skills, and job market outcomes of young people.[96] A study of high school students who participated in a Wisconsin youth apprenticeship in printing documented participant earnings levels substantially above expected earnings for similar youth (Orr et al., 1994). Anecdotal evidence suggests that youth apprenticeships motivate participants to do better in school and to pursue difficult courses broadly related to their occupational interests.

Well-structured career-focused programs can potentially enhance character as well as occupational skills, in ways most relevant to the occupations and tasks that engage young people. Halpern (2009) undertook in-depth, observational studies of high school youth apprenticeships over a three-year period. He analyzed 24 separate programs involving nearly

95. We have benefited from the commentary of Robert Lerman in preparing this subsection. See Lerman (2013) for a discussion of related issues.

96. Students involved in Wisconsin's Youth Apprenticeship Program believed their worksite learning experiences were excellent, with 84%–86% reporting that they enabled them to improve their problem-solving and teamwork skills (Scribner and Wakelyn, 1998). Students reported gaps between their work-based and school-based learning. But interviews with instructors and employers indicated that apprentices improved their social and interpersonal skills, developed independent decision-making skills, and increased their self-confidence and self-esteem. However, one should be wary of self-reports. Students in the Cambridge-Somerville program reported satisfaction with the program, even though objective evaluations of it were negative (McCord, 1978).

500 apprentices and conducted over 300 hours of observation and over 90 interviews with adult mentors, staff, program directors, and students. One program, called After School Matters, engaged inner-city Chicago high school students in a one- to two-year program for two to three afternoons a week in fields such as video and computer technology, culinary arts, and design. Halpern also followed students in other programs, including Wisconsin's youth apprenticeship program.

Halpern's qualitative analysis of these programs is rich and difficult to summarize. Nonetheless, several perspectives are worth noting. He gives many examples of how apprentices gradually develop expertise in an occupation as well as in problem-solving skills. They acquire self-confidence, teamwork, the ability to take direction and take initiatives, and other non-cognitive skills. He notes that participating youth see themselves as judged by their ability to meet or exceed the established standards of a discipline, including meeting deadlines and facing genuine constraints and unexpected difficulties that arise in the profession. To quote Halpern, "Young people learn through observation, imitation, trial and error, and reiteration; in other words through force of experience." Adult mentors scaffold the discipline protocol for the apprentice, sequencing and controlling task demands to keep them on the constructive side of difficulty. They direct apprentices' attention, demonstrate new points, and sometimes collaborate with them.

Utilizing workplaces as learning locations is motivated by evidence of the importance of occupational and character skills. Workplace-oriented training can help youth attain development goals such as personal autonomy, efficacy, motivation, realism, optimism, and knowledge of vocations. It facilitates matching between workers and firms, and motivates adolescents to acquire relevant academic and character skills. Evidence from other countries shows that workplace-based learning helps students develop an occupational identity, a professional ethic, and self-esteem based on accomplishment (Rauner, 2007). We review some of the better documented programs in this section.

9.9.3.1 Career Academies

Career Academies provide evidence that integrating career development into a standard high school can have long-term labor market benefits. These academies operate within regular high schools and prepare students for postsecondary education and employment. In addition to regular high school courses, Career Academies offer courses that are career- or occupation-focused (Kemple and Willner, 2008). Individual academies focus on preparing students for participation in particular industries such as finance, health science, hospitality, and tourism. They include activities that might enhance character skills in the workplace (Kemple and Snipes, 2000). Career Academies have many features in common with European apprenticeship programs that are discussed below in Section 9.10.

Compared to other high schools, Career Academies expose students to career-oriented activities, including job shadowing, career fairs, job search workshops, resume preparation, and interview preparation. Students work together in teams when relating their experiences. A recent evaluation based on random assignment estimates the effects of Career Academies on labor market, educational, and social outcomes (Kemple and Willner, 2008). Table 9.10 shows the difference in outcomes between the control and treatment groups. Career Academies have positive and sustained impacts on earnings and employment among young men but have no impact on high school completion rates and postsecondary educational enrollment and attainment rates.[97] Treatment group participants are more likely to live independently with children and a spouse/partner. Young males in the treatment group are more likely to get married and become custodial parents. For females, most effects are positive but not statistically significant.

Career Academies likely benefit their students by improving character skills. The program improves earnings for males in the long run, even though it does not improve educational attainment or scores on achievement tests. The Career Academies include activities that are designed to improve character. Internships may teach students the importance of perseverance and Conscientiousness, along with other occupation-related skills that improve their labor market readiness. Programs that integrate school and work not only motivate students to learn relevant academic material but also integrate adolescents into the larger society and teach children the skills valued in the workplace and in society at large.

9.9.3.2 Year-Up Program

The Year-Up program provides low-income, mostly black and Hispanic 18- to 24-year-olds with full-time classes and six-month internships. To enter the program, applicants must submit a written essay, letters of reference, a high school transcript, and attendance records (Grobe, Rosenblum, and

---

97. The percentage gains in earnings were highest for the students facing the highest risk of dropping out of school. Young women did not experience any statistically significant gains in earnings. Given that only 55% of the treatment group actually finished the full curriculum of the Career Academy, the earnings gains likely understate the actual impact of full participation.

Table 9.10 Summary of Treatment Effects from Career Academies within 96-month Follow-up after Scheduled High School Graduation

Outcome	Males	Females
Labor Market (49–96 Months)		
Monthly Earnings ($)[a]	361**	118
Months Employed (#)	2.8***	−0.3
Average Hours Worked per Week (#)	4.1***	0.2
Average Hourly Wages ($)	0.6	0.7
Educational Attainment (after 96 Months)		
High School Diploma	−0.4	0.2
GED	3.6	1.3
Certificate/License	2.0	0.1
AA Degree	−1.0	1.8
BA Degree	−2.2	−1.6
Family Formation (after 96 Months)		
Married and Living Together	9.0**	1.5
Custodial Parent	11.5***	3.7
Noncustodial Parent	−6.4**	0.2

Source: Kemple and Willner (2008).
Notes: Impact estimates are regression-adjusted to control for background characteristics of the sample and for the clustering of students within schools and random assignment years. (a) Nonworkers were assigned a value of "0" for monthly earnings.
*10% significance; **5% significance; ***1% significance.

Weissman, 2010). Given the requirements, Year-Up applicants may be more motivated than their peers.

During the first six months of the program, students take classes involving business writing, time management, teamwork, problem solving, and conflict resolution (Grobe, Rosenblum, and Weissman, 2010). To remain in the program, students must maintain high attendance rates, be on time, and complete assignments (Roder and Elliot, 2011). Students who complete classes are placed in internships with companies (Roder and Elliot, 2011). Participants continue to attend a weekly class during their internships where they share experiences about their internships, work on their resumes, do mock job interviews, and look into postsecondary options. The technical skills training component of the program includes instruction in word processing, spreadsheet, and presentation software. Some students learn about computer installation and repair, and other students learn how to track portfolios.

Table 9.11 Impacts of the Year-Up Program

Outcome	Treatment	Control	Treatment Effect
Hourly Wage at Current or Most Recent Job	12.58	10.32	2.26***
Annual Earnings during Year after Program [a]	15,082	11,621	3,461*
Employed during Year after Program	86	83	3
Works Full-Time	67	55	12*
Works in Information Technology	22	2	20[†]
Works in Investment Operations	15	0	15[†]

Source: Roder and Elliot (2011).
Notes: (a)The annual earnings calculations include nonworkers.
*10% significance; **5% significance; ***1% significance; [†]No measure of statistical significance reported.

Roder and Elliot (2011) study the effect of Year-Up on labor market outcomes one year after the end of the program. Qualified applicants on the waiting list were assigned to treatment or control groups. Table 9.11 summarizes the effects of the program two years after random assignment (one year after the end of the program). The treatment group has higher annual earnings, primarily due to their increased hourly wages. The employment rates are similar between the treatment and control groups, although the treatment group was more likely to have full-time jobs. The earnings and wage benefits arise from improvements in job quality. Compared to the control group, more members in the treatment group find higher paying jobs in information technology and investment operations. About a quarter of the treatment group is hired by the employer sponsoring their internship.

The one-year follow-up is too short to determine whether the program has lasting effects, but some evidence suggests that the benefits might be more permanent than other similar programs. The Job Corps primarily improves earnings in the short run by increasing employment (Schochet, Burghardt, and McConnell, 2008). In contrast, Year-Up increases hourly wages (Roder and Elliot, 2011). If these wage increases reflect increased human capital formation, the benefits likely last longer. Many employers of interns later hired their trainees.

The evaluation has no direct measures of character skills, but it does provide clues that the program affected character in ways that lead to better outcomes in the job market. Year-Up students were taught that appropriate behavior, dress, and communication are important for success.

9.9.3.3 Dominican Youth Employment Program

A recent study by Gertler and Martinez (2012) evaluates the Dominican Youth Employment program. The intervention targets unemployed youth (ages 16–29) without a high school diploma. In the evaluation, youth were assigned to one of three groups: a group that received vocational skill training, life skills training, and an internship; a group that received life skills training and an internship; or a control group. The vocational training is available in a variety of fields, including cosmetology, sales, tourism, and electricity. The life skills training focuses on building self-esteem and capacities for communication, conflict resolution, time management, and teamwork. The internship takes place at a private company and lasts 240 hours.

Table 9.12 summarizes treatment effects from the program 18 months after assignment for the group that received both treatments ("Life + Vocation") and the group that only received life skills training ("Life Only"). Females in both treatment groups have higher employment rates, higher earnings, and fewer pregnancies than their control group counterparts. These differences are statistically significant when compared with the control group. The difference in impact between the two treatment groups is only statistically significant for preventing pregnancies. Since both treatment groups benefit equally, the program likely helps females by improving character through work experience rather than through the receipt of

Table 9.12 Summary of Treatment Effects from the Dominican Youth Employment Program 18 Months after Assignment

	Males		Females	
Outcome	Life + Vocation	Life Only	Life + Vocation	Life Only
Worked during Last Week (%)	−8.3**	−3.8	6.4**	7.2***
Searching for Job in Last Week (%)	6.8*	5.3	−4.5	−1.6
Monthly Wage Income	676	−414	456**	518**
Expect Better Employment (%)[a]	3.8**	1.9	2.9**	3.2**
Number of Children	—	—	−0.13*	−0.15**

Source: Roder and Elliot (2011).
Notes: The reported estimated effects come from a linear probability model. The tests of significance assume that the errors are clustered at the course level. (a) The variable takes the value of 1 if the respondent reports that they expect their employment to be improved a year from now and a value of 0 if they expect it to be the same or worse. *10% significance; **5% significance; ***1% significance.

vocational training. For males, life skills training had no effect, while the combined training produced negative impacts. Given that the males who received vocational training report that they are actively looking for work and that they believe that their employment outcomes will improve, the authors of the evaluation speculate that vocational training might have raised the labor market prospects of male participants.

9.9.3.4 Self-Sufficiency Project

The Canadian Self-Sufficiency Project (SSP) provides direct evidence that working improves character. The program provided earnings supplements to single parents on welfare if they found full-time jobs and agreed to leave welfare. New enrollees were told that if they remained on welfare a year later, they would have the chance to participate in the SSP program. After a year, they were either assigned to a treatment group that would receive an earnings subsidy for three years if they worked full time or to a control group that would not.[98]

Assessing the effect of employment on skills is complicated by the possibility of reverse causality. Just as employment might affect skills, skills might affect employment. The SSP program provides a way to study the effects of exogenous variation of employment status on skills. Gottschalk (2005) uses assignment status in the experiment as an instrumental variable for employment to estimate the effect of employment on Locus of Control (the extent to which people feel they have control over their lives).[99] After 36 months, those who received the subsidy were more likely to have an improved Locus of Control, suggesting that work can improve this character skill. This finding supports the earlier evidence that work-based education can improve character.

Other studies evaluate the labor market benefits of the program. The findings are mixed. Michalopoulos et al. (2002) evaluate the labor market benefits of the program. During the three-year eligibility period, SSP had significant positive impacts on employment, earnings, and reduced welfare use. However, the effect faded. Nevertheless, the children of participants who were in preschool at randomization performed better in school. At the 36-month follow-up, the children of mothers in the treatment group scored 10 percentage points higher on a test of math skills ($p < 0.05$)[100] and

98. See Michalopoulos et al. (2002) for a detailed description of the program.

99. Locus of Control is related to Big Five Neuroticism. See Almlund et al. (2011) for a discussion.

100. The report does not specify the nature of the math skills test.

about ⅛ of a standard deviation higher on a vocabulary test, but this difference is not statistically significantly different from zero.[101]

Later studies investigate short- and long-term treatment effects for the take-up group (the members of the treatment group who qualified for the supplements). Zabel, Schwartz, and Donald (2010) find that the take-up group was 25% more likely to be employed after 52 months. Another study by Zabel, Schwartz, and Donald (2013) shows that, although the overall treatment effect on the wages of the take-up group is small, there is heterogeneity in the impact of SSP on wages between "incentivized" and "nonincentivized" take-up groups.[102] For the incentivized program group the absolute wage progression was 10.8%–11.5% compared to 1.9%–2.2% for the control group, while for the nonincentivized take-up group, the absolute wage progression was 11.2%–12.2% compared to 8.2%–11.6% for the control group. Card and Hyslop (2009) find that SSP increased welfare participation in the first year after initial entry and lowered it over the following five years even after SSP payments ended, although the effect largely disappeared after seven years.

9.10 Apprenticeship Programs[103]

Apprentices are employees who have formal agreements with employers to carry out a recognized program of work-based and classroom learning. Apprenticeships typically begin in late adolescence or early adulthood. The training is highly structured, with a well-designed curriculum usually lasting three to four years. It is common for apprentices to spend three to four days per week at workplaces, acquiring knowledge and undertaking productive work involving gradually increasing levels of complexity. Classroom instruction in theoretical and general studies takes place at vocational schools one to two days per week. Apprentices participate in the production process, work with a trainer who is often a mentor, and ultimately gain sufficient occupational mastery to become certified by an external body (Wolter and Ryan, 2011). The emphasis is on occupational skills, but apprentices are likely to improve character and other generic

101. The Peabody Picture Vocabulary Test-Revised was used to measure vocabulary.

102. "Incentivized take-up group"—individuals who were induced by the program to find full-time jobs during a 13-month eligibility window and who would not otherwise have worked full time. "Nonincentivized take-up group"—members of the program group who would leave welfare and work full-time regardless of the SSP program.

103. The commentary and text of Robert Lerman was helpful in preparing this section. See Lerman (2013).

employment skills as well, including those most relevant for their chosen occupation. The training is employer-led and thus sensitive to market demands and less costly to the government than full-time schooling. Career Academies and apprenticeship programs share many features in common. They train participants in the skills of specific occupations, supplement the training with general education, and provide guidance and mentoring for participants.

Apprenticeship training is common in many countries, reaching 55%–70% of youth in Austria, Germany, and Switzerland. The scale of apprenticeship varies widely across countries. Apprenticeships as a share of the total labor force are about 3.7%–3.9% in Australia and Germany, about 2.3%–2.5% in Canada and England, and 1.7% in France, but only about 0.3% in the United States.[104]

Given the concern that apprenticeships train workers too narrowly and make apprentices less adaptable to a changing labor market, in evaluating apprenticeship programs it is important to follow those completing apprenticeships over long time horizons. At a minimum, an evaluation has to find an appropriate comparison group, estimate costs to firms, workers, and the government, and take account of the heterogeneity of occupations used for apprenticeships.

Several studies of apprenticeship training in European countries find high rates of returns to participants, often in the range of 10%–15%.[105] Bougheas and Georgellis (2004) find that about 70% of apprentices were in full-time employment immediately after training. Cooke (2003) shows that apprentices do not initially earn more than other workers, but experience greater wage growth.

One recent study of apprenticeship training analyzes small Austrian firms that eventually failed. It compares the wages of apprentices who started well before the firm failed (and thus who had a long period in apprenticeship training) with wages of apprentices who spent less time in training because the firm failed earlier in their apprenticeship period (Fersterer, Pischke, and Winter-Ebmer, 2008). Estimates suggest that for a three- to four-

---

104. Apprenticeships have expanded rapidly in several countries, including Australia (rising from 157,000 in 1996 to 515,000 in 2012) and in England (rising from 53,000 in 1990 to 614,000 in 2012) (National Apprenticeship Service, 2012; National Centre for Vocational Education Research, 2012). Along with the increasing roles of apprenticeship in Australia and England have come initiatives to upgrade the quality of their programs (McDowell et al., 2011).

105. See, for example, Adda et al. (2013); Bougheas and Georgellis (2004); Clark and Fahr (2002); and Winkelmann (1996).

year apprenticeship, post-apprenticeship wages are 12%–16% higher than they would otherwise be. Since the worker's costs of participating in an apprenticeship are often minimal, the returns are high.

What about job and occupational mobility? Buechtemann, Schupp, and Soloff (1993) find that about 80% of apprentices join the firm where they apprenticed after completing the program. In order to examine the adaptability of apprenticeship training, researchers (Clark and Fahr, 2002; Geel and Backes-Gellner, 2009) identified groups of skills that are required for each occupation. Changing occupations may not imply a significant change in the types of expertise required because of the overlap of skill requirements across occupations. While only 42% of apprentices stay in their initial occupation, nearly two-thirds remain with the apprentice occupation or another occupation requiring a similar mix of skills (Geel and Backes-Gellner, 2009). When apprentices move to another occupation that requires similar skills, their wages increase. Those trained in occupations with more specific skills are most likely to remain in their initial occupation or move to occupations within the same cluster.[106]

Germany has formally integrated apprenticeship programs into its educational system with apparent success. In Germany, there are three types of secondary schools: low (Hauptschule), medium (Realschule), and high (Gymnasium). Students who graduate from any of these secondary schools qualify to participate in the dual apprenticeship program. Those who graduate from higher quality schools have more prestigious vocational options.[107] The apprenticeships typically last about three years during which participants spend one to two days per week in a part-time vocational training school. They work the remaining time (Franz and Soskice, 1995).

Harhoff and Kane (1997) argue that apprentices occupy a similar place in the German economy as high school graduates occupy in the American economy. They find that apprentices earn about 19% more than those completing 10 or fewer years of school but 47% less than college graduates, whereas in the United States high school graduates earn about 23% more than those who complete 10 or fewer years of school but 42% less

---

106. Clark and Fahr (2002) also find that the wage penalty of departing from the occupation for which apprentices trained varies with the distance away from the original occupation and that there is no penalty at all from displacement into a somewhat related occupation. Among the former apprentices changing occupations, about two of five report using many or very many of the skills from their apprenticeship and another 20% used some of the skills.

107. See Franz and Soskice (1995) for a detailed description of the program.

than those who complete college. The estimates are similar over the life cycle.

Adda et al. (2013) estimate that participating in the German apprenticeship program yields a 5%–10% annual rate of return. This estimate includes the return to character skills which the authors do not isolate from the other benefits of the program. It also includes the return to the education and job training received, which likely produces skills valued in the labor market.

Some American apprenticeships are also promising. Hollenbeck (2008) estimates rates of return to various types of job training in Washington State. He compares outcomes of apprentices to those of other workers with similar backgrounds and earnings histories. His results show that apprenticeship training yields higher returns than other training or postsecondary (mostly community college) occupational programs. For apprenticeships, the social and governmental rates of return are large (over 20%) within the first 2.5 years after apprentices exit the program.

Another, more recent study of apprenticeship in 10 American states documents large and statistically significant earnings gains from participating in an apprenticeship (Reed et al., 2012). The study estimates how the length of participation in an apprenticeship affects earnings, holding constant the pre-enrollment earnings of apprenticeship participants. Six years after starting a program, the earnings of the average apprenticeship participant (average duration in an apprenticeship) are 40% higher than the earnings of nonparticipants with the same pre-apprenticeship history.

Workplace-based education is promising. It breaks down the artificial barrier between the culture of high schools and that of the rest of society documented in Coleman (1961). It motivates adolescents to learn relevant academic skills and gives mentoring and guidance to participants, many of whom come from disadvantaged families where such guidance is missing.

9.11 Other Curricula That Have Been Applied to Multiple Age Groups

9.11.1 TOOLS OF THE MIND

A random assignment evaluation of *Tools of the Mind* provides evidence that character skills can be fostered. *Tools of the Mind* is a program that attempts to teach preschool and early primary schoolchildren to regulate their social and cognitive behaviors. The curriculum encourages children to role-play and learn in groups with other children. In short-term follow-ups, several studies show that it improves classroom behavior as well as executive functioning, defined as higher-level cognitive skills, including inhibitory control, working memory, and cognitive flexibility.[108] Similar findings are reported for the Montessori preschool curriculum (Lillard and Else-Quest, 2006).

However, the evidence on the program is not all favorable.[109] There are few long-term evaluations of it. As noted by Heckman, Pinto, and Savelyev (2013), the Perry curriculum and the *Tools of the Mind* curriculum have common intellectual origins, so the positive long-term evidence on Perry arguably transfers to forecasting the likely long-run effects of *Tools of the Mind.*

9.11.2 STUDIES THAT TEACH THE INCREMENTAL THEORY OF INTELLIGENCE

Several studies examine the effect of teaching students that capabilities are malleable and that learning can change the structure of the brain (the "incremental theory of intelligence"). Dweck (2007) presents an extensive discussion of this approach. The focus in this intervention is on promoting cognition, but the measures used to evaluate the interventions include achievement tests and grades that are also determined by character skills. Some of this research also measures perseverance. The theory underlying the intervention is that children who believe that cognitive ability is a fixed trait might have little incentive to improve it.

The "mindset" interventions implement the logic of Figure 9.1. Effort and character skills determine performance on tasks, including performance on grades and achievement tests. Motivating greater effort enhances performance, and the "mindset" intervention is one such motivational exercise. At issue is whether the enhanced effort, however motivated, has lasting consequences. Unfortunately, all of the follow-ups are short-term in nature, so the important question—do these motivational programs have lasting consequences?—remains unanswered.[110]

Table 9.13 summarizes the results from three evaluations of these programs. Aronson, Fried, and Good (2002) evaluate an intervention in which college students were taught the incremental theory of intelligence. As a way to internalize the information, the participants were instructed to write a

---

108. Barnett et al. (2006, 2008); Bodrova and Leong (2001, 2007); Diamond et al. (2007).

109. See the study by Farran, Lipsey, and Wilson (2011).

110. Motivation research (Deci, 1971; Deci and Ryan, 1985) suggests that intrinsic rewards have longer lasting consequences than extrinsic rewards (e.g., payments or punishment).

Table 9.13 Evidence on the Treatment Effects of Teaching That Intelligence Is Malleable

Intervention	Follow-up	Main Results	Source
College students were taught the incremental theory of intelligence and wrote letters to a middle school student explaining the theory on three occasions over a one-month period.	2 quarters[a]	0.20–0.27 point increase in GPA ($p < 0.05$)[b]	Aronson et al. (2002)
Seventh graders received explanations of the incremental theory of intelligence via two 90-minute, in-person meetings with a mentor and weekly emails during the school year.	1 year	0.64 standard deviation increase on math score for boys ($p < 0.10$), 1.13 standard deviation increase in TAAS math scores for females ($p < 0.01$), and 0.52 standard deviation increase in reading scores ($p < 0.05$)[c]	Good et al. (2003)
Seventh graders attended a weekly, 25-minute class that explained the incremental theory of intelligence.	1 semester	0.53 point increase in math GPA ($p < 0.05$)	Blackwell et al. (2007)

Notes: (a) The intervention began at the beginning of the winter quarter, and grades were measured at the end of the spring quarter. (b) A range is given because the effect size differs across races and between different types of comparison groups. Not all of the effects are significant at the 5% level. (c) The authors do not estimate separate effects for males and females on the reading score.

letter that explains the theory to a low-performing middle school student. At the end of the next academic quarter, the average GPA in the treatment group was modestly higher than in the control group. There was no follow-up.

Good, Aronson, and Inzlicht (2003) study an intervention in which seventh-grade students were taught the incremental theory of intelligence. At the end of the year, students who learned about the incremental theory of intelligence performed somewhat better on the math and reading sections of the Texas Assessment of Academic Skills (TAAS) achievement test. The effect was strongest for girls.

Blackwell, Trzesniewski, and Dweck (2007) evaluate a program in which seventh graders are taught about the incremental theory of intelligence through a series of class sessions. The treatment group and control group participated in eight 25-minute classroom sessions that had similar course material about the physiology of the brain, study skills, and antistereotypic thinking. Only the treatment group was taught the incremental theory of intelligence. After one term, the treatment group improved its math GPAs relatively more than the control group.

While these studies are promising, their follow-ups are very short. The longest follow-up is a year after the beginning of the program. For example, it is possible that the interventions increased motivation in the short run, much like the studies in which children are incentivized using M&M candies. In addition, while the effects are statistically significant, they are relatively small. It is unknown whether the benefits outweigh the costs. None of the studies of the "mindset" interventions report a rate of return. The mechanism by which reported results are produced is not analyzed.[111]

9.12 The Effects of Education and Parental Investment on Character and Cognition

Studies that analyze the consequences of parental and schooling investment demonstrate their causal effects on promoting cognitive and character skills. Heckman, Stixrud, and Urzúa (2006) estimate the effect of schooling in creating cognitive and character skills, controlling for the problem of reverse causality that schooling may be caused by skills. Specifically, they estimate the effect of schooling on Self-Esteem and Locus of Control, character skills related to Neuroticism.[112] Figures 9.14 and 9.15 show the effect of education on measures of these skills: Schooling improves both character and cognitive skills. In results that are not displayed, they show that these traits, in turn, boost a variety of labor market and social outcomes at age 30.[113]

Cunha, Heckman, and Schennach (2010) estimate a causal model of parental investment using longitudinal data on the development of children with rich measures of parental investment and child skills. It estimates the model of Figure 9.9. They show that skills are self-productive and exhibit dynamic complementarity; levels of skills at one age affect the

---

111. Hunt (2012), a leading authority on intelligence, provides a trenchant assessment of this group of interventions and in particular the work of Dweck.

112. The Rosenberg Self-Esteem Scale assesses the degree of approval or disapproval of oneself (Rosenberg, 1965). The relationship between these measures and the Big Five traits of Neuroticism is discussed in Almlund et al. (2011). See Table 9.1.

113. Both Heckman et al. (2011) and Heckman, Stixrud, and Urzúa (2006) use an identification strategy employing matching on proxies for unobserved skills that corrects for measurement error and the endogeneity of schooling.

Figure 9.14 Causal Effect of Schooling on ASVAB Measures of Cognition

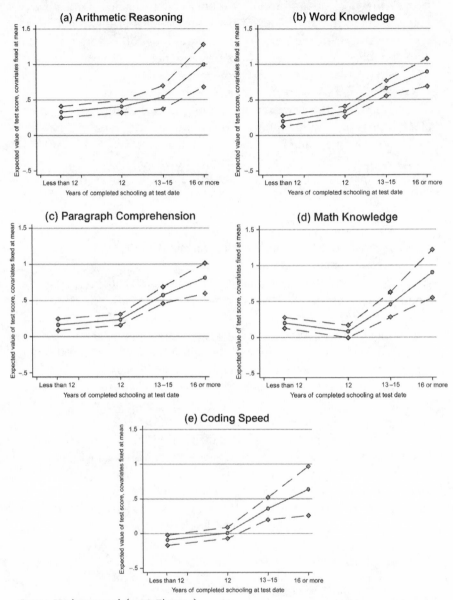

Source: Heckman et al. (2006, Figure 4).
Notes: Mean effect of schooling on components of the ASVAB. The first four components are averaged to create males with average ability. We standardize the test scores to have within-sample mean zero and variance one. The model is estimated using the NLSY79 sample. Solid lines depict average test scores, and dashed lines, 2.5%–97.5% confidence intervals. Regressors are fixed at means.

Figure 9.15 Causal Effect of Schooling on Two Measures of Character

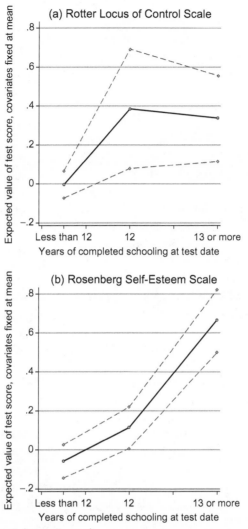

Source: Heckman et al. (2006, Figure 5).

Notes: Effect of schooling on socioemotional scales for males with average ability, with 95% confidence bands. The locus of control scale is based on the four-item abbreviated version of the Rotter Internal-External Locus of Control Scale. This scale is designed to measure the extent to which individuals believe they have control over their lives through self-motivation or self-determination (internal control), as opposed to the extent to which individuals believe that the environment controls their lives (external control). The self-esteem scale is based on the 10-item Rosenberg Self-Esteem Scale. This scale describes a degree of approval or disapproval toward oneself. In both cases, we standardize the test scores to have within-sample mean zero and variance one, after taking averages over the respective sets of scales. The model is estimated using the NLSY79 sample. Solid lines depict average test scores, and dashed lines, 2.5%–97.5% confidence intervals. Regressors are fixed at means.

productivity of future investments at later ages and hence help determine the evolution of future skills through direct and cross effects. For example, more motivated children learn more.

The authors find that it is more difficult to compensate for the effects of adverse environments on cognitive skills in adolescence than it is to build cognitive skills at earlier ages. Thus the early years are sensitive periods for cognitive skills. This finding is consistent with the high-rank stability of cognitive skills after age 11 or so; it also helps to explain the evidence on ineffective cognitive remediation strategies for disadvantaged adolescents documented in Cunha et al. (2006), Knudsen et al. (2006), and Cunha and Heckman (2007).

Character skills foster cognitive development. Greater malleability of character skills is found over longer stretches of the life cycle than for cognitive skills. This occurs in part because new aspects of character emerge with maturity and can be influenced.[114] Investment in character skills in the early years has a higher economic return than investment in the later years because it builds the base for subsequent investment. Nonetheless, the productivity of later-age investment in character skills is substantial. If the early years have been compromised, it is more effective in the adolescent years to focus on developing character skills rather than on cognitive skills.[115]

Heckman et al. (2011) estimate a sequential model of education to study the effects of education on a variety of outcomes, controlling for cognitive and character skills and the endogeneity of education. Correcting for selection into education, they find that early cognitive and character skills have substantial causal effects on schooling, labor market outcomes, adult health, and social outcomes and that education at most levels causally produces benefits in labor market, health, and social outcomes. They also study the effects of schooling on measures of adult character and find substantial impacts.

Jackson (2013) estimates a valued-added model of the effect of ninth-grade math and English teachers on student cognitive and noncognitive (character) skills as measured by absences, suspensions, grades, and grade progression. Similar models have been adopted by school districts to assess the teacher's impact on student achievement test scores and to determine

---

114. Borghans et al. (2008).

115. Cunha, Heckman, and Schennach (2010) report that 16% of the variation in educational attainment is explained by adolescent cognitive skills, 12% is due to adolescent socioemotional traits (character skills), and 15% is due to measured parental investments.

teacher bonuses.[116] Jackson estimates a bigger effect of teachers on character skills than on cognitive skills.[117] Estimated teacher effects on cognition and character are only weakly correlated with each other, suggesting that some teachers improve one dimension of skill without improving the other. These findings imply that using achievement tests alone to assess teacher effectiveness would miss important dimensions of teacher quality.

Coleman, Hoffer, and Kilgore (1982), Neal (1997), and Bryk, Lee, and Holland (1993) document the benefits of Catholic education in terms of scores on achievement tests.[118] It has long been speculated that Catholic schools mold character through creating a more disciplined environment and through teaching moral values. However, to our knowledge, there are no direct estimates of the effects of religious education on character. Typical of the entire literature on evaluation of schools, these studies focus on the effects of Catholic schools on test scores and schooling.

Arum (2005) documents the decline of disciplinary practices in American schools arising in part from legal and legislative developments originating in the 1960s that increased the rights of students and circumscribed teachers from using traditional measures of enforcing discipline. He cites evidence showing that greater discipline improves test scores and behavior and promotes greater high school graduation.[119]

Some modern schools have shown how it is possible to integrate character education into schools. The Knowledge Is Power Program (KIPP) is a group of public charter middle schools that are designed to improve educational outcomes for low-income families. Tough (2012) discusses how the first wave of KIPP students excelled at taking achievement tests but dropped out of college at disappointingly high rates. In response, KIPP schools started to emphasize character skills, "grit, self-control, social intelligence (including self-advocacy), zest, optimism, and gratitude, that enable students to stick with college even in the face of considerable obstacles" (The KIPP Foundation, 2011). Their motto is: *Work hard. Be nice.*

Evidence on the efficacy of KIPP is lacking. An evaluation of KIPP schools suggests that it has improved achievement test scores three years after

116. See, for example, the Teacher Advancement Program in Chicago Public Schools (Glazerman and Seifullah, 2012).

117. The estimates are from teacher "fixed-effect" models.

118. Neal (1997) corrects for the selection effect that Catholic schools can expel unruly and undisciplined students. Uncontrolled comparisons could show a spurious positive effect of Catholic schools that do not reflect their true effect on any given person.

119. DiPrete, Muller, and Shaeffer (1981).

students enter the program.[120] A recent report from KIPP found that 33% of the students graduate from a four-year college, which is less than their goal of 75% but is four times higher than the rate for students with comparable backgrounds (The KIPP Foundation, 2011). However, these evaluations are based on comparing KIPP students to students in other schools; some have argued that KIPP students have higher levels of starting achievement and that KIPP selects more motivated students and parents into their schools.[121] A recent randomized trial evaluation of KIPP (Mathematica, 2013) found that KIPP boosted achievement test scores but had mixed effects on character skills. For example, participants in KIPP were more likely to lie to their parents or quarrel with them (Tuttle et al., 2013).

Similar to KIPP, a recent intervention in Chicago attempts to foster character skills. The OneGoal program selects and trains high school teachers to help students apply to colleges, improve grades and test scores, and, importantly, *persist* through college. It serves low-income schools in Chicago, most of which have college enrollment rates of less than 50%. Like KIPP, it attempts to cultivate character skills (Tough, 2012). So far, OneGoal appears to be successful: 94% of OneGoal participants attend college, and 85% of the college enrollees complete the first year.[122] While there have been no long-term evaluations of KIPP or OneGoal that account for selection bias, these programs show that it is possible to openly emphasize character in schools without infringing on the rights of students or families or violating the boundaries between church and state. These efforts can be viewed as secular versions of moral and character education that do not introduce religion into schools.

9.13 Summary

This chapter reviews recent literature on the economics and psychology of character skills and how interventions can develop character. Character skills predict later-life outcomes with the same, or greater, strength as measures of cognition.

Character is a skill—not a trait. It can be enhanced, and there are proven and effective ways to do so. Character is shaped by families and social environments. At any age, character skills are stable across different tasks, but performance on any task depends on multiple skills as well as the effort

---

120. Tuttle et al. (2010).

121. Carnoy et al. (2005).

122. See http://www.onegoalgraduation.org/onegoal-results/. The OneGoal students are not old enough to estimate college graduation rates.

expended on it. Effort, in turn, depends on the incentives offered to perform the task. Since all measures of character and cognition are measures of performance on some task, it is necessary to standardize for incentives, effort, and other skills in measuring any particular character or cognitive skill. Despite these difficulties, reliable measures of character have been developed, although there is always room for improvement.

Though stable at any age, skills are not set in stone over the life cycle. Both cognitive and character skills can change. Parents, schools, and social environments shape them, although there are important genetic influences. Skill development is a dynamic process. The early years are important in laying the foundation for successful investment in the later years. While there is hard evidence on the importance of the early years in shaping all skills, some character skills are more malleable than cognitive skills at later ages.

This chapter reviews a variety of interventions targeted to different stages of the life cycle. Long-term evaluations of early childhood programs are more numerous. There is substantial evidence that high-quality early childhood programs have lasting and beneficial effects on character skills. The evidence on interventions in elementary schools shows lasting benefits of interventions that primarily operate through boosting character skills.

There are few long-term evaluations of adolescent interventions. The available evidence suggests a much greater benefit from programs that target character skills compared to the benefits of programs that mainly target cognition and academic learning. Workplace-based programs that teach character skills appear to be the most effective remediation interventions for adolescents. They motivate acquisition of work-relevant skills and provide discipline and guidance for disadvantaged youth that is often missing in their homes or high schools.

The available evidence suggests that the most successful remediation programs are not as effective as the most successful early childhood programs. Building an early base of skills that promote later-life learning and engagement in school and society is a better strategy. Prevention is more effective than remediation.

BIBLIOGRAPHY

Abbott, R. D., J. O'Donnell, J. D. Hawkins, K. G. Hill, R. Kosterman, and R. F. Catalano (1998). Changing teaching practices to promote achievement and bonding to school. *American Journal of Orthopsychiatry 68*(4), 542–552.

Achenbach, T. M., and L. A. Rescorla (2001). *Manual for ASEBA School-Age Forms and Profiles.* Burlington, VT: Research Center for Children, Youth and Families.

Ackerman, P. L., and E. D. Heggestad (1997). Intelligence, personality, and interests: Evidence for overlapping traits. *Psychological Bulletin 121*, 219–245.

Adda, J., C. Dustmann, C. Meghir, and J.-M. Robin (2013). Career progression, economic downturns, and skills. Unpublished manuscript, Institute for Fiscal Studies, London UK.

Almlund, M., A. Duckworth, J. J. Heckman, and T. Kautz (2011). Personality psychology and economics. In E. A. Hanushek, S. Machin, and L. Wößmann (Eds.), *Handbook of the Economics of Education*, Volume 4, pp. 1–181. Amsterdam: Elsevier.

American Psychiatric Association (1994). *Diagnostic and Statistical Manual of Mental Disorders: DSM-IV* (4th ed.). Washington, DC: American Psychiatric Association.

Aronson, J., C. B. Fried, and C. Good (2002). Reducing the effects of stereotype threat on African American college students by shaping theories of intelligence. *Journal of Experimental Social Psychology 38*(2), 113–125.

Arum, R. (2005). *Judging School Discipline: The Crisis of Moral Authority.* Cambridge, MA: Harvard University Press.

Ayllon, T., and K. Kelly (1972). Effects of reinforcement on standardized test performance. *Journal of Applied Behavior Analysis 5*(4), 477–484.

Barnett, W. S., K. Jung, D. J. Yarosz, J. Thomas, A. Hornbeck, R. Stechuk, and S. Burns (2008). Educational effects of the Tools of the Mind curriculum: A randomized trial. *Early Childhood Research Quarterly 23*(3), 299–313.

Barnett, W. S., D. J. Yarosz, J. Thomas, and A. Hornbeck (2006). Educational effectiveness of a Vygotskian approach to preschool education: A randomized trial. Technical report, National Institute for Early Education Research, Rutgers, The State University of New Jersey.

Barrick, M. R., and M. K. Mount (1991). The Big Five personality dimensions and job performance: A meta-analysis. *Personnel Psychology 44*(1), 1–26.

Barton, P. (2006). *High School Reform and Work: Facing Labor Market Realities.* Princeton, NJ: Educational Testing Service.

Becker, A., T. Deckers, T. Dohmen, A. Falk, and F. Kosse (2012, July). The relationship between economic preferences and psychological personality measures. *Annual Review of Economics 4*, 453–478.

Benda, B. B. (2005). The robustness of self-control in relation to form of delinquency. *Youth & Society 36*(4), 418–444.

Besharov, D. J., P. Germanis, C. A. Higney, and D. M. Call (2011). Houston parent child development center. Working Paper 17, University of Maryland, School of Public Policy, Welfare Reform Academy.

Binet, A., and T. Simon (1916). *The Development of Intelligence in Children (The Binet-Simon Scale).* Psychological Science. Baltimore, MD: Williams & Wilkins Co.

Blackwell, L. S., K. H. Trzesniewski, and C. S. Dweck (2007). Implicit theories of intelligence predict achievement across an adolescent transition: A longitudinal study and an intervention. *Child Development 78*(1), 246–263.

Bloom, D., A. Gardenhire-Crooks, and C. L. Mandsager (2009). Reengaging high school dropouts: Early results of the National Guard Youth ChalleNGe program evaluation. Report, MDRC. Last accessed online February 11, 2013. http://www.mdrc.org/sites/default/files/full_491.pdf.

Bodrova, E., and D. J. Leong (2001). *Tools of the Mind: A Case Study of Implementing the Vygotskian Approach in American Early Childhood and Primary Classrooms.* Geneva: International Bureau of Education, UNESCO.

Bodrova, E., and D. J. Leong (2007). *Tools of the Mind: The Vygotskian Approach to Early Childhood Education.* Upper Saddle River, NJ, Pearson Education.

Borghans, L., A. L. Duckworth, J. J. Heckman, and B. ter Weel (2008, Fall). The economics and psychology of personality traits. *Journal of Human Resources* 43(4), 972–1059.

Borghans, L., B. H. H. Golsteyn, J. J. Heckman, and J. E. Humphries (2011a). Identification problems in personality psychology. *Personality and Individual Differences 51*(3: Special Issue on Personality and Economics), 315–320.

Borghans, L., B. H. H. Golsteyn, J. J. Heckman, and J. E. Humphries (2011b). Reinterpreting estimated effects of cognition on social outcomes. Unpublished manuscript, Department of Economics, University of Chicago.

Borghans, L., B. H. Golsteyn, J. J. Heckman, and H. Meijers (2009, April). Gender differences in risk aversion and ambiguity aversion. *Journal of the European Economic Association 7*(2–3), 649–658.

Borghans, L., H. Meijers, and B. ter Weel (2008, January). The role of noncognitive skills in explaining cognitive test scores. *Economic Inquiry 46*(1), 2–12.

Bouchard, T. J., and J, C. Loehlin (2001, May). Genes, evolution and personality. *Behavior Genetics 31*(3), 243–273.

Bougheas, S., and Y. Georgellis (2004). Early career mobility and earnings profiles of German apprentices: Theory and empirical evidence. *Labour 18*(2), 233–263.

Bowen, W. G., M. M. Chingos, and M. S. McPherson (2009). Test scores and high school grades as predictors. In *Crossing the Finish Line: Completing College at America's Public Universities*, pp. 112–133. Princeton, NJ: Princeton University Press.

Bowlby, J. (1951). Maternal care and mental health. Bulletin, World Health Organization, Geneva, Switzerland.

Boyle, S. H., R. B. Williams, D. B. Mark, B. H. Brummett, I. C. Siegler, and J. C. Barefoot (2005). Hostility, age, and mortality in a sample of cardiac patients. *American Journal of Cardiology 96*(1), 64–66.

Breitmayer, B. J., and C. T. Ramey (1986, October). Biological nonoptimality and quality of postnatal environment as codeterminants of intellectual development. *Child Development 57*(5), 1151–1165.

Breuning, S. E., and W. F. Zella (1978). Effects of individualized incentives on norm-referenced IQ test performance of high school students in special education classes. *Journal of School Psychology 16*(3), 220–226.

Bridgeman, B., J. B. Blumenthal, and S. R. Andres (1981). Parent Child Development Center: Final evaluation report. Report, ETS Research.

Bryk, A. S., V. E. Lee, and P. B. Holland (1993). *Catholic Schools and the Common Good.* Cambridge, MA: Harvard University Press.

Buechtemann, C. F., J. Schupp, and D. J. Soloff (1993). Roads to work: School-to-work transition patterns in Germany and the United States. *Industrial Relations Journal 24*(2), 97–111.

Campbell, F., G. Conti, J. Heckman, S. Moon, R. Pinto, and E. Pungello (2012). The long-term health effects of early childhood interventions. Under review, *Economic Journal*.

Campbell, F., G. Conti, J. J. Heckman, R. Pinto, and E. Pungello (2013). Early childhood investments substantially boost adult health. Unpublished manuscript, University of Chicago, Department of Economics. Under review, *Science*.

Campbell, F. A., E. P. Pungello, S. Miller-Johnson, M. Burchinal, and C. T. Ramey (2001, March). The development of cognitive and academic abilities: Growth curves from an early childhood educational experiment. *Developmental Psychology 37*(2), 231–242.

Campbell, F. A., C. T. Ramey, E. Pungello, J. Sparling, and S. Miller-Johnson (2002). Early childhood education: Young adult outcomes from the Abecedarian Project. *Applied Developmental Science 6*(1), 42–57.

Canli, T. (2006). *Biology of Personality and Individual Differences.* New York: Guilford Press.

Card, D., and D. R. Hyslop (2009). The dynamic effects of an earnings subsidy for long-term welfare recipients: Evidence from the self sufficiency project applicant experiment. *Journal of Econometrics 153*(1), 1–20.

Carneiro, P., and R. Ginja (2011, January). Preventing behavior problems in childhood and adolescence: Evidence from Head Start. Unpublished manuscript, University College London.

Carneiro, P., and R. Ginja (2012, January). Long term impacts of compensatory preschool on health and behavior: Evidence from Head Start. IZA Discussion Paper 6315, Institute for the Study of Labor (IZA).

Carneiro, P., and J. J. Heckman (2003). Human capital policy. In J. J. Heckman, A. B. Krueger, and B. M. Friedman (Eds.), *Inequality in America: What Role for Human Capital Policies?*, pp. 77–239. Cambridge, MA: MIT Press.

Carnoy, M., R. Jacobsen, L. Mishel, and R. Rothstein (2005). *The Charter School Dust-up.* Washington, DC: Economic Policy Institute.

Carroll, J. B. (1993). *Human Cognitive Abilities: A Survey of Factor-Analytic Studies.* New York: Cambridge University Press.

Chetty, R., J. N. Friedman, N. Hilger, E. Saez, S. W. Diane, and D. Yagan (2011). How does your kindergarten classroom affect your earnings? Evidence from Project STAR. *Quarterly Journal of Economics 126*(4), 1593–1660.

Clark, D., and R. Fahr (2002, February). The promise of workplace training for non-college bound youth: Theory and evidence from German apprenticeship. CEP Discussion Paper 518, Centre for Economic Performance, London School of Economics and Political Science, London, UK.

Clingman, J., and R. L. Fowler (1976). The effects of primary reward on the I.Q. performance of grade-school children as a function of initial I.Q. level. *Journal of Applied Behavior Analysis 9*(1), 19–23.

Cloninger, C. R., D. M. Svrakic, C. Bayon, and T. R. Przybeck (1999). Measurement of psychopathology as variants of personality. In C. R. Cloninger (Ed.), *Personality and Psychopathology*, pp. 33–66. Washington, DC: American Psychiatric Press.

Coleman, J. S. (1961). *The Adolescent Society: The Social Life of the Teenager and Its Impact on Education.* New York: The Free Press of Glencoe.

Coleman, J. S., T. Hoffer, and S. Kilgore (1982). *High School Achievement: Public, Catholic, and Private Schools Compared.* New York: Basic Books.

Cooke, L. (2003). A comparison of initial and early life course earnings of the German secondary education and training system. *Economics of Education Review 22*(1), 79–88.

Costa, P. T., and R. R. McCrae (1992a). Four ways five factors are basic. *Personality and Individual Difference 13*(6), 653–665.

Costa, P. T., and R. R. McCrae (1992b). *Revised NEO Personality Inventory (NEO PI-R) and the NEO Five-Factor Inventory (NEO-FFI) Professional Manual.* Odessa, FL: Psychological Assessment Resources.

Cunha, F., and J. J. Heckman (2007, May). The technology of skill formation. *American Economic Review 97*(2), 31–47.

Cunha, F., and J. J. Heckman (2008, Fall). Formulating, identifying and estimating the technology of cognitive and noncognitive skill formation. *Journal of Human Resources 43*(4), 738–782.

Cunha, F., and J. J. Heckman (2009, April). The economics and psychology of inequality and human development. *Journal of the European Economic Association 7*(2–3), 320–364. Presented as the Marshall Lecture, European Economics Association, Milan, Italy, August 29, 2008.

Cunha, F., J. J. Heckman, L. J. Lochner, and D. V. Masterov (2006). Interpreting the evidence on life cycle skill formation. In E. A. Hanushek and F. Welch (Eds.), *Handbook of the Economics of Education*, Chapter 12, pp. 697–812. Amsterdam: North-Holland.

Cunha, F., J. J. Heckman, and S. M. Schennach (2010, May). Estimating the technology of cognitive and noncognitive skill formation. *Econometrica 78*(3), 883–931.

Currie, J., and D. Thomas (1995, June). Does Head Start make a difference? *American Economic Review 85*(3), 341–364.

Deci, E. L. (1971). Effects of externally mediated rewards on intrinsic motivation. *Journal of Personality and Social Psychology 18*, 105–115.

Deci, E. L., and R. M. Ryan (1985). *Intrinsic Motivation and Self-Determination in Human Behavior.* New York: Plenum Press.

DeLong, J., and K. Magin (2009, Winter). The U.S. equity return premium: Past, present and future. *Journal of Economic Perspectives 23*(1), 193–208.

Deming, D. (2009, July). Early childhood intervention and life-cycle skill development: Evidence from Head Start. *American Economic Journal: Applied Economics 1*(3), 111–134.

Devlin, B., M. Daniels, and K. Roeder (1997). The heritability of IQ. *Nature 388* (6641), 468–471.

DeYoung, C. G., J. B. Hirsh, M. S. Shane, X. Papademetris, N. Rajeevan, and J. R. Gray (2010). Testing predictions from personality neuroscience: Brain structure and the Big Five. *Psychological Science 21*(6), 820–828.

Diamond, A., S. Barnett, J. Thomas, and S. Munro (2007). Preschool program improves cognitive control. *Science 318*(5855), 1387–1388.

DiPrete, T. A., C. Muller, and N. Shaeffer (1981). *Discipline and order in American high schools*. Washington, DC: National Center for Education Statistics. Contractor Report from NORC.

Duckworth, A. (2012, November). Reference bias. Presented at the University of Chicago.

Duckworth, A. L., C. Peterson, M. D. Matthews, and D. R. Kelly (2007, June). Grit: Perseverance and passion for long-term goals. *Journal of Personality and Social Psychology 92*(6), 1087–1101.

Duckworth, A. L., P. D. Quinn, D. R. Lynam, R. Loeber, and M. Stouthamer-Loeber (2011). Role of test motivation in intelligence testing. *Proceedings of the National Academy of Sciences 108*(19), 7716–7720.

Durlak, J. A., R. P. Weissberg, A. B. Dymnicki, R. D. Taylor, and K. B. Schellinger (2011). The impact of enhancing students social and emotional learning: A meta-analysis of school-based universal interventions. *Child Development 82*(1), 405–432.

Dweck, C. S. (2007). *Mindset: The New Psychology of Success*. New York: Ballantine Books.

Eckenrode, J., M. Campa, D. W. Luckey, C. R. Henderson, R. Cole, H. Kitzman, E. Anson, K. Sidora-Arcoleo, and D. L. Olds (2010, January). Long-term effects of prenatal and infancy nurse home visitation on the life course of youths: 19-year follow-up of a randomized trial. *Journal of the American Medical Association 164*(1), 9–15.

Edlund, C. V. (1972). The effect on the behavior of children, as reflected in the IQ scores, when reinforced after each correct response. *Journal of Applied Behavior Analysis 5*(3), 317–319.

Engle, P. L., M. M. Black, J. R. Behrman, M. Cabral de Mello, P. J. Gertler, L. Kapiriri, R. Martorell, M. Eming Young, and The International Child Development Steering Group (2007, January). Strategies to avoid the loss of developmental potential in more than 200 million children in the developing world. *The Lancet 369*(9557), 229–242.

Engle, P. L., L. C. H. Fernald, H. Alderman, J. Behrman, C. O'Gara, A. Yousafzai, M. Cabral de Mello, M. Hidrobo, N. Ulkuer, I. Ertem, and S. Iltus (2011, October). Strategies for reducing inequalities and improving developmental outcomes for young children in low-income and middle-income countries. *The Lancet 378*(9799), 1339–1353.

Epstein, S. (1979). The stability of behavior: I. On predicting most of the people much of the time. *Journal of Personality and Social Psychology 37*(7), 1097–1126.

Farran, D. C., M. W. Lipsey, and S. Wilson (2011, August). Experimental evaluation of the Tools of the Mind pre-k curriculum. Technical report, Peabody Research Institute Report.

Fersterer, J., J.-S. Pischke, and R. Winter-Ebmer (2008). Returns to apprenticeship training in Austria: Evidence from failed firms. *Scandinavian Journal of Economics 110*(4), 733–753.

Fitzenberger, B., and A. Kunze (2005). Vocational training and gender: Wages and occupational mobility among young workers. *Oxford Review of Economic Policy 21*(3), 392–415.

Flynn, J. R. (2007). *What Is Intelligence?: Beyond the Flynn Effect*. New York: Cambridge University Press.

Franz, W., and D. W. Soskice (1995). The German apprenticeship system. In *Institutional Frameworks and Labor Market Performance*, Chapter 8, pp. 208–234. New York: Routle.

Friedlander, D., and G. Hamilton (1996, Fall). The impact of a continuous participation obligation in a welfare employment program. *Journal of Human Resources 31*(4), 734–756.

Friedman, D., and A. H. Streicher (1985). Reliability of scores for fiscal year 1981 Army applicants: Armed Services Vocational Aptitude Battery forms 8, 9, and 10. Technical report, Defense Technical Information Center.

Friedman, H. S., and L. R. Martin (2011). *The Longevity Project: Surprising Discoveries for Health and Long Life from the Landmark Eight-Decade Study.* New York: Hudson Street Press.

Garces, E., D. Thomas, and J. Currie (2002, September). Longer-term effects of Head Start. *American Economic Review 92*(4), 999–1012.

Geel, R., and U. Backes-Gellner (2009). Occupational mobility within and between skill clusters: An empirical analysis based on the skill-weights approach. Economics of Education Working Paper Series 0047, University of Zurich, Institute for Strategy and Business Economics (ISU).

Gertler, P., J. Heckman, R. Pinto, A. Zanolini, C. Vermeersch, S. Walker, S. M. Chang, and S. Grantham-McGregor (2013). Labor market returns to early childhood stimulation: A 20-year followup to an experimental intervention in Jamaica. Working Paper 19185, NBER.

Gertler, P., and S. Martinez (2012). Vocational and life skills in youth training: A randomized experiment in the Dominican Republic. Presented at the IZA/ World Bank/OECD Conference on Activation and Employment Support Policies, Bahcesehir University, Istanbul, Turkey, May 1, 2012.

Glazerman, S., and A. Seifullah (2012). An evaluation of the Chicago teacher advancement program (Chicago TAP) after four years. Final Report 06736-520, Mathematica Policy Research.

Goldammer, C. (2010). Skills, investment, and race: Evidence from the ECLS-K. Unpublished manuscript, University of Chicago, Department of Economics.

Goldin, C., and L. F. Katz (2008). *The Race between Education and Technology.* Cambridge, MA: Belknap Press of Harvard University Press.

Goldschmidt, P., and D. Huang (2007). The long-term effects of after-school programming on educational adjustment and juvenile crime: A study of the LA's BEST after-school program. Technical report, National Center for Research on Evaluation, Standards, and Student Testing (CRESST), Los Angeles, CA.

Good, C., J. Aronson, and M. Inzlicht (2003). Improving adolescents' standardized test performance: An intervention to reduce the effects of stereotype threat. *Applied Developmental Psychology 24*(6), 645–662.

Gottfredson, M. R., and T. Hirschi (1990). *A General Theory of Crime.* Palo Alto, CA: Stanford University Press.

Gottschalk, P. (2005). Can work alter welfare recipients' beliefs? *Journal of Policy Analysis and Management 24*(3), 485–498.

Gough, H. G., and A. B. Heilbrun (1983). *The Adjective Check List Manual.* Palo Alto, CA: Consulting Psychologists Press.

Grantham-McGregor, S., Y. B. Cheung, S. Cueto, P. Glewwe, L. Richter, and B. Strupp (2007). Developmental potential in the first 5 years for children in developing countries. *The Lancet 369*(9555), 60–70.

Grantham-McGregor, S. M., C. A. Powell, S. P. Walker, and J. H. Himes (1991). Nutritional supplementation, psychosocial stimulation, and mental development of stunted children: The Jamaican study. *The Lancet 338*(8758), 1–5.

Griffin, M., J. J. Heckman, and S. Moon (2013). Preschool curricula. Unpublished manuscript, University of Chicago.

Griffiths, R. (1954). *The Abilities of Babies.* London, UK: University of London Press.

Grobe, T., E. Rosenblum, and T. Weissman (2010). *Dollars and Sense: How "Career First" Programs Like Year Up Benefit Youth and Employers.* Boston: Jobs for the Future.

Groot, W. (2000). Adaptation and scale of reference bias in self-assessments of quality of life. *Journal of Health Economics 19*(3), 403–420.

Haggerty, K., R. Kosterman, R. F. Catalano, and J. D. Hawkins (1999). Preparing for the drug free years. Juvenile Justice Bulletin, U.S. Department of Justice, Office of Justice Programs, Office of Juvenile Justice and Delinquency Prevention, Washington, DC.

Halpern, R. (2009). *The Means to Grow Up: Reinventing Apprenticeship as a Developmental Support in Adolescence* (1st ed.). Critical Youth Studies. New York: Routledge.

Hansen, K. T., J. J. Heckman, and K. J. Mullen (2004, July–August). The effect of schooling and ability on achievement test scores. *Journal of Econometrics 121*(1–2), 39–98.

Hanushek, E. (2003, February). The failure of input-based schooling policies. *Economic Journal 113*(485), F64–F98.

Harhoff, D., and T. J. Kane (1997). Is the German apprenticeship system a panacea for the U.S. labor market? *Journal of Population Economics 10*(2), 171–196.

Harter, S. (1985). *Manual for the Self-perception Profile for Children.* Denver, CO: University of Denver.

Hawkins, J. D., R. F. Catalano, R. Kosterman, R. D. Abbott, and K. G. Hill (1999). Preventing adolescent health-risk behaviors by strengthening protection during childhood. *Archives of Pediatrics and Adolescent Medicine 153*(3), 226–234.

Hawkins, J. D., R. Kosterman, R. F. Catalano, K. G. Hill, and R. D. Abbott (2005). Promoting positive adult functioning through social development intervention in childhood. *Archives of Pediatrics and Adolescent Medicine 159*(1), 25–31.

Hawkins, J. D., R. Kosterman, R. F. Catalano, K. G. Hill, and R. D. Abbott (2008). Effect of social development intervention in childhood 15 years later. *Archives of Pediatrics and Adolescent Medicine 162*(12), 1133–1141.

Hawkins, J., E. Von Cleve, and R. Catalano, Jr. (1991). Reducing early childhood aggression: Results of a primary prevention program. *Journal of the American Academy of Child and Adolescent Psychiatry 30*(2), 208–217.

Heckman, J. J. (2008, July). Schools, skills and synapses. *Economic Inquiry 46*(3), 289–324.

Heckman, J. J., J. E. Humphries, S. Urzúa, and G. Veramendi (2011). The effects of educational choices on labor market, health, and social outcomes. Unpublished manuscript, University of Chicago, Department of Economics.

Heckman, J. J., and T. Kautz (2012, August). Hard evidence on soft skills. *Labour Economics 19*(4), 451–464. Adam Smith Lecture.

Heckman, J. J., and D. V. Masterov (2007). The productivity argument for investing in young children. *Review of Agricultural Economics 29*(3), 446–493.

Heckman, J. J., S. H. Moon, and R. Pinto (2012). The effects of early intervention on abilities and social outcomes: Evidences from the Carolina Abecedarian study. Unpublished manuscript, University of Chicago.

Heckman, J. J., S. H. Moon, R. Pinto, P. A. Savelyev, and A. Q. Yavitz (2010a, February). The rate of return to the HighScope Perry Preschool Program. *Journal of Public Economics 94*(1–2), 114–128.

Heckman, J. J., S. H. Moon, R. Pinto, P. A. Savelyev, and A. Q. Yavitz (2010b, August). Analyzing social experiments as implemented: A reexamination of the evidence from the HighScope Perry Preschool Program. *Quantitative Economics 1* (1), 1–46.

Heckman, J. J., R. Pinto, and P. A. Savelyev (2013). Understanding the mechanisms through which an influential early childhood program boosted adult outcomes. Forthcoming, *American Economic Review.*

Heckman, J. J., J. Stixrud, and S. Urzúa (2006, July). The effects of cognitive and noncognitive abilities on labor market outcomes and social behavior. *Journal of Labor Economics 24*(3), 411–482.

Heine, S. J., E. E. Buchtel, and A. Norenzayan (2008). What do cross-national comparisons of personality traits tell us? The case of Conscientiousness. *Psychological Science 19*(4), 309–313.

Heine, S. J., S. Kitayama, D. R. Lehman, T. Takata, E. Ide, C. Leung, and H. Matsumoto (2001). Divergent consequences of success and failure in Japan and North America: An investigation of self-improving motivations and malleable selves. *Journal of Personality and Social Psychology 81*(4), 599–615.

Heine, S. J., D. R. Lehman, K. Peng, and J. Greenholtz (2002, June). What's wrong with cross-cultural comparisons of subjective Likert scales? The reference-group effect. *Journal of Personality and Social Psychology 82*(6), 903–918.

Herrnstein, R. J., and C. A. Murray (1994). *The Bell Curve: Intelligence and Class Structure in American Life.* New York: Free Press.

Hieronymus, A. N., E. F. Lindquist, and H. D. Hoover (1980). *Iowa Tests of Basic Skills: Primary Battery.* Iowa City, IA: Houghton.

Hillage, J., J. Regan, J. Dickson, and K. McLoughlin (2002). Employers skill survey: 2002. Research Report RR372, Department for Education and Skills.

Hirschi, T., and M. Gottfredson (1993). Commentary: Testing the general theory of crime. *Journal of Research in Crime and Delinquency 30*(1), 47–54.

Hogan, J., and B. Holland (2003). Using theory to evaluate personality and job-performance relations: A socioanalytic perspective. *Journal of Applied Psychology 88*(1), 100–112.

Hollenbeck, K. (2008). State use of workforce system net impact estimates and rates of return. Technical report, Upjohn Institute. Presented at the Association for Public Policy Analysis and Management (APPAM) Conference, Los Angeles, CA.

Holmlund, H., and O. Silva (2009). Targeting non-cognitive skills to improve cognitive outcomes: Evidence from a remedial education intervention. Discussion Paper 4476, IZA.

Holt, M. M., and T. R. Hobbs (1979). The effects of token reinforcement, feedback and response cost on standardized test performance. *Behaviour Research and Therapy 17*(1), 81–83.

Holzer, H. (1997). Is there a gap between employer skill needs and the skills of the work force? In A. Lesgold, M. Feuer, and A. Black (Eds.), *Transitions in Work and Learning: Implications for Assessment*, Chapter 2, pp. 6–33. Washington, DC: National Academy Press.

Howard, K. S., and J. Brooks-Gunn (2009). The role of home-visiting programs in preventing child abuse and neglect. *The Future of Children 19*(2), 119–146.

Huang, D., B. Gribbons, K. S. Kim, C. Lee, and E. L. Baker (2000). A decade of results: The impact of the LA's BEST after school enrichment program on subsequent student achievement and performance. Technical report, UCLA Center for the Study of Evaluation, Graduate School of Education and Information Studies, Los Angeles, CA.

Huang, D., K. S. Kim, A. Marshall, and P. Pérez (2005). Keeping kids in school: An LA's BEST example—a study examining the long-term impact of LA's BEST on students' dropout rates. Technical report, National Center for Research on Evaluation, Standards, and Student Testing (CRESST), Los Angeles, CA.

Hunt, E. (2012). Improving intelligence. Presented at the American Psychological Association Annual Meeting, Sunday, May 27, 2012, Chicago, IL.

Jablonka, E., and G. Raz (2009). Transgenerational epigenetic inheritance: Prevalence, mechanisms, and implications for the study of heredity and evolution. *The Quarterly Review of Biology 84*(2), pp. 131–176.

Jackson, C. K. (2013). Non-cognitive ability, test scores, and teacher quality: Evidence from 9th grade teachers in North Carolina. Working Paper 18624, NBER.

John, O. P., A. Caspi, R. W. Robins, and T. E. Moffitt (1994). The "little five": Exploring the nomological network of the five-factor model of personality in adolescent boys. *Child Development 65*(1), 160–178.

John, O. P., and S. Srivastava (1999). The big five trait taxonomy: History, measurement and theoretical perspectives. In L. A. Pervin and O. P. John (Eds.), *Handbook of Personality: Theory and Research*, Chapter 4, pp. 102–138. New York: Guilford Press.

Johnson, A. W. (1999). Assessing the impact of the sponsor-a-scholar youth mentoring program on student performance. Technical Report 355, Mathematica Policy Research.

Johnson, D., and T. Walker (1991). A follow-up evaluation of the Houston parent child development center: School performance. *Journal of Early Intervention 15*(3), 226–236.

Jolly, R. (2007). Early childhood development: The global challenge. *The Lancet 369*(9555), 8–9.

Kagitcibasi, C., D. Sunar, and S. Bekman (2001). Long-term effects of early intervention: Turkish low-income mothers and children. *Journal of Applied Developmental Psychology 22*(4), 333–361.

Kagitcibasi, C., D. Sunar, S. Bekman, N. Baydar, and Z. Cemalcilar (2009). Continuing effects of early enrichment in adult life: The Turkish Early Enrichment Project 22 years later. *Journal of Applied Developmental Psychology 30*(6), 764–779.

Kahne, J., and K. Bailey (1999). The role of social capital in youth development: The case of "I Have a Dream" programs. *Educational Evaluation and Policy Analysis* 21(3), 321–343.

Kemple, J., and J. C. Snipes (2000). Career academies: Impacts on student engagement and performance in high school. Report 03/2000, MDRC.

Kemple, J., and C. Willner (2008). Career academies: Long-term impacts on labor market outcomes, educational attainment, and transitions to adulthood. Report 06/2008, MDRC.

Kern, M. L., and H. S. Friedman (2008). Do conscientious individuals live longer? *Health Psychology* 27(5), 505–512.

Kettner, N. (1976). Armed Services Vocational Aptitude Battery (ASVAB form 5): Comparison with GATB and DAT tests: Final report for period May 1975–October 1976. Technical report, DTIC Document: Department of Defense, Department of the Air Force, Air Force Systems Command, Air Force Human Resources Laboratory.

The KIPP Foundation (2011). The promise of college completion: KIPP's early successes and challenges. Report, The KIPP Foundation, San Francisco, CA.

Kitzman, H., D. L. Olds, R. Cole, C. Hanks, E. Anson, K. Arcoleo, D. W. Luckey, M. Knudtson, C. R. Henderson, and J. Holmberg (2010, May). Enduring effects of prenatal and infancy home visiting by nurses on children: Follow-up of a randomized trial among children at age 12 years. *Journal of the American Medical Association* 164(5), 412–418.

Knudsen, E. I., J. J. Heckman, J. Cameron, and J. P. Shonkoff (2006, July). Economic, neurobiological, and behavioral perspectives on building America's future workforce. *Proceedings of the National Academy of Sciences* 103(27), 10155–10162.

Krueger, A. B. (2003, February). Economic considerations and class size. *Economic Journal* 113(485), F34–F63.

Kubzansky, L. D., D. Sparrow, P. Vokonas, and I. Kawachi (2001). Is the glass half empty or half full? A prospective study of optimism and coronary heart disease in the normative aging study. *Psychosomatic Medicine* 63(6), 910–916.

Lake, A. (2011). Early childhood development—global action is overdue. *The Lancet* 378 (9799), 1277–1278.

Lally, J. R., P. L. Mangione, and A. S. Honig (1987). *The Syracuse University Family Development Research Program: Long-Range Impact of an Early Intervention with Low-Income Children & their Families.* San Francisco, CA: Center for Child and Family Studies, Far West Laboratory for Educational Research and Development.

Lang, F. R., D. John, O. Lüdtke, J. Schupp, and G. G. Wagner (2011). Short assessment of the Big Five: Robust across survey methods except telephone interviewing. *Behavior Research Methods* 43(2), 548–567.

Lapsley, D., and D. Yeager (2012). Moral-character education. In I. Weiner, W. Reynolds, and G. Miller (Eds.), *Handbook of Psychology*, Volume 7 of *Educational Psychology*, Chapter 7, pp. 117–146. New York: John Wiley and Sons.

Larson, G. E., D. P. Saccuzzo, and J. Brown (1994). Motivation: Cause or confound in information processing/intelligence correlations? *Acta Psychologica* 85(1), 25–37.

Lemann, N. (1999). *The Big Test: The Secret History of the American Meritocracy.* New York: Farrar, Straus and Giroux.

Lerman, R. I. (2013). Are employability skills learned in U.S. youth education and training programs? Under review, *IZA Journal of Labor Policy.*

Likert, R. (1932). A technique for the measurement of attitudes. *Archives of Psychology 22* (140), 55.

Lillard, A., and N. Else-Quest (2006). The early years: Evaluating Montessori. *Science 313* (5795), 1893–1894.

Lleras, C. (2008). Do skills and behaviors in high school matter? The contribution of noncognitive factors in explaining differences in educational attainment and earnings. *Social Science Research 37* (3), 888–902.

Ludwig, J., and D. L. Miller (2007). Does Head Start improve children's life chances? Evidence from a regression discontinuity approach. *Quarterly Journal of Economics 122* (1), 159–208.

Lutz, M. N., J. Fantuzzo, and P. McDermott (2000). *Adjustment Scales for Preschool Intervention.* Philadelphia: University of Pennsylvania.

Mallar, C., S. Kerachsky, C. Thornton, and D. Long (1982). Evaluation of the impact of the Job Corps program: Third follow-up report. Technical Report PR82-05, Mathematica Policy Research, Inc., Princeton, NJ.

Martin, L. R., H. S. Friedman, and J. E. Schwartz (2007). Personality and mortality risk across the life span: The importance of conscientiousness as a biopsychosocial attribute. *Health Psychology 26* (4), 428–436.

Martins, P. S. (2010). Can targeted, non-cognitive skills programs improve achievement? Discussion Paper 5266, IZA.

McAdams, D. P. (2006). *The Person: A New Introduction to Personality Psychology* (4th ed.). Hoboken, NJ: John Wiley and Sons.

McCord, J. (1978). A thirty-year follow-up of treatment effects. *American Psychologist 33* (3), 284–289.

McCord, J., and W. McCord (1959). A follow-up report on the Cambridge-Somerville youth study. *Annals of the American Academy of Political and Social Science 322* (1), 89–96.

McCormick, M. C., J. Brooks-Gunn, S. L. Buka, J. Goldman, J. Yu, M. Salganik, D. T. Scott, F. C. Bennett, L. L. Kay, J. C. Bernbaum, C. R. Bauer, C. Martin, E. R. Woods, A. Martin, and P. H. Casey (2006, March). Early intervention in low birth weight premature infants: Results at 18 years of age for the Infant Health and Development Program. *Pediatrics 117*(3), 771–780.

McDowell, J., D. Oliver, M. Persson, R. Fairbrother, S. Wetzlar, J. Buchanan, and T. Shipstone (2011). A shared responsibility: Apprenticeships for the 21st century. http://www.australianapprenticeships.gov.au/faq/documents/apprenticeshipsforthe21stcenturyexpertpanel.pdf, last accessed February 11, 2013.

McLanahan, S. (2004, November). Diverging destinies: How children are faring under the second demographic transition. *Demography 41* (4), 607–627.

Michalopoulos, C., D. Tattrie, C. Miller, P. K. Robins, P. Morris, D. Gyarmati, C. Redcross, K. Foley, and R. Ford (2002). Final report on the self-sufficiency project for long-term welfare recipients. Report, Social Research and Demonstration Corporation.

Millenky, M., D. Bloom, and C. Dillon (2010). Making the transition: Interim results of the National Guard Youth ChalleNGe evaluation. Report 05/2010, MDRC.

Millenky, M., D. Bloom, S. Muller-Ravett, and J. Broadus (2011). Staying on course: Three-year results of the National Guard Youth ChalleNGe evaluation. Report 06/2011, MDRC.

Mischel, W. (1968). *Personality and Assessment.* New York: John Wiley and Sons.

Mischel, W., O. Ayduk, M. G. Berman, B. J. Casey, I. H. Gotlib, J. Jonides, E. Kross, T. Teslovich, N. L. Wilson, V. Zayas, and Y. Shoda (2011). 'Willpower' over the life span: Decomposing self-regulation. *Social Cognitive and Affective Neuroscience* 6(2), 252–256.

Moon, S. H. (2012, July). Time to invest in disadvanted young children. *Samsung Economic Research Institute Quarterly* 5(3), 50–59.

Mroczek, D. K., and A. Spiro (2007). Personality change influences mortality in older men. *Psychological Science* 18(5), 371–376.

Myers, R. (1992). *The Twelve Who Survive: Strengthening Programmes of Early Childhood Development in the Third World.* New York: Routledge/UNESCO.

National Apprenticeship Service (2012). History of apprenticeships. http://www .apprenticeships.org.uk/About-Us/History-of-Apprenticeships.aspx, last accessed February 11, 2013.

National Centre for Vocational Education Research (2012). Historical time series of apprenticeships and traineeships in Australia from 1963. http://www.ncver.edu .au/publications/2329.html.

Naumann, L. P., and O. P. John (2011). Toward a domain-specific approach to cultural differences: The influence of cultural values and reference-group standards on self-reported personality. Unpublished manuscript, Sonoma State University, Department of Psychology.

Neal, D. A. (1997, January). The effects of Catholic secondary schooling on educational achievement. *Journal of Labor Economics* 15 (1, Part 1), 98–123.

Nelsen, B. (1997). Should social skills be in the vocational curriculum? Evidence from the automotive career field. In A. M. Lesgold, M. J. Feuer, and A. M. Black (Eds.), *Transitions in Work and Learning: Implications for Assessment, Papers and Proceedings.* Washington, DC: National Academy Press.

Niles, M. D., A. J. Reynolds, and M. Nagasawa (2006). Does early childhood intervention affect the social and emotional development of participants? *Early Childhood Research and Practice* 8(1), 34–53.

Nisbett, R. E. (2009, February). *Intelligence and How to Get It: Why Schools and Cultures Count.* New York: W. W. Norton.

Nisbett, R. E., J. Aronson, C. Blair, W. Dickens, J. Flynn, D. F. Halpern, and E. Turkheimer (2012). Intelligence: New findings and theoretical developments. *American Psychologist* 67(2), 130–159.

Nyhus, E. K., and E. Pons (2005). The effects of personality on earnings. *Journal of Economic Psychology* 26(3), 363–384.

Olds, D. L. (2006). The Nurse-Family Partnership: An evidence-based preventive intervention. *Infant Mental Health Journal* 27(1), 5–25.

Olds, D. L., H. Kitzman, R. Cole, C. Hanks, K. Arcoleo, E. Anson, D. W. Luckey, M. Knudtson, C. R. Henderson, J. Bondy, and A. J. Stevenson (2010, May). Enduring effects of prenatal and infancy home visiting by nurses on maternal life course and government spending: Follow-up of a randomized trial among children at age 12 years. *Journal of the American Medical Association 164*(5), 419–424.

Olds, D. L., H. Kitzman, R. Cole, J. Robinson, K. Sidora, D. W. Luckey, C. R. Henderson, C. Hanks, J. Bondy, and J. Holmberg (2004, December). Effects of nurse home-visiting on maternal life course and child development: Age 6 follow-up results of a randomized trial. *Pediatrics 114*(6), 1550–1559.

Olds, D. L., H. Kitzman, C. Hanks, R. Cole, E. Anson, K. Sidora-Arcoleo, D. W. Luckey, C. R. Henderson, J. Holmberg, R. A. Tutt, A. J. Stevenson, and J. Bondy (2007, December). Effects of nurse home-visiting on maternal and child functioning: Age 9 follow-up of a randomized trial. *Pediatrics 120*(4), 832–845.

Olds, D. L., J. Robinson, L. Pettitt, D. W. Luckey, J. Holmberg, R. K. Ng, K. Isacks, K. Sheff, and C. R. Henderson (2004, December). Effects of home visits by paraprofessionals and by nurses: Age 4 follow-up results of a randomized trial. *Pediatrics 114*(6), 1560–1568.

Organization of Economic Cooperation and Development (2001). OECD employment and labour market statistics. Data available from http://www.oecd-ilibrary.org/employment/data/oecd-employment-and-labour-market-statistics_lfs-data-en.

Orr, L., H. Bloom, S. Bell, W. Lin, G. Cave, and F. Doolittle (1994). *The National JTPA Study. Impacts, Benefits, and Costs of Title II-A.* Bethesda, MD: Abt Associates.

Peng, K., R. E. Nisbett, and N. Y. Wong (1997). Validity problems comparing values across cultures and possible solutions. *Psychological Methods 2*(4), 329–344.

Petersen, A. C., J. E. Schulenberg, R. H. Abramowitz, D. Offer, and H. D. Jarcho (1984). A self-image questionnaire for young adolescents (SIQYA): Reliability and validity studies. *Journal of Youth and Adolescence 13*(2), 93–111.

Pratt, T. C., and F. T. Cullen (2000). The empirical status of Gottfredson and Hirschi's general theory of crime: A meta-analysis. *Criminology 38*(3), 931–964.

Rauner, F. (2007). Vocational education and training—a European perspective. In A. Brown, S. Kirpal, and F. Rauner (Eds.), *Identities at Work*, Volume 5 of *Technical and Vocational Education and Training: Issues, Concerns and Prospects*, pp. 115–144. New York: Springer.

Raven, J., J. C. Raven, and J. Court (1988). *Manual for Raven's Progressive Matrices and Vocabulary Scales.* San Antonio, TX: Harcourt Assessment.

Raven, J. C. (1962). *Advanced Progressive Matrices: Sets I and II* (Revised ed.). London: H. K. Lewis.

Reed, D., A. Yung-Hsu Liu, R. Kleinman, A. Mastri, D. Reed, S. Sattar, and J. Ziegler (2012). An effectiveness assessment and cost-benefit analysis of registered apprenticeship in 10 states. Mathematica Final Report 06689.090 and 40096, Mathematica Policy Research.

Reynolds, A. J. (1994). Effects of a preschool plus follow-on intervention for children at risk. *Developmental Psychology 30*(6), 787–804.

Reynolds, A. J. (1995). One year of preschool intervention or two: Does it matter? *Early Childhood Research Quarterly 10*(1), 1–31.

Reynolds, A. J. (2000). *Success in Early Intervention: The Chicago Child-Parent Centers.* Lincoln: University of Nebraska Press.

Reynolds, A. J., and J. A. Temple (1998, February). Extended early childhood intervention and school achievement: Age thirteen findings from the Chicago longitudinal study. *Child Development 69*(1), 231–246.

Reynolds, A. J., J. A. Temple, S.-R. Ou, I. A. Arteaga, and B. A. B. White (2011, July). School-based early childhood education and age-28 well-being: Effects by timing, dosage, and subgroups. *Science 333*(6040), 360–364.

Reynolds, A. J., J. A. Temple, D. L. Robertson, and E. A. Mann (2001, May). Long-term effects of an early childhood intervention on educational achievement and juvenile arrest—a 15-year follow-up of low-income children in public schools. *Journal of American Medical Association 285*(18), 2339–2346.

Reynolds, A. J., J. A. Temple, D. L. Robertson, and E. A. Mann (2002). Age 21 cost-benefit analysis of the Title I Chicago Child-Parent Centers. *Educational Evaluation and Policy Analysis 24*(4), 267–303.

Reynolds, A. J., J. A. Temple, B. A. White, S.-R. Ou, and D. L. Robertson (2011, January/February). Age 26 cost-benefit analysis of the Child-Parent Center early education program. *Child Development 82*(1), 379–404.

Roberts, B. W. (2009). Back to the future: Personality and assessment and personality development. *Journal of Research in Personality 43*(2), 137–145.

Roberts, B. W., N. R. Kuncel, R. L. Shiner, A. Caspi, and L. R. Goldberg (2007, December). The power of personality: The comparative validity of personality traits, socioeconomic status, and cognitive ability for predicting important life outcomes. *Perspectives in Psychological Science 2*(4), 313–345.

Roberts, R. D., G. N. Goff, F. Anjoul, P. C. Kyllonen, G. Pallier, and L. Stankov (2000). The Armed Services Vocational Aptitude Battery (ASVAB): Little more than acculturated learning (Gc)!? *Learning and Individual Differences 12*(1), 81–103.

Roder, A., and M. Elliot (2011). A promising start: Year-Up's initial impacts on young adults' careers. Technical report, Economic Mobility Corporation.

Rodríguez-Planas, N. (2010). Mentoring, educational services, and economic incentives: Longer-term evidence on risky behaviors from a randomized trial. Discussion Paper 4968, IZA.

Rodríguez-Planas, N. (2012, October). Longer-term impacts of mentoring, educational services, and learning incentives: Evidence from a randomized trial in the United States. *American Economic Journal: Applied Economics 4* (4), 121–139.

Rosenberg, M. (1965). *Society and the Adolescent Self-Image.* Princeton, NJ: Princeton University Press.

Rothstein, R., Jacobsen, R. and Wilder, T. (2008). Grading education: Getting accountability right. New York: Economic Policy Institute and Teachers College Press.

Ryan, R. M., and E. L. Deci (2000). Intrinsic and extrinsic motivations: Classic definitions and new direction. *Contemporary Educational Psychology 25*(1), 54–67.

Rutter, M. (2006). Implications of resilience concepts for scientific understanding. *Annals of the New York Academy of Sciences 1094*(1), 1–12.

Salgado, J. F. (1997). The five factor model of personality and job performance in the European Community. *Journal of Applied Psychology 82*(1), 30–43.

Schmidt, F. L., and J. Hunter (2004). General mental ability in the world of work: Occupational attainment and job performance. *Journal of Personality and Social Psychology 86*(1), 162–173.

Schmitt, D. P. (2002). Are sexual promiscuity and relationship infidelity linked to different personality traits across cultures? Findings from the International Sexuality Description Project. *Online Readings in Psychology and Culture 4* (Unit 4), 1–22. Retrieved from http://scholarworks.gvsu.edu/orpc/vol4/iss4/4.

Schmitt, D. P., J. Allik, R. R. McCrae, and V. Benet-Martínez (2007). The geographic distribution of Big Five personality traits: Patterns and profiles of human self-description across 56 nations. *Journal of Cross-Cultural Psychology 38*(2), 173–212.

Schochet, P. Z., J. Burghardt, and S. Glazerman (2001). *National Job Corps Study: The Impacts of Job Corps on Participants' Employment and Related Outcomes.* Princeton, NJ: Mathematica Policy Research, Inc.

Schochet, P. Z., J. Burghardt, and S. McConnell (2008, December). Does Job Corps work? Impact findings from the National Job Corps Study. *American Economic Review 98*(5), 1864–1886.

Schulz, R., J. Bookwala, J. E. Knapp, M. Scheier, and G. M. Williamson (1996). Pessimism, age, and cancer mortality. *Psychology and Aging 11*(2), 304–309.

Schumacher, R. (2003). Family support and parent involvement in Head Start: What do Head Start program performance standards require? Technical Report, Center for Law and Social Policy.

Scribner, J. P., and D. Wakelyn (1998). Youth apprenticeship experiences in Wisconsin: A stakeholder-based evaluation. *The High School Journal 82*(1), 24–34.

Secretary's Commission on Achieving Necessary Skills (1992). *Learning a Living: A Blueprint for High Performance: A SCANS Report for America 2000.* Washington, DC: U.S. Government Printing Office.

Segal, C. (2008, October). Working when no one is watching: Motivation, test scores, and economic success. Economics working papers, Department of Economics and Business, Universitat Pompeu Fabra, Barcelona, Spain.

Shure, M. B., and G. Spivack (1988). Interpersonal cognitive problem solving. In R. H. Price, E. L. Cowen, R. P. Lorion, and J. Ramos-McKay (Eds.), *14 Ounces of Prevention: A Casebook for Practitioners*, Chapter 6, pp. 69–82. Washington, DC: American Psychological Association.

Social and Character Development Research Consortium (2010, October). Efficacy of schoolwide programs to promote social and character development and reduce problem behavior in elementary school children. Research Report NCER 20112001, National Center for Education Research, Institute of Education Sciences, U.S. Department of Education.

Sroufe, L. A. (1997, Spring). Psychopathology as an outcome of development. *Development and Psychopathology 9*(2), 251–268.

Sroufe, L. A., B. Egeland, E. Carlson, and W. A. Collins (2005). *The Development of the Person: The Minnesota Study of Risk and Adaptation from Birth to Adulthood.* New York: Guilford Press.

Stasz, C. (2001). Assessing skills for work: Two perspectives. *Oxford Economic Papers 53*(3), 385–405.

Sylva, K. (1997). The quest for quality in curriculum. In L. J. Schweinhart and D. P. Weikart (Eds.), *Lasting Differences: The High/Scope Preschool Curriculum Comparison Study through Age 23*, pp. 89–93. Ypsilanti, MI: High/Scope Press.

Temple, J. A., and A. J. Reynolds (2007). Benefits and costs of investments in preschool education: Evidence from the child-parent centers and related programs. *Economics of Education Review 26*(1), 126–144.

Terman, L. M., and M. A. Merrill (1960). *Stanford-Binet Intelligence Scale: Manual for the Third Revision Form L-M.* Boston: Houghton Mifflin.

Thaler, R. H. (2008, July). A short course in behavioral economics. Edge Master Class, Sonoma, CA, July 25–27, 2008.

Tierney, J. P., J. Baldwin-Grossman, and N. L. Resch (1995). Making a difference: An impact study of Big Brothers Big Sisters. Report, Public/Private Ventures.

Tough, P. (2012). *How Children Succeed: Grit, Curiosity, and the Hidden Power of Character.* Boston: Houghton Mifflin Harcourt.

Tuttle, C. C, G. Brian, P. Gleason, V. Knechel, I. Nicholas-Barrer, and A. Resch (2013). KIPP middle schools: Impacts on achievement and other outcomes. Executive Summary. Mathematica Policy Research.

Tuttle, C. C., B.-R. Teh, I. Nichols-Barrer, B. P. Gill, and P. Gleason (2010). Student characteristics and achievement in 22 KIPP middle schools. Report 06441.900, Mathematica.

Tyler, Ralph W. (1973). Assessing Educational Achievement in the Affective Domain. *National Council on Measurement in Education 4* (3).

Walker, G. C., and F. Vilella-Velez (1992). *Anatomy of a Demonstration: The Summer Training and Education Program (STEP) from Pilot through Replication and Postprogram Impacts.* Philadelphia, PA: Public/Private Ventures.

Walker, S., T. Wachs, S. Grantham-McGregor, M. Black, C. Nelson, S. Huffman, H. Baker-Henningham, S. Chang, J. Hamadani, B. Lozoff, J. Meeks Gardner, C. Powell, A. Rahman, and L. Richter (2011). Inequality in early childhood: Risk and protective factors for early child development. *The Lancet 378*(9799), 1325–1338.

Walker, S. P., S. M. Chang, C. A. Powell, and S. M. Grantham-McGregor (2005). Effects of early childhood psychosocial stimulation and nutritional supplementation on cognition and education in growth-stunted Jamaican children: Prospective cohort study. *The Lancet 366*(9499), 1804–1807.

Walker, S. P., S. M. Chang, C. A. Powell, E. Simonoff, and S. M. Grantham-McGregor (2007). Early childhood stunting is associated with poor psychological functioning in late adolescence and effects are reduced by psychosocial stimulation. *The Journal of Nutrition 137*(11), 2464–2469.

Walker, S. P., S. M. Chang, M. Vera-Hernández, and S. Grantham-McGregor (2011). Early childhood stimulation benefits adult competence and reduces violent behavior. *Pediatrics 127*(5), 849–857.

Walker, S. P., T. D. Wachs, J. M. Gardner, B. Lozoff, G. A. Wasserman, E. Pollitt, J. A. Carter, and The International Child Development Steering Group (2007, January). Child development: Risk factors for adverse outcomes in developing countries. *The Lancet 369*(9556), 145–157.

Walsh, D. A. (2005). *Why Do They Act That Way? A Survival Guide to the Adolescent Brain for You and Your Teen* (1st ed.). New York: Free Press.

Washington Workforce Training Board (2008). Washington State employers workforce needs and practices survey. Statewide report.

Webb, E. (1915). Character and intelligence. *British Journal of Psychology Supplement 1*(3), 1–99.

Westat (2010). Head Start Impact Study: Final report. Contract 282-00-0022, U.S. Department of Health and Human Services.

Westwood, A. (2004). Skills that matter and shortages that don't. In C. Warchust, I. Grugulis, and E. Keep (Eds.), *The Skills that Matter.* New York: Palgrave-Macmillan.

Winkelmann, R. (1996, July). Employment prospects and skill acquisition of apprenticeship-trained workers in Germany. *Industrial and Labor Relations Review 49*(4), 658–672.

Wolter, S. C. and P. Ryan (2011). Apprenticeship. In S. M. Eric A. Hanushek and L. Woessmann (Eds.), *Handbook of the Economics of Education*, Volume 3 of *Handbooks in Economics*, Chapter 11, pp. 521–576. San Diego: Elsevier.

Young, M. E. (1996). *Early Childhood Development: Investing in the Future.* Washington, DC: World Bank.

Zabel, J., S. Schwartz, and S. Donald (2010). The impact of the Self-Sufficiency Project on the employment behaviour of former welfare recipients. *Canadian Journal of Economics 43*(3), 882–918.

Zabel, J., S. Schwartz, and S. Donald (2013). An analysis of the impact of the Self-Sufficiency Project on wages. *Empirican Economics 44*(1), 231–259.

Zemsky, R. (1997). Skills and the economy: An employer context for understanding the school-to-work transition. In A. Lesgold, M. Feuer, and A. Black (Eds.), *Transitions in Work and Learning: Implications for Assessment.* Washington, DC: National Academy Press.

10

WHAT SHOULD BE DONE?

JAMES J. HECKMAN, JOHN ERIC HUMPHRIES, AND TIM KAUTZ

10.1 What Should Be Done

Character and intellect are twin pillars supporting flourishing lives. American public policy neglects character and focuses on intellect. Achievement tests embody this vision. Scores on achievement tests have become the measure of man.

The GED program implements this vision. High school dropouts are certified to be equivalent to conventional high school graduates based only on their performance on an achievement test. Achievement tests do not measure many of the skills needed to graduate from high school, or succeed in life. The GED exam does not measure the skills that cause high school students to show up to school on time, persevere in tasks, follow rules, and cooperate with their teachers or fellow students.

This book demonstrates the danger of our national preoccupation with achievement tests. As a group, GEDs are about as smart as high school graduates but lack the character skills of graduates. GEDs earn less than high school graduates and drop out of everything they start. After adjusting for their greater cognitive ability, GEDs earn at the same level as other dropouts. The same deficits in skills that cause many GED recipients to drop out of high school cause them to fail to persist in marriage, employment, or the military.

Character matters. It is an essential ingredient of successful lives. It can be measured. It can be fostered. Families, schools, and communities are major producers of character. There are effective programs that develop character and can supplement challenged schools and families.

Assessments of schools and skill development programs should be made more comprehensive. Achievement tests should be supplemented with objective measures of character that have been shown to predict important schooling, labor market, and social outcomes.

Character can be fostered without infringing on the autonomy of students or the sanctity of families. Many American families are struggling and need assistance. The programs discussed in this book are noncompulsory. Many engage parents on a voluntary basis.

Character education should complement cognitive education in schools. While preparing for achievement tests might build some character skills, the skills so cultivated do not cover the wide range of character skills that are valued in the labor market. There is no evidence that preparing for the GED exam produces long-term gains in cognition or character.

Research in neuroscience, psychology, and economics shows that character skills are more malleable in adolescence than are cognitive skills. Although the early years are important for creating both kinds of skills, the greater malleability of character at later ages suggests that adolescent remediation efforts should focus on creating character. Mentoring and monitoring adolescents in workplace-based environments can foster skills by demonstrating their relevance.

This book has important lessons for public policy toward the GED program. The GED certificate is not equivalent to a high school degree. Counting GEDs as high school graduates hides problems and overstates American progress in raising high school graduation rates. Counting GEDs as high school graduates gives a misleading impression of the effectiveness of public policies. For example, the Job Corps was originally perceived to be a successful program in large part because it produced GED recipients. Long-term evaluations show that the Job Corps is ineffective. Faith in the GED motivates government efforts to funnel billions of dollars into failed programs. Belief that GED certification solves the high school dropout problem diverts policymakers from seeking effective solutions.

With its promise of a cheap route to high school equivalency, the GED induces students to drop out of high school. The GED program deceives and misrepresents its recipients. It bundles hardworking dropouts who have turned their lives around with people who are good test takers but who lack character.

Passing the GED test does not establish readiness for college. Of the GED recipients who attend college, half drop out in the first year, most in the first semester. Few GED recipients are adequately prepared for the rigors of college. Even hardworking and persistent GED recipients often struggle with college because they are several academic years behind high school graduates when they enter college. The promise of a college degree that motivates many GED certifiers is usually unfulfilled. This deception is costly because students forgo earnings and pay tuition.

In 2014, the GED Testing Service will introduce a new GED exam. The new exam is computer-based and its content is aligned with the Common Core high school curriculum. The new exam will put more emphasis on problem-solving skills and aims to measure more effectively college and career readiness. The new GED exam will not address the skill deficits that prevent many GED recipients from succeeding in college. Many GEDs will still lack the character skills necessary for success. If the exam's content is more difficult, those who pass will have higher cognitive skills, yet, as shown in this book, more than cognition matters.[1] Making the exam more difficult in the cognitive dimension will not address the problem of deficits in character not captured by the exam.

America is a second-chance society. The GED program should be retained as a second-chance option for those who want to turn their lives around. Women appear to be the primary beneficiaries, although even for them any benefit from GED certification comes mainly through opening doors and facilitating access to jobs—not in securing higher paying jobs.

For most people, the GED offers false promises. While second chances should be encouraged, the second chance should not encourage failure on the first chance. High school students should not be encouraged to earn GEDs instead of completing high school.

GED certification should be more tightly age restricted. Many high school students have not matured. For this reason, there are age restrictions on drinking, smoking, joining the military, and driving. Raising the minimum age for GED certification would reduce the high school dropout rate. At the very least, high school students who plan to earn a GED should receive mandatory counseling so that they are well informed about the difference between earning a GED and completing high school. They should know the opportunities they foreclose by dropping out of high school. People who earn the GED as a stepping stone to postsecondary education should be warned that passing the GED test does not establish readiness for college.

10.2 Specific Policy Recommendations about the GED

We make the following specific policy recommendations about the GED.

1. GED recipients should not be considered high school graduates in social statistics or when evaluating the success of government programs. Counting GED recipients as high school graduates paints a false picture of the American educational system and conceals inequality. It also misdirects government funding.

---

1. Note that a shift towards problem-solving skills does not mean the new test will be harder for dropouts to pass. The difficulty of passing is determined by both the difficulty of the content and by the number of questions that test takers must answer correctly.

2. GED preparation centers should be eliminated from high schools. The minimum age required to take the exam should be raised, so that test takers are more mature when they take it. Students who plan to take the GED should receive mandatory counseling to inform them of the options that they are foreclosing.

3. Refine the signal sent by the GED test to include assessments of character and to distinguish GED recipients with serious seat time and study time from other dropouts who GED certify.

4. Recognize that the problems associated with the GED will not be fixed by raising the passing threshold on the same kind of achievement test. The 2014 GED exam may be more cognitively challenging, but it will continue to test only a subset of the skills necessary for success in life.

10.3 General Policy Recommendations about Character Skills

We make the following general policy recommendations about character skills.

1. Character skills should be measured and integrated into school accountability systems and in evaluations of all skill programs. There are reliable ways to do so. The assessments of schools, preschools, and other skill-formation activities should be based on objective inventories such as those suggested by Ralph Tyler (1940)—one of the creators of the modern achievement test—and operationalized and validated in the recent literature. This broader notion of assessment should recognize that all "tests" measure performance on tasks. Inventories of character should be based on what is revealed from behavior. The distinction between "tests" and "behaviors," while entrenched in the psychology literature, is misleading and falsely elevates the importance of measures based on tests (including self-reports of personality and reports by observers) over measures based on behaviors.

2. Recognize that families are major producers of character skills, that schools work with what families send them, and that many American families are stressed. Programs that support family life and that encourage parenting and parent–child attachment are effective in promoting both cognitive and character skills.

3. Secular programs to foster moral and character education in schools should be implemented and evaluated. These efforts can compensate, in part, for the challenges facing modern American families. Introducing discipline in the school will likely build character skills.

4. Recognize that effective adolescent remediation programs should focus on promoting character skills. Encourage workplace-based adoles-

cent remediation programs that foster character and that recognize the greater malleability of character skills than cognitive skills at later stages of childhood.

BIBLIOGRAPHY

Tyler, R. W. (1940, September). The place of evaluation in modern education. *The Elementary School Journal 41*(1), 19–27.

CONTRIBUTORS

Eric Grodsky is Associate Professor of Sociology at the University of Wisconsin–Madison. Most of his research focuses on inequality in higher education, including work on affirmative action, socioeconomic inequalities in college attendance and completion, changes in the role of merit in these processes over time, and the role of information about the college readiness and college-preparatory behavior of high school students. Grodsky is currently studying the relationship between adolescent sexual activity and educational attachment and achievement and the effects of college remediation on persistence and time to degree. He is also designing and fielding a follow-up to the High School and Beyond study.

Andrew Halpern-Manners is an Assistant Professor in the Department of Sociology at Indiana University. His research focuses on family and school effects on children's academic outcomes and on methodological issues surrounding longitudinal data analysis. His recent work includes "The Effects of Family Member Migration on Education and Work among Nonmigrant Youth in Mexico" (*Demography*), "Panel Conditioning in a Longitudinal Study of Chilean Adolescents' Substance Use: Evidence from an Experiment" (*Social Forces*), and "Panel Conditioning in Longitudinal Studies: Evidence from the Current Population Survey" (*Demography*). He is currently working on developing a dynamic model of contextual effects on individuals' educational attainments and academic performance.

James J. Heckman is the Henry Schultz Distinguished Service Professor of Economics and Public Policy at the University of Chicago, where he has served since 1973. In 2000, he won the Sveriges Riksbank Prize in Economic Sciences in Memory of Alfred Nobel. Heckman directs the Economics Research Center in the Department of Economics and the Center for Social Program Evaluation at the Harris School for Public Policy. In addition, he is Professor of Science and Society at University College Dublin and a Senior Research Scholar at the American Bar Foundation. His work has been devoted to the development of a scientific basis for economic policy evaluation. His recent research focuses on inequality, human development and life-cycle skill formation, with a special emphasis on early childhood. Heckman has published over 300 articles and several books. He has received numerous awards for his work, including the John Bates Clark Medal in 1983, the Jacob Mincer Award for Lifetime Achievement in 2005, the 2005 and 2007 Dennis Aigner Award for Applied Econometrics from the *Journal of Econometrics*, the Ulysses Medal from the University College Dublin in 2006, the 2007 Theodore W. Schultz Award, the Gold Medal of the President of the Italian Republic in 2008, and the Distinguished Contributions to Public Policy for Children Award from the Society for Research in Child Development in 2009.

John Eric Humphries is a National Science Foundation Graduate Research Fellow in the Department of Economics at the University of Chicago. His research interests include educational choice, the origins of inequality, and the role of personality in social and economic outcomes. His published research includes work on the General Educational Development test, educational choice, the role of cognitive and noncognitive skills in later-life outcomes, and the combination of skills measured by grades and achievement tests. He holds an M.A. in Economics and an honors A.B. in Economics from the University of Chicago.

Tim Kautz is a Ph.D. candidate in the Economics Department at the University of Chicago and a National Science Foundation Fellowship recipient. His research interests include education, inequality, and health. Previously, he conducted policy research at Stanford University's Center for Health Policy and Acumen LLC. He holds a B.A. in Economics from Stanford University and an M.A. in Economics from the University of Chicago.

Paul A. LaFontaine is an Industry Economist at the Federal Communications Commission. He has a B.A. in mathematics from the University of Chicago and an M.A. in economics from UCLA. He previously worked with Heckman on the study of U.S. educational trends and the evaluation of social programs aimed at low-skilled workers. This work is published in the *Journal of Labor Economics* and the *Review of Economics and Statistics.* His current work focuses on topics in Telecommunications Policy, Antitrust and other aspects of Industrial Organization economics. He currently resides in Washington, D.C.

Janice H. Laurence is an Associate Professor in the College of Education at Temple University. Previously, she served as the Director of Human Resource Development for the Army's Human Terrain System and as the Director of Research and Analysis within the Office of the Under Secretary of Defense (Personnel and Readiness). Dr. Laurence spent much of her career as a social science contract researcher concentrating in the military setting. She is the lead editor for the *Oxford Handbook of Military Psychology* published in 2012. Dr. Laurence holds an M.A. and a Ph.D. in Industrial-Organizational Psychology from George Mason University, an M.A. in Experimental Psychology from Temple University, and a B.A. in Psychology from Temple University.

Lois M. Quinn is a senior scientist with the University of Wisconsin-Milwaukee Employment and Training Institute, a department that addresses the workforce training, transportation, and education needs of Wisconsin workers. She holds a Ph.D. in urban studies from UW-Milwaukee, where her 1990 dissertation topic was "GED: The Test that Became an Institution." Her current research and technical assistance work focuses on labor force drilldowns and job vacancy surveys for the Milwaukee Area Workforce Investment Board, assessments of socioeconomic issues impacting children and families in Milwaukee public schools, reentry program evaluations for the Wisconsin Department of Corrections, and asset-building research for the NAACP.

Pedro L. Rodríguez is an Assistant Professor and the Academic Coordinator of the International Center for Energy and Environment (CIEA) at the Institute of Advanced Studies in Administration (IESA) based in Caracas, Venezuela. Rodríguez obtained his bachelor's degree in economics from the University of Chicago in 2007 and an MPhil in economics from the University of Cambridge in 2010. His current research focuses on the political economy of resource wealth management in developing countries. He is currently co-authoring a book on Venezuela's experience managing its oil wealth.

John Robert Warren is Professor of Sociology at the University of Minnesota. His research focuses on the roles of education and health in stratifying life outcomes and in reproducing inequality across generations. His recent work focuses on the measurement of states' grade retention and high school completion rates; the consequences of high school exit examinations; the magnitude of panel conditioning biases in longitudinal surveys; the correlates of childhood sickness in the nineteenth century; and the effects of lifetime trajectories of work and family roles on subsequent outcomes. He is the incoming Editor of *Sociology of Education* and has recently served on the editorial boards of *Social Forces, Educational Evaluation and Policy Analysis,* and the *Journal of Health and Social Behavior.*

INDEX

by behavioral patterns, 139, *140,*
141–142, 148, 149, 150, 155, 156, 157,
158, 190, *237, 238,* 238–239, *242, 243,*
244, 272, 280

by cognitive ability, 111, 141–145, *143,*
144, 152, 160–168, *161,* 171, 185, 191,
242, 243, 245

by earnings, 111, 112, 156, 171, *172–173,*
174, *176,* 177–183, 187, 188–189, 190,
191, 192, 193, *194–195,* 196–201,
208–209, 219, 242–243, 244

by noncognitive skills, 145–147,
148–151, 156, *157,* 160–168,
256–258

by postsecondary (educational and
nonacademic) performance, 157,
158, 160–168, 171, *176,* 177–183, 185,
193, *194–195,* 196–209, 216–217, *219,*
220, *221–223,* 223–224, *225–232,*
233–236, *242–243,* 244

by survival rates, 233, *234,* 235–236,
235n54, 236n55

by work experience, *172–173,* 174,
191–192, 193–195, 196–200, 206–207,
208–209, 223–225, *227–232,* 233,
234–235, 236, 236n55, *242–243,* 244,
244n67, 245, *246–247,* 248–254

drop out of higher education, 177,
182, 233

drop out of marriage (divorce), 177, 236

drop out of the military, 177, 233

families of GED recipients vs. HSGs,
7, 25, 28

female, 141, 143, 145n15, 147, 152, 155–156,
160, 162, 163, 166, 433

are more likely to participate in the
labor force, 178, 180–181, 244, 259

are primary beneficiaries of GED,
178, 259, 433

do not earn higher hourly wages,
178, 181, 185, 196, 212, 224, 233, 259,
261n87, 433

have better social skills, 256, *258*

have higher annual incomes, 177, 233,
244, 245, 259

more likely to attempt further education, 177, 188, 205–206

more likely to be employed, 180, 183,
193, 196, 212, 236n56, 244, 248, 249,
255, 259

pregnancy, 141, 155–157, 162–163,
163n46, 166

drop out due to, 5, 32, 179, 183,
254–255, 256, 259, *296*

supply more labor, 171, 180, 212, 233

women (but not men) benefit,
32, 46

have lower discounted earnings,
177–178, 182, 217, *219,* 220, 259

immigrants, 33, 185, 189–190

male, 141, 143, 145n13, 157, *158,* 160, 162,
162n44, 163, 181

higher cognitive ability, 181, 248, 259

more likely to attempt further education, 181, 188, 205–206

male-female comparison, 141, 152, 157,
160, 163–165

social skills, 256–257

mental and physical health, 236–239

performance of

veterans, 139, 139n1, 168, 168n48

vs. high school graduates, 142–143,
145

vs. other high school dropouts,
142–43, 145

postsecondary education, attainment
of, 143, 145, 145n11, 182, 432

delay in time, between earning GED
and further educational attainment, 177–178, 182, 216

reasons for dropping out, 139–141,
155–156, 162, 166, 295–296, 314–315

school-related behavior, 146–147, *150,*
155, *157*

survival rates, 233–236, 235n54, 236n55

teenagers, 123–131

GED Testing Service (GEDTS), 9, 57–58, 77,
80, 86, 92, 98n12, 117n28, 123n40, 201, 284,
287, 294, 295, 318, 319, 324, 335, 432

GEDTS Annual Reports, *303*

General education curriculum, 58–62,
66–67, 76

German Socio-Economic Panel (GSOEP).
See **Data sets**

GI Bill. *See* **Military**
Government
Congress, 70, 270, 284
Department of Defense (DoD), 270, 284, 285, 287
state departments of education, 58, 62, 73, 78, 80, 91–92, 301n11
adoption of GED credential, 58, 73, 78–81, 85–86
Common Core of Data (CCD), 301, 301n11, 301n14, *302, 305, 306,* 310–311, *312, 313*
U.S. Census Bureau, 301n13, 313n35, *314*
U.S. Department of Education, *296*
Grover, Herbert, 57, 98
Guaranteed Student Loans, default rates, 96

Herrnstein, Richard, and Murray, Charles, 5–6, 44
High school
at-risk students, 295, 309
black-white gap in educational attainment, 9, 35
Common Core curriculum, 432
diploma, 295, 309, 312, *312*
wartime diplomas, 72–74, 78, 99
dropout problem, 341, 344–345
incentives, 8, 36, 46, 294–295, 299
dropout rates, *297,* 301–302, *302,* 304, *305–306,* 311n30
causality between GED age requirements and dropout rates, 297
causality between GED passing standards and dropout rates, 293–297, *296,* 299, *302,* 304, *305,* 315
Common Core of Data (CCD), 301, 301n11, 301n14, *302, 305, 306,* 310, 311, *313*
sensitivity to migration, 301–302, 302n15
graduation rate, 109, 294–295, 301, 309, 312–315, *314,* 316
determinants, 141, 160, *161,* 162, 162n44, 166–168
measurement of, 133–134
graduation standards, 110, 130–131

other alternative credentials, 270–271, *272–273,* 277, 280, 285n9, 312, 344
home school, 270, 271, *272–273*
reasons for dropping out, 139, *140,* 141, 155–157, *158,* 160, 162–163, 163n46, 166, 293–296, *296*
pregnancy, 5, 32, 179, 183, 254–255, 256, 259, 296, *296*
seat time in high school, 4, 22, 59, 179, 293n2, 434
High school exit examinations (HSEEs), 25, 46–47, 131, *131,* 322–323, 304, 318
cost of implementing, 334–335
difficulty of, 318–319, 322–323, 323n5, *328,* 329, 330, *330,* 331, *332, 333*
effect of, on graduation rates, 318, 3 21–322, *327*
history of, 319, 323, *330*
pass rates, 320n2, 321
relationship between, and GED testing, 318–322, 324–325, 327, *328,* 329–330, *330,* 331, *332,* 333–335
re-testing, 319, 319n1, 320
specific performance targets for schools, 321
types, 319, 323, 323n6, 335
High Scope Foundation, *377. See also* **Interventions,** early childhood programs, Perry Preschool Program; infant and model preschool programs
High-stakes tests. *See* **High school exit examinations (HSEEs)**
Hutchins, Robert Maynard, 66–67

Immigration Act of 1990, 123
Intelligence. *See* **Cognitive skills**
Interventions, 345, 366–372, 383, 387
adolescent interventions, 9, 45, 387–401
mentoring, 387, 388–391, 432
Big Brothers Big Sisters, *368–370,* 389–391
EPIS Program, *368–370,* 391
Quantum Opportunity Program, *368–370,* 388–389
workplace-based, 432, 434–435